NOTABLE
TWENTIETH-CENTURY
LATIN AMERICAN
WOMEN

NOTABLE TWENTIETH-CENTURY LATIN AMERICAN WOMEN

A Biographical Dictionary

Edited by
CYNTHIA MARGARITA TOMPKINS
and
DAVID WILLIAM FOSTER

Greenwood Press
Westport, Connecticut • London

Library of Congress Cataloging-in-Publication Data

Notable twentieth-century Latin American women : a biographical dictionary / edited by
Cynthia Margarita Tompkins and David William Foster.
    p. cm.
   Includes bibliographical references and indexes.
   ISBN 0–313–31112–9 (alk. paper)
   1. Women—Latin America—Biography. 2. Latin America—Biography. I. Tompkins,
Cynthia, 1958– II. Foster, David William.
   CT3290.N68   2001
   920.72'098—dc21   00–027631

British Library Cataloguing in Publication Data is available.

Library of Congress Catalog Card Number: 00–027631
ISBN: 0–313–31112–9

First published in 2001

Greenwood Press, 88 Post Road West, Westport, CT 06881
An imprint of Greenwood Publishing Group, Inc.
www.greenwood.com

Printed in the United States of America

The paper used in this book complies with the
Permanent Paper Standard issued by the National
Information Standards Organization (Z39.48–1984).

10 9 8 7 6 5 4 3 2 1

Contents

Contents

Preface

Notable Twentieth-Century Latin American Women is a celebration of women conjoined by their common struggle against discrimination. Some overcame racism, a few, compulsive heterosexuality. But most have experienced multiple oppressions. Given the current economic crisis in Latin America, most struggle against poverty and unemployment. Many have experienced and continue to experience political repression and human rights violations. The women featured in this volume have challenged the status quo, have given voice to others, have fought for human dignity, and have reconfigured the social imaginary. More important, the contemporary women in this book continue to do so.

The editors have identified outstanding women in the fields of politics, the visual arts, religion, government, education, literature, popular culture, and the sciences. While certain categories, such as politics and government, appear to be part of a continuum, political engagement does not assure access to power. Other fields, such as theater, seem to be rendered invisible by these categories, since inclusion in literature erases or diminishes the importance of their performance. Several categories were used to define some individuals, which proves that single labels fail to encompass the achievements of these outstanding women.

Except where information is unavailable, each entry of *Notable Twentieth-Century Latin American Women* includes biographical data, family background, education, career highlights, obstacles encountered, and the personal life of each woman featured. The editors strove for inclusiveness regarding race and ethnicity, class, political ideology, religious persuasion, and sexual orientation. Most of the women featured were born after 1900. Despite the desire to represent all Latin American countries, inclusiveness is limited to Spanish- and Portuguese-speaking peoples, which curtailed the incorporation of notable women of Hispanic origin who write primarily in English.

In selecting seventy-two entries, the editors canvassed other experts in the field to arrive at the best representation of the countries included. Furthermore, to enhance the interdisciplinary nature of the text, the editors invited Jane S. Jaquette, a leading expert in the fields of Latin American studies and women's studies, to write an introduction that would set the achievements of these remarkable women in a historical context.

This celebration of outstanding Latin American women is intended to increase their visibility, to raise consciousness about the issues they confront, and, given the trying conditions most of these notable women have experienced and continue to experience, to honor their daily struggle. The scarcity of bibliographical citations in some cases and the number of citations in Spanish and Portuguese speak both to the limited available resources in English and to the groundbreaking nature of this volume.

Acknowledgments

There are too many people to thank in ventures such as these. The editors are particularly grateful to the contributors, since this project could have never come to fruition without them. Additionally, we wish to show our appreciation for the overwhelming support of our colleagues who responded to the calls placed in the newsletter of the *Latin American Studies Association*, in *PMLA*, and in the electronic lists generated by *Feministas Unidas*, and the LASA Gender Section. The difficulty of the selection process surely suggests that the women featured in this volume are merely the tip of the iceberg. The editors render their heartfelt thanks to the experts in the field who generously contributed to the narrowing down of the paradigmatic representatives for each country. Robson Camargo's advice regarding Brazil especially comes to mind. Among graduate students at Arizona State University, Juana Suárez was instrumental in the areas of popular culture, the visual arts, and the selection of the entries on Colombian women. In addition to identifying contributors for those fields, Suárez proved to be extremely resourceful in locating photographs. David R. Miller's contribution was significant because of painstaking reading of the manuscript striving for stylistic conformity. Additionally, Miller devoted much time and energy to identifying images and scanning them. Likewise, Cecilia Rosales meticulously read the manuscript and scanned pictures. Preparation of the index included assistance from Monica Castillo and Mikel Imaz.

Introduction: Women in Latin America

Few North Americans can name a famous Latin American woman other than Eva Perón. And, if her name is recognized, it is largely because the American pop star Madonna a few years ago made a movie of Andrew Lloyd Webber's musical *Evita*, based on her life. Many North Americans regard Latin American women in a negative way, oppressed by machismo or controlled by the Catholic Church.

These views, of course, are inadequate and inaccurate. Latin American women have a rich history and a dynamic present. This biographical dictionary honors a small but impressive sample of notable Latin American women who made their mark in the twentieth century; it represents a diverse range of women and their accomplishments in fields ranging from politics to literature and contemporary music. This introduction will give some historical sense of women's roles in the region and put the lives of the women represented here into a fuller contemporary context.

This work highlights women who have become well known as leaders and activists, as writers and public servants. The history of women in Latin America, however, is not only the history of the famous, but also of the nameless: indigenous women who resisted the conquest and remained the backbone of Indian communal life for centuries; women who came as slaves from Africa to a world controlled by the Spanish and the Portuguese; women who came as immigrants, not only from Spain, but also from Italy, Germany, the Middle East, and Asia; women who farmed and managed businesses; and women who struggled to support their families and survive, then and now.

Latin Americans are keenly aware of their past, and, as we will see, women have been important actors at critical points in the region's history. Latin Americans often contrast their own experiences with those of their more powerful neighbors to the north. From its birth as a nation, the United States has been a great power in the making, but Latin Americans have always been subjected to outside powers, from the Spanish and Portuguese in the colonial period to the growing dominance of the "Colossus of the North" in the nineteenth and twentieth centuries. North American and European economic power conditioned and, many would say, hindered Latin American economic development, which in turn distorted the region's political evolution. The countries of Latin America vary widely on all dimensions—political, economic, and demographic— but the relatively slow pace of development and repeated economic crises throughout the region have maintained rather than ameliorated historic inequalities of income and opportunity. These difficulties have not similarly restricted Latin American cultural production, which often draws on the dramatic geography of the continent; on the stark social contrasts between rich and poor, urban and rural, indigenous, black and white; and on the rich mental landscapes of its novelists, poets, songwriters, and essayists. Latin Americans historically have had a significant impact on international affairs, particularly in their contributions to international law. In both cultural and legal arenas, women are strongly represented.

Despite, or perhaps because of dependence on the United States, many Latin Americans criticize the materialism, individualism, and secularism that characterize much of U.S. culture today. By contrast, they regard their own cultures as more concerned with community and family, more religious, and more connected to European political and intellectual currents. These value differences have helped form and consolidate regional and national identities, and they also have important gender dimensions. These must be borne in mind when observing how women enter the public sphere—as guerrilla fighters or politicians, novelists, or artists.

Two notable women from the colonial past, La Malinche and Sor Juana Inés de la Cruz, illustrate two contrasting but enduring poles of women's identities in Latin American culture. Women were important figures during the conquest, and they were critical to the survival of native populations and cultures. Perhaps the most notorious woman of the conquest period is La Malinche. A Tabascan (Tabasco, Mexico) by birth, she was captured and enslaved in the warfare among groups prior to the conquest of Mexico. La Malinche was sold to conquistador Hernán Cortés as he was making his way from the Mexican Atlantic coast to the interior to confront Monteczuma, the leader of the Aztecs. With her help, Cortés was able to translate the Aztec language Nahuatl and thus interpret and anticipate Aztec reactions to his campaign, giving him an immense advantage. La Malinche bore Cortés a son and was rewarded by the Spanish Crown with land in her own name. A heroine to the Spanish, she is regarded by contemporary Mexicans as a traitor—but also as a dramatic figure and a symbol of the conquest of the native peoples by Europeans.

Juana Ramírez de Asbaje, known to us as Sor Juana Inés de la Cruz, left a less ambiguous heritage. As a young woman in the mid-seventeenth century, she became part of the Spanish viceregal court in Mexico City. Choosing not to marry, she joined a convent, where she was able to develop her talents as a writer and a poet. Sor Juana is also known for her essays, the most famous of which eloquently defends the right of women to be educated and to speak—rights that few women could then claim. In the last years of her life, Sor Juana gave up her worldly passion for learning and sought spiritual strength in fasting and self-abnegation. She died from a disease she caught while nursing her sister nuns during an epidemic that swept Mexico City.

Octavio Paz, the Mexican essayist, wrote in *El laberinto de la soledad* (The Labyrinth of Solitude, 1950) that La Malinche represents the "female" vulnerability of Latin America, and especially Mexico, conquered by the Spanish but after independence increasingly dominated by an expansionist United States. La Malinche fulfills the theme, so powerful in Western thought, of woman as traitor, an image as old as the biblical Eve. In Paz's view, the story of La Malinche is the beginning of a narrative of loss and betrayal, one that helps explain specific characteristics of Mexican identity, but that also helps us understand the broader Latin American cultural themes.

Sor Juana, in contrast, represents woman in her most positive light. Sor Juana combines the purity of the nun—in association with the still compelling image of the Madonna in Latin America—and the life of the mind. The life of the mind has a deep significance in a culture where, as was true in classical Greece, the writer is more respected than the merchant, the farmer, or the craftsman. Sor Juana combined both these compelling characteristics in one exemplary life, made more perfect by her choosing spiritual commitment over her intellectual pursuits. In doing so, she fulfilled in the most dramatic way a norm for female behavior that persists to this day: the ideal woman chooses self-sacrifice over self-fulfillment.

Sor Juana and La Malinche represent contrasting yet recurring archetypes that still influence the roles of women. When women rebel and seek their own voices, they do so in dialogue with these normative possibilities, and within the larger cultural and nationalist expectations they represent.

WOMEN IN THE NATIONAL PERIOD: THE NINETEENTH AND EARLY TWENTIETH CENTURIES

From 1810 to 1825, women were actively engaged in wars of independence against the Spanish, who were then ruled by Joseph Bonaparte who had been placed on the throne after Napoléon Bonaparte had conquered Spain. After an epic campaign, Generals José de San Martín and Simón Bolívar combined their forces to defeat the Spanish, and the countries of the region followed the lead of the United States and Haiti in declaring independence from their colonial rulers. (The ties of Puerto Rico and Cuba to Spain were not severed until the Spanish American War of 1898.) As was the case in the American Revolution, the independence wars forged important elements of each country's national identity. In contrast to the United States, however, there were many more celebrated heroines. Policarpa Salavarrieta, Josefa Ortiz de Domínguez, and Manuela Sáenz, to name a few, were among those who fought courageously for independence and, as historian Francesca Miller reminds us, ironically, for the "rights of *man*" (1991, 32).

Although all the newly independent Latin American states established constitutions based on the U.S. model, they could not legislate democratic governments or egalitarian political cultures. In fact, the most successful governments in the region were run by caudillos, military strongmen who used force, not votes, to stay in power and prop up the landholding elites, often with the overt support of a conservative Catholic Church. Some caudillos became modernizing dictators and won support by enforcing peace and encouraging economic growth. In contrast to the United States, where civilian rule was firmly established during the course of the nineteenth century, in the same period Latin American armies came to be seen as stabilizing forces. Many of the region's constitutions were rewritten to give the military the right to intervene whenever civilian politics threatened to dissolve into chaos, threatening peace and national security. Military rule denied political participation to all, but even civilian governments during this period did not allow illiterates (largely the rural poor) or women to vote.

By the late nineteenth century, women's suffrage had become a global cause, and many notable Latin American women were deeply involved in the struggle for women's rights in the broadest sense—legal and economic, as well as political. As would be true later, during the UN Decade for Women (1975–1985), Latin American women were active in international movements and played visible roles in regional organizations such as the Pan American Union and in international organizations such as the Women's International League for Peace and Freedom.

The twentieth century brought about fundamental changes in social conditions in much of the region. The Latin American economies had always been dependent on agriculture both for subsistence and for income from such agricultural exports as coffee and sugar and from minerals, including copper and tin. The large-scale agricultural holdings that had been consolidated during the colonial period produced semifeudal social relations, with peasants—often Indians or blacks—at the bottom.

By the mid-twentieth century, the rigid structures of rural life were challenged by population growth and by successive waves of rural-urban migration that brought about significant shifts in values, family organization, and patterns of employment. In the 1970s, Mexico City, São Paulo, Buenos Aires, and other urban centers rivaled the largest U.S. cities in size and social complexity, although a much higher proportion of individuals were living in poverty in Latin American cities.

Several factors prevented Latin American nations from following the path of industrial development characteristic of the United States and Northern Europe. Export earnings and capital flows remained tied largely to traditional agricultural and mineral exports. Industrial development, encouraged by governments eager to employ urban migrants and increase standards of living, was based on "import substitution"— that is, on replacing manufactured imports from abroad with home-produced products, often of higher price and lower quality. Few manufacturing concerns became sufficiently competitive to export their products abroad (the key to the development success stories of East Asian countries, beginning with Japan), and Latin America remained highly dependent on the North for capital and new technology.

Industrial development was stunted as a result. Industrial expansion absorbed most of the capital available for investment, leaving little to modernize agriculture. The rural exodus, which far outran the ability of the cities to supply industrial and professional jobs, produced chronic underemployment. Many were forced to engage in such marginal economic activities as street vending and small-scale crafts production, and many families survived because of women's meager earnings in the burgeoning "informal sector." Eventually, because of the lack of agricultural investment, countries that had been able to grow their own food began to depend on food imports, and women often joined movements to push the government to control the prices of basic necessities. The gap between rich and poor, established first under colonial rule and maintained during the semifeudal hacienda system throughout the nineteenth century, took on its present form, which is visible to any traveler to the region: urban dynamism and abject rural poverty, as well as pockets of conspicuous wealth surrounded by the favelas, *barriadas*, and barrios, or shantytowns, so characteristic of Latin American cities. Shantytowns replaced haciendas as the most salient feature of Latin American life.

Nonetheless, during much of the twentieth century, Latin America as a region was ahead of many other regions of the global south. The countries of the Southern Cone, especially Argentina, enjoyed high levels of per capita income and were regarded as having entered a viable path to development that would eventually be followed by all the economies of the region. In contrast to the many new nations that emerged from colonial status after World War II, Latin American countries had long been sovereign nation-states, experienced in international affairs. Latin American statesmen—and women—helped create institutions of global governance, like the League of Nations (in the 1920s) and the United Nations. In fact, it was Latin American women who, as delegates to the conference establishing the United Nations in 1945, persisted until sex discrimination was explicitly banned by the UN Charter.

FROM SUFFRAGE TO SOCIAL MOBILIZATION

The right to vote is clearly an important test of women's status although experiences in both the United States and Latin America demonstrate that it must be backed by political mobilization to modify laws and policies and to ensure that these are implemented. Despite the long history of women's activism, it was not until the early 1960s that all women of the region had acquired the right to vote. Although women's suffrage is generally viewed as a logical consequence of modernization, in 1929 Ecuador (still among the least developed of the countries of the region) was the first country to give women the vote.

Several countries, including Brazil, Uruguay, and Cuba, adopted women's suffrage in the 1930s, during the political crises sparked by the Great Depression, and El Salvador, the Dominican Republic, Panama, and Guatemala followed suit during World War II. Still others waited until after the war, including several of the most economically advanced: Venezuela and Argentina in 1947, Chile and Costa Rica in 1949, and Mexico in 1953. The last country in the region to allow women to vote was Paraguay, in 1961 (Miller 1991, 96).

Even when they could not vote, women were often active leaders of major political parties. In the 1940s, Magda Portal became one of the top officials of Peru's APRA party, which was gaining popularity for its support of workers' and peasants' rights and for its opposition to U.S. imperialism. Although she was not a feminist, Portal eventually left the party on the grounds that women were being ignored. Women could not vote in Peru until 1955.

Ironically, the radical parties, which were committed to eliminating class differences and officially supported the Marxist position on equality for women, often joined the conservative parties in resisting women's suffrage. Conservatives thought that women should not vote on principle, but leftist parties feared, not unreasonably it turned out, that women would vote more conservatively than men and reduce their chances of winning. In general, women were given the vote when the party or co-alition in power concluded it was in their interest to do so, not because they had any deep commitment to women's rights.

The most visible and powerful political woman of the twentieth century was undoubtedly Eva Perón of Argentina, who rescued her husband from political defeat, then organized a women's party to strengthen her husband's proworker, quasi-fascist Peronist party. Evita had been successful at mobilizing the working class and the urban poor, and she regarded women as an underexploited political resource. The Peronists also experimented with gender quotas. Today, under a new Peronist leadership, Argentina is again leading the way on quotas. All political parties are required to nominate women candidates for 30% of their seats. Nine other countries have adopted quotas, but Argentina's law is still the most strictly enforced, and today women occupy nearly 30% of the seats in the Argentine Congress.

Although women as a group may tend to vote more conservatively, individual women in impressive numbers have joined leftist parties and even guerrilla armies. The Cuban revolution was just a beginning; since 1960, guerrilla movements have actively recruited women and included them in their top political and military leadership. Women writer-activists like Rigoberta Menchú Tum and Domitila Barrios de Chúngara have become prominent voices for the rights of peasants, miners, and indigenous peoples.

During the last few decades, several women have been candidates for president in a number of countries, and three women have served in that role. Isabel Perón, Juan Domingo Perón's second wife, was elected vice president and then became president when Perón died in 1974. Like Lidia Geiler, who became president of Bolivia in 1979, Isabel was later overthrown by a military coup. The only woman president to serve out her term is Violeta Barrios de Chamorro, the widow of a martyred newspaper editor in Nicaragua, who was elected president in 1990. She appealed to voters as the person who could help heal the deep rift between the leftist Sandinistas and the opposition.

The political mobilization of Latin American women grew to a crescendo of women organizing in the last quarter of the twentieth century. Women's movements played a critical role in the processes of democratization and demilitarization throughout the region, from the Southern Cone to Central America.

The degree of women's politicization is unprecedented, but it has taken place under conditions quite different from those in the United States and Northern Europe. In Latin America, women's movements have emerged as part of broad coalitions formed to end military rule. The Mothers and Grandmothers of the Plaza de Mayo of Argentina, who drew public attention to the "dirty war" of military repression by demonstrating week after week for the return of their children and husbands, are the best-known Latin American women's groups. Similar women-led human rights groups formed in other countries, including Chile, El Salvador, and Guatemala.

At the same time, experiencing extreme economic hardship during the "Lost Decade" of the 1980s, poor urban women organized to feed their families in communal kitchens and through Glass of Milk movements in the shantytowns of Peru and Chile. Women's organizations formed to address a range of survival issues, from food prices to reproductive health. Although some groups would later find themselves in conflict with the Catholic Church over issues like divorce and abortion, many women organized with its early support in a period when the Church encouraged lay activism in part to fulfill its post–Vatican II commitment to the poor, in part to oppose military rule, and in part to offset the inroads being made by evangelical Protestant groups. At the same time, small but vocal feminist circles began to develop feminist thought and to organize research-action groups to address Latin American realities. Taken together, the activities of these groups began to be perceived as a social movement, and it changed the public perception—and the perceptions of many women themselves—that women are politically passive and powerless.

From the beginning, class was a central issue for Latin American women's movements, and rural-urban and racial differences emerged as the movements grew and gained political clout. Alliances have been common between urban and rural poor women and upper-middle class, professionally educated women. But support from middle-class women, an important constituency for the women's movement in the North, has usually been weak and ambivalent. In fact, these disparate groups were united as much by their opposition to military dictatorship as by their agreement on a woman's—much less a feminist—agenda. Women in the region have often mobilized as mothers, not only as mothers of the disappeared, but also as mothers organizing to respond to the so-called structural adjustment policies that cut government budgets and social programs. The new austerity has threatened family survival and increased unemployment, forcing more women into the informal sector.

WOMEN'S ACHIEVEMENTS

In the areas of education, politics, and the creative arts, as well as others, Latin American women's achievements are worthy of global recognition. Writers, activists, and professionals—"feminine" and "feminist"—are building richer institutional resources and changing the image of women, creating new opportunities throughout the region.

Education

During the course of the twentieth century, the gender barriers to education were gradually removed, although effective access to university education is still sharply limited by income. By mid-century, especially in the most developed cities in the Southern Cone, Latin American women had already achieved what many North American women were just beginning to fight for: equal access to professional careers, even in the male-dominated professions of law and medicine. By century's end, the number of girls and women in school equaled or exceeded male attendance at all levels from primary school through university. Education is critical to improving women's status. Such issue as gender bias in educational materials, educational tracking, and discrimination in the classroom, as well as in the labor market, are beginning to receive the systematic attention that issues of women's economic participation and human rights had previously gained.

Politics

In addition to making women a political force to be reckoned with, and their success in shifting cultural norms about gender, women's movements have helped shape the agendas of the reconstituted democratic governments in the region. They have established women's councils and ministries to develop women's legislation and to lobby for women's rights and interests in virtually every country, and they have made violence against women a major issue throughout the region. But like other social movements, women's groups have had to adjust their demands to the needs of the broader coalitions of which they were a part. When democratic institutions were reestablished, women had to work through the political parties to bring forward needed legislation and to build support for their issues.

The traditional parties were often resistant to women's issues, however, and early attempts to elect more women to national legislatures ended in failure. Many groups, including women's groups, felt marginalized by the democratic politics they had fought so hard to achieve. The economic crisis that sharply reduced economic growth in the region during the 1980s also produced reverses in government spending on health, education, and social safety nets, policies of critical concern to women. Some women's groups have disappeared, and others have professionalized, recognizing that sustained pressure on legislatures and government agencies is the only way to ensure that women's issues will continue to be addressed. Many groups are concerned about maintaining their autonomy, fearing too close relations with governments and too much dependency on international financing from foundations and other donor agencies that have embraced women's groups as evidence of the emergence of healthy civil societies in the region.

Increasingly, parties are adopting gender quotas and, whether or not the women elected under quotas are sympathetic to women's concerns, the evidence from other countries and regions shows that women of all political persuasions approach politics differently from men, and this can change legislative priorities. Gender quotas are a political experiment that will have implications for politics in the region and worldwide.

Finally, women's issues are most successfully addressed when they are part of a broader process of building coalitions. In the past several years, women have been active in, and have worked with, a variety of other groups and social movements, from human rights, environmental, and indigenous groups to those focused on gay and lesbian rights and health issues, including AIDS. Coalitions make it easier to generate awareness, create legislative alliances, and gain the active support of the president or his staff, often a critical factor for success.

Culture

These dramatic changes in women's educational opportunities and political roles have not occurred in a cultural vacuum. What is perhaps most striking about the past three decades is the degree to which women's traditional roles have changed in attitudes and social practices visible in every country and at every level of society. From soap operas to novels, popular songs, and even television advertising, traditional images and expectations for women are being challenged and redefined.

Women writers and artists have played a major part in changing gender roles in the United States and Northern Europe, beginning in the nineteenth century. Today women novelists, poets, artists, and playwrights are among the most important sources of innovation and debate on gender roles in Latin America today.

The range of Latin American women writers and artists and their creative ways of renegotiating women's identities are widely appreciated in Latin America and beyond. Such poets and novelists as Rosario Castellanos, Elena Poniatowska, Diamela Eltit, Clarice Lispector, and Isabel Allende, to name just a few, have made significant contributions to this process of cultural construction and challenge. Of the women profiled in this volume, 70 percent have made their mark in the cultural sphere. These creative women can draw on a rich cultural heritage and a long tradition linking art and politics together to change public perceptions and reshape social norms.

Women in twentieth-century Latin America have shown remarkable resilience and adaptability, while retaining a sense of pride and a deep commitment to their history, their national and regional and ethnic identities, and the broader world community. The pace of women's activism picked up in the last quarter of the twentieth century, and Latin American women are again receiving the kind of global recognition they enjoyed a century ago, magnified by the numbers of women involved, their wider class and ethnic origins, and the quality of their achievements. The twentieth century was a century of struggle but also of advance; the twenty-first century represents both a promise and a challenge.

—Jane S. Jaquette

NOTABLE
TWENTIETH-CENTURY
LATIN AMERICAN
WOMEN

CLARIBEL ALEGRÍA
(May 12, 1924–   )

Nicaragua/El Salvador:
Author, Poet, Political Activist

Claribel Alegría, author, poet, and political activist in Latin American causes, was born in Estelí, Nicaragua. She considers herself, however, a Salvadoran, and Salvadoran literary histories routinely include her. In fact, the wide array of Alegría's poetic, narrative, and testimonial work has El Salvador and its history as its privileged point of reference.

Her childhood memories in the Western city of Santa Ana and her proximity to the events that had as their epicenter the peasant insurrection of January 1932 in El Salvador served as the background for what might be her most important novel, *Cenizas de Izalco* (Ashes of Izalco, 1966). This novel brought Alegría and her husband, American journalist and writer Darwin J. Flakoll, international notoriety.

Her given name was Clara Isabel Alegría. Mexican intellectual José Vasconcelos, while on his way through El Salvador, gave her her literary name when she was still very young. Vasconcelos also wrote the preface to *Anillo de silencio* (Ring of Silence), her first collection of poems, which was published in Mexico in 1948. Two other people were influential during Alegría's formative period: Salvadoran writer and painter Salarrué, whom she had known since childhood as a family friend, and Spanish writer Juan Ramón Jiménez, who became her energetic tutor after they met in Washington, D.C., around 1943. It was at the home of Jiménez and his wife Zenobia Camprubi that Alegría was initiated into universal poetry and art. Jiménez edited the first collection of her poems written during those three years under his tutelage.

In September 1947 Alegría met Flakoll and married him three months later. Theirs was a fruitful relationship that produced, among other things, four children and over a dozen jointly written novels, narratives, *testimonios* (literally testimonials, but a type of documentary writing considered a separate cultural genre in Latin America), and English translations of Central American poets. The couple took a long journey through various American and European countries. In 1951 they established their residence in Mexico City, where they cultivated a close friendship with writers Augusto Monterroso, Juan José Arreola, and Juan

Claribel Alegría. Photo by Giuseppe Dezza. Courtesy of Dirección de Publicaciones e Impresos, CONCULTURA.

Rulfo. Alegría and Flakoll introduced these and many other Latin American writers to the English-speaking world in their anthology *New Voices of Hispanic America*, published in Boston in 1962. They also lived in Chile, and later in Montevideo (1958–1960) and in Buenos Aires (1960–1962), where they made long-lasting friendships with Chilean poet Nicanor Parra, Argentine writer Julio Cortázar, and Uruguayan writer Mario Benedetti.

The advent of the Cuban Revolution in 1959 substantially modified Alegría's thought and way of life. Her affinity for the revolutionary cause and her husband's position in a diplomatic post for the U.S. government put their marriage at odds. In 1962 the U.S.–supported Bay of Pigs invasion disillusioned Flakoll, who gave up the diplomatic service. Upon their return to the United States, Flakoll obtained a job as a correspondent which took them to Paris. The Cuban Revolution demonstrated to Alegría, at the time, the possibility of putting an end to military dictatorships and it brought back her childhood memories related to the 1932 peasant insurrection. It was then that *Cenizas de Izalco* was written.

In 1966 the couple established their residence on the island of Mallorca, off the coast of Spain, first in Palma Nova and later in Deià, where the British poet Robert Graves lived. Alegría and Flakoll translated Graves's poetry into Spanish for the first time, and Flakoll published his translations in Barcelona in 1984. Meanwhile, Alegría's poetry continued to gain international recognition. In 1978 her collection of poems *Sobrevivo* (I Survive) won the Cuban Casa de Las Américas (House of the Americas) award.

But once again, revolutionary outbursts disrupted their lives. In July 1979, after the victory of the Sandinista Revolution in Nicaragua, they decided to go there to write an extensive testimonial work. After several months in Nicaragua, they returned to Mallorca to write the book. In 1981 they published *No me agarran viva* (They Won't Take Me Alive), the first in a series of texts related to the Salvadoran political reality. In 1982 they decided to reside permanently in Nicaragua where they integrated themselves into the revolution and participated in solidarity activities with El Salvador and other Latin American countries. In 1995, after Flakoll's death, Alegría initiated a permanent migration giving conferences and poetry recitals throughout the United States and Europe. In 1998 the University of Eastern Connecticut awarded her a Doctorate Honoris Causa.

Further Reading

Boschetto-Sandoval, Sandra M., and Marcia Phillips McGowen, eds. *Claribel Alegría and Central American Literature: Critical Essays*. Athens: Ohio University Center for International Studies, 1994.

Craft, Linda J. "Claribel Alegría: Family Ties/Political Ties." In *Novels of Testimony and Resistance from Central America*. 72–105. Gainesville: University Press of Florida, 1997.

Miguel Huezo Mixco

ISABEL ALLENDE
(August 2, 1942–   )

Chile: Author

The best-selling Chilean novelist Isabel Allende was born in Lima, Peru, where her father, Tomás Allende, was serving as a diplomat. Allende is a second cousin of the first democratically elected Marxist-socialist president in Chile, Salvador Allende Gossens, whose presidency and life were terminated during the 1973 coup d'état. Like many other Chilean writers, Allende became an author of literature in exile.

Allende completed her secondary studies at a private school in Santiago de Chile. Due to the diplomatic career of her stepfather, Ramón Huidobro, Allende also spent several years in Bolivia and Lebanon, where she attended a U.S. binational private school and an English private school, respectively. After the completion of her secondary studies, Allende worked as a bilingual secretary at the Santiago Office of the Food and Agriculture Organization (FAO) of the United Nations (1967–1974), for a women's magazine, *Paula*, for a children's magazine, *Manpato*, and for Channels 7 and 13 as an interviewer in Santiago.

In 1975 Allende went into exile in Venezuela. In 1981 Allende began a letter addressed to her dying grandfather in Santiago, which became her best-seller novel *La casa de los espíritus* (The House of the Spirits, 1982), which brought Allende international attention. Since 1987 Allende has resided in California, where she dedicates herself to her writing, lectures, and conferences at numerous universities.

Allende's principal novels are *La casa de los espíritus, De amor y sombra* (Of Love and Shadows, 1984), *Eva Luna* (Eva Luna, 1987), *Cuentos de Eva Luna* (The Stories of Eva Luna, 1989), *El plan infinito* (The Infinite Plan, 1991), *Paula* (Paula, 1994), *Afrodita* (Aphrodite, 1996), and *La hija de Fortuna* (Fortune's Daughter, 1999).

Allende has received such prestigious awards as the Grand Roman d'Evasion Prize (1984), the Freedom to Write Pen Club (1991), the Brandeis University Major Book Collection Award (1993), the Gabriela Mistral Award (1994), and the Dorothy and Lillian Gish Prize (1998). She has also received various book of the year awards and other recognitions, and she holds six honorary doctorates. Allende was visiting professor of creative writing at Montclair State University (1985), the University of Virginia (1986–1987), Barnard College (1988), and the University of California at Berkeley (1989).

Although Allende's literary awards as well as her honorary degrees are numerous, some literary critics have alleged that her works are imitations of Nobel laureate Gabriel García Márquez's masterpiece *Cien años de soledad* (One Hundred Years of Solitude, 1967). This criticism alludes to Allende's use of the elements of so-called magical realism. Some critics agree that the lack of originality of resources and themes is Allende's main weakness. Nevertheless, it must also be stated that Allende was the first Latin American female author to write internationally best-selling novels. In addition, two of her books, *The House of the Spirit* and *Of Love and Shadows*, have been made into films, and her novel *Eva Luna* is currently being made into a film.

In spite of the criticism about Isabel Allende's originality, she fulfilled her tacit mission of denouncing the atrocities committed in the 1973 coup d'état in Chile; its abuses, tortures, murders, and exiles are presented in *The House of the Spirits, Of Love and Shadows*, and *Eva Luna*. In these,

Allende describes her new surroundings, her past years in Chile, her recollections of Chile while residing in exile in Venezuela, and finally her life in San Rafael, California. Allende's writing has become the repository of an array of sad emotions resulting from her father's abandonment of the family during her childhood, her witnessing of the fall of 150 years of democracy in Chile brought about by the socioeconomic interests of a few Chilean aristocrats and U.S. businessmen, her having to leave her family and culture to escape from the fear of threats to an unknown land and society where she suffered economic hardship, losing her beloved grandfather, the impotence of not being allowed to enter her native country again, divorcing her first husband, Miguel Frías, while in Venezuela, and finally the agony and helplessness of losing her daughter Paula, who died after a year of being in a coma.

Prominent in Allende's works are her mastery of the language and her rich use of depictions which enliven her characters and give the reader a clear-cut image and background of each character. Another outstanding characteristic of Allende's novels is the presence of autobiographical elements, which are expressed in a very forthright manner. Allende does not hesitate to portray a homosexual hairdresser as one of her characters (in *Of Love and Shadows*), a rape committed by Esteban Trueba and the grotesque depictions of an elderly overweight woman's lack of personal hygiene (*The House of the Spirits*), her father, while serving as a diplomat in Peru, as the center of a scandal when he is caught in a sexual encounter with a man from Lima's elite (*Paula*).

Allende's fiction has been translated into twenty-five languages, and her popularity has allowed her to live a comfortable life, all of which has allowed her to be active in several philanthropic activities and in establishing the Isabel Allende Foundation and the Paula Scholarship fund.

Further Reading

Hart, Patricia. *Narrative Magic in the Fiction of Isabel Allende*. Rutherford, N.J.: Fairleigh Dickinson University Press, 1989.
Rodden, John. *Conversations with Isabel Allende*. Austin: University of Texas Press, 1999.

Gregory D. Lagos-Montoya

ALICIA ALONSO

(December 21, 1921–   )

Cuba: Dancer, Choreographer, and Educator

Alicia Alonso, a former prima ballerina, is known for international successes as a dancer, her founding of classical ballet schools in Cuba, and her Cuban-inspired choreography.

The name Alonso came from Fernando Alonso, her husband and professional associate until 1975, when they divorced. Alicia Martínez del Hoyo was born in Marianao, Cuba. In 1929 her father, a veterinary doctor in the army, was commissioned by the government to make a purchase of Spanish horses. The family settled in Spain for several years, where Alicia took lessons in Spanish classical dance. Back in Havana in 1931 she registered in a classical dance course taught by Nikolai Yavorsky. Also in that year, she attended a performance given by Antonia Mercé, known as La Argentina, a mythical Spanish dancer who made a deep impression on her.

In 1932 she gave her first dance solo when she played the role of Oiseau Bleu in Pyotr Ilich Tchaikovsky's classical ballet *Sleeping Beauty*, which was choreographed by Yavorsky. In 1937, still a student with Yavorsky, she was chosen to dance in Tchaikovsky's *Swan Lake* with Robert Belsky, a famous dancer with the Russian Ballet of Montecarlo. Although the critics declared that the young novice was certainly worthy of her famous male counterpart, the road to becoming a professional was not an easy one. Her biographer, Pedro Simón, has written that at that time Cuba was by no means a country capable of fostering a talent in classical dance. Furthermore, the traditional middle class still held prejudices against the theater, instilled by the colonial clergy.

In search of more promising horizons she moved to New York, which was not yet the art emporium it became after World War II. In order to survive, Alonso resorted to performing in musical reviews. At the same time she was taking lessons from the best dance teachers available in the city, including Enrico Zanfretta (representative of the already almost extinct Italian school), Alexandra Fedorova (herself a former pupil of Mikhail Fokine, the outstanding Russian choreographer), and Muriel Stuart (a direct heir to the great Russian ballet dancer Anna Pavlova's

Alicia Alonso. Courtesy of Photofest.

knowledge). All of them admired the young Cuban's amazing physical and creative qualities. From her teachers, Alonso assimilated and synthesized a series of classical principles from different schools and created her own personal style. Overcoming all obstacles—among them the birth of her only daughter—Alicia began to promote herself as one of the most promising figures of the incipient American ballet.

In 1939, while working for Lincoln Kirsten in his rather modest American Ballet Caravan, she was discovered by Léonide Massine, the great figure of the Russian Ballet of Montecarlo, who offered her a costardom in Manuel de Falla's *El sombrero de tres picos* (The Three Cornered Hat) and Nikolai Rimsky-Korsakov's *Capriccio Espagnol*. Cleverly, Alonso declined the offer and stayed with Kirsten, who allowed her to pursue an experimentality that she still needed in order to explore her possibilities both as a dancer and as a choreographer.

In 1940 Alonso entered the Ballet Theatre of New York (later named American Ballet Theater), which already had outstanding choreographers, designers, musicians, and instructors. There she spent two decades that were crucial for her integral formation and promotion; she also acquired extensive choreographical knowledge from costar Anthony Tudor, the British dancer and choreographer who was incorporating a new theatrical language to ballet. Alonso's first great triumph took place in 1943 when she was called upon to replace an ailing Alicia Markova, the great British ballerina, in the main role of Adolphe Charles Adam's *Giselle*, which allowed her to demonstrate her absolute mastery of both movement and pantomime.

In 1942 she began to promote dance in Havana, where, together with the Spanish actor Juan Martínez Allende and the Cuban writer Alejo Carpentier, she founded a cultural group called Agrupación La Silva (i.e., "The Poetic Forest," in Spanish), for whom she choreographed *La condesita* (The Little Countess), based upon a piece by the Catalan composer Joaquim Nin.

In 1943, after having declined costardom four years before, she joined Massine in *Capriccio Espagnol* as his dancing partner. Because that choreography demanded a knowledge of Spanish classical dance, she consulted with two famous Spanish dancers, Vicente Escudero and Encarnación López, known as a La Argentinita. She later worked with the Russian painter Marc Chagall in the designs for *Aleko*, a creation by Massine based on a Rimsky-Korsakov score.

The list of choreographers for whom Alonso danced is vast. Among all of them, Mikhail Fokine provided her with the most emblematic choreography of her entire career, such as Adam's *Giselle*, based on a popular Germanic legend. It premiered in 1943 with Anton Dolin as her partner. This ballet, which accentuates the romanticism of the original folktale, has been incorporated into the repertoire of the operas of Los Angeles, Paris, and Vienna, among others. *Giselle*, in which Alicia played a wide range of characters of variable complexity, remains the most beloved of her roles.

If both Tudor and Massine were important influences on Alonso's peculiar scenography, no less important was George Balanchine, an outstanding master, musician, and choreographer, who created for Alonso some successful ballets based on the music of Tchaikovsky and Igor Stravinsky. Through Balanchine Alonso learned a better use of music in the language of dance. Equally fruitful was her association with the American choreographer Agnes de Mille, who was fond of historical and folkloric subjects, and for whom Alonso danced in *Fall River Legend* by Morton Gould and Oliver Smith in 1948.

The American Ballet Theater took Alonso to the most important stages in the world. She had already reached full stardom. In 1946 the London critics acclaimed her as "prima ballerina assoluta" (Siegel 1979, 37). Then she took the American Ballet Theater to Havana, where she was warmly applauded and given important official decorations. Thanks to Alonso, Cuba discovered its passion for classical dance. In 1948 Alonso created Ballet Alicia Alonso in Havana, which she was able to fund by means of her many contacts abroad. In 1956, after renaming it Ballet de Cuba, she created a series of choreographies inspired in local folklore and using autochthonous musical elements, including *Fiesta negra* (Black Fiesta) and

Sonsoro Cosogno, both by Alberto Alonso, Alicia's brother-in-law. Alonso soon received a warning from the Intelligence Services of dictator Fulgencio Batista that Alberto Alonso's choreography *Antes del alba* (Before the Dawn) had a destabilizing message. When she ignored the warning, the authorities deprived Ballet de Cuba of its meager state funding and soon after Cuban theaters were officially forbidden to accept her performances.

Alonso became an exile and took the best of Ballet de Cuba's components and settled in the United States. Soon after, the Ballet de Cuba's successful performances at Moscow's Bolshoi, Leningrad's Kirov, and the Opera Theater of Kiev confirmed both Alonso's mastery and the Ballet of Cuba's quality. In her visits to the Soviet Union, she had access to the great centers for the formation of talent, allowing her to observe and adopt a series of teaching techniques then unknown in America.

With the Cuban Revolution in 1959, she decided to return to her native island, where she then founded the Alicia Alonso School of Dance. She soon received the encouragement and protection of the socialist authorities and thereafter she renamed her company Ballet Nacional de Cuba. Defying old racist prejudices she opened both her ballet and school of dance to students of all races and social backgrounds, making talent the supreme criterion for admission. In 1960 she severed her connections with the American Ballet Theater to devote herself to promoting Cuban ballet. In that same year the U.S. Department of State denied her an entry visa. She rejected lucrative American offers to defect, oriented her Cuban National Ballet toward Europe and the rest of the world, and began a series of cooperative efforts with Maurice Béjart's Ballets, the Royal Ballet of Denmark, the Imperial Ballet of Tokyo, and the Ballet of the Scala di Milano, and she established special relations in 1972 with the Paris Opera.

In 1975, after several years of being denied an entering visa by the U.S. State Department, she received an invitation to attend a special gala celebrating the thirty-fifth anniversary of the American Ballet Theater, which owed much of its fame to her. New appearances in America followed, especially those at the Metropolitan during the 1970s, where she presented her own choreographies of Georges Bizet's *Carmen* and *Giselle*. In 1978 she took her Cuban National Ballet to the Kennedy Center, with enormous success.

Today, the Cuban ballet school's methodology and principles are appreciated and followed by many teaching institutions of the world, especially in Latin America and Spain. In 1993 the City University of Madrid created a professorship of dance, the Cátedra de Danza Alicia Alonso, under Alonso's patronage and advice. In her catalogue of choreographies, many of them incorporated into the repertoires of the most famous theaters in the world, mention must be made of Léo Delibes's

Coppelia (1948); Frédéric Chopin's *Les Sylphides* (The Sylphs, 1948); Ernesto Lecuona's *Estampas cubanas* (Cuban Sketches, 1953); Tchaikovsky's *Swan Lake* (1954), *The Nutcracker* (1973), and *Sleeping Beauty* (1974); Adam's *Giselle* (1973); Ludwig Minkus's *La Bayadère* (The Indian Dancer, 1976) and *Don Quixote* (1988); and Gaspar Angiolini's *Dido abbandonata* (Dido Abandoned, 1773).

She has been distinguished with an extremely long list of decorations, both Cuban and international. No other prima ballerina in the world has continued her choreographical and dancing activities for such a long period—from the early 1930s to the present. Alonso incorporated diverse traditions into her career. However, Alonso not only excelled as a prima ballerina but also succeeded in transmitting her enthusiasm to a number of younger artists in the Ballet School she founded in Cuba, the youngest and most promising one in the small circle of world-class ballet schools.

Further Reading

Arnold, Sandra Martin. *Alicia Alonso, First Lady of Ballet*. New York: Walker, 1993.
Gámez, Tana de. *Alicia Alonso at Home and Abroad*. New York: Citadel Press, 1971.
Siegel, Beatrice. *Alicia Alonso, the Story of a Ballerina*. New York: F. Warner, 1979.
Terry, Walter. *Alicia and Her Ballet Nacional de Cuba*. Garden City, N.Y.: Anchor Books, 1981.

Manuel García Castellón

ELVIA ALVARADO
(January 25, 1940–   )

Honduras: Social Activist, Political Activist

Elvia Alvarado, a peasant leader and social activist in rural Honduras, was born in 1938 to a poor, landless peasant family. Her father worked as a day laborer for a large landowner, and her mother raised chickens and pigs and baked bread for sale at the market. A small garden supplemented their meager food supply. The family lived in the village of Lejamani near the state capital of Comayagua. Elvia Alvarado was one of seven children raised by their mother after her parents separated. She was the only child to attend school, and although the highest level offered in her village school was second grade, she attended for five years in order to learn as much as possible from the limited resources available. At the age of fifteen, she had the first of her six children, all of whom

Elvia Alvarado. Photo by Medea Benjamin. Courtesy of Speak Out.

she has brought up without significant support from their father. When
her youngest children were very small they lived with their grandmother
for two years while Alvarado worked as a live-in cook and servant in
Comayagua and sent her salary home to support them. During those
years she had a free weekend once every three months to visit her children in Lejamani.

A turning point in Alvarado's life occurred during her mid-thirties
when she joined a mothers' club sponsored by the Catholic Church.
These clubs brought together poor women in rural villages for the primary purpose of improving nutrition for children through education,
community gardens, and distribution of donated food. The women also
discussed other problems that they faced in their community, such as
the lack of medical care, safe drinking water, jobs, roads, schools, and
other public services. After being elected president of her local club, the
Church invited Alvarado to participate in a week-long workshop where
she received training to serve as an organizer of mothers' clubs in other
villages in her region of Honduras. The club experience and the leadership training awakened a new awareness of the need for far-reaching
social, economic, and political changes in her country. Alvarado worked
for a number of years under the auspices of the Catholic Church, traveling to remote areas and organizing women to carry out nutrition programs. These trips required a minimum stay of three days per village in

order to develop contacts and establish a rudimentary organization, which meant long absences from her home and family. Through the clubs the women's consciousness of their situation soon went beyond a concern about the lack of food for their children to fundamental questions about the structures of power and wealth in Honduras that result in a stratified and unequal society.

In 1977, when the Church ended its support of the mothers' clubs, Alvarado and the other grassroots leaders decided to create their own women's organization, the Federation of Campesina Women (FEHMUC). Alvarado worked with FEHMUC for several years, setting up food cooperatives and gardens and organizing women into effective advocates for their communities. However, the problem of the unequal distribution of land and the poverty of the landless peasant majority presented obstacles to progress that cooperatives and small gardens could not address. With this larger problem in mind, Alvarado joined the National Campesino Union (UNC), and in 1985 she was a founder of the National Congress of Rural Workers (CNTC). These are grassroots organizations that work to recover unproductive agricultural land and put it into the hands of the peasants using the procedures established by the Agrarian Reform Law of 1975.

The Agrarian Reform Law stipulates that agricultural lands, whether private or state owned, must be kept in productive use. Uncultivated lands may be identified, investigated, and ultimately turned over to peasant families, who are then entitled to technical assistance from government agronomists and loans for seed and equipment. In order to process claims under the law, the people work with the National Agrarian Institute (INA). Due to corruption and the very lengthy legal process, little if any land is legally acquired in this manner. When title is granted, the technical assistance and loans are slow to come forth. The UNC and the CNTC have therefore developed the strategy of land recoveries, direct actions to take over lands in which Alvarado has often played a leading role. In a land recovery, a group of peasant families moves onto uncultivated land and begins to live there and to plant crops. They meet with varying degrees of opposition from the landowners and the police, but they persist in appealing to their rights under the law and in establishing a visible presence on the land. At times their settlements and crops are repeatedly destroyed by the landowners, but they return to reestablish their claim. This technique sometimes leads the authorities to grant legal ownership to the peasants, and it has proved to be their most effective instrument of change. However, not all land recoveries are successful, and the peasants often suffer violence at the hands of the landowners. In one early land recovery in which Alvarado participated, a peasant leader was shot and killed by a sniper. In other cases, multiple killings have been carried out against the peasants who are occupying disputed land.

Land recoveries and other organizing activities of the CNTC constitute the primary social justice work carried out by Alvarado. Due to her ongoing efforts and her visibility as a regional leader of the CNTC, she has been the target of persecution by the government. She was jailed at least six times in the 1980s, and she reports being tortured while in detention on one occasion. Nevertheless, she remains committed to struggling for change through peaceful means such as land recoveries, marches, sit-ins, and hunger strikes. Besides opposition from the government and land-owners, Alvarado perceives that peasant groups working for change face obstacles from within their own ranks that must be overcome. The low level of formal education is one impediment that must be addressed through training of peasant leaders, and the sexism of a patriarchal society is an obstacle to the full participation of women in the struggle. Alvarado is dedicated to strengthening the role of women through her own example and through practical organizing activities. The CNTC does not receive any funding from the government. It relies on dues paid by its own members, and it gets some support from international solidarity groups. The lack of funds to pay for lawyers and to compensate the organization's leaders is another significant obstacle to its work.

In 1986 Alvarado agreed to collaborate with the writer Medea Benjamin to produce her life story. The book *Don't Be Afraid Gringo* was first published in 1987 by the Institute for Food and Development Policy, and it was reissued by Harper & Row in 1989. Alvarado thus joined the ranks of Latin American women who have found a way to make their voices heard outside of their immediate communities through the writing of testimonial autobiographies. *Don't Be Afraid Gringo* is unique in that it directly addresses a U.S. audience, with the objective of educating them about her country and about the reality of U.S. intervention in Central America. In the 1990s Alvarado has continued to bring word of the situation of Honduran peasants and the negative impact of the increasing U.S. military presence there to an international audience through speaking tours in the United States. Appearing before community, church, and union groups and college and university audiences, she talks about Honduras and her work there and appeals to her listeners to advocate for change in the policies of their own government. The devastating hurricane of 1998 caused a terrible loss of life, and it destroyed roads, bridges, crops, and entire villages throughout Honduras. Alvarado is in the forefront of efforts to raise funds and material aid to meet the urgent task of rebuilding Honduras, a process that most observers estimate will take over a decade to complete. Alvarado is both an exceptional and a typical representative of women of her social class in Central America who live a daily struggle for existence and yet who, when given the smallest opening, effectively utilize their skills and their experiences to challenge the status quo and to work for social and economic change.

Further Reading

Alvarado, Elvia, and Medea Benjamin. *Don't Be Afraid Gringo: A Honduran Woman Speaks from the Heart.* New York: Harper & Row, 1989.

Beth E. Jörgensen

ALBALUCÍA ANGEL MARULANDA
(September 27, 1939–   )

Colombia: Author

A conscious experimenter in the field of literature, a gifted singer, and a tireless traveler, Angel Marulanda was born in the heart of the coffee-growing region of Colombia: the city of Pereira, in the state of Risaralda. Her career as a writer covers several decades, and she is undoubtedly a prominent figure in the literature of Colombia and the continent. Angel's work includes a small volume of short stories titled *¡Oh Gloria inmarcesible!* (Oh, Boundless Glory, 1979) and the novels *Los girasoles en invierno* (Sunflowers in Winter, 1970), *Dos veces Alicia* (Alice, Twice Over, 1972), *Estaba la pájara pinta sentada en el verde limón* (The Petite Painted Bird Perched on the Green Lemon Limb, 1975), *Misiá señora* (Missus-Lady, 1982), and *Las andariegas* (The Wayfarers, 1984). Her theater pieces include *Siete lunas y un espejo* (Seven Moons and a Mirror, 1984) and *La Manzana de piedra* (The Stone Apple, 1983).

Angel's great-grandparents were the founders of Pereira, the provincial town where she grew up. She was the daughter of Margarita Marulanda and Gustavo Angel, who were from upper-class families dedicated to commerce and business. Her father persuaded her to study commerce and she received a degree as technician in commerce and became the manager of her father's business when she was sixteen.

Known to many as Albalú, she was very close to her paternal grandmother who rewarded her every time she read a page of the Bible, even though she had little or no money. Angel's relationship with her mother, however, was marked by tension and silence.

Later on, when Angel chose to be a writer, her grandmother's way of

Albalucía Angel Marulanda. Courtesy of
Olga Angel.

talking and her sayings found their way into Angel's fiction. Besides the
Bible, Angel was nurtured by *Thousand and One Nights*, the lives of Saint
Francis of Assisi and Teresa of Avila, and such popular publications as
Argentine magazines *Billiken* and *Leoplán*, especially the latter since it
offered the classics in western literature. The images of saints, heroes,
and heroines left an imprint in her writing.

Angel's childhood was spent between the small town of Pereira and
the countryside. On her father's farm she was in contact with nature,
and she liked to tame horses. Her beloved river and trees would reappear in her literary production. Angel continues to keep close to nature. Even at public events it is not unusual to see her holding some
fragrant rose sticks, which she uses as a source of energy and as a connection to nature.

In contrast to the freedom experienced at the farm, her early school
years were rigid and controlled. She went to a religious school in Pereira,
which was run by Swiss Franciscan nuns whose command of Spanish
was extremely limited. School is not favorably portrayed in her fiction.
Besides excelling academically, Angel enjoyed music and sports. Angel,
who still sings and plays the guitar, depended on her music for economic
survival while she was living in Paris.

Neither these activities nor her inclination to write were encouraged by her family. One of the most powerful obstacles Angel encountered was the strong opposition of her family to her desire to become a writer. Her family either ignored or criticized her novels. In the face of her mother's and her siblings' criticism, Angel left for Europe to become a writer. In 1975, when her novel *Estaba la pájara pinta sentada en el verde limón* was awarded the Vivencias (Experiences) literary prize in Colombia, María Isabel Mejía, the mayor of Cali, stated that Angel was in exile because she was not accepted by her generation and that she had no one with whom to share her work and culture in Colombia.

The publishing world has proved challenging too. Argos Vergara, which published *Estaba la pájara pinta sentada en el verde limón, Misiá señora,* and *Las andariegas,* went bankrupt. None of these books has been reprinted. *Estaba la pájara pinta sentada en el verde limón* and *¡Oh gloria inmarcesible!* were published in paperback, thanks to Gloria Zea, the director of the Colombian Institute of Culture (Colcultura) at the time. In Colombia Angel's work has neither enjoyed wide distribution nor acceptance. Harsh and uninformed criticism, mostly by male readers in Colombia, is grounded in the critics' suspicions of lesbianism. However, some of her less accessible novels, such as *Misiá señora* and *Las andariegas,* are beginning to receive critical attention.

Angel has used her travels as a source of inspiration. Voyages of women through space and time are central to her novels *Los girasoles en invierno* and *Las andariegas.* Angel's circuitous journeys started within Colombia. First she went to Barranquilla on the Atlantic coast and then to Bogotá, where she attended the University of the Andes. She began to study history, literature, and art history, but she had to return to Pereira under pressure from her father, because she was still a minor.

Her family disapproved of her links with the members of the Nadaista movement who aggressively challenged bourgeois conventions. The Nadaistas represented a late avant-garde movement close to the Beatniks and other similar movements in Latin America. Angel was very close to the poet Gonzalo Arango, the founder of the group.

Despite her family's attempt to restrain her, Angel returned to the University of the Andes. She took up art and art history under the tutelage of the Argentine critic and writer Marta Traba, who was a powerful influence on Angel. As Angel's role model, mentor, and friend, Traba introduced her to the rigors of academia hoping to turn her into an art critic. For some time Angel would send art reviews while visiting museums and studying art at La Sorbonne and at the University of Rome. But this was not Angel's real passion.

As encouraging as Traba was in the area of art history, she, however, also opposed Angel's desire to be a writer. Despite feelings of loyalty and indebtedness, Angel persisted. In 1975 her novel *Estaba la pájara pinta sentada en el verde limón* was awarded the Vivencias literary prize in Colombia. This luminous moment was darkened by a wave of unexpected and corrosive publicity. The headlines of the June 14, 1975, edition of *El pueblo* (The People), a newspaper from Cali, portrayed her as "crazy" and added that according to one of the judges for the prize, the novel "was not original." It was also said that Angel was a *"rancheras"* (Mexican *corridos*) singer in Europe, an occupation too mundane and bohemian for a woman of the upper class. This was aimed at diminishing the merits of a novel written by a woman while maintaining the male-dominated Colombian literary canon. The Vivencias prize created a scandal, but it did not produce a forum for critical readings; consequently, the novel had some difficulties in being published.

Albalucía Angel has come to represent female transgression, marginality, and audacity as well the inner power of following a dream. The quality of her work is a direct result of an honest and real love and disposition for writing. No matter how poor, lonely, or isolated, Angel has made herself in her own terms. Even though her work has not been widely available and accepted in Colombia, she still wants to show that literature remains her desire and her utopia; in literature, she cannot be disenfranchised.

After a long hiatus, Angel is writing a new book. *Aratia* is semiautobiographical. The ability to persevere despite setbacks is a quality that identifies Albalucía Angel both in the literary world and in her personal life. She is a pioneer and a role model. For her, writing is a self-fulfilling experience. Therefore, each one of her literary works is a high peak. Since she never knows if she would ever write another, each is written "as if it were the last" (personal communication, 1999).

Further Reading

Araujo, Helena. "Oppression, Tradition, Transgression in Some Colombian Female Novelists." In *Splintering Darkness. Latin American Women Writers in Search of Themselves*, edited by Lucía Guerra Cunningham, 131–42. Pittsburgh: Latin American Literary Review Press, 1990.

García Pinto, Magdalena. "Albalucía Angel." In *Women Writers of Latin America: Intimate Histories*, translated by Trudy Blach and Magdalena García Pinto, 45–78. Austin: University of Texas Press, 1991.

Williams, Raymond. "Women Writing in the Americas: New Projects of the 1980s." In *The Novel in the Americas*, 119–50. Niwot, Colo.: University Press of Colorado, 1992.

Myriam Osorio

LAURA ANTILLANO

(August 8, 1950–)

Venezuela: Author, Journalist, Educator

Laura Antillano, who was born in Caracas, Venezuela, is a professor, writer, and journalist. When she completed the fifth grade, she moved to Maracaibo. Her mother, Lourdes Armas, was a painter, and her father, Sergio Antillano, a journalist. Both were members of Taller Libre de Arte (Free Art Studio), an important art group in the 1940s. From her mother, Antillano inherited a curiosity for reading, the ability to narrate, and her interest in art; from her father, she inherited an interest in journalism and the media. Her love for literature emerged at an early age. She remembers writing in notebooks when she was about eleven years old; this time became the starting point of her literary work. At the age of fifteen, she began writing for newspapers and, at eighteen, the prestigious publishing house Monte Avila published her first book. This precocious inclination for writing forced Antillano to face her first challenge: to enter the world of journalism and literature as a young woman in Venezuela during the 1960s.

In 1967 Antillano began her studies at the University of Zulia, where she soon established the Teatro de Títeres (Puppet Theater), and became the director as well as head scriptwriter, positions she held until 1975. While at the university, she also began a Sunday program on the radio called *Reporte Especial* (Special Report). In 1971 she graduated with a degree in Hispanic literature.

Her first book, *La bella epoca* (Belle Epoque), published in 1969, is a collection of short stories. Here she developed some of the stylistic features that would be found in future works, such as her interest in children's and women's issues; the combination of nostalgic, poetic, and tragic views; her preference for short and dense narrative; and the use of sober, elaborate, and suggestive language. In 1971 her first novel was published, *La muerte del monstruo-come-piedras* (Death of the Rock-eating Monster), which concerns children's issues. From an autobiographical and testimonial point of view, Antillano does not limit herself to facing reality, but provides a vast historical view that blends both a nostalgic perspective of childhood and concern for the future.

During the 1970s, Antillano began to travel abroad, to Germany, Spain,

Laura Antillano. Courtesy of Argenis Agudo.

Austria, Argentina, Mexico, and Cuba, where she participated in several conferences and gave lectures. She spent eight months in Rome, where she wrote a collection of short stories, *Un carro largo se llama tren* (A Long Car Is Called a Train). In 1973 she went to Chile, where she took literature classes under the direction of Antonio Skármeta and Luis Domínguez. In 1975 she started teaching literature at the University of Carabobo, Valencia, and later became director of cultural affairs in the Department of Education and chair of the Department of Languages and Literature. In 1975 she also returned to her journalistic activities at the newspaper and radio, almost always placing an emphasis on culture. In the daily newspaper *Hora cero* (Zero Hour), she wrote a weekly column dedicated to children; she also wrote a literary and cultural column. Children are a constant theme throughout Antillano's works; two of them especially reveal her creativity: *Una vaca querida* (A Dear Cow; 1996), and the essay "¡Ay! Qué aburrido es leer: El hábito lector y el cuento de la infancia" (Oh! Reading Is So Boring: Reading Habits and Children's Stories, 1991). She also wrote a daily column for the newspaper *El carabobeño* (Carabobo Daily), and she now writes for the Fundarte magazine *Criticarte* (Criticism/Art), for the journal *Imagen* (Image) on literature, and for the magazine "Pandora" of the newspaper *El Nacional*.

In 1980 Antillano moved to the United States, where she completed a Master of Arts degree in Latin American literature in 1981 at the University of Oregon. In 1992 she completed another master's degree, this time at the University of Zulia, with a major in Venezuelan literature.

Antillano also works with cinema. Her involvement in Venezuelan cinema and television has been prolific and rewarding. As a scriptwriter she worked with Olegario Barrera on the film *Pequeña revancha* (Small Revenge, 1985) and with Emilia Anguita on the short *Entre líneas* (Between the Lines, 1982). Adapting several of Venezuelan Rómulo Gallegos's short stories for television was a gratifying experience for her. She also wrote television scripts for soap operas and a children's series for Radio Caracas Television. Written works that reflect her involvement in cinema include *Cuentos de película* (Movie Stories, 1985) and articles published in movie magazines, such as *Encuadre* (Frame).

In 1988 Antillano published her second novel, *Perfume de gardenia* (A Gardenia's Perfume). This novel demonstrates how much the author has grown, not only in technique, but also in structure complexity. However, she reached maturity as a novelist with her third novel, *Solitaria. Solidaria* (Lonely. Understanding, 1990), which revolves around the female character and reflects one of Antillano's main interests: historical re-creation. What stands out is the complex relationship between time and space, the blending of reality and fiction, and the ability to create a poetic atmosphere in which language—natural, spontaneous, and suggestive—is a fundamental element. Her interest in history is also reflected in her short stories, such as "Tuna de mar" (Tuna of the Sea).

From 1989 to 1992, Antillano continued to work on cultural activities. She directed the Literary Supplement of *El otro papel* (The Other Paper) of the Maracaibo daily newspaper *Crítica* (Criticism), she wrote a column called "La palmera luminosa" (The Shiny Palm Tree), and she established a publishing house called La Letra Voladora (The Flying Letter). She also developed a literary workshop at the Centro de Bellas Artes (Fine Arts Center) in Maracaibo. When she returned to Valencia in the early 1990s, Antillano was elected chair of the Department of Venezuelan and Ibero-American Literatures at the University of Carabobo. She also organized a literary workshop in her home.

From 1994 to 1997, Antillano was in charge of the Literary Supplement *Letra inversa* (Inverted Letter) of the daily newspaper *Notitarde* (Afternoon News). In 1995 she was elected graduate coordinator of Venezuelan literature at the University of Carabobo, a position she holds to this day. In 1997 she returned to her work on the radio, this time with a program called *La palmera luminosa* (The Shiny Palm Tree) at the Cultural Radio Station at the same university. Soon afterward she created an educational program called *Taller literario* (Literary Workshop), and she currently works on both programs. She writes a column for *Notitarde* and, in addition to these activities, in 1998 she was elected director of culture at the University of Carabobo.

Antillano has published seventeen books and has received several awards, both for her work in literature and for her journalistic and cultural activities. In 1998 she was the first woman to win the XXXIII Concurso de Cuentos (33rd Award for Short Stories) for "La luna no es pan-de-horno" (The Moon Is Not Oven Bread). She also won the Premio de Periodismo Especializado Pancho Silbino (The Pancho Silbino Award for Specialized Journalism). In 1996 she received the Premio Regional de Literatura (Regional Award for Literature) from the government of Zulia State for prose, and in 1997, she was recognized nationally for her literary work at the Mariano Picón Salas Biennial in Mérida. At this ceremony, Antillano expressed her thoughts on literature and her creative work: her work is nothing more than the answers to questions raised by living daily reality, and it is a sample of her nonconformity and rebellion within society. For Antillano, writing is a subversive act in the sense that it represents opposition to any kind of hegemonic power. This opposition to power, in a broad sense, is the reason she writes.

Antillano belongs to the outstanding group of Latin American intellectuals and writers who are totally committed to their country and their time. Her ongoing educational and creative efforts represent an attempt to overcome a troubled reality with the specific goal of creating a project for the future.

Further Reading

Antillano, Laura, and Kathy Leonard. "Gone with the Wind." In *The Movies: Texts, Receptions, Exposures*, edited by Laurence Goldstein and Ira Konigsberg, 240–43. Ann Arbor: University of Michigan Press, 1996.

Gary, Edith Dimo. "La marginalidad como autorepresentación en la escritura de Laura Antillano." *Alba de América: Revista literaria* 14, nos. 26–27 (1996): 373–79.

Rivas de Wesolowski, Luz Marina. "La perspectiva marginal de la historia en la obra de Laura Antillano." *Venezuelan Literature and Arts Journal* 2, no. 1 (1996): 15–31.

Roberto Fuertes-Manjón

DÉBORA ARANGO

(November 11, 1907–   )

Colombia: Artist

Débora Arango, a controversial painter who challenged the Colombian cultural status quo, was born in Medellín, the eighth of the twelve children of Elvira Pérez and Cástor Arango, a businessman. Arango contracted malaria at an early age and a change of climate was the only cure known at the time. Her elementary education was thus interrupted by frequent periods spent with relatives living in the countryside. Upon her return to Medellín to pursue her high school degree, she met the Italian nun María Rabaccia, who discovered Arango's ability as a painter. Because the aftereffects of her illness set her back repeatedly, after six years Arango abandoned her studies to devote herself completely to painting.

Arango's work brings up questions about our own view of morality, and hers is the kind of work that will never suit everybody's taste. As a result, she has been both flatly rejected and attacked by the establishment and ignored by critics to minimize the value of her work. Active at a moment, and in a society, that wanted only to maintain the status quo, she and her work were rejected both by government and church. From the beginning, it was clear that the strong opinions voiced in her paintings were directed against the ruling classes and a moralistic society that did not want to be confronted with the reality and the changes that were taking place in the country and the world at the time.

The moment in history when Arango began to show her works is of extreme importance to understand the reactions to her paintings. In the 1930s, after forty-five years of government by the extreme right, the centrist Liberal party had regained access to power in Colombia. Whereas the defeated party had tried to keep the status quo for decades, the new government attempted to bring to the forefront all sorts of political and social issues. In Arango's native region of Antioquia, the struggle between the old and the new was as obvious and visible as it was in the rest of the country, if not more so owing to the conservative ideals of the people of the region.

At the same time, these were crucial times for the development of

Colombian painting. The influential work of Pedro Nel Gómez and Ignacio Gómez Jaramillo heralds changes in art, marking the beginnings of modern painting in the country. Far from the traditionalistic Círculo de Bellas Artes (Fine Arts Circle) centered in the capital city of Bogota, these artists were able to avoid both the rigidity of the Academics and the local color of the Bachues, an artistic movement searching for a truly American style and rejecting any foreign or European model, with the concomitant search for an art rooted in the vernacular and ecology. Finding inspiration in the modernistic art they had previously seen in Europe, their work was fueled mainly by social issues. By the 1930s, though, artists who took on social or political themes in their work were being harassed and persecuted all over Europe. Nationalistic movements flourished which, more often than not, put art at the service of the state. Most commonly, the chosen means of expression were realism and monumentalism: artistic expressions that tend to lack any criticism or individualism. Here the objective was to show the might of the state, whether it be the socialist or the fascist state, and deviations were hardly tolerated.

In Colombia any initiative in favor of change was quickly exposed to the criticism of the conservatives. In exactly this social theme Arango found the material for her paintings. The years between 1937 and 1944 are of extreme importance for her; these years show the deep mark on her artistic career. The artists of her generation were then regarded as a continuation, in the field of the aesthetics, of the political ideas of the newly elected Liberal party. In 1940 Laureano Gómez, head of the opposition, seized an opportunity to take on the ministry of education by allowing an Arango show to take place in the foyer of the Teatro Colón in Bogotá. The next day, the exhibition had to be taken down amid the intense pressure from the conservative Bogotá society. The paintings were then taken to the senate, at the request of the opposition, as proof of the lack of morality of the Ministry of Education, which had granted permission for the show to take place in a state-sponsored venue. In 1937 Arango participated in a show, together with some other former and current students of Pedro Nel Gómez, at the Palacio de Bellas Artes (Palace of Fine Arts) in Medellín. After the success of the show, the master painter asked the group to explore the nude figure in their paintings as a further step in their artistic development. The suggestion was quickly rejected by everybody but Arango, who made the nude a central point of her career.

From her other mentor, the painter Eladio Vélez, she learned to master her preferred medium, the watercolor, and discovered her passion for portraiture. Eladio Vélez's world was one of tranquil existence in deep contrast with the expressionistic temperament of Pedro Nel Gómez, from whom Arango learned to improvise and be creative with pigments. Most important, from Gómez she learned to disregard beauty in favor of a new aesthetic of the ugly that she would develop during her career. Neither master left on her a mark stronger than that of her own will: her use of her peculiar sense of color, the choice of subjects straight from the marketplace, the portrayal of prostitutes and policemen were all of her own volition, a most expressionistic way of expression.

For her, expressionism was all around to be explored. It was an integral yet hidden part of all individuals, a twist of the talk, a shade of everybody's soul. Her interest was to go past the beauty of the surface to reach the hidden psyche; the beauty of the naked body as she painted it in *Bailarinas en reposo* (Dancers at Rest, 1939) could be as inspiring as the strength of such portraits as *Actriz retirada* (Veteran Actress, 1944). Her nudes are open; they never try to hide their nakedness. Her women are never ashamed of their sexuality, and their pubic hair reveals more than it hides. This is equally true of their direct and open gaze, in contrast with the timid and moralizing nudes of her male contemporaries, let alone the still lives of other female painters. Arango's women stare at us and hold their gaze up even though, or perhaps because, they are naked.

This transgression of the academic rules made her an easy target. Any transgression of the norm becomes an aggression against society. These painted women are stating their independence and showing their emancipation in both the sexual and the intellectual fields, something unheard of in Colombian society of the 1930s, much less meriting being represented on a canvas and by a woman moreover. But at the same time that Arango does not judge the individuals who sit for her, she does not condone their faults either. In her bizarre and mad women and her prostitutes, there is always an element of evilness and eroticism, feelings that the conservative society of her time did not want to acknowledge as inherent to human nature, hence, her art had to be stigmatized and rejected. The nude was acceptable only so long as it did not cross the lines established by society. Her two mentors, Pedro Nel Gómez and Eladio Vélez, clearly understood the unspoken limits and never dared to cross the invisible line. Vélez's women are nothing but an excuse for him to show his mastery at the medium, and his women are unnamed models who have no stories to tell us, mere clichés that do not dare to reveal their souls. Gómez's women, on the other hand, are mythical figures that could not be farther from the human race. *La Patetarro* (1958) and *Barequera* (1963) are the subject of long-standing folk legends that are only nominally related to the rest of the female gender, in deep contrast with Arango's everyday women.

The validity of her art has been constantly denied or plainly ignored as though nonexistent even as late as the late 1970s. Even otherwise enlightened people like the critic **Marta Traba**, who promoted the modern art of the likes of Fernando Botero and Alejandro Obregón, side-stepped the issue of Arango's work. It is only after the 1980s that Arango's work has been reviewed and offered again to public view. In 1984 the Biblioteca Luis Angel Arango (Luis Angel Arango Library) and the Museo de Arte Moderno de Medellín (Medellín Museum of Modern Art), which holds a large number of her pieces in its permanent collection, presented two retrospective exhibitions of her works. In 1995 two new large shows were held, one of which consisted of never-before-seen drawings, followed by a retrospective in 1996 at the Museo de Arte Moderno de Medellín. In contrast, and as proof that fear about her art is still alive, the Colombian government refused to include her work in the Biarritz Art Festival of 1995 because of fear of controversy and the possibility that the subjects of her paintings would project a bad image of the country.

Further Reading

Arango, Débora. *El arte de la irreverencia*. Medellín, Colombia: Secretaría de Educación y Cultura de Medellín, 1997.

González, Beatriz. *Débora Arango, exposición retrospectiva*. Bogotá, Colombia: Banco de la República, Biblioteca Luis Angel Arango, 1996.

Londoño Vélez, Santiago. *Débora Arango: Vida de pintora*. Santafé de Bogotá, Colombia: Ministerio de la Cultura, 1997.

Ruiz Gómez, Darío, et al. *Débora Arango*. Medellín, Colombia: Museo de Arte Moderno de Medellín; Bogotá, Colombia: Villegas Editores, 1986.

Rubén D. Durán

VIOLETA BARRIOS DE CHAMORRO

(?, 1929–   )

Nicaragua: Politician

Violeta Chamorro, who served as president of Nicaragua from 1990 to 1996, was the first woman ever elected president of a Latin American country. Chamorro, or Doña Violeta as she was generally called, was an apparently unlikely president. Until she ran for president in 1990, she had never run for electoral office, nor had she participated for any significant period of time in politics. It was precisely her ability, however, to stand above politics, as a maternal reconciler, that made Chamorro such a powerful candidate in a country that had just endured a decade of civil war.

Born in the Nicaraguan province of Rivas to a wealthy landowning family, she attended Catholic grade schools in Nicaragua and then spent several years in boarding school in the United States, initially at Our Lady of the Lakes, near Austin, Texas, then at Blackstone in Virginia. At the age of eighteen, while she was studying at Blackstone, her father died. His death led to the end of her formal education, and she returned to Nicaragua to live with her mother.

On December 8, 1950, Violeta Barrios married Pedro Joaquín Chamorro, the coeditor of the daily newspaper *La prensa* (The Press), who became editor and owner of the newspaper upon his father's death in 1952. Throughout the twenty-seven years of their marriage, she always played the role of loyal wife and mother to their four children (Pedro Joaquín, born in 1951; Claudia, born in 1953; Cristiana, born in 1954; and Carlos Fernando, born in 1956). Despite her efforts to live the quiet, private life of wife and mother, politics continually intruded upon her life because of her husband's active involvement in the effort to end the Somoza family dictatorship, a dictatorship that had ruled over Nicaragua since 1936.

As editor in chief of *La prensa*, the only opposition newspaper in the country, Pedro Joaquín Chamorro used his position to publicize the abuses of the Somoza dictatorship. But merely publicizing the abuses of the Somoza family was not enough to end the family's rule over the country, given their willingness to use violence and electoral fraud to maintain their power. So in 1954 and 1959, Pedro Joaquín Chamorro, along with other opposition activists, participated in failed attempts to overthrow the Somozas through military means. For his efforts to end the dictatorship, Pedro Joaquín Chamorro paid a high price: repeated arrests, torture, and imprisonment for four years.

During the years in which Pedro Joaquín Chamorro was one of Nicaragua's most prominent political activists, his wife was supportive but largely uninvolved in politics. The only exception to that rule occurred when Chamorro joined her husband when he fled into exile in Costa Rica in 1956. Though he hesitated to bring her along on the risky voyage across the river separating Nicaragua and Costa Rica, she convinced him that she had to do it, that accompanying him was her wifely duty. "I had sworn when I married Pedro that I would always be by his side, 'till death do us part,' and I really believed in that" (Barrios de Chamorro 1996, 69). In the years following their return to Nicaragua, she continued to support her husband without directly participating in his work, focusing her energies instead on her role as mother and housewife until 1978.

Then, one day, an event occurred that forever changed the course of

Chamorro's personal history, and that of her country. While driving to his office at *La prensa* on January 10, 1978, Pedro Joaquín Chamorro was strafed with machine-gun fire from passing cars. When she heard about his death, his wife returned immediately from Miami, where she and her daughter Cristiana had been shopping in preparation for Cristiana's wedding to Antonio Lacayo.

Chamorro's murder was a major turning point in Nicaraguan politics, an event that is often identified as one of the final straws that brought down the Somoza dictatorship. While the Somozas had regularly murdered their political opponents, they had been clever enough to spare opponents who were as wealthy and internationally connected as Pedro Joaquín Chamorro. His murder signaled a change in the dictatorship and a new level of brutality that set off the final round of urban insurrections that would force Anastasio Somoza to flee the country a year and a half later.

In his place, a guerrilla organization, the Sandinista Front for National Liberation (Frente Sandinista de Liberación Nacional, or FSLN) took over. The FSLN had been seeking to overthrow the dictatorship since it was founded in 1961, and by 1979 it enjoyed the support of a broad cross-section of Nicaraguan society, including significant sectors of the middle and upper classes. While the Somoza dictatorship might not have fallen without the insurrection that began in response to Pedro Joaquín Chamorro's murder, the force of the insurrection certainly would have remained ineffective and unchanneled without the FSLN and its nearly two decades of guerrilla experience.

Recognizing that their support cut across class and political lines, and seeking to maintain such support in the difficult work of rebuilding the country, the ruling committee, or junta, that the Sandinistas created in July 1979 also cut across class and political lines. Three of the members of the junta—Daniel Ortega, Moisés Hassan, and Sergio Ramírez—represented the left wing of the anti-Somoza coalition; the other two member—Alfonso Robelo and Violeta Barrios de Chamorro—represented the conservative opposition to Somoza.

The junta was inherently unstable from the beginning: the three leftists envisioned that Somoza's overthrow would permit a revolutionary transformation of Nicaraguan society: the two conservatives had a narrower view of the political reforms that would follow the end of the Somoza dictatorship. Unhappy with the Sandinista's efforts to transform political and economic structures, Chamorro resigned less than a year after the end of the Somoza regime.

While Chamorro withdrew from public life in the 1980s, her children continued to play prominent roles in politics, on opposing sides. Cristiana and Carlos Fernando were both newspaper editors: Cristiana for the anti-Sandinista *La prensa*, and Carlos Fernando for the official Sandinista newspaper, *Barricada* (Barricade). Pedro Joaquín and Claudia were even more directly involved in politics: he was a commander of the armed opposition to the Sandinistas, known as the Contra (Against), and she was Sandinista ambassador to Spain and Cuba during the 1980s.

In 1990 Violeta Chamorro reentered formal politics when she ran for president. Running on the promise to end the Contra war and repair the economy, she portrayed herself as the loyal widow and traditional mother who would reconcile the Nicaraguan family just as she had reconciled her own politically torn family. She won the election with nearly 55 percent of the vote.

During her six years in office, Chamorro clearly oversaw the fulfillment of her first electoral promise: to end the Contra war. It ended in part because the Contras agreed to demobilize once their political opponents, the Sandinistas, were no longer in office and, most significantly, because the primary funder of the Contra's war efforts—the Bush administration—no longer was interested in promoting the war once its preferred candidate, Violeta Barrios de Chamorro, was inaugurated as president.

Yet Chamorro turned out to be far more independent of the United States than the Bush administration had expected, and she resisted pressure from Washington to return rapidly to something approximating the prerevolutionary status quo. During much of her term in office, she even allied with some Sandinistas in the National Assembly against far rightwing members of her own political coalition, the UNO (Unión Nacional Opositora). To a significant extent, Chamorro's term could be considered a success in political terms, as she oversaw the end of the Contra war and the consolidation of electoral democracy. But her record was far less clear in economic terms.

When Chamorro took office, she had to deal with a huge foreign debt and an economy weakened by years of war. She implemented a severe structural adjustment program, slashing budgets for state agencies, firing thousands of state workers, privatizing state agencies, and cutting the services and credit that had made the Sandinista agrarian reform viable. Social inequality only increased under her watch, and the most basic necessities became luxuries: "per capita food consumption fell by 31 percent between 1990 and 1992" (Robinson 1997, 40).

Many of the economic policies that Violeta Barrios de Chamorro carried out were typical of those carried out throughout the hemisphere in the 1990s in response to pressures created by the international debt and the international lending agencies; in some sense, these structural adjustment policies were not under her control. Her ideological actions, especially her gender policies, provide a more interesting measure of her presidency since those were the policies that she did control.

One might think that, since she was a woman, Chamorro would have strongly promoted gender equality, but that was not the case. Many of her policies—eliminating antidomestic violence programs, firing day care workers, promoting traditional gender roles in grade school text-books—had the effect of increasing gender inequality. Furthermore, Chamorro always maintained a safe distance from the feminist movement that grew rapidly during her administration. As she once told a reporter, "I am not a feminist nor do I wish to be one. I am a woman dedicated to my home" (quoted in Kampwirth 1998, 264). Ironically, dedication to her home, to upholding her late husband's ideals, and to reconciling her politically divided children took her far from the seclusion of domestic life. Doña Violeta did not run again in 1996 although she still has a public presence as an opponent to the pact that President José Arnoldo Alemán Lacayo (1996–present) of the liberal party negotiated with Daniel Ortega of the Sandinista Front in 1998–2000.

Further Reading

Barrios de Chamorro, Violeta, with Sonia Cruz de Baltodano and Guido Fernández. *Dreams of the Heart: The Autobiography of Violeta Barrios de Chamorro of Nicaragua*. New York: Simon and Schuster, 1996.

Edmisten, Patricia Taylor. *Nicaragua Divided: La Prensa and the Chamorro Legacy*. Pensacola: University of West Florida Press, 1990.

Heyck, Denis Lynn Daly, ed. "Violeta Chamorro." In *Life Stories of the Nicaraguan Revolution*, 37–52. London: Routledge, 1990.

Kampwirth, Karen. "Feminism, Antifeminism, and Electoral Politics in Postwar Nicaragua and El Salvador." *Political Science Quarterly* 113, no 2. (Summer 1998): 259–79.

———. "The Mother of the Nicaraguans: Doña Violeta and the UNO's Gender Agenda." *Latin American Perspectives* 23, no. 1 (January 1996): 67–86. Issue 88.

Robinson, William. "Nicaragua and the World: A Globalization Perspective." In *Nicaragua Without Illusions: Regime Transition and Structural Adjustment in the 1990s*, edited by Thomas W. Walker, 23–42. Wilmington, Del.: Scholarly Resources, 1997.

Rushdie, Salman. "Doña Violeta's Version." In *The Jaguar Smile: A Nicaraguan Journey*, 145–53. New York: Penguin Books, 1998.

Williams, Harvey. "Violeta Barrios de Chamorro." In *Women in World Politics*, edited by Francine D'Amico and Peter Beckman, 31–43. Westport, Conn.: Bergin and Garvey, 1995.

Karen Kampwirth

DOMITILA BARRIOS DE CHÚNGARA

(May 7, 1937–)

Bolivia: Author, Political Activist

A testimonial writer and political activist, Barrios de Chúngara was born into a very poor family. Her father was originally a farmer, in Toledo (Bolivia), but after he served in the war against Paraguay, which ended in 1936, he lost all his possessions. Nonetheless he married and in 1942 went to work at the mines known as Siglo XX (Twentieth Century). Because of his political activism, he was put on a black list that did not allow him to work as a miner, and he had to move to the colder mining region of Pulacayo, where he worked as a tailor.

Barrios de Chúngara had a troubled childhood. Her mother died in 1947 when she was only ten, and she finished primary school through great effort, which in her social context constitutes a major achievement (many women in her condition remain illiterate). Barrios studied at the public school Escuela Luis María Sola de Pulacayo. She had few female peers at school, since people in the mines considered it unnecessary for women to read and write and since such process would only hinder them from acquiring the more useful skills required to become good wives. Girls at school were mostly the children of more privileged families, and miners' or lower-class workers' daughters were rare. Barrios de Chúngara's father had very advanced ideas for his time and class: he taught his children that a woman and a man have the same responsibilities and rights.

In 1958 Barrios married and moved to Siglo XX. She had eleven children; seven of them are still alive. In Siglo XX she started to work in the union movement. In 1963 she was an active member of the Comité de Amas de Casa de Siglo XX (Housewives Committee of the Twentieth Century). Two years later (1965), she was elected the general secretary of the committee. The committee put a lot of pressure on the government to improve the miners' situation. Since Barrios was the visible head of this movement, she was imprisoned and tortured for speaking up against the "Massacre of San Juan" (June 24, 1967), which took place during the dictatorial regime of General José Barrientos. In order to destroy her work with the committee, she was confined to Yungas, a tropical region,

Domitila Barrios de Chúngara.
Photo by Fabiola Fernández Salek.
Courtesy of Domitila Barrios de
Chúngara.

where there are no mines and she would be unable to pursue her political and sociological work with the people. After Barrios de Chúngara
returned to Siglo XX in 1977, she again took the position of general secretary of the Comité de Amas de Casa de Siglo XX. In 1985 she moved
to Cochabamba as a result of "relocalization," through which, owing to
economic reforms, the government laid off thousands of mine workers.
Her husband remains in Siglo XX because he is unwilling to adapt to a
new place.

In 1975 the United Nations invited Barrios de Chúngara to participate
in the International Women's Year Tribune which took place in Mexico.
Her intervention was polemical because she contested the main speakers'
articulation of women's problems and argued that they represented only
upper-class professionals who did not deal with the economic and social
problems confronted by poor women. The publicity generated was re-

directed by Brazilian educator Moema Viezzer, and the outcome was the testimonial book *"Si me permiten hablar . . ." Testimonio de Domitila, una mujer de las minas de Bolivia (Let Me Speak! Testimony of Domitila, a Woman of the Bolivian Mines)*, published in 1977. In this book, Barrios de Chúngara describes her life in the mines and denounces the abuses of the government against the working-class sector, especially the miners. This testimony also shows the work carried out by labor unions to protect the rights of the workers and their families.

Barrios de Chúngara's first testimonial book was translated and published in several languages. The English translation was published in 1978. In 1985, David Acebey, a Bolivian journalist, published with Barrios de Chúngara *¡Aquí también Domitila!* (Here Domitila Also!). This book, which did not have the impact of the previous one, was only recently translated into German and Dutch. This book concerns her experiences during exile. Finally, Barrios de Chúngara published *La mujer y la organización* (Women and Organization, 1980), which is not a testimonial, but rather her own ideas and a discussion about the role of the woman in society.

Barrios de Chúngara speaks very humbly about her personal achievements and considers that every honor she has earned belongs not only to her but also to the people. The historic hunger strike she undertook with four other women (Aurora de Lora, Angélica Flores, Nelly de Panigua, and Luzmila de Pimentel) on December 28, 1977, brought together 4,000 strikers and lasted twenty-three days. The strikers demanded from the government general amnesty, reinstatement of the jobs of people linked to politics, withdrawal of the army from the mines, and authorization to reestablish the labor unions. The pressure of the strike finally overthrew Hugo Banzer's military regime. Clearly, this is one of Barrios de Chúngara's biggest political achievements. In a way, Bolivia's democracy owes a debt to her.

In 1978 she entered the political arena and ran unsuccessfully as a candidate for vice president (with Casiano Amurrio as the candidate for the presidency) for the political party Revolutionary Left Front.

Barrios de Chúngara has received various awards and has been invited to give speeches in several countries. In 1979 she was invited to Venezuela to the World Conference on Exile and Solidarity. In 1980 she was invited to the United Nations Decade for Women Conference held in Denmark. In 1981, in Austria, she received the Bruno Kreisky prize for the publication of her first book. In 1983 she was invited to address the Sixth Assembly of the World Council of Churches. Finally, in 1995, she received the award given by the Women's World Summit Foundation "To the Creativity of Women in the Rural Setting."

While Barrios de Chúngara was in Denmark in 1980, the military regime of Luis García Meza took over the government, and she was commissioned by the Central Obrera Bolivia (Bolivian Workers Union), the strongest workers' union in Bolivia, to denounce the atrocities being committed by the military against the mine workers (imprisonment, torture, and rape). In Copenhagen she organized a women's march to sway the 2,000 UN delegates, even though she feared reprisals against her own family in Bolivia at that time. After this campaign, she was not allowed to return to Bolivia, where her family remained until they were allowed to leave the following year. The family lived in Europe, primarily Sweden, until 1983. Throughout this period, Barrios de Chúngara went to different European countries (Germany, France, Italy, England, and Spain) to lobby against the military regimes in her country.

Back in Bolivia the Escuela Móvil Domitila (Domitila Mobile School) was founded in 1990 with twelve members, although it is currently reduced to two (Domitila herself and Félix Ricablez) due to the lack of resources. The creation of this program was conceived as imperative in the mines, where people face a daily political and social struggle. The idea behind the workshops given in the Escuela Móvil Domitila is to broaden the vision of the workers, helping them understand the macrostructures of the society, so they might begin to fight for their rights. The first organizational bulletin called *Imilla* (Quechua for young single woman) was edited in 1993, and by January 1999 200 bulletins had been published. Scarce resources make the publication very primitive; nonetheless, it is a way of documenting the progress of this school. The school, which was financed initially by Barrios de Chúngara's earnings from her first book, now lacks a formal budget.

Barrios de Chúngara receives no income from the government, and she and the school survive on money sent by her children in Sweden and personal Bolivian friends in Denmark. The premises, phone, and postal box do not belong to the institution, but they are rented and located in a popular sector of Cochabamba, which also serves as her house. The reduced budget of the school has forced her to charge for transportation costs and all travel expenses, when she is invited to give a workshop.

Barrios de Chúngara has had a difficult life, and because of her active participation in political movements and labor unions against the government, she has faced imprisonment, exile, and even torture. Despite all this, she has managed to establish a small front of her own in the fight for her beliefs and the right to teach others all that experience and the school of life have taught her. Unfortunately, she has been marginalized from the possibility of having a more active role in the decisions of Bolivian political life.

Barrios de Chúngara believes that one of the greatest obstacles faced by humanity is the fear implemented by the systems that repress the freedom of action and speech. She considers that socioeconomic status, and not gender, is responsible for the social isolation of women. She believes that the indigenous Andean society was more equal regarding the condition of women and that patriarchal hierarchy and machismo were imported and established during the American conquest by the Spaniards.

Further Reading

Barrios de Chúngara, Domitila, with Moema Viezzer. *Let Me Speak! Testimony of Domitila, a Woman of the Bolivian Mines.* New York: Monthly Review Press, 1978.

Browdy de Hernández, Jennifer. "Of Tortillas and Texts: Postcolonial Dialogues in the Latin American Testimonial." In *Interventions: Feminist Dialogues on Third World Women's Literature and Film,* edited by Ghosh Bishnupriya and Bose Brinda, 163–84. New York: Garland, 1997.

Gutiérrez Villalobos, Sonia. "Reading Cultural Difference: 'Let Me Speak!' and 'I Rigoberta Menchú' in the U.S." Ph.D. diss., University of Massachusetts, 1995.

Sanjinés, Javier. "From Domitila to 'los relocalizados': An Essay on Marginality in Bolivia." *Translation Perspectives* 6 (1991): 185–96.

Strom, Linda. "Personal Stories in Political Times: Rereading Women's Working-Class Narratives." Ph.D. diss., University of Oregon, 1993.

Fabiola Fernández Salek

GIOCONDA BELLI
(December 9, 1948–   )

Nicaragua: Poet, Author, Political Activist

Gioconda Belli is a prominent Nicaraguan feminist poet and a militant political activist. "And God Made Me a Woman": With this poem, Gioconda Belli opened her first published collection of poetry, *Sobre la grama* (On the Grass, 1974), and it is an appropriate starting point to understanding the woman and her work. Her exuberant celebration of feminine sexuality immediately provoked a national scandal when this collection first appeared in Nicaragua. The magnitude of such an event can be better understood if one considers that in Nicaragua, unlike many other countries, poetry is an integral part of everyday culture. In fact, poetry is a staple of daily newspapers, and as a result it is not unusual to find that a majority of the general population, regardless of social

Gioconda Belli. Courtesy of Margarita
Montealegre.

status, is familiar with their national poets. Given the widespread popularity and diffusion of poetry, the publication of *Sobre la grama* was an
important event which proved that women could write poetry equal in
quality to that of their male counterparts.

Belli admits that she enjoyed the scandal elicited by her first collection.
With the ensuing discussion of Belli's work came the recognition that
Nicaragua had, for the first time in its history, an impressive group of
women poets, including Ana Ilce Gómez, Michele Najlis, Daisy Zamora,
Vidaluz Meneses, Yolanda Blanco, and Rosario Murillo. Belli and these
women share a love of poetry and a commitment to social change. In
fact, Belli acknowledges that she discovered political militancy and po-
etry at about the same time. As a result, many of these women, including
Belli, not only wrote poetry but also occupied important positions in the
Sandinista revolutionary movement.

Belli's personal background seemed an unlikely one to produce a revolutionary. Raised in an upper-class Nicaraguan family that opposed the
Somoza regime, she was educated in Nicaragua, Spain, and the United
States. After completing an advertising course in the United States, she
returned to work in Nicaragua, where she married "well" at eighteen.
Nevertheless, money and privilege could not allow her to ignore the
poverty and political repression suffered daily by thousands of poor Nicaraguans. At the same time, she awakened to the repression of women

caused by traditional societal roles. Her autobiographical first novel, *La mujer habitada* (The Inhabited Woman, 1988) explores in detail this two-fold road to feminine and national liberation. The protagonist, Lavinia, initially establishes her independence by moving into her late aunt's house and living alone, much to her parents' concern. Soon, however, she realizes that her personal independence is but a first step in what ultimately becomes her public transformation into a revolutionary. Rather than remaining focused on her career and sexual freedom, Lavinia is transformed into an instrument of political struggle, an urban guerrillera, fighting to liberate her country. Parallel to Lavinia's growth and transformation is the story of a Nauhuatl Indian woman, Itza, who comes to inhabit Lavinia, thereby connecting the main protagonist of the novel to the ongoing resistance of the indigenous population to foreign domination.

Like Lavinia, Belli gradually evolved into a young woman aware of her country's overwhelming social problems. Shortly after the birth of her daughter, Maryam, Belli met Camilo Ortega, who was instrumental in getting her involved with the then underground FSLN (Frente Sandinista de Liberación Nacional, or Sandinista National Liberation Front) in 1970. She entered a period during which she led a double life as a respectable married woman and a participant in the revolutionary movement. As her activities increased, she was more and more at risk in Nicaragua, and she found it difficult to remain married to a man who opposed her political involvement. In 1975 she was forced into exile in Costa Rica and Mexico. During this time, far from her children and family, she traveled extensively, giving public speeches on the Sandinista struggle against the injustices committed by the Somoza regime.

Before the triumph of the Sandinista Revolution in 1979, Belli published two collections of poetry. Her first book, *Sobre la grama*, was awarded the Mariano Gil Prize of the National Autonomous University of Nicaragua in 1972 and was published in 1974. In her interviews with Margaret Randall, Belli explains that *Sobre la grama* excludes mention of her political involvement in order to protect herself and to allow herself a "cover" in order to continue her work with the Sandinistas. Instead, this book reflects the intimate discoveries of the poet:

I wrote out of all the euphoria I felt at being alive, at being a woman, a mother— it was deeply erotic poetry, in the broadest sense of that term. Not only in the sexual sense to which it's often limited. I was singing out of my pleasure at being alive, of feeling glad to be a woman and living in a time when things were happening that promised such important changes. (quoted in Randall 1984, 145)

In contrast to these poems, her second book of poetry, *Línea de fuego* (Line of Fire), which received the Casa de las Américas Prize for Poetry from

Cuba in 1978 and was published that same year, is more focused on the Nicaraguan revolutionary struggle.

After the Sandinista victory in 1979, Belli occupied important posts in the new government and continued to write and publish poetry. Her first position was to take over, direct, and organize the television system. After this first assignment, she held a series of positions in the Ministry of Planning, the Department of Analysis and Propaganda, the Electoral Commission, and the Council of Political Parties. In retrospect, Belli acknowledges that, in spite of the Sandinista rhetoric that stressed the equality of women, she experienced sexual discrimination several times when she was passed over in favor of men for leadership roles. When she complained to her superiors, they justified their actions by claiming that their society was a sexist one (Randall 1994, 178).

Meanwhile, Belli continued to write and publish poetry. Her books *Truenos y arco iris* (Thunder and Rainbow, 1982) and *De la costilla de Eva* (From Eve's Rib, 1986) reflect the difficulties in this period of constructing a new society that respects all its members. Nevertheless, Belli's political candor eventually led her to express disappointment with the revolutionary leaders' declining interest in women's issues. Her poem "Desolaciones de la revolución" (Revolutionary Disillusions), which appeared in her anthology of poems, *El ojo de la mujer* (Woman's Eye, 1991), reflects her feelings of abandonment by the FSLN leaders. The electoral campaign in 1989, before the defeat of Daniel Ortega, convinced her that the Sandinista leadership had strayed from the needs and wants of the people they proposed to represent. Moreover, she was disappointed in their refusal to promote a woman to the national directorate of the FSLN.

From the late 1980s to the present, Belli has been principally concerned with writing novels. Her first one, *La mujer habitada*, received great critical acclaim and was soon translated into German, English, Italian, Danish, Finnish, Turkish, Greek, and Dutch. While this novel explores the parallel struggles of Lavinia to free both herself and her country, Belli's second novel, *Sofía de los presagios* (Sophie of the Prophecies, 1990), concentrates on the issues of sexual oppression in Nicaragua and the discovery of magic. Rather than finding liberation in a national movement, Sofía charts her own personal path that leads her to construct a new life for herself and her daughter, free from the repression she experienced as a woman. More recently, Belli has published her third novel, *Waslala: Memorial del futuro* (Waslala: Memorial to the Future, 1996), which deals with the search of a futuristic utopia, and a children's book, *El taller de las mariposas* (The Butterflies' Workshop, 1994).

Since the mid-1990s, Belli had divided her time between Nicaragua and Los Angeles. Her most recent publication of poetry, *Apogeo* (Zenith, 1997), which includes poems written from 1987 to 1997, confronts many of the misconceptions of aging that women approaching their forties and fifties face. This collection, in essence, continues her celebration of women that began with *Sobre la grama*. Her most recent work, a memoir entitled *Trespassing: A Woman's Memoir of Love and War*, was published in Spain and the United States in 2000.

Among the awards and honors she has received during her career as a poet and novelist are the Mariano Fiallos Gil Prize of the National Autonomous University of Nicaragua in 1972, the Casa de las Américas Prize for Poetry from Cuba in 1978, the Ebert Prize from Germany in the novel category in 1989, and the Anna Seghers prize, also from Germany, in 1989.

Further Reading

Beverley, John, and Marc Zimmerman. *Literature and Politics in the Central American Revolutions*. Austin: University of Texas Press, 1990.

Craft, Linda J. *Novels of Testimony and Resistance from Central America*. Gainesville: University Press of Florida, 1997.

Moyano, Pilar. "The Transformation of Nation and Womanhood: Revisionist Mythmaking in the Poetry of Nicaragua's Gioconda Belli." In *Interventions: Feminist Dialogues on Third World Women's Literature and Film*, edited by Bishnupriya Ghosh and Brinda Bose, 79–95. New York: Garland, 1997.

Randall, Margaret. *Risking a Somersault in the Air: Conversations with Nicaraguan Writers*. San Francisco: Solidarity Publications, 1984.

———. *Sandino's Daughters Revisited*. New Brunswick, N.J.: Rutgers University Press, 1994.

Rodríguez, Ileana. "Giaconda Belli: Urban House/Nation—Domi Nostre." In *House/Garden/Nation*, translated by Robert Carr and Ileana Rodriguez, 165–97. Durham, N.C.: Duke University Press, 1994.

Frances Jaeger

MARÍA LUISA BEMBERG
(April 14, 1922–May 7, 1995)
Argentina: Director, Social Activist

Pioneering feminist film director María Luisa Bemberg was born in Buenos Aires into one of the wealthiest families between 1930 and 1945 in Argentina. Bemberg's childhood and teenage years took place within the cultural background of the conservative conventions of aristocracy. Unlike her two brothers, she and her sister were deprived of going to

María Luisa Bemberg. Courtesy of Museo
del Cine "Pablo C. Ducros Hicken,"
Buenos Aires.

high school. From her early years, several governesses were in charge of
her education.

With the overthrow in 1943 of conservative president Ramón Castillo,
the Bembergs' economic interests were seriously affected, and several
family members left the country. During this time, Bemberg met her
future husband, Carlos Miguens, a young man from her social class, who
was studying architecture. From a historical perspective, the date chosen
for the wedding was paradigmatic because it was celebrated on October
17, 1945, the day when popular masses arrived in Buenos Aires to demand the release of Juan Domingo Perón from jail. Because of the riots
the wedding was celebrated in Bemberg's home on Talcahuano Street.

When Perón took the presidency, the Bembergs' economic interests
continued to erode. Bemberg's parents left for France, and she and her
husband spent several years in Francisco Franco's Spain.

In 1954 Bemberg decided to separate from her husband. The future
movie director began to reconsider several issues linked to her female
condition and her life experience. As she reconsidered her female condition, the reading of Simone de Beauvoir's *The Second Sex* gave her some
key concepts to reconsider her views about the world. "Ideas should be
lived," a phrase from *The Human Condition* by novelist, art critic, and

film director André Malraux, exercised a strong influence on the re-orientation of her life (Bemberg March 1990, 6–11).

In 1960 she was part of the group that staged Friedrich Dürrenmatt's *The Visit of the Old Lady* (1958) at the Astral Theater. This group experience allowed her to channel her creativity. She was in charge of the costume design, which was praised by the press. After that, she founded the Teatro del Globo (Globe Theater) with Catalina Wolff. This five-year commitment led her to explore the interaction of staging, lighting, and directing. Later on, she complemented this experience by studying with Lee Strasberg, one of the founders of the Group Theatre and instrumental in devising the Actor's Studio method in New York.

In 1969, toward the end of the military government of Juan Carlos Onganía, two key events took place in Bemberg's life: she was one of the founders of the UFA (Unión Feminista Argentina, or Argentine Feminist Union) and she submitted a short play, *La margarita es una flor* (The Daisy Is a Flower), to the literary contest organized by the newspaper *La nación* (The Nation). Even though the play did not receive the award, movie director Raúl de la Torre suggested that Bemberg rework it into a script for a movie. *Crónica de una señora* (Chronicle of a Lady, 1970), Bemberg's debut in the motion picture world, centers on Finita, the protagonist's story, who like Bemberg was conditioned by an extremely traditional education. This screenplay offers the key to all of her other films, for her female characters are victimized by a system that oppresses women.

During the advertising campaign for this film, Bemberg talked about her activist feminism, which made headlines and stigmatized her career. Her feminist activism, however, was remarkably moderate. The director understood that feminism was not restricted to fighting against "male chauvinism." Bemberg also rejected "extreme feminism," although she pointed out that she understood the anger of these women even though she did not share their goals (Bemberg 1983, 78–81).

In 1972 she directed a short film titled *El mundo de la mujer* (Woman's World), shot at the Exposición Femimundo (Woman's World Exposition) held in Buenos Aires. Bemberg considered this film a feminist pamphlet. Exposición Femimundo allowed for a critique of the social expectations of femininity (cooking, makeup, appliances, and the like). In 1974 she wrote the script for another movie, *Triángulo de cuatro* (Four-Way Triangle), directed by Fernando Ayala.

Her second short film, *Juguetes* (Toys), was released that year. *Juguetes* shows that children's games are not innocent. Through toys and games, girls are socialized into the closed world of the house, while boys are nurtured to compete and explore the world. In 1974 she announced the filming of the movie *Señora de Nadie* (Mrs. Nobody) as a coproduction with Spain, but the project was not approved by the National Institute of Cinematography, which was controlled by the military dictatorship, and the film remained on hold for five years.

As the scriptwriter of two movies, and the director of two shorts, Bemberg understood that her stories could not be directed by a man, since the logic of a male perspective would prevail and detract from the presentation of key issues by her female characters. This awareness of difference as identity and as worldview and her opposition to the dominant male viewpoint led Bemberg to direct her subsequent projects herself.

Momentos (Moments), her first motion picture, was released in 1980. It develops an intimate and, according to the director, a "timidly feminist" story about a middle-class married woman who has an affair and dares to be honest with herself and others (Bemberg 1982, 56–60). *Señora de Nadie* was finally filmed and released in 1982. In this case, again within an intimate framework, Bemberg tells the story of a married woman who leaves when she discovers that her husband is cheating on her, and she starts to live out her emotions. This is the story of a woman who dares to transgress middle-class rules. For Bemberg, this film could be considered a feminist film. The claims of the female characters in these two movies are always uttered on behalf of honor and dignity, concepts that unequivocally refer to the sociocultural perspective from which the director is observing the world. The name Leonor (perhaps referring to *el honor*, or honor), the name of the main character in the film *Señora de Nadie*, played by Luisina Brando, was chosen to pay homage to the poet Leonor Calvera, who for years worked to write a book documenting the predicament of women in Argentina. The autobiographical references were underlined by filming the final scene at the facilities of the producer's office.

After this movie, Bemberg considered working with a biography of Alfonsina Storni, Juana Manuela Gorriti, **Victoria Ocampo**, or Camila O'Gorman. With *Camila* (1984), Bemberg understood that she was leaving feminist movies behind. This film addresses the tragic relationship between Camila O'Gorman and the priest Ladislao Gutiérrez within the nineteenth-century background of the dictatorship of Juan Manual de Rosas. This allowed the director to show a woman confronting traditional institutions: family, church, and state. She later regretted the ending of the movie, the romantic promise of eternal love whispered after Camila and Ladislao have been executed. Bemberg promised herself not to repeat this concession to the box office (Bemberg March 1990, 6–11).

Her fourth movie, *Miss Mary* (1986), probably the most autobiographical, recreates the events of an aristocratic family of landowners in the Argentina of the 1930s and 1940s, evoked by the memories of a governess as she packs her luggage to return to England at the end of the war. The complex sociopolitical background of the Peronist era she is forced to witness is superficially elaborated because of Bemberg's own class limitations.

In 1986 she shot *Yo, la peor de todas* (I, the Worst of All), based on Mexican writer Octavio Paz's 1982 text *Sor Juana Inés de la Cruz, o las trampas de la fe* (Sor Juana Inés de la Cruz, or the Traps of Faith). She coauthored the script with Uruguayan playwright Antonio "Taco" Larreta. Production problems delayed the shooting of the film for two and a half years.

Bemberg's statements to the press reflect a significant distance from her previous moderation when she begins to attack the patriarchy. Bemberg considers Sor Juana "the first feminist of the American continent," who, because of her need for knowledge, becomes a nun and confines herself to a convent, looking for the "calm silence of the books" (Bemberg January 1990, 1–2). In her conception of Sor Juana's character, some correspondences with Bemberg's own life could be observed: both women were self-taught, transgressive, and devoted to their work. Sor Juana was one of the most illustrious voices of the Spanish Baroque; Bemberg was the first Argentine woman who developed a movie career from her personal point of view.

Between 1988 and 1991, Bemberg was a member of the advisory committee of the International Festival of Movies Made by Women. This dynamic exchange led Bemberg to show a particular interest in the work of such directors as Margaret Von Trotta, Helma Sanders, and Yutta Bruckner, all from Germany, and Chantal Ackerman from Belgium because of their controversial perspectives. She also announced her next project, an "iconoclast comedy" whose plot she handed to Dacia Maraini, who had worked as a scriptwriter with Margaret Von Trotta (Bemberg March 1990, 6–11). Moreover, she announced the shooting of a telefilm for an American producer based on a story by Beatriz Guido. She was not able to carry out either of these projects.

In her last movie, *De eso no se habla* (We Don't Talk about That, 1993), moving away from her initial moderation, she addressed the right to be different. At this point, the ideological and cultural parameters that Bemberg had inherited from her social class generated conflict and tension with her feminist axioms. The mother (again called Leonor, played, as in *Señora de Nadie*, by Luisina Brando) is burdened with the restrictions of her education and cultural inheritance, and she proposes a differential practice framed by domestic values. The daughter (called Charlotte) finally destroys her marriage and locates her freedom in the entertainment realm by joining a circus. This proposal is unusual and paradoxical because the daughter is a dwarf, so it attaches a differential value to otherness. This esthetic anti-ideological configuration limits Bemberg's discourse because she resorts to features bordering on the grotesque to represent otherness.

El impostor (The Impostor, 1997), an unfinished project resumed by Alejandro Maci (her assistant director in *De eso no se habla*), was shot after Bemberg's death.

Bemberg died of cancer on May 7, 1995, curiously and paradoxically, the day that is remembered for the birth of Eva Duarte de Perón, the final irony of the Peronist story that she decided not to tell.

Further Reading

Bemberg, María Luisa. "Interview." *Revista La Semana* (September 1982): 56–60.
———. "Interview." *Revista Mujer* (September 1983): 68–81.
———. "Interview." *Diario Clarín* (January 1990): 1–2.
———. "Interview." *Revista La Nación* 1078 (March 1990): 6–11.
Ciria, Alberto. "Historia, sexo, clase y poder en los films de María Luisa Bemberg." In *Más allá de la pantalla: Cine argentino, historia y política*, ch. 4. Buenos Aires, Argentina: Ediciones de la Flor, 1995.
Fontana, Clara. *María Luisa Bemberg*. Buenos Aires, Argentina: Centro Editor de América Latina, 1993.
Foster, David William. "*Camila:* Beauty and Bestiality." In *Contemporary Argentine Cinema*, 14–26. Columbia: University of Missouri Press, 1995.

Horacio Campodónico

MARÍA LUISA BOMBAL
(June 8, 1910–May 6, 1980)
Chile: Author

A prolific woman of letters whose work illuminated the relations between the sexes in Chile, María Luisa Bombal was born in Viña del Mar, Chile. Bombal's upbringing was typical of that of many young women of the Chilean upper-middle class during the first half of this century. She attended a private Catholic school run by French nuns who stressed the importance of music and literature in her education. Four years after her father's death in 1919 she and her twin sisters attended school abroad at the Notre Dame de l'Assomption and Saint Geneviève. Bombal was especially attracted to French dramatist Pierre Corneille's tragedies and the rich world of nineteenth-century novelists: Honoré de Balzac, Gustave Flaubert, Prosper Mérimée, and Stendhal (Marie-Henri Beyle). Blanca Antes, her mother, exposed her to German and Scandinavian literature. Hans Christian Andersen's fairy tales, in particular, influenced her own work.

Although her mother was able to secure a comfortable life for her family in Paris, she decided to return to Chile in 1928. Bombal remained behind to pursue a degree in literature at the Sorbonne. She soon became interested in the theater though her family did not consider acting a suitable activity for "decent" women. Without informing her mother, she interrupted her studies at the Sorbonne and registered at L'Atelier, a prestigious theater school where Antonin Artaud and Jean Louis Barrault were also students. Her experiment came to an abrupt end when friends of the family spotted her on stage during a performance and informed her mother, and she was made to return to Chile in April 1931.

Back in Santiago, Bombal continued with her theater avocation, working with Vera Zouroff and Luis Pizarro Espoz, who were intent on modernizing the Chilean theater. Bombal's experience with the French literary scene proved valuable to them. She received the leading role in Franz Molnar's *Olimpia* and a secondary part in Marcel Achard's *Juan de Luna*. Despite her success, Bombal did not return to the stage after the summer break; she argued that she was not a very good actress, that she was too intellectual and too distant.

On the day she arrived in Chile from France, Bombal met Eulogio Sánchez, a twenty-eight-year-old engineer who was estranged from his wife. Bombal fell in love with him, but her commitment to him was not fully reciprocated. This failed relationship, which had a profound and long-lasting effect on her, largely informed her understanding of intergender relationships. Because of Sánchez's inability to commit to their future together, Bombal attempted to take her life by shooting herself, but she only injured her shoulder. Eight years later, however, long after they had severed their romantic ties, she shot Sánchez while he was walking on a busy Santiago street. Sánchez was hospitalized for a few weeks but he did not press charges against Bombal.

After her failed suicide attempt, in an effort to afford her a new start, Chilean poet Pablo Neruda, whose literary circle Bombal frequented, invited her to join him and his wife in Buenos Aires. It was in his apartment that "La Mangosta," as Neruda called her, wrote *La última niebla* (The Last Mist); its first publication in 1935 included a preface by Norah Lange. While in Buenos Aires she was a close friend of Jorge Luis Borges, who did not believe that the plot of her second novel, *La amortajada*, would work; **Victoria Ocampo** published the novel under the imprint of her literary review, *Sur* (South). She was briefly married to painter Juan Larco. Her previous experience in the theater was important for her involvement with cinema during her stay in Buenos Aires. First she wrote film reviews for Victoria Ocampo's *Sur*. Then director Luis Saslavsky commissioned from her the script of *La casa del recuerdo* (The House of Memory), with Libertad Lamarque in the leading role, which opened to great critical acclaim in Buenos Aires in March 1940.

When her marriage to Larco failed, Bombal was ready to leave Buenos Aires, since it was difficult to make a living there. Unable to relocate in Chile after the shooting of Sánchez, Bombal departed in 1942 for the United States, where she dubbed films intended for the Chilean market. She was also employed by Sterling to create advertisements. Overwhelmed by loneliness and depression, she resorted to alcohol, as she had done previously in Buenos Aires. In New York, she met Fal de Saint Phalle, an investor twenty-five years her elder, who in 1944 became her husband and lifelong companion. Fal convinced her to submit *La última niebla* to Paramount Pictures, which liked the novel and requested its translation. This led to *House of Mist*—"her Hans Christian Andersen tale"—which, although related to and based on *La última niebla*, is a different novel. Although Paramount Pictures paid Bombal the handsome sum of $125,000 for it, the film was never made.

Before her fortieth birthday, Bombal had already written her major works; she continued to rework some of her shorter pieces such as "La historia de María Griselda" (María Griselda's Story, 1946), and began *El canciller* (The Chancellor), a novel she never finished. She also worked on three plays in English and wrote film scripts for Hollywood. She frequently, however, became prey to long bouts of depression that lured her back to alcohol. After her husband's death in 1969 and her estrangement from Brigitte, her daughter, Bombal returned to Chile. Despite the widespread recognition of her work there she was repeatedly denied the Premio Nacional de Literatura (National Prize in Literature). Bombal worked on the translation of *House of Mist* and on *Caín*, another novel; she would finish neither. Her liver function began to deteriorate, and on May 6, 1980, Bombal died of a stomach hemorrhage.

Bombal's work, especially *La última niebla, La amortajada*, and "El árbol" (The Tree, 1939), proposed a new aesthetic within Chilean letters, parting ways with the prevailing *criollismo* (nationalistic local color) that centered on the landscape and the life of the land. *La última niebla* was enthusiastically reviewed by Amado Alonso, one of the most prestigious Hispanic scholars of the day. This first novel and *La amortajada*, her second work, are lyrical novels that, unlike the fiction of *criollismo*, underscore the unreal as natural. Ana María's contemplation of her life from the realm of death in *La amortajada* and the protagonist's dream of a lover who fulfills her yearning for erotic satisfaction in *La última niebla* (much like Brígida's or María Griselda's connection with nature) highlight the existence of levels of reality usually absent from the fiction of *criollismo*. Although many of her fictional settings, as in *criollismo*, take place in the countryside, her works focus on the plight of female protagonists who are unable to find realization and fulfillment in the male-dominated worlds they inhabit. The female protagonists of *La última niebla*, *La amortajada*, "El árbol," *La historia de María Griselda*, and "Las islas nuevas" (New Islands, 1939) clearly demonstrate that there is an insurmountable void between the ways in which males and females understand the world. Women are intuitive, intimately connected to nature, to the realms of imagination, myth, and dream. Men are bound to the material, to the objects of civilization, and they are ruled by the dictates of logic. In "El árbol," for example, Brígida is an impulsive young woman who yearns for the attention and love of an older husband who, under the guise of work and professional commitments, avoids her. Silence becomes both a manifestation of withdrawal from a milieu in which women feel estranged and a rejection of a discourse that is inadequate for expressing female experience. Bombal's characters resort to other forms of expression; some arise from deeply set regions of the unconscious, as in *La última niebla*, others from her characters' ability to connect intimately with nature, as in "El árbol," "Las islas nuevas," and *La historia de María Griselda*.

Bombal's critique of the patriarchy is underscored by the fact that most of her female characters appear to be locked in a set of particular circumstances. Men are the axis of most of her heroines' lives, but their love is unrequited because men's lives acquire meaning in the outside world and not in the intimacy of love. Women are pawns. In *La última niebla*, Daniel marries the heroine in order to fill the void left by his first wife's death. The anonymous protagonist is a substitute for his dead wife's body.

Most of Bombal's female characters passively accept the immutability of their destinies and withdraw to the regions of their imagination or to the realm of nature. In *La última niebla*, the heroine finds fulfillment in a dream lover. Both Brígida in "El árbol" and María Griselda in *La historia de María Griselda* become one with nature. Ana María, the protagonist of *La amortajada*, remains frustrated by a loveless marriage and an unconsummated affair. Even when Bombal's heroines act, as does Regina in *La última niebla*, who fills the void left by her husband's disinterest with a lover, they are unable to exert change and remain imprisoned by a system that ignores their needs.

Furthermore, Bombal's heroines do not generally connect with other women, and when they do, as they do in *La última niebla*, their relationship becomes adversarial. In "El árbol," Brígida is isolated from her five older sisters. It is not until *House of Mist* that Bombal's female characters seek solace in the company of other women. Helga is welcomed by the three young sisters who run Daniel's house. Her relationship with Daniel's twin is significant because it encourages Helga to be independent and to recognize her value as an individual.

House of Mist is especially relevant within Bombal's work because it develops her thinking about power relationships between men and women. Although critics have rightly stated that Bombal's fiction successfully portrays the situation of women under patriarchal society without proposing alternatives, *House of Mist* begins to address some of these issues. Thus, Bombal's opus is an important antecedent to both Chilean and Spanish American women's literature that developed in the following decades, and it is central to the understanding of its development.

Further Reading

Adams, M. Ian. "María Luisa Bombal: Alienation and the Poetic Image," In *Three Authors of Alienation*, 15–35. Austin: University of Texas Press, 1975.

Agosín, Marjorie, *María Luisa Bombal: Apreciaciones críticas*. Elena Gascón-Vera, and Joy Renjilian-Burgy, eds. Tempe, Ariz.: Bilingual Press/Editorial Bilingüe, 1987.

Gálvez Lira, Gloria. *María Luisa Bombal: Realidad y fantasía*. Potomac, Md.: Scripta Humanistica, 1986.

Guerra Cunningham, Lucía. *La narrativa de María Luisa Bombal: Una visión de la existencia femenina*. Madrid: Editorial Playor, 1980.

———. "Visión de lo femenino en la obra de María Luisa Bombal: Una dualidad contradictoria del ser y el deber-ser." *Revista chilena de literatura* 25 (April 1985): 87–99.

Patricia Rubio

HEBE DE BONAFINI
(December 4, 1928–   )

Argentina: Political Activist, Educator

Hebe de Bonafini—or Hebe María Pastor, her maiden name, or Kika Pastor, as she was known before she became a member of the Madres de Plaza de Mayo (Mothers of the Plaza de Mayo)—is a tireless activist in the fight for human rights, liberty, and justice. Even after serving as president of the Mothers of the Plaza de Mayo Association and receiving international praise and recognition and countless awards, Bonafini insists that she is just a mother and a housewife.

In addition to her duties in the Mothers of the Plaza de Mayo, she is a permanent member of the Committee against Torture in New York City and a former professor at the Cátedra de Derechos Humanos (Chair of Human Rights) in the Department of Communications at the National University of La Plata. She was an original member of the Encuentro Internacional de Madres que Luchan (International Encounter of Mothers Engaged in Struggle) in Paris in 1994 and a godmother for the Buenos Aires Journalist's Union (UPTBA). To raise awareness about human rights, Bonafini has addressed national legislatures in Australia, Bolivia, Brazil, Denmark, Germany, Israel, Italy, the Netherlands, Sweden, Spain, and Venezuela. She has participated in university conferences in Argentina and abroad since 1979 and has served as an advisor for academic theses written about the Mothers of the Plaza de Mayo from a variety of disciplines in Argentina, France, Germany, and Venezuela.

Bonafini was born in La Plata, Buenos Aires. Her working-class family lived in a two-room home with a sheet-metal roof. Since her parents could not afford to send all of their children to high school, only her brother was given the chance. She learned weaving at the María Josefa Rosello Institute. Both rich and poor students attended the trade school, which was run by nuns, but the poor students received their lessons in exchange for doing chores at the school. Hebe and her friend Queca later wove ponchos which sold very well.

Bonafini met her first and only boyfriend, Humberto Bonafini (or Toto), when she was fourteen years old. A seventeen-year-old boy from her neighborhood, he was poor and uneducated. The couple was engaged on December 29, 1942, and married seven years later in a civil ceremony on November 9, 1949. Wearing a borrowed gown, Bonafini was married in the San Francisco de La Plata church on November 12, 1949. The couple's first child, Jorge, was born on December 12, 1950, and their second son, Raúl, was born two-and-a-half years later on July 3, 1953. As their family grew, they moved out of her parents' home to a small house in City Bell. Their daughter María Alejandra was born on August 30, 1965.

Throughout her life, Bonafini has worked creatively to make ends meet. When her children were young, she and her husband made fireworks to sell during Christmas and New Year's Eve. She also made pastries, built walls, installed windows, and worked with her husband in a mechanic's shop. She continued to sell clothes in the streets.

Both of Bonafini's sons attended the National University of La Plata in the 1970s. Jorge studied physics, and Raúl studied natural sciences. Both of them joined the student movement. They told her they were participating in the political process so that others could have a better future. Jorge worked in an adult literacy program. Her sons were not the only politically active members of the family. Bonafini's brother, Walmer, was a union member, and their cousin was a member of Montoneros, the Peronist guerrilla group of the 1960s and 1970s. He was murdered by the state-sponsored paramilitary organization Triple A in 1975. When he was finishing school and becoming increasingly committed to political activism, Jorge married María Elena Bugnone, a classmate from the university and a member of the movement.

Because of their activism, both of Bonafini's sons were targeted. The military broke into Jorge's house and destroyed his two years' worth of research. He was taken into custody on February 8, 1977, by a group of men in civilian clothes who took him away unconscious. Raúl told his parents to demand habeas corpus. Feeling pressure from the increasingly repressive government, Raúl went underground in early winter 1977. He kept intermittent contact only with his younger sister Alejandra. He disappeared on December 6, 1977. Jorge's wife María Elena disappeared from a bar in Lomas de Zamora on May 25, 1978.

Bonafini found out that many people had been taken to the army's First Regiment in Palermo. She asked to speak with someone there, but she was told she would have to wait. Finally, Bonafini recognized a woman who seemed to be making the same trips to the army regiment. As they shared their experiences, they discovered they were searching for the same explanations from the government. Bonafini learned that there was a group of other women in the same situation. In this way, Bonafini met with the women who would become the nucleus of the Mothers of the Plaza de Mayo.

The Mothers began to march in the Plaza de Mayo in front of the Casa Rosada (Pink House, the Argentine seat of the Executive Branch) in Buenos Aires every Thursday beginning April 30, 1977. They chose to meet in the Plaza de Mayo because it gave their cause public exposure. Though the military did not block them from gathering, they did encircle the Plaza so that it would not appear to be a demonstration. Soon after the Mothers organized and began to win recognition for their activities, a young blonde man joined the group claiming that his brother had disappeared. Known as Gustavo Niño, he became a close friend of Azucena Villaflor, one of the group's founders.

A group of several Mothers and French nuns gathered at the Santa Cruz Church to collect donations to publish their open letter to the president. With Gustavo Niño's collaboration, the military arrested and made all of these women "disappear." Bonafini suggested halting the Mothers' activities to search for their colleagues, but Villaflor disagreed, insisting on continuing with their efforts. On December 10, 1977, International Human Rights Day, the newspapers published the Mothers' letter with the names of all of their missing family members and their demand for justice. That same day, Villaflor, who had gone to get a newspaper, disappeared. Her commitment was an inspiration for the remaining members of the Mothers of the Plaza de Mayo.

Bonafini pressured the Mothers of the Plaza de Mayo to build alliances. The Mothers also decided to travel abroad to spread the word. They traveled to the United States and Italy in the late 1970s. In Washington, D.C., they met with representatives from the U.S. Department of State and Massachusetts Senator Edward Kennedy. In Italy, Bonafini and the other Mothers met with the minister of foreign relations, spoke in the Parliament, and had a brief encounter with Prime Minister Sandro Pertini. The pope was unable to meet with them, but the Mothers had a meeting with Argentine Cardinal Eduardo Pironio. The military government was fully aware of their activities.

The Mothers' increasing international visibility marked the beginning of a series of accomplishments. They registered the Mothers of the Plaza de Mayo Association and they elected an eleven-member commission on August 22, 1979. The association rented a small apartment in Buenos Aires, and it organized demonstrations in which members marched in silence. The international press filmed these marches. By this time, neither the government nor the police could stop them. When Adolfo Pérez Esquivel received the Nobel Peace Prize, Bonafini and other Mothers accompanied him to Sweden to accept the award. The Mothers also participated in human rights commissions, and they joined the protests against the Falklands conflict with Britain in 1982.

In 1981 Bonafini's husband Toto fell ill. Committed to tending to him, Bonafini told the Mothers that she had to abandon her struggle for the association temporarily. The other Mothers traveled to La Plata. Toto died in September of the following year.

The Mothers of the Plaza de Mayo split. The Línea Fundadora (Founding Line) supported the exhumation of the bodies of those who had disappeared and the distribution of economic compensation. The other wing, headed by Bonafini, refused to collaborate with a supposedly democratic government that had pardoned assassins. The Mothers stated that their children were not dead as long as a single assassin was free.

Currently, the Mothers of the Plaza de Mayo Association hold their commission meetings on Tuesday afternoons. They also maintain a web page (www.madres.org) and host literature classes, literary workshops, a newspaper, and other publications. In addition, before they go to the Plaza de Mayo to march, the Mothers meet to discuss current events and newspaper articles, and to define the organization's political line. The Mothers' radical political positions and their ongoing activism have attracted many young people to the organization. A group of children of the disappeared, now adolescents, has formed the H.I.J.O.S. Association (in Spanish, the acronym spells children), which works arm and arm with the Mothers of the Plaza de Mayo.

Bonafini has received numerous awards from organizations around the world. She was presented the Medalla de Oro de la Ciudad (Gold Medal of the City) from the Ayuntamiento de Castelldefels (Castelldefels City Hall) in Barcelona, Spain; the Sajarov, for Freedom of Thought, from the European Parliament; and the Orden José Rafael Verona (Order of José Rafael Verona) from the Organización Latinoamericana de Estudiantes in Cuba (Latin American Student Organization). Bonafini was also granted honorary citizenship from the city of Santos in Brazil and the René Sand for Contributions to the Fight for Human Rights in Berlin, Germany.

Further Reading

Bouvard, Marguerite Guzman. *Revolutionizing Motherhood: The Mothers of Plaza de Mayo*. Wilmington, Del.: Scholarly Resources, 1994.
Mellibovsky, Matilde. *Circle of Love over Death*. Willimantic, Conn.: Curbstone Press, 1997.

María del Mar López-Cabrales

Rosa María Britton
(July 28, 1936–   )

Panama: Author, Playwright, Physician

As a woman who has excelled in two very different fields—medicine and literature—Rosa María Britton occupies a unique position in Latin America. She has received numerous medical awards and is a prolific and well-known novelist, playwright, and short story writer.

Born in Panama to a middle-class family who owned a small factory producing women's clothing, Britton grew up comfortably. Although the family income hardly allowed for luxuries, it did provide for a large and varied family library. Both her parents were avid readers, and as a result Britton was encouraged to read extensively. By the age of ten she had already read works by Émile Zola, Jules Verne, Guy de Maupassant, Benito Pérez Galdós, and Oscar Wilde. Britton credits her mother's progressive thinking for inspiring her to study. Her parents had met in New York City, where Britton's mother, dissatisfied with her own Panamanian teacher certification, had gone to study in the 1920s. When the stockmarket crashed in 1929, she abandoned her studies to learn a practical trade that would allow her to support herself. She met Britton's father, a Cuban, at the clothing factory where they both worked. They married, returned to Panama in 1931, and opened their own clothing factory.

Nevertheless, Britton's mother had ambitions that compelled her to insist her children follow a more demanding school curriculum than the one offered in Panama at the time. As a result, Britton left Panama at a young age in order to attend the best high school in Havana, Cuba, where she lived for seven years. After graduating as valedictorian, she began her medical studies in Cuba, but these were cut short by the Cuban Revolution in 1959. Britton consequently left Cuba to study in Madrid, where she stayed for eight years, married an American engineer, and earned her medical degree. Afterward, she continued her studies in gynecology and oncology in New York City.

Britton credits her success as a doctor to her mentor, Dr. Harry Greene, a famous oncologist, whose assistance and support allowed her to overcome the many obstacles she faced in New York as the only woman and the only foreigner in a surgical specialty. As an example of gender discrimination, Britton tells of the times when Greene brought her to meetings of the New York Tumor Society held at the Princeton Club (which did not allow women) by sneaking her through its kitchen. Nevertheless, her constant curiosity, positive attitude, superior skill as a surgeon, and boundless energy helped her to overcome these difficulties. She became the chief resident in Brooklyn Jewish Medical Center, established a private practice in Queens, and served as an attending physician and clinical professor in Downstate Medical School.

Shortly after the birth of her second child, Britton's husband was offered a position with the Canal Company in Panama. Since the lack of proper child care in the United States was making her professional life more complicated, her husband convinced her to return to Panama in 1973. Upon returning, Britton began working in the only cancer hospital in the country. As the director of the National Oncological Institute of Panama for eighteen years, she has received numerous medical awards in Latin America. For three years (1993–96) she was president of the Latin American Federation of Cancerology Societies (FLACSA) and was the Panamanian representative of the American College of Obstetrics and Gynecology (1996–2000).

While it was easy for Britton to find work in Panama because she was the only U.S.–trained cancer specialist, she spent most of her professional career fighting various governments in order to raise funds to improve her hospital. Another important contribution was *La costilla de Adán* (Adam's Rib, 1985), a handbook on women's bodies and sexuality that Britton wrote in an accessible literary style in response to women's ignorance about their own bodies. While *La costilla de Adán* is a practical book that explains women's health to a nonspecialized audience, it recognizes the particular obstacles faced by Latin American women in terms of their health and sexuality. This book was very well received, and Britton is currently working on an updated version.

Rosa María Britton. Photo by Javier Macias. Courtesy of Foto el Halcon SA.

Although Britton's family had always encouraged her to read and she had been writing since high school, she did not begin writing in earnest until 1978 as a way to escape the boredom of numerous bureaucractic meetings. What began as a short story eventually developed into a novel that her secretary insisted she enter in the prestigious national Ricardo Miró literary competition. To her surprise, this first novel, *El ataúd de uso* (Used Coffin), won the Miró prize in 1982 and was published in 1983. This historical novel explores the period of Panamanian independence and subsequent U.S. domination from the turn of the century until World War II through the lives of the inhabitants of an imaginary coastal town, Chumico. By focusing on the principal characters, Manuel and Carmen, an Afro-Panamanian fisherman and a white schoolteacher who marry despite family opposition, Britton manages to incorporate the themes of racism, machismo, religion, and politics in Panamanian society. This novel is now part of the national school curriculum and is read by all Panamanian schoolchildren.

Inspired by her initial literary success, Britton has continued writing. Her first novel was soon followed by *El señor de las lluvias y el viento* (The Master of the Rain and the Wind, 1984), which was awarded a Miró in 1984. This work interweaves the lives of three separate protagonists: Andrés, a lovelorn medicine man; Alicia, a mulatto nurse who as a young orphan traveled to the United States to become a nun only to fall in love with a man incapable of overcoming his family's prejudices in order to marry her; and José, whose infidelity provokes the attack of his long-suffering wife and whose stay in the hospital brings Alicia and Andrés together at last. The well-developed principal and secondary characters in search of love and happiness allow the author to delve into the themes of love, infidelity, racial discrimination, and magic. This novel is also part of the national school curriculum.

Britton's literary successes continued with three more Miró prizes: one for short story in 1985 ("¿Quién inventó el mambo?," or Who Invented the Mambo?) and two for drama in 1986 and 1987 (Esa esquina del paraíso, or That Corner of Paradise, and Banquete de despedida, or Farewell Banquet). Of these works, Esa esquina del paraíso deserves special mention because of its treatment of racism in both Panama and the United States. The main protagonist is a mulatto woman who attempts to marry an American serviceman during World War II by passing as a Caucasian. This play shows the impact of U.S. racial segregation as it influences attitudes about race in Panamanian society: the main protagonist feels she must deny a part of herself in order to fit into the American way of life. Another drama, Miss Panamá Inc. (1992), is a ferocious critique of beauty pageants and their effect on women.

More recently, Britton has published a historical novel, No pertenezco a este siglo (I Don't Belong to This Century, 1989), which deals with the independence of Panama from Colombia as seen through the eyes of a conservative Colombian politician, and two collections of short stories, La muerte tiene dos caras (Death Has Two Faces, 1988) and Semana de la mujer y otras calamidades (Women's Week and Other Calamities, 1995). The former explores the theme of death in a series of different guises, such as the Chinese worker on the Panamanian railroad of the nineteenth century who uses opium to escape the harsh working conditions that eventually kill him, or the poor Panamanian black woman who slowly bleeds to death because she has prostituted herself shortly after an operation in order to feed her children. The second collection explores the difficulties faced by Latin American women as they attempt to construct their own independent identities in the face of discrimination and machismo. Finally, her latest and most autobiographical novel, Todas íbamos a ser reinas (We Were All Going to Be Queens, 1997), deals with the fate of five young women who formed a profound friendship at their boarding school in Batista's Cuba. The novel traces their dreams and disappointments as reality forces them to discover that the world is not the way they imagined it when they were coming of age in the safe, cloistered atmosphere of their Catholic convent school. The novel also manages to capture the ambience of reckless excess in prerevolutionary Cuba as well as the sombre, oppressive atmosphere of Francisco Franco's Spain.

In addition to her five Miró awards, Britton won the Golden Pen Award in Panama in 1998 for having sold more books than any other national author. While Britton continues to work full-time as a physician, she sees her primary vocation as a writer and plans to continue writing indefinitely. According to Britton, "[Writing] gives me the opportunity to be and to transform myself into everything and nothing, man or woman, present or future, bird or serpent, anything that the imagination and the written word tells me. After all, it's the only thing that remains in the end" (personal communication, 1999).

Further Reading

López-Cruz, Humberto. "Factores discursivos en la narrativa de Rosa María Britton: Feminismo y negritud." *SECOLAS Annals: Journal of the Southeastern Council on Latin American Studies* 29 (1998): 55–60.

———. "La negritud como la historia no oficial en las dos primeras novelas de Rosa María Britton." *Romance Notes* 39, no. 1 (1998): 53–59.

Frances Jaeger

JULIA DE BURGOS
(February 14, 1914–August 4, 1953)
Puerto Rico: Author, Poet

A poet who found emotional solace in her work and became a patriotic symbol in Puerto Rico, Julia de Burgos was born in Barrio Santa Cruz, Carolina, on the northern coast of Puerto Rico. Her parents, Francisco Burgos Hans and Paula García, were very poor, and she was the oldest of thirteen siblings, of whom only seven survived. Burgos studied at a rural public school in Barrio Santa Cruz and also in Río Grande. After graduating with honors in 1927, she joined the Superior School at the University of Puerto Rico. In 1931 she received the Superior School Diploma and a scholarship to study at the University of Puerto Rico. She received her teaching certificate in 1933, and one year later she started working as a Milk Station employee for the Puerto Rico Economical Rehabilitation Agency (PRERA) at Comerío, where children of poor families received free breakfasts.

Burgos married twice. When she was twenty she married Rubén Rodríguez Beauchamp, whom she divorced three years later. When PRERA was closed in 1935, she started teaching at the rural school in Barrio

Julia de Burgos. Courtesy of Ateneo Puertorriqueño.

Cerro Arriba, Naranjito. During these months she wrote "Río Grande de
Loíza" (Main River of Loíza) and took a nursery school education course
at the University of Puerto Rico. Burgos met and befriended Puerto Rican
poets Luis Llorens Torres, Luis Palés Matos, Evaristo Ribera Chevre-
mont, and others. In 1936 she published the poem "Es nuestra la hora"
(Ours Is the Hour) and gave a speech, "La mujer ante el dolor de la
Patria" (Women in the Face of Puerto Rican Suffering), at the first general
assembly of United Front for the Constituent Convention, at the Puerto
Rican Athenaeum. While living on Luna Street, in Old San Juan, she
worked at the School of the Air on some educational programs under
the Department of Public Instruction. During that year, she wrote four
short dramas: *Llamita quiere ser mariposa* (Little Flame Wants To Be a
Butterfly), *Paisaje marino* (Marinescape), *La parranda del sábado* (Saturday
Bash), and *Coplas Jíbaras para ser cantadas* (Peasant Verses for Singing).
She also took a survey of English literature and a contemporary civilization course at the University of Puerto Rico. By 1937 she had finished
Poemas exactos a mí misma (Exact Poems to Myself), a typewritten book
that was eventually lost. She read books by Stephen Zweig, Friedrich
Nietzsche, Immanuel Kant, Anatole France, and Oscar Wilde. This same
year she published poems in the Puerto Rican newspaper *El imparcial*

(The Impartial) and the Puerto Rican published literary journal *Renovación* (Renovation). "Poema al hijo que no llega" (Poem to an Unarrived Son), in which she expresses her frustration of not having a child, appeared in the magazine *El poeta de hoy* (Today's Poet).

In 1938 she met the love of her life, Juan Isidro Jimenes Grullón, a Dominican medical doctor and sociologist who was married to Cuban Ana María Sabater. Burgos took courses in Hispanic language and literature as well as the history of Hispanic America at the University of Puerto Rico. Three years before she had found out that her mother had cancer. She published *Poema en veinte surcos* (Poem in Twenty Furrows) and sold it personally throughout the island. With the benefits she obtained, she partially paid the bills incurred by her mother's illness, but Doña Paula died the following year. Burgos published other poems in *Renovación* (1938) and *Puerto Rico ilustrado* (Puerto Rico Illustrated, 1939) and in 1939 was honored with a recital at the Puerto Rican Athenaeum, where the poet herself read "Mi madre y el río" (My Mother and the River). In December of the same year, she published *Canción de la verdad sencilla* (Song of the Simple Truth, 1939), a book for which she received a $500 prize awarded by the Puerto Rican Literature Institute in 1940. On January 18, 1940, she arrived in New York City, where fifteen days later she was interviewed by the newspaper *La prensa* (The Press). She participated in a conference organized by Jimenes Grullón at the Chilean Workers Club by reciting her poem "Main River of Loíza." On February 23 Carmen Rodríguez recited her poems at the Master Theater, and some weeks later, the Association of Puerto Rican Journalists and Writers paid homage to Burgos along with Antonio Coll y Vidal. She worked for the United States census until April 16, and the following day she gave a recital of her poems at the Master Theater. She arrived in Cuba on June 26, along with Jimenes Grullón, where she was interviewed by the magazines *Carteles* (Posters) and *Vanidades* (Vanities). There she met such Cuban intellectuals as Juan Marinello, Juan Bosch, Raúl Roa, and Manuel Luna. She gave a speech to the children of the Cuban Civic-Military School entitled "Mensaje de un niño puertorriqueño a un niño cubano" (Message from a Puerto Rican Child to a Cuban Child). By September she was about to finish her book of poems *El mar y tú* (The Sea and You) and announced another book entitled *Campo* (Countryside). On January 23, 1941, she published a sonnet dedicated to José Martí in *Oriente* (East), a newspaper in Santiago de Cuba, and in March she sent three certified copies of *El mar y tú* to the Latin American Writers Conference held on April 15 in Puerto Rico. She then moved to Havana, where she took courses in humanities at the University of Havana. There, she participated in public seminars on the independence of Puerto Rico.

In 1942 Burgos met the Chilean poet Pablo Neruda, who promised to write a prologue to her book *El mar y tú*. Meanwhile her private life began to disintegrate. Jimenes Grullón's family did not approve of their affair, and he temporarily abandoned her. Disappointed, she left Cuba and went to New York, where she held several modest jobs. She often felt exiled and homesick in the big city.

In 1943 she married Armando Marín, a musician from Vieques, and she began to work as an editor for *Pueblos hispánicos* (Hispanic Peoples) the following year. She took care of Llorens Torres, who was in a clinic in New York. Beginning on August 26, she lived in Washington, D.C., with her husband, where she worked as an office clerk for the coordinator of inter-American affairs. Washington depressed her even more than New York; she called it "the capital of silence," and she looked forward to returning to Puerto Rico. After meeting Spanish poet Juan Ramón Jiménez, Burgos returned to New York, and in 1946 the Institute of Puerto Rican Literature granted her a journalism award for her article "Ser o no ser es la divisa" (To Be or Not To Be, That Is the Motto), which had appeared the previous year in *Semanario hispano* (Hispanic Weekly). Other homages followed. Meanwhile, her alcohol dependency degenerated into cirrhosis of the liver. She experienced problems with her vocal cords and was admitted to several hospitals. In 1947 she attended a lecture given by her ex-lover, Juan Jimenes Grullón, who had arrived with his wife.

In 1952 she read her *Homenaje al cantor de Collores* (Homage to the Singer of Collores) on a radio program dedicated to Llorens Torres. Her sister tried in vain to have the Library of Puerto Rican Authors publish *El mar y tú*. During the first months of 1953 Burgos underwent surgery on her vocal cords and remained secluded at the Goldwater Memorial Hospital, on the outskirts of New York. Her physical and mental health deteriorated, and she left the hospital several times. In February she wrote a poem in English, "Farewell in Welfare Island," in which she denounced her desperate situation. Once again, poetry was her only haven: the poem reconciled her with death, which had become her obsession. In May she left the hospital and lived with her family in Brooklyn. She died under tragic circumstances. One day in July she was found unconscious on 105th Street and Fifth Avenue. She was taken to the Harlem Hospital, where she was pronounced dead. Later, pneumonia was identified as the cause of death. The deceased had no identification and was taken to the morgue. A month later, the picture of the body helped solve the mystery. Immediately thereafter, a committee was formed in Puerto Rico to bring her home. The Puerto Rican Athenaeum and the Society of Journalists honored her posthumously. In a letter to her sister she had asked to be buried in her native country so, following her wishes, she was buried in a humble tomb in the Municipal Cemetery in Carolina.

Burgos belongs to the generation of 1930, also known as the "generation in crisis." She has become a symbol in Puerto Rico thanks to her profound patriotism and her ideas about national independence. Apart from the respect for her poetry, her situation as a lonely and suffering woman, her solidarity, and her will to struggle mirror the collective conscience of thousands of Puerto Ricans outside the island. The reader can identify with her longing for self-definition and liberation, her feelings of frustration and love, and her sympathy for the poor and oppressed, the victims of racial discrimination and the dead of the Spanish Civil War. However, according to Matilla and Silén, "She was ignored by critics, silenced by institutes and cast aside by local poets who drove her to an alcoholic state that frightened the Puerto Rican bourgeoisie" (1972, xvi). She relieved her frustrations through her poetry. As a consequence, her life and her writings are inseparable. Her existential anguish, her solitude, and her disagreement with the conditions of contemporary women in her society all found expression in her books. In *Poema de veinte surcos* (1938), published when she was twenty-four, she protested against imperialism and devoted much space to her feminist and nationalistic ideals in favor of independence leader Pedro Albizu Campos. It included two of her most celebrated poems: "A Julia de Burgos" (To Julia de Burgos) and "Yo misma fui mi ruta" (I Was My Own Path). In *Canción de la verdad sencilla*, a book inspired by Jimenes Grullón, her erotism prevailed. She set aside her previous commitment to sociopolitical struggles and chose a more intimate and optimistic tone. Several critics have pointed out the neoromantic traits of her poetry. However, her posthumous book, *El mar y tú; otros poemas* (The Sea and You; Other Poems, 1954), is a song of disillusionment to the lost love. Poetry became her release for the pain caused by the betrayal and abandonment of her lover. Her final alcohol dependency and self-destruction were most likely born out of her lifelong struggles in her interpersonal relationships.

Further Reading

Matilla, Alfredo, and Iván Silén. *The Puerto Rican Poets/Los Poetas Puertorriqueños: The First Bilingual Anthology Covering the Entire Range of Puerto Rican Poetry of This Century*. New York: Bantam Books, 1972.

Sievert, Heather Rosario. "Between the Woman and the Poet: The Abyss of Julia de Burgos." In *Actas del Congreso Internacional Julia de Burgos*, edited by Edgar Martínez Masdeu, 201–12. San Juan, Puerto Rico: Ateneo Puertorriqueño, 1993.

Umpierre, Luz María. "Metapoetic Code in Julia de Burgos' *El mar y tú*: Towards a Revision." In *Retrospect: Essays on Latin American Literature*, edited by Elizabeth Rogers and Timothy Rogers, 85–94. York: South Carolina Spanish Literature Publication Company, 1987.

Zavala-Martínez, Iris. "A Critical Inquiry into the Life and Work of Julia de Burgos." In *The Psychosocial Development of Puerto Rican Women*, edited by Cynthia García Coll and María de Lourdes Mattei, 1–29. New York: Praeger, 1989.

Ignacio López-Calvo

LYDIA CABRERA

(May 20, 1900–September 19, 1991)

Cuba: Author, Ethnologist

An interpreter of Afro-Cuban culture and an ethnologist, Lydia Cabrera was born with the twentieth century in Havana, Cuba, the seventh child of Raimundo Cabrera and Elisa Bilbao. Her father, a well-known lawyer, politician, and writer, had a great influence on her. When she was thirteen, she began to write humorous and ironic chronicles about Cuban social life, published under the pseudonym Nena en Sociedad (Little Girl in Society), in her father's journal *Cuba y América* (Cuba and America).

Cabrera continued writing her column until 1916 and also wrote for the *Diario de la Marina* (Navy Daily). Always interested in art and drawing, she contributed illustrations to her father's journal and to *Social*. She also accompanied him to meetings of the prestigious Sociedad Económica del País (National Economic Society), an association established by Cuban landowners for the purpose of developing agriculture and industry. Because of his participation in politics, her father had to leave Cuba in 1917, and Lydia accompanied her parents into exile.

In 1918 they returned to Cuba and, without her father's consent, she studied art at the San Alejandro Academy. She later founded the Asociación de Arte Retrospectivo (Association of Retrospective Art), and in 1922, in order to finance a study trip to France, she established her own company, Alyds, devoted to interior decoration and the importation of European furniture. After her father's death in 1923, Cabrera left for Paris to pursue a degree in Oriental art at the Louvre. She also took courses at the Contemporary Academy, directed by French painter Fernand Léger, and became interested in African art.

On her return to Cuba in 1930, Cabrera undertook a sustained interpretation of Cuban-African culture and established contact with the Yorubas (Black Cubans), who in time passed on to her, in spoken form, knowledge of their culture. At this time, she began collecting African tales and initiated her own research into religions, customs, and language vocabularies, stimulated by the pioneering work of her brother-in-law, Fernando Ortiz, on Cuban-African culture.

In 1936 her first book of fiction was published in Paris by Gallimard, translated by Francis de Miomandre as *Contes nègres de Cuba* (Black Stories from Cuba), which had already been published separately in such

Lydia Cabrera. Courtesy of Mariela A. Gutiérrez.

French literary journals as *Cahiers du sud* (Southern Notebooks), *Revue de Paris* (Paris Review), and *Les Nouvelles littéraires* (New Writers). These twenty-two stories were poetic transcriptions of the myths, the magic world, and the folklore of Afro-Cuban culture. With their borrowed Lucumí words, terms from one of the languages spoken by people of African descent in Cuba, they revealed with humor, wit, and wisdom a world of human beings and animals—the *jicotea* (tortoise) and the *majá* (a thick-bodied snake)—of proverbs and songs.

Cabrera dedicated these stories to a close friend, Venezuelan writer Teresa de la Parra, who had encouraged her to have them published. Gabriela Mistral, the Chilean writer who was also her friend, wrote to her from Nice to insist that she have them published in Spanish as well, and in 1940 the Cuban edition, *Cuentos negros de Cuba*, appeared with a preface by Fernando Ortíz. In his introduction, Ortíz calls this the first work on Afro-Cuban culture produced by a Havana-born writer, a woman whom he himself had initiated into the world of Afro-Cuban folklore. Ortíz also speaks of the literary qualities and values of the book, calling the collection of stories a new chapter in the literature of Cuba.

Cabrera's work formed a part of Cuban avant-garde interest in African culture. Along with the writings of Alejo Carpentier, Nicolás Guillén,

Amadeo Roldán, and Wifredo Lam, it (re)created its words and symbols. Cabrera continued to study its linguistic and anthropological characteristics during the 1930s, 1940s, and 1950s. In spite of the fact that she lacked formal ethnological training, she became, nevertheless, a respected ethnologist and writer.

Her *Pourquoi contes nègres de Cuba* (Why Black Stories from Cuba) appeared in 1954 and was also translated by Miomandre for Gallimard in a collection edited by Roger Caillois. *El monte* (The Forest) came out in her own publishing house, Eds. C. R., in 1954, as did *Refranes de negros viejos* (Old Black Sayings) a year later; *Anago: Vocabulario lucumí* (Anago: Lucumí Vocabulary) was published with a preface by Roger Bastide in 1957, and *La sociedad secreta Abakuá* (Abakua Secret Society) in 1959.

El monte is one of Cabrera's most important books. Its subject is the music, religion, superstition, and folklore of Cuban blacks and of the Cuban people. "El monte" is a temple of symbolic connotation, a place of spirituality and magic for the Cuban black. Unfortunately still unpublished in English, *El monte* had two editions in Italian while Cabrera was still alive. An unauthorized Cuban edition of 1989 went out of print but was later to be found secondhand at a high price. In Miami, the book had six additional editions between 1968 and 1986.

Since her return to Cuba in the 1930s and throughout the 1940s and 1950s, Cabrera had books published abroad and by her own publishing house. She also wrote articles for national and international journals and acted as a consultant for the National Institute of Culture (1952–1959). Her love for art, however, never waned, and she pursued with passion her abiding interest in antiques and Cuban furniture, in buildings, houses, and decor. She and her lover and partner, historian María Teresa de Rojas, called Titina, helped restore one of Havana's most beautiful eighteenth-century residences, the Palacio Pedroso, and San José, a villa in Marianao (a Havana suburb) owned by María Teresa de Rojas.

Cabrera spent much of her time traveling throughout the island in search of pieces that would fit into the Cuban colonial and Creole style she had created at San José. There, she and Rojas lived and worked in a wonderfully artistic atmosphere: while Rojas pursued her own paleographic research, Cabrera conducted her ethnological research and wrote books. The two women transformed the eighteenth-century villa into a sort of living museum of Cuban artistic tradition and style.

Cabrera was the friend of many well-known intellectuals from Cuba and abroad. She was a friend of the Spanish playwright and poet Federico García Lorca, attended Teresa de la Parra in her illness, corresponded with Gabriela Mistral, and was friendly with Cuban painters Wifredo Lam and Amélia Peláez. Fernando Ortíz, as well as Cuban novelists Alejo Carpentier and José Lezama Lima, wrote with enthusiasm of her work. Spanish philosopher María Zambrano considered her a poet of metamorphosis.

With the advent of the Cuban Revolution of 1959, Cabrera's life underwent an important change. She and Titina Rojas left the island in 1960 and lived in Miami until their deaths. Cabrera, who was by then sixty years old, had to endure the loss of personal friends and surroundings and of contact with the Cuban cultural world. During her self-imposed exile, she continued to write and publish; she gave interviews; and she saw the publication of new editions of her books, not only in Spanish but also in English. She received honors; her work continued to merit critical and academic acclaim; and her short stories were published in anthologies in the United States.

When she left Cuba, Cabrera had managed to take documents and manuscripts with her. With that rich and valuable fund of information she was able to write other works well into her sixties and beyond: *Otán Iyebiye* (a history of gems and their meaning); *Ayapá, cuentos de Jicotea* (Ayapá, Stories of Jicotea—stories with animal and human characters); *La laguna sagrada de San Joaquín* (The Sacred Lagoon of San Joaquín—Cuban photos); *Yemayá y Ochún* (Yemayá and Ochún—about Yoruba's female goddesses, the *orichas*); *Anaforuana* (about the initiation ritual into the secret society of Abakua); several books on the rules of different religions (*Palo Monte Mayombe, Regla, Lucumí*), a book of short stories (tales for adults and children); and a Congolese dictionary.

In an interview that probed whether she was satisfied with her life, Cabrera provided a thoughtful answer. She replied that she has been happy, maybe too happy; she thanks God for the good and the bad years. She does not consider herself ambitious: she has never asked for what she could not have. She even thanks God for the experience of having lost everything; everything except her sense of humor (Hiriart 1978, 179).

The stability of her family upbringing, the intellectual environment of her childhood, the early access to books and culture all helped her form a strong personality, but her natural sense of humor brightened Cabrera's work and life. The intimate bonding with her Cuban heritage and her dedication to making a place in the culture of Cuba for its African heritage became part of her independent way of facing her own life and molding it.

Studying art without parental consent, establishing her own private business, going to Paris on her own, daring to penetrate, as a white bourgeois woman, the Afro-Cuban world, having her own publishing house, and choosing an unconventional private life all speak of Cabrera's personal autonomy and explain her position within the Cuban avant-garde. Her contribution to Cuban culture and her accomplishments are related to her appearing in a world in which the definition of Cuba as a nation and of Cuban cultural identity were central to the discourse of the day. Her personal interest in those issues and her assiduous efforts came together to meet the luck and good fortune of being born at the right moment in the right place.

Further Reading

Costa Willis, Miriam de. "Folklore and the Creative Artist: Lydia Cabrera and Zora Neale Hurston." *College Language Association Journal* 27, no. 1 (1983): 81–90.

Hiriart, Rosario. *Lydia Cabrera: Vida hecha arte.* New York: E. Torres, 1978.

Levine, Suzanne Jill. "A Conversation with Lydia Cabrera." *Review: Latin American Literature and Arts* 31 (1982): 13–15.

Valdés-Cruz, Rosa. "The Short Studies of Lydia Cabrera: Transposition or Creations." In *Latin American Women Writers—Yesterday and Today*, edited by Yvette Miller and Charles Tatum, 148–54. Pittsburgh: Latin American Literary Review Press, 1977.

Nara Araújo

MARÍA CANO

(August 12, 1887–April 26, 1967)

Colombia: Political Leader

María de los Angeles Cano Márquez was the most important Colombian socialist leader of the 1920s. She was born in Medellín and died in the same city. In contrast to many wealthy families from Antioquía who lived from mining, cattle, or commerce, hers was an educated and influential family of writers, journalists, musicians, photographers, and painters.

Unlike many women of her time, she grew up in an intellectual environment and was exposed to public debate. During the 1920s, she was involved in political circles influenced by the Bolshevik Revolution of 1917 in Russia.

Public life and literary activity are intertwined in María Cano's case. In cooperation with other intellectuals from Medellín, Cano not only began a literary circle called Cyrano, but also founded the homonymous magazine. From an art-for-art's-sake position she turned to socially committed writing. By 1922 Fita Uribe and María Eastman, two other writers from Antioquia, and Cano worked in *El correo liberal* (The Liberal Mail), which was a progressive, democratic, and very popular newspaper. Other women writers in different regions of the country soon imitated their literary activities. As a poet, Cano was influenced by other Latin American poets such as Argentine Alfonsina Storni, Uruguayans Delmira Agustini and Juana Ibarbourou, and, particularly, Chilean Gabriela Mistral. Unfortunately, most of Cano's work remains disseminated in journals, newspapers, and literary magazines. In her development as a socialist leader, she abandoned the intimate and erotic tone of her poetry and prose. Often times, in the pursuit of workers' rights, Cano neglected the vindication of women's rights. Given the traditional roles women were relegated to, Cano became a symbol for rebellious women, so much so that Antioquía parents sought to prevent their daughters from becoming *mariacanos* (i.e., like María Cano).

Cano was particularly concerned about the workers' access to education. At the Public State Library, she read to the workers to raise their cultural awareness. She also visited their houses where she learned about their harrowing living conditions. In the beginning, she turned to philanthropy, providing food and clothes to those in need. Social activism was not unusual at the time. While the dominant class in Antioquia was conservative and Christian, there was no sharp division between socialist and Catholic principles. Thus, groups like Acción Social Católica (Catholic Social Action) got the workers organized by the 1920s. On May 1, 1925 (Labor Day in Colombia), the workers named Cano Revolutionary Red Flower because of her work in their behalf to improve their living conditions. Yet Cano succeeded in displacing women's participation from the emblematic connotations of the Revolutionary Red Flower title to real social activism. She started visiting factories, denouncing unfair working conditions and organizing at a grassroots level.

During the intense social and political upheaval in the Colombia of the 1920s, Cano became a social public speaker and a revolutionary leader. She went to the political rallies that targeted the most important concentrations of workers in spite of the lack of access between the different geographical regions and the precarious conditions of highways and transportation.

Cano's rallies began with a visit to the mines of Sevilla and Remedios, in Antioquia. Her agenda was restricted to human rights, especially overthrowing the death penalty. She succeeded in obtaining the liberation of Raúl Eduardo Mahecha, a labor leader who had been in prison since the first oil strike in 1924. By 1925 Cano had reached out to labor movements beyond Antioquia. In 1926 the Confederación Obrera Nacional (National Workers Confederation, or CON) made her responsible for organizing the regional representation of Antioquía at the Third National Labor Congress. Her participation in labor meetings and demonstrations placed her at the same rank as socialist leaders such as Mahecha, Ignacio Torres Giraldo, and Tomás Uribe Márquez. This congress was significant on two counts: Cano was appointed to interview the secretary of government to demand the release of political prisoners, specifically Vicente Adame and the legendary indigenous leader Manuel Quintín Lame. For the first time in the history of Colombia, a woman occupied a leadership position in a political organization. The Partido Socialista Revolucionario (Revolutionary Socialist party, or PSR), which would become the Colombian Communist party in 1930, also arose from the congress.

The third rally was to take place in Cundinamarca and Boyacá, but the authorities showed hostility toward this socialist group. They were expelled from Boyacá. Torres Giraldo was imprisoned. Upon his release, Torres Giraldo and Cano remained in hiding. Cano started organizing the fourth rally that would take place in Barrancabermeja, an important oil town near the central Magadalena valley. The location was significant because the workers of the Tropical Oil Company (a subsidiary of Jersey Standard) were organizing a second strike. Cano's anti-imperialist speeches were crucial to the organization of labor unions along the Magdalena River. The national repercussions of the strikes led to state repression. President Miguel Abadía Méndez and Ignacio Rengifo, the secretary of defense, quashed the military counterattack. By the end of January, the PSR strikes had been suppressed. Cano was under surveillance and forbidden to speak publicly.

Nonetheless, the PSR and the CON instructed Cano to continue with the fifth rally to be held along the western rim of the country. Her leadership was proven in Manizales, where she succeeded in holding the audience's attention in spite of military attempts to disperse the crowd. The rally concluded when Cano joined the PSR convention in La Dorada, an important fluvial port on the Magdalena River. The convention did not take place as planned because some of the organizers had been imprisoned. With the support of some military factions of the Liberal party, the PSR split into the Comité Central Conspirador Colombiano (Colombian Central Organizing Committee). Nonetheless, Cano remained faithful to the political and ideological principles of the original PSR. With other members of the Regional of Antioquia, she founded La justicia (Justice), the party newspaper. In addition to contributing to this paper, Cano contributed to other similar publications such as La humanidad (Humanity), Vox populi, and Nueva era (New Era).

After visiting the tobacco zone of Santander and the coffee plantations, she went on her last rally. Cano and Torres Giraldo went to the banana zone where the United Fruit Company operated. This was also the site of the most powerful labor unions at the time. Her visit galvanized 30,000 workers of the Unión Sindical de Trabajadores del Magdalena (Magdalena Syndicated Workers Union). Meanwhile, the government countered the threat of an imminent "communist" upheaval with the ley *heroica*, a law designed to combat international communism. During the second half of 1928, Cano devoted her energy to fight this law and to support Nicaraguan rebel leader Sandino's struggle for national sovereignty in Nicaragua. The workers' demonstrations continued in the banana zone, only to meet a bloody end on December 6, 1928, when soldiers fired into a mass of strikers gathered in Ciénaga, a historical episode immortalized in Gabriel García Márquez's *Cien años de soledad* (One Hundred Years of Solitude, 1967). To date, the number of victims remains controversial. Although Cano and Torres Giraldo were in Medellín at the time of the massacre, they were imprisoned together with other PSR leaders. These events, coupled with the economic recession of the 1930s, brought about the end of the political activity of the CON and led to the splitting of the PSR. Both Cano and Torres Giraldo were charged with conspiracy. Her attempts to clear up the charges in writing were unsuccesful. Together with other PSR leaders, Cano was politically isolated. Her attempts to return to politics in 1934 were unsuccessful too. She worked for the Antioquia State Press, where she was promoted to the Library Department.

After 1947 she appeared on the public scene on several occasions. The Alianza Femenina de Medellín (Medellín Women's Alliance) recognized her contributions in 1945. She was appointed as speaker for the Organización Democrática de Mujeres de Antioquia (Democratic Organization of Antioquia Women) on March 8, 1960. By the time of her death in 1967, revolutionary movements had taken different paths. Colombia had experienced an undeclared civil war known as La Violencia (The Violence), the repercussions of which continue to this day. On the other hand, the National Front, the institutionalized bipartisan coalition regime that guaranteed political power to the two traditional Colombian political parties (Liberal and Conservative) had succeeded in remaining in power for the third time.

Further Reading

DeJong, Jana Marie. "Recuperación de las voces de una década: feminismo y literatura femenina en los años veinte." In *Literatura y diferencia. Escritoras colombianas del siglo XX*, edited by María Mercedes Jaramillo et al., 1.31–55. Bogotá, Colombia: Ediciones Uniandes and Editorial Universidad de Antioquia, 1995.

Marín Taborda, Jorge Iván. *María Cano en el amanecer de la clase obrera*. Bogotá, Colombia: Librería Sindical Colombiana, 1985.

———. "María Cano. Su época, su historia." In *Las mujeres en la historia de Colombia*, 156–72. Bogotá, Colombia: Grupo Editorial Norma, 1995.

Velásquez Toro, Magdala. "María Cano pionera y agitadora social de los años 20." *Revista credencial de historia* (January–December 1990). http://www.banrep.gov.co/blaavirtual/credencial/hcano.htm

Juana Suárez

NANCY CÁRDENAS
(May 29, 1934–March 22, 1994)
Mexico: Playwright, Director

Among the most renowned playwright directors in the intellectual Mexican arena in the twentieth century is Nancy Cárdenas. She was born in the northern Mexican state of Coahuila, in the city of Parras; she died after decades of battling cancer. Cárdenas practiced a variety of professions ranging from playwright, poet, journalist, radio, television, and film critic, to theatrical actress and director. As a theatrical director, Cárdenas received "all the awards that the Mexican associations bestow" (Garza, 1991, 2; author's translation), and as a poet, she wrote two books that depicted erotic lesbian love. Among her most important achievements was her establishment of feminist militancy in Mexican theater, not only because of the subject matter she chose to write about and direct, but also because of her total commitment to freedom from conventionalism. (Garza 1991, 3).

In an interview, Cárdenas recalled her childhood in Parras, "a little town 400 years old, a million trees, a population of 20 thousand, and a single road leading in and out of it" (Martínez, "Homenaje," 11; author's translation). It was here that she lived until she was fifteen. Later she moved to Mexico City, where she pursued her academic education and obtained her doctorate in liberal arts with a specialization in dramatic arts from the National Autonomous University of Mexico (UNAM). Subsequently, she obtained a postdoctoral fellowship at Yale University, which enabled her to study cinematography and theatrical direction at the Center for Cinematographic Studies in Poland.

In 1971 Cárdenas initiated the fight against homosexual prejudice in Mexico and in favor of human rights for all men and women, irrespective of their sexual preferences. A militant advocate from that time forward, Cárdenas openly entered into a discourse on lesbianism through her work as a director and playwright, as well as through her work as a poet. This is apparent in the theatrical trilogy she directed: *Claudine*, a musical comedy based on the novel *Claudine á l'école* (Claudine at School) by the French writer Colette; *Las amargas lágrimas de Petra Von Kant* (The Bitter Tears of Petra Von Kant) by the German director W. R. Fassbinder; and her own piece, *El día que pisamos la luna* (The Day We Landed On

Nancy Cárdenas. Courtesy of Lilia Cárdenas Martínez and Juan Miguel Abad
Cárdenas.

the Moon), in which she depicts four lesbians of distinct ages and personalities who share a lone characteristic: they are interested only in the
feminine world and love between women. Further evidence of her discourse on lesbianism is illustrated both in her erotic lesbian poems that
appeared in the *Anuario de poesía 1990* (1990 Poetry Annals, 1991) and
also in her most extensive poetic work, *Cuaderno de amor y desamor* (Notebook of Love and Unlove, 1994), which was published posthumously,
with an introduction by her very dear friend, Carlos Monsiváis. Her
ideology regarding lesbianism in literature has been evident since the
publication of her poem "Amor de verano" (Summer Love) in 1981, in
which she signifies the importance of identification between the author
and the poetic voice in lesbian writing.

Cárdenas's ideology was greatly influenced by the progressive family
in which she grew up and the liberal environment that surrounded her.
It was in this atmosphere that the spirit of struggle and rebellion that
characterized her during her life was initiated. Her fierce attitude is evident in her battle for human rights in the social arena for men and
women, homosexuals and heterosexuals. Cárdenas's political views also
showed up in her professional career in the theater, permeating the plays
she chose to write and direct.

She began to write plays during her first year of college, after several months of working as a radio actress. During her early years in the theater, she worked with poetry and theater groups from the university. Even though these groups were university affiliated and not professional, their performances were attended by wide-ranging audiences. From 1970 onward, she wrote and directed productions for independent theater groups. However, she occasionally returned to perform and direct at the university, taking professional actors along with her. When asked if she identified with a particular school or generation, Cárdenas replied that she did not, given that over the years her aesthetics and preoccupations were significantly different from those of her university colleagues, who later became the theatrical Mexican intelligentsia (Martínez, "Homenaje," 11). Cárdenas's colleagues, José Luis Ibáñez, Héctor Mendoza, and Juan José Gurrola, had all obtained significant prestige and had active careers in the Mexican theatrical world.

Perhaps these last statements explain why the work of Cárdenas did not inspire a great body of literary criticism in her day, in spite of her having earned numerous awards, including best direction from the ACT 1971, Asociación de Críticos de Teatro (Association of Theatre Critics), for *El efecto de los rayos gama sobre las caléndulas* (The Effect of Gamma Rays on Man-in-the-Moon Marigolds), by Paul Zindel; best direction from the ACT 1973 for *Aquelarre* (Witches' Sabbath), by Friederich Zauner; best direction from the ACT 1975 for *Cuarteto* (Quartet), by E. A. Wilehead; best direction from Premio El Heraldo 1981 for *Las amargas lágrimas de Petra Von Kant* (The Bitter Tears of Petra von Kant), by R. W. Fassbinder.

Despite the fact that during her early years Cárdenas was writing, directing, and producing in a lively environment influenced by the theater of the absurd, it is more than possible that the fact that she was addressing gay and lesbian themes in a different way from traditional approaches made her unclassifiable and, for the same reason, made her motives invisible to theatrical critics. When she was asked about whether a tradition of lesbian literature, theater, or art existed in Mexico, Cárdenas admitted to shaping the first generation of lesbian voices of her time (Martínez, "Homenaje," 12). Cárdenas not only wrote about gay and lesbian topics in her artistic work, she also fought publicly for the rights of all people. In her poetic and theatrical work dealing with lesbian and homosexual subject matters, Cárdenas proposes worlds in which the characters, even while suffering, maintain the possibility of new beginnings. By contrast, the heterosexual characters in her work seem to be predisposed to encountering worlds of misfortune and incomprehension.

Just before her death, Cárdenas finished the script for a movie dealing with a gay theme. She also oversaw the premiere of a comedy, *Todo en un día* (All in One Day), about the profession of sexology and its familial and social repercussions.

Her influence has been deeply felt in the social and intellectual environment in Mexico. There is a sociohistorical and cultural organization in cyberspace named after her which seeks to inform and promote gay rights, culture, and literature.

Further Reading

Centro de Documentación y Archivo Histórico Lésbico de México "Nancy Cárdenas." http://www.laneta.apc.org/cdahl/cdahleng.htm. May 28, 1999.

Garza, Mabel. "Hablemos de teatro con Nancy Cárdenas." *El Reporte Teatral* 1 no. 5 (1991): 1–3

Martínez, Elena M. "Cárdenas, Nancy (Mexico; 1934)." In *Latin American Writers on Gay and Lesbian Themes: A Bio-Critical Sourcebook*, edited by David William Foster, 100–102. Westport, Conn.: Greenwood Press, 1994.

———. "Homenaje: Hablando con Nancy Cárdenas." *fem* 18, no. 134 (1994): 11–12.

Guadalupe Cortina

MARÍA MERCEDES CARRANZA
(March 24, 1945–)

Colombia: Poet, Journalist, Political Activist

María Mercedes Carranza, the most authoritative voice in contemporary Colombian poetry, belongs to the "disenchanted" generation of poets. This generation, which began publishing in the 1970s, includes such writers as Giovanni Quessep, Harold Alvarado Tenorio, Juan Manuel Roca, Juan G. Cobo-Borda, Mario Rivero, and Darío Jaramillo-Agudelo. Rivero and Jaramillo-Agudelo both had an important influence on her work.

As Carranza alleges, her generation was marked by the "political and cultural impact of the Cuban Revolution, the Frente Nacional (National Front), the political crisis of the traditional parties and the left, the increasing urbanization of the country, the zenith of the mass media, . . . [and] the *boom* of the novel, that relegated poetry to a second or third place" (Rincón 1986, 5–6).

She was the only daughter among three siblings, from a Catholic fam-

María Mercedes Carranza. Courtesy of
Gilma Suárez.

ily of peasant origins. Her father, the poet Eduardo Carranza (1913–
1985), was a cultural consular representative. Because of his position, she
spent a good part of her youth abroad: she lived in Chile (1946–1948)
and later in a postwar fascist Spain (1951–1958), idealized in her memory
as "an isolated country outside of the society of consumerism" (personal
interview, 1999).

She grew up under the protective figure of a politically conservative
father—although a tolerant one—who initiated her in the secrets of the
Prado Museum and Spanish and French classical literature. At the same
time, he transmitted to her his passion for detective novels. Among the
many writers and artists who visited her father, she remembers Gerardo
Diego, Dámaso Alonso, Jorge Gaitán Durán, and especially the painter
Débora Arango, who did a full-length portrait of her in a red dress,
which she remembers as being the bright image of those days (personal
interview, 1999).

Especially influential in her life was the writer Elisa Mujica (1918–),
her maternal great-aunt who was living in Spain at that time: "The fable
of my childhood is knitted with the legends and stories that she told me;
with her I discovered the power of language" (personal interview, 1999).
Later, while studying in a school run by nuns, with her brothers away
at boarding school, and amidst domestic problems between her parents,
she found poetry in the pages of Rubén Darío in her father's library, "the
place of solitary games with books" (personal Interview, 1999). With that
time period in mind, she edited a collection of juvenile literature in 1982,

Colección Instituto Colombiano de Bienestar Familiar de literatura infantil (Colombian Institute of Family Welfare Collection of Children's Literature). The return to Colombia was not easy: "When I returned, I still played with dolls and didn't know how babies were born. I left Spain and my childhood; I experienced a terrible cultural nostalgia that I confronted with a resolution to belong to this country" (personal interview, 1999).

Before finishing high school in Colombia, she decided to become a bilingual secretary, which was a fairly common vocation for women with intellectual aspirations at that time. Her mother, Rosa Coronado, convinced her to continue her studies with the promise of sending her to Spain. After graduating and with the financial support of a scholarship, she returned to Spain and studied philosophy and literature in the Central University of Madrid. In Spain, she met the poet Juan Luis Panero, who would later become her second husband (1977–1978), and throughout the year she mixed classes in Latin and history of art with a bohemian lifestyle that somewhat overshadowed her studies. Between 1965 and 1987 (intermittently), she completed her degree in philosophy and literature at the University of the Andes in Bogotá.

Although Carranza initiated the canonical feminine presence in Colombian poetry, and her work contains a feminist agenda, she rejects this type of recognition. She considers it self-discriminatory to speak of "feminist poetry" and sees feminism as an "imported" and elitist schema that "hides—at least in our countries—the actual causes of social inequality of women," which essentially reside, according to Carranza, in "great social inequalities and profound class differences" (Carranza, "Feminismo y poesía," 341–45).

Her first book, *Vainas* (Stuff, 1972), ironically subverted patriotic icons ("De Boyacá en los campos" [From Boyaca in the Country]) and the manners of the establishment ("Aquí con la señora Arnolfini" [Here with Mrs. Arnolfini]), but it also ridicules the "secondary role assigned to women within a patriarchal society" (Alstrum 1991, 521) and the rhetorical commonplace of the so-called ethereal woman.

Conscious that "every moment there are new ways/to say the same old things" ("Se lo voy a decir" ["I Am Going to Tell You"], *Vainas* "seeks to revoke poetry's sanctified language and reinvent it from zero" (Jaramillo-Agudelo 1991, 27), using a deliberately colloquial language that fractures the rhetorical grandiloquence of previous poetry.

Carranza bares herself with an ironic gesture that reaches her own poetry and herself in an autobiographical confession, without cynicism or bitterness. Her iconoclastic attitude is not inherited from the vanguardistic pretensions of Nadaism (a poetic movement of the 1960s), but rather from the antipoetry of Nicanor Parra and the playful yet melancholic tone of Julio Cortázar.

A reader of French from a young age, she was influenced by the existentialism of Albert Camus and the work of Simone de Beauvoir, to which she added the Catalan anarchism, and the 1960s, a decade of which she feels herself a daughter (personal interview, 1999).

Fear is a recurrent theme in Carranza's poetry in *Tengo miedo* (I Am Afraid, 1983). In these poems, the body and the gaze are inhabited by fear. Love gives way to the encroaching and all-encompassing political violence. Fear also roams the spaces of the metaphorical city of identity, an architectural mirror. Irony gives way to anguish over the disaster of the present. Not even the word saves the narrator.

Within the context of Colombian poetry, *Hola soledad* (Hello Solitude, 1987) is one of the most renowned books on the theme of love. This theme recurs in *Amor y desamor* (Love and Disenchantment, 1994); nonetheless, rather than desire the thematic axis is the "deterioration of hope, ... the deterioration of love, the deterioration of one's self" (Carranza, qtd. in Rincón 1986, 5) and the fatality of death ("Canción de domingo" Sunday's Song). A claustrophobic and inhospitable symbolic space defines her homeland; Colombia is a house of colonial walls that "started falling down centuries ago" ("La patria" [My Motherland]).

The horror of a widespread Colombian war is made evident in *El canto de las moscas* (The Song of the Flies, 1998), a book that while doing an inventory of the toponymy of violence also celebrates the melopoeia of the names of twenty-four Colombian towns ("Ituango").

Carranza maintains that even the poet who—in poetry—takes refuge from the social delirium has an intimate relation with the political and economic violence of the present (*Revista Casa Silva* 1990, 6–8): "In Colombia whatever geography—whether poetic or not—is a geography baptized with violence and blood. I chose the names of the towns for their beauty and to speak of life, but I know that beauty and life are memories of death" (personal interview, 1999).

Carranza's poetic exercise of pessimism contrasts with her optimism in the work to which she has dedicated herself since 1984. She is the founder director of Casa de Poesía Silva (Silva House of Poetry) in Bogotá, named after poet José Asunción Silva, who lived and committed suicide in that house. The institution is devoted to stimulating the study and enjoyment of poetry—especially in the popular sectors—through free services (library, audio library), events (recitals, workshops, discussions, festivals), research, and publications.

Carranza is criticized simultaneously and contradictorily for promoting the institutionalization and populist mass consumption of poetry, and for leading what has been called a high-culture project. She defends the necessity to lobby the state and political and economic groups in order to obtain resources for Silva House. With respect to doing "poetic demagogy," she affirms that poetry is a social practice of communication and solidarity, above and beyond "specialized" reading of "select" poetry in academic circles (*Revista Casa Silva* 1992, 7–9; 1994, 9; 1995, 9–10; 1998, 9–11). When confronting the critics who feel that she is biased toward high culture, she replies,

What I promote is not for the poets, nor for the professors, it is for the public, a public that in diverse sociocultural strati produces, reads, and has and experiences poetry. What is elitist is not to promote poetry, but to think that poetry (or the aesthetic) is only for the initiated. (personal interview, 1999)

Other than her work at Silva House, Carranza considers cultural journalism to be the central activity of her life. She directed the literary pages "Vanguardia" (Vanguard) of the newspaper *El siglo* (The Century) in Bogotá and "Estravagario" (neologism=An Account of Extravagances) of the newspaper *El pueblo* (The People) in Cali. For thirteen years she was chief editor of the magazine *Nueva frontera* (New Frontier). She currently writes for *Semana* (Week).

In 1990 she joined the Alianza Nacional M-19 (M-19 National Alliance), which resulted from the integration of the guerrilla group M-19 into the democratic system. She was one of four women among the seventy-four members elected for the National Constitutional Assembly which, in 1991, proclaimed a new constitution. In the Assembly, she urged the participation of the FARC, the major guerrilla group in Colombia that did not have confidence in the peace process after the assassination of more than 1,500 members of the Unión Patriótica (Patriotic Union), a left-wing political party.

The *Asamblea* [Assembly] tried to offer a way out of the war; but in Colombia there exists neither the political will nor the economic conditions for peace. While we spoke of reconciliation in the *Asamblea*, President César Gaviria bombarded "Casa verde," the center of operations for the FARC. (personal interview, 1999)

She has voted against the constitutional ban on abortion, has defended women's and children's rights, religious freedom and the secular state (officially Catholic in the previous constitution), cultural pluralism, and the freedom of information, and she has insisted on the democratization of mass-media ownership. Risking her life, Carranza voted publicly, along with four others, to maintain the option of the extradition of Colombians as a legal tool against the Mafia of drug traffickers, alleging respect for international treaties, impunity in the face of terrorism, and loyalty to the cause of her friend Luis Carlos Galán (1943–1989), who was assassinated by Mafia hitmen while a presidential candidate.

After the assembly, she abandoned politics and returned to the helm of Silva House:

Here I will be, working in what I believe in while my faith lasts, reading Darío and Neruda as if I were encountering them for the first time in my father's library, and living poetry, stubbornly, as a social experience of beauty within language. (personal interview, 1999)

Further Reading

Alstrum, James-J. "Generación Golpe de Dados." *Historia de la poesía colombiana.* Bogotá, Colombia: Ediciones Casa Silva, 1991. 512–27.

Carranza, María Mercedes. "Feminismo y poesía." In *Literatura y diferencia: Escritoras colombianas del siglo XX,* edited by María Mercedes Jaramillo, Betty Osorio-de-Negret, and Angela Inés Robledo, 341–45. Bogotá, Colombia: Uniandes, 1995.

———. "Carta abierta a quien quiera leerla." *Revista Casa Silva: La Poesía es de todos* 2 (1989): 5–7.

———. "La poesía en la hora de los asesinos." *Revista Casa Silva: La Poesía: Resistencia en la tierra* 3 (1990): 6–8.

———. "El país se desintegra señores." *Revista Casa Silva: La Poesía . . . locura* 6 (1992): 7–9.

———. "Contra la violencia confortable." *Revista Casa Silva: Poesía, el oficio más antiguo del mundo* 7 (1994): 8–10.

———. "¡Fuera verdad tanta belleza!" *Revista Casa Silva: Caza de poesía* 8 (1995): 7–10.

———. "Alzados en almas." *Revista Casa Silva: Alzados en almas* 12 (1998): 9–11.

Crow, Mary, ed. *Woman Who Has Sprouted Wings: Poems by Contemporary Latin American Women Poets.* Pittsburgh: Latin American Literary Review Press, 1984. 71–77.

Jaramillo-Agudelo, Dario. "La desconfianza con las palabras." *Golpe de dados* 19, no. 60 (1991): 26–30.

Perico, Carmen-Sofia. "El amor en la poesía de María Mercedes Carranza." *RLA: Romance Languages Annual* 3 (1991): 561–66.

Rincón, María Cristina, and Guillermo Bernal. "¿Desencantadas de qué?" *Magazin Dominical* 165 (1986): 5–7.

Tono, Lucía. "La poesía de María Mercedes Carranza: Palabra, sujeto y entorno." In *Literatura y diferencia: Escritoras colombianas del siglo XX,* edited by María Mercedes Jaramillo, Betty Osorio-de-Negret, and Angela Inés Robledo, 16–47. Bogotá, Colombia: Uniandes, 1995.

Carlos Jáuregui

ROSARIO CASTELLANOS
(May 25, 1925–August 7, 1974)

Mexico: Poet, Author, Journalist, Diplomat

Fiction writer, poet, essayist, journalist, diplomat, university professor, and the most prominent feminist from Latin America during the middle years of this century, Rosario Castellanos grew up in the rural Mexican state of Chiapas. Her father was a landowner and engineer and worked as a math teacher. When her younger brother died, her parents never recovered from their loss; Rosario claimed never to have recovered from his death or from her parents' avowed preference for the male heir, now deceased. The unhappiness and solitude of these early years were to become dominant themes in her writings.

The family lost their Chiapas property as a result of the land reform programs that followed the Mexican Revolution, and they relocated in Mexico City, where Castellanos remained despite brief absences. Her parents died within a few months of each other in 1948, leaving her with limited financial means. The budding writer suffered tremendous loneliness, but she soon discovered the camaraderie of intellectuals and authors who became known as the Generation of 1950. Her sense of humor, biting irony, and capacity for scorn, which helped her live through difficult times, made her popular with readers. Most of her poetry can be found in the largely chronological collection *Poesía no eres tú, obra poética 1948–1971* (You Are Not Poetry, Poetic Work), published in 1972. One of her first books of poetry, *Apuntes para una declaración de fe* (Notes for a Declaration of Faith, 1948), meditates abstractly on solitude and death. Whereas her first published writings were poems, and she is best known as a poet, all her works reflect her lifelong social activism.

Submitted to the National Autonomous University of Mexico (UNAM), Mexico's premier university, her 1950 thesis in philosophy focuses on the canonical rejection of the artistic production of women and the nonobjectivity of common critical practices detrimental to women artists. After the radicalizing experiences of the student revolts in 1968 and stints on U.S. campuses, these themes would reappear with particular vehemence in four later books: (1) a collection of short fiction about urban women, *Album de familia* (Family Album, 1971); (2) essays on women writers, *Mujer que sabe latín* (Woman Who Knows Latin, 1971); (3) a journalism miscellany collected before her death but published posthumously, *El mar y sus pescaditos* (The Sea and Its Little Fishes, 1975); and (4) a feminist farce, *El eterno femenino* (The Eternal Feminine, 1975). A good sampling appears in English in *A Rosario Castellanos Reader*, edited by Maureen Ahern (1988). One of her most interesting biographers, the Mexican novelist **Elena Poniatowska**, writes that women's liberation in Mexico on the national level truly began in 1971 when Castellanos gave a lecture at the National Museum of Anthropology and History

denouncing injustice against women and declaring that there is no equality when one [sex] can have an education and the other not; when one can work and the other only fulfills a duty unworthy of remuneration, housework; when one is the owner of his body and uses it however he wishes and the other reserves her body not for her own ends but so that he may accomplish processes alien to her will. (Poniatowska 1985, 46; author's translation)

A lifelong admirer of the Chilean poet and Nobel prize winner Gabriela Mistral, Castellanos showed an affinity with and affection for great female intellects and historical figures from Mexico (Sor Juana Inés de la Cruz, Marina/la Malinche), Latin America (**María Luisa Bombal, Clarice Lispector**), the United States (Emily Dickinson), and Europe (Simone Weil, Simone de Beauvoir).

After graduating in 1950, Chayo or Chayito (as she was known to her friends) received a scholarship for graduate study in Madrid awarded by the Hispanic Cultural Institute. She studied philosophy and aesthetics and later traveled and wrote poetry. Unfortunately, soon afterward she was diagnosed with tuberculosis. While ill, she accepted the government post of director of cultural activities in the Chiapanecan Institute of Arts and Sciences in Tuxtla Gutiérrez, the capital of Chiapas state. Returning to Chiapas allowed her to devote time to improving the lot of the marginalized Mayans around her. Because she was not recovering, she returned to Mexico City where she was admitted to a sanatorium. Able to leave after a few months, she underwent another year of rest at home before her recovery was complete. Her creative activities of this period included dramatic monologues imagining the voices of famous women of literature and history (Salome, Judith, Eve, Sor Juana). In 1953 she received funding to research "the cultural contributions of women" (Bonifaz 1990, 29).

During 1954 and 1955, a Rockefeller Foundation fellowship allowed her to write her first novel, *Balún-Canán* (The Nine Guardians, 1957). Tremendously successful with critics, this autobiographical fiction was translated into several European languages and won the Mexican Critics award for 1957 and the Chiapas Prize in 1958. Like her poetry collection, *El rescate del mundo* (Rescuing the World, 1953), *Balún-Canán* treats the relations between races and cultures in the predominantly Indian region of Chiapas. The point of view of a small girl in the fiction allows for an innocent and unjaundiced eye to be turned unflinchingly toward the cruel practices and long-standing tradition of subjecting Indians and women to silence and powerlessness.

Castellanos published *Poemas 1953–1955* (Poems, 1957), which was closely followed by another poetry collection, *Al pie de la letra* (The Exact Words, 1959). The former was written in Mexico City and the latter after her 1955 return to Chiapas. During this period (1955–1956), her longest return to her home state, the National Indian Institute was her employer, offering her the opportunity to have a base in San Cristóbal de las Casas while traveling to remote hamlets and villages on her cultural mission. Although there is controversy regarding her knowledge of native languages, at this time she was in charge of the Guiñol Theater, a traveling puppet show in Tzotzil and other Indian languages, for which she authored didactic pieces raising awareness about political rights, hygiene, agricultural methods, and nutrition. Her works were probably translated before being staged, although her friend Oscar Bonifaz writes that she translated the Mexican constitution into Tzotzil (Bonifaz 1990, 33, n15).

Back in Mexico City, Castellanos married Ricardo Guerra, a professor of philosophy. After two miscarriages she gave birth to a son, Gabriel. The marriage was not a happy one. The injustices she had seen haunted her. The title of her first of three collections of stories, *Ciudad real* (City of Kings, 1960) refers to San Cristóbal. These ten brief, incisive narratives that Castellanos considered mere sketches manifest a critical and ironic attitude toward stereotyped, oppressive, or insensitive attitudes and actions by those of all races in Chiapas. The poems of *Lívida luz* (Livid Light, 1960) reflect her new desire to write with a "coldness" and "commitment" about Chiapas. Castellanos reported in an interview: "In those places of struggle, brutality has arrived at its most heart-rending extreme" (Carballo 415, qtd. in English in Bonifaz 1990, 34, n18). Soon thereafter Castellanos's most important novel, *Oficio de tinieblas* (The Book of Lamentations, 1962), appeared. Based on a historical account of an 1867 Tzotzil rebellion, this long novel received the prestigious Sor Juana Inés de la Cruz Prize for Literature and the Xavier Villaurrutia Prize.

When asked in a 1965 interview whether she was happy being included by critics as an indigenist writer, Castellanos vehemently denied belonging to the indigenist movement:

I do not believe my inclusion is valid because what is understood as indigenist literature corresponds to a series of schema, to a Manichean conception of the world, in which the good and the bad are divided by the color of the skin, and naturally the good are the Indians because they are the victims, and the bad people are the whites because they are the ones who exercise power, who have authority and money. (Cresta de Leguizamón 1976, 4; author's translation)

Instead, in Castellanos, the struggle for power, dignity, and survival plays itself out between strongly drawn characters who have been marked by the racism, sexism, and economic power that hurts (the Indians, women) or helps (the whites, men) them. While Castellanos never ignored social context as a shaping force, she sought to portray the "essential ambiguity of human beings," capable both of incredible sacrifice while suffering hardship and of harming the weakest among us because we have been abused (Cresta de Leguizamón 1976, 4). Her preference for ambiguity and personal choice in her portrayals of injustice remains in *Los convidados de agosto* (The Guests of August, 1964) and in *Album de familia* (1971), set in Mexico City. During the most successful period of her life, she received the Trouyet Award, presented to her by the famous writer Agustín Yáñez, and the Sourasky Prize for her literary accomplishments.

Upon her return to Mexico City in 1958, Castellanos began collaborating with journals and newspapers. In 1961 she began to work for the National University of Mexico, first as press and information director, then as a professor of comparative literature. After several years, she abruptly resigned the directorship in support of the university president, who had been summarily removed from office during the student protests of the 1960s. In 1967 she accepted a series of visiting professorships in the United States at the Universities of Wisconsin, Indiana, and Colorado. Under Mexico's next president, Luis Echeverría Álvarez, Castellanos was appointed ambassador to Israel in 1971. She had just finished a feminist farce, *El eterno femenino* (1975; "The Eternal Feminine," 1988), when she died after an unusual accident at home. Still wet from the shower, she tried to change a lightbulb and was electrocuted. There are those who argue that Castellanos committed suicide that day, but the circumstances seem to indicate otherwise.

Rosario Castellanos's novels, short stories, poems, and essays consistently retain autobiographical elements, especially on the subjects of Chiapas and feminism, but she is largely remembered as a public intellectual who contributed to her country's constant search for justice in the face of the intransigent forces of subtle corruption and brute force which prevented certain of its citizens from enjoying the full exercise of their rights and their voice.

Further Reading

Ahern, Maureen, ed. *A Rosario Castellanos Reader: An Anthology of Her Poetry, Short Fiction, Essays, and Drama*, translated by Maureen Ahern et al. Austin: University of Texas Press, 1988.

Bonifaz Caballero, Oscar. *Remembering Rosario*, edited and translated by Myralyn Allgood. Potomac, Md.: Scripta Humanistica, 1990.

Cresta de Leguizamón, María Luisa. "En recuerdo de Rosario Castellanos." *La Palabra y el Hombre* 19 (July–September 1976): 3–18.

Lindstrom, Naomi. *Women's Voice in Latin American Literature.* Washington, D.C.: Three Continents Press, 1989. 48–70.

O'Connell, Joanna. *Prospero's Daughter: The Prose of Rosario Castellanos.* Austin: University of Texas Press, 1995.

Poniatowska, Elena. "Rosario Castellanos: ¡Vida nada te debo!" In *¡Ay, vida, no me mereces!*, 45–132. México, D.F.: Joaquín Mortiz, 1985.

Diane E. Marting

CELIA CRUZ
(October 21, 1924?–   )

Cuba: Singer

For almost fifty years singer Celia Cruz has graced the stages of such varied cultural and musical capitals as London, Cali (Colombia), Cannes, and Brasília (Brazil), and she is considered the Queen of Salsa. With her trademark wigs, fabulous costumes, and wide, gap-toothed smile dissolving into a full-blown speaker system that belts out solemn chants in Yoruba, playful *guarachas* (a type of popular song) from the Cuban countryside, or salsa's throbbing *soneos* (vocal improvisations), Celia Cruz's career has defied the boundaries of music and gender, pushing back the borders into the center stage. She has musically reinvented herself while maintaining a solid base in the traditional rhythms of her native Cuba. With more than seventy albums, honorary doctoral degrees from Yale University and most recently one from the University of Miami, a Grammy award, and ten Grammy nominations, the Smithsonian Institution's Lifetime Achievement Award, the National Medal of the Arts, the Hispanic Heritage Lifetime Achievement Award, and the Hispanic Women Achievers Award, Cruz has proven herself to be a pioneering force in the male-dominated world of salsa music. She is one of the few artists whose fans encompass four generations.

Cruz does not reveal her age (some estimate the year of her birth to be between 1916 and 1929), but the year generally accepted is 1924. Born into a large family in modest Santo Suárez, a neighborhood of Havana, Cuba, Cruz originally had plans of becoming a schoolteacher, but her talent for singing led her to participate in a series of local competitions

Celia Cruz. Courtesy of Photofest.

on Cuban radio. In 1941 one of these competitions was for the radio show *La hora del té* (The Tea Hour) transmitted by Radio García Cerra, in which her cousin entered her after hearing her sing. She won a first place and was assured of steady performances on Cuban radio. The 1940s were the golden years of radio in Cuba. Radio Progreso was the lead radio station in popular music, and the 1940s saw the birth of the mambo. The island was opening up to musicians and performers worldwide who were lured by the skyrocketing salaries and the exciting nightlife. Bolero music was given a facelift by new, younger composers, and Cuba was fast becoming the music and performance capital of the Caribbean. Cruz could not have chosen a better moment to start her career. During these years she performed in reputable theaters such as the Teatro Fausto and the Teatro Auditorium, and in 1947 Cruz enrolled at the National Conservatory of Music in Havana and studied voice and music theory.

If the 1940s were the golden years of radio in Cuba, the 1950s brought forth the development of a mass television culture along with the importance of performance in a city that demanded decadence and high living. It was during this time that the cabarets and casinos flourished in Havana, drag queen shows were a booming business, and the cha-cha-cha and the pachanga became world-renowned rhythms.

In 1950 Cruz's career came to a decisive turning point when she returned to Cuba after an engagement in Lima. Rogelio Martínez, the leader of one of the most respected bands in Cuba, the Sonora Matancera, the stars of Radio Progreso, had heard Celia perform in a show at the notorious Cabaret Tropicana. The band wanted to replace Myrta Silva, their leading female voice, who was returning to her native Puerto Rico. Martínez took Celia to Radio Progreso for an audition, and she was hired on the spot with an exclusive contract. Throughout the 1950s, Celia toured with the Sonora Matancera to the United States, Europe, Mexico, and South America, while maintaining her Cuban audience in performances at the Cabaret Sans Souci, the Teatro Martí, the Teatro Nacional de La Habana, the Cabaret Bambú, the Teatro Blanquita, and the Cabaret Tropicana. Cruz's partnership with the Sonora Matancera lasted well into the 1970s, making her one of the most marketable and respected salsa singers.

In 1960, nearly a year after the Cuban Revolution, while on an engagement in Mexico with the Sonora Matancera, Cruz and the band decided to stay in Mexico for a year and later make the United States their home. Shortly afterward, in the United States, Cruz married the man who would be her right hand, musically as well as emotionally, Pedro Knight, the lead trumpet of the Sonora Matancera; this became one of the most successful and legendary marriage partnerships in salsa history. They made New York City their permanent home base. In the 1960s, aided by the exodus of hundreds of Cuba's most gifted musicians and the emergence of the new music of the Puerto Rican barrio, New York became what Havana had been in the 1950s: the new capital of Latin music. Cruz took advantage of this opportunity to play the U.S. Latin club circuits while touring Latin America with the Sonora Matancera. By 1965 Cruz had signed a contract with Secco Records that lasted for a year, during which she recorded some of her most memorable Afro-Cuban albums, including *Homenaje a los santos con Celia Cruz* (Homage to the Saints with Celia Cruz), *Homenaje a los santos con Celia Cruz Vol. II*, and *Homenaje a Yemayá de Celia Cruz* (Celia Cruz's Homage to Yemayá).

In 1966 Celia left Secco Records and signed with Tico Records, a label that represented the real mambo kings of the times: Tito Puente, Tito Rodríguez, and Machito. Celia recorded thirteen albums with the Tico label, seven of which she recorded with Tito Puente. The Celia-Tito records remain some of their most critically acclaimed albums: *Cuba y Puerto Rico son* (Cuba and Puerto Rico Rhythm), *El Quimbo Quimbumbia, Alma con Alma* (Soul to Soul), and *Algo especial para recordar* (Something Special to Remember). In the early 1970s, Celia switched record labels again, this time to Vaya Records, a subsidiary label of Fania Records, the most important salsa record label in New York. In 1973 the pianist and bandleader Larry Harlow cast her as Gracia Divina (Divine Grace) in his opera *Hommy* a Latin-style adaptation of The Who's rock opera *Tommy*) at Carnegie Hall. She was an instant success, and it gave her an opportunity to demonstrate her abilities as a singer and performer.

By 1974 Cruz's career was skyrocketing. She teamed up with Dominican Johnny Pacheco, the owner of La Fania Records as well as a top flutist and percussionist, and they recorded a concept album of old Cuban *sones* (the Cuban antecedent of salsa) that instantly went gold, *Celia y Johnny* (Celia and Johnny). The importance of this first gold record had a lot to do with the fact that Pacheco's music was along the lines of the traditional Sonora Matancera, with similar orchestral arrangements done in a new style, but with the definite feeling of old-time Cuban rhythm. Some believe that it was a commercial strategy on the part of Pacheco who, by bringing Celia on board, was trying to recreate the past glories of the Sonora Matancera while setting her up to be the main attraction of the Fania All Stars, a group of artists signed by the Fania label who joined efforts occasionally to produce the most star-studded concerts in the history of salsa. Celia made two more record-breaking hit albums with Pacheco, which would include some of her best-known songs, including *Quimbara, Toro mata* (The Bull Kills) and *Tres días de carnaval* (Three Days of Carnival).

After Cruz made her last album with Pacheco, she was featured with the Fania All Stars. Not only was she the only woman in the all-male ensemble, she was the featured singer, the heart and soul of the Fania All Stars. After recording her trademark song, *Bemba colorá* (Red Lips), with the Fania All Stars, she went to number one and became the undisputed Queen of Salsa. Celia's remarkable voice, charisma, and her thirty years of experience in the music industry had finally paid off. With the Fania All Stars, Celia toured England, France, and Africa, placing salsa on the international sphere, and when the Fania All Stars eventually broke up in the early 1980s, Cruz remained one of the label's most bankable performers. During that time, Celia continued to collaborate individually with other Fania artists, including Willie Colón and Papo Lucca y la Sonora Ponceña.

By the 1980s and 1990s, Celia had begun to experiment with different musical approaches. She sang a duet with former Talking Head David Byrne for the 1986 Jonathan Demme film *Something Wild*. The next year Celia performed in a special segment of the Grammy awards with her longtime friend and collaborator Tito Puente. In 1998 she flew to Argentina to record four songs with the Latin ska band Los Fabulosos Cadillacs. The album *Vasos vacíos* (Empty Glasses), the song that gave the album its title, instantly became a hit in Argentina as well as in the United States. She won her first Grammy in 1989 for the album *Ritmo en el corazón* (Rhythm of the Heart), which she recorded with Latin Jazz great Ray Barretto. Celia, who admits she speaks little or no English, has appeared in two American films, *The Mambo Kings* (1992), playing a nightclub owner, and *The Perez Family* (1995), playing a *santera* (priestess in the Afro-Cuban religion called Santería). She learned her lines phonetically for both roles.

Cruz has been an active force in Latin music since the beginning of her career in the 1940s. Her contralto voice and *soneos* have been unparalleled in the salsa music world. She is also devoted to humanitarian causes including AIDS fund-raising and the League against Cancer. Whether in music or in life, Cruz has been not only a survivor but a true winner. She is loved internationally by millions of people not only because of her music, but for her incredible warmth and humility. Cruz continues to produce best-selling albums and still performs throughout Latin America and the United States. She lives in Fort Lee, New Jersey, with her husband, and she has formed her own production company, Azucar Productions.

Further Reading

Aparicio, Frances R. *Listening to Salsa: Gender, Latin Popular Music, and Puerto Rican Cultures.* Hanover, N.H.: New England University Press, 1998.
Boggs, Vernon. *Salsiology: Afro-Cuban Music and the Evolution of Salsa in New York City.* New York: Greenwood Press, 1992.
Falcón, Rafael. *Salsa: A Taste of Hispanic Culture.* Westport, Conn.: Praeger, 1988.

Chiara Merino Pérez

ANDREA ECHEVERRI
(?, 1965–   )
Colombia: Singer, Artist

Andrea Echeverri is the most important Latin American female rock music interpreter. She is also a ceramist from the University of Los Andes, Bogotá, and she has attended classes at Plymouth College of Art and Design in England. She participated in different collective exhibitions in Colombia between 1986 and 1992 and held individual ones in Bogotá and Medellín. Although her career as a ceramist was interrupted by her musical activities, Echeverri often maintains that ceramics is her real vocation and profession and that she will return to it when the time comes to leave the musical scene graciously. There are, however, many intersections between Echeverri's ceramic work and the topics of her songs;

for example, the use of pastiche to incorporate religious motifs in a kitschy way. Both in her artwork and in her music, Echeverri underlines the hybrid nature of Latin American culture by incorporating the past rather than refusing it or mocking it. In this way, Echeverri creates a confluence of themes and periods, together with an irreverent criticism of conservative, religious, and patriarchal institutions. This artistic technique is also apparent in her musical videos, mainly the ones created for her first three compact discs, widely diffused by MTV.

Despite her unique talent as a ceramist, it is music that has really marked the path of fame for Echeverri. As the leader of the Colombian band Aterciopelados (The Velvety Ones), she has added her name to a list of former and contemporary Latin American *rockeras* (female rock personalities), including Julieta Venegas, Betsy Pecanis, Rosa Adame, and Vilma and the Vampires. Echeverri's name stands out because of her particular style, which combines a very clever public persona and a rebellious look, and she has an array of extremely witty and insightful songs that have inaugurated a different chapter in the history of rock in Spanish, one of the most revolutionary and controversial musical genres in Latin America. On the other hand, despite the eclectic nature of her music, Echeverri does ascribe to the definition of rock in Spanish; the aforementioned singers are often considered merely pop singers.

Rock in Spanish is an example of transculturation that has resulted in a mix of U.S. rock with different kinds of Latin American rhythms, whether in their pure forms or in already revisited versions. Although dates on the origins of rock in Spanish range from the 1950s to the 1960s, it was around 1985 that the recording label Ariola coined it as *rock en tu idioma* (rock in your language). By that time, there was a proliferation of Mexican, Chilean, and Argentine rock bands, and despite being considered an alternative form of music, rock in Spanish has been widely dominated by male voices and male groups. Although both Echeverri and the band acknowledge the influence of such rockers as Charly García, Gustavo Cerati, and Fito Paez and the influence of bands like Soda Estéreo and El Último de la Fila, the style of Aterciopelados is closer to the Mexican group Café Tacuba with plenty of similarities both in form and content. Famous traditional rhythms (such as boleros, *rancheras, danzones*) with contemporary musical forms such as rock and punk combine to produce compositions that sing, in very ironical lyrics, about everyday political and social situations, resulting in a mestizo rock. As the only rock in a Spanish band led by a woman, this Colombian group has a substantially different production from other Latin American rock bands. The chief reason is the feminist agenda of the group, which is closely related to its popularity.

Echeverri claims that her musical career began as a hobby. As a child, Echeverri took guitar lessons. Her mother, also a singer and music fan, inspired her to sing popular Latin American rhythms such as boleros, *baladas*, and *rancheras*. Although she got away from music while she studied art, she came back to it spurred by Bogotá's intense nightlife in the 1980s. She was also motivated by the richness of Colombian musical heritage, a conspicuous motif in her musical production.

In 1990 Echeverri joined talents with Colombian musician Héctor Buitrago and started the band Delia y los Aminoácidos (Delia and the Aminoacids). Their musical production was highly influenced by punk and hard core, pretty much along the lines of Buitrago's work with La Pestilencia, his former band. Later, they became the Aterciopelados with two other musicians. The mix of Buitrago's background and Echeverri's predilection for Latin American and Colombian popular rhythms has generated interesting rearticulations of *vallenato, cumbia*, Latin ska, bolero, and other regional Colombian (and Latin American) musical forms with transgressive results. Because of Echeverri's interests and concerns, the repertoire of Aterciopelados places particular emphasis on women's issues. Most of their songs are about women and about their relationships with men. They censure domestic abuse, denounce misogyny, and overdramatize passionate love and the tradition of romantic love as portrayed in Latin American musical history. By doing so, Echeverri has become a feminist icon (although the term is not to her liking) on the Latin American musical scene (Suárez, in press). The feminist stance of Aterciopelados provides a critical view of different social and political issues. Both as the singer and the main voice of the group, and as the composer of many of the lyrics, Echeverri occupies multiple subject positions, such as the difficult girl, the femme fatale, the political commentator, the ecologist, the new age follower, the defendant of native indigenous cultures, and the passionate lover.

Aterciopelados produced their first compact disc in 1993, *Con el corazón en la mano* (With Heart in Hand). This experimental production, recorded in an underground studio, was intended to be a demo, but it reached the Colombian top ten and attracted the attention of the recording label BMG. Likewise, MTV showed interest in the video productions of Aterciopelados, which are typically mininarratives that cast Echeverri as protagonist. Aterciopelados produced a second compact disc in 1995 entitled *El Dorado*, and in 1996 they traveled to London for the production of *La pipa de la paz* (The Peace Pipe), which became a disco de oro (gold platter) in Colombia and earned them their first nomination for a Grammy award in the category of Best Album Latin/Alternative Rock. Even though the titles of the second and third compact discs apparently refer to contemporary Colombia, the lyrics of the songs may easily describe common situations of other Latin American countries and even of other latitudes. Songs like *No futuro* (No Future) and *Quemarropa* (Point Blank) call for peace and a solution to violent political situations; *Colombia co-*

nexión (Colombian Connection) and *Expreso Amazonia* (Amazonian Express) satirize the neoliberal vision of tourist investment in Latin America; *Miss panela* (Miss Brown Sugar) criticizes the absurdity of beauty pageants; *El Dorado* and *La pipa de la paz* are a celebration of the indigenous cultures in Latin America; *La voz de la patria* (The Voice of the Fatherland) criticizes the official nature of the news as transmitted by the ideological apparatus of the state, a debate that finds echoes in many transnational frontiers. Of course, central to the repertoire are songs like *Cosita seria* (Serious Stuff), *No necesito* (I Don't Need Your Approval), *La culpable* (Guilty), and *Chica difícil* (Difficult Girl), which reaffirm women's agency by attacking domestic violence, sexual harassment, and *piropos* (flattering remarks made to women in Latin American streets which often carry sexual connotations). The video production for *Cosita seria* is a narrative in which a man is emasculated for insulting Echeverri and a friend as they wander around a very popular neighborhood in Bogotá.

Echeverri and Aterciopelados's fourth production was *Caribe atómico* (Atomic Caribbean), again nominated for the Grammy award in 1998. Aesthetically, this compact disc distances itself from the former kitsch techniques, opting for props that reassemble images from a futuristic film. Although some fans and music critics believe that Echeverri's work with the band is becoming too serious, the change is more a token of musical evolution. As the title suggests, *Caribe atómico* is committed to the environment. The content of the songs is similar to former productions. The aesthetics of the two videos for this compact disc has changed but with a specific purpose. *El estuche* (The Case) criticizes constructing the female body for male visual pleasure, and it calls for strengthening women's notions of self. Rather than the urban mix that characterizes the former videos, Echeverri appears in a plastic bubble (a case) with plenty of makeup and in segments of the video with a hairdo reminiscent of Medusa. In spite of her enhanced beauty, the images of the video emphasize the character's encapsulation and entrapment. In contrast to the striking artificiality of her makeup in this video, Echeverri returns to her neon grunge style in the video for *Maligno* (Evil) and to miniperformances with Buitrago to narrate the song plot.

The change is also a result of the band's participation in a global economy. Their web site attests to their technological interest, and their links highlight their commitment to different social causes. Aterciopelados frequently participates in concerts and festivals organized for social and political causes. The Lilith Fair Festival, which brings together internationally renowned female singers, invited Echeverri and her band to attend in 1999. They also participated in the recording of an international tribute to Chilean poet Pablo Neruda. In the closed world of Argentine rock, Aterciopelados was one of the few foreign bands invited to the musical tribute to Sandro, a very popular singer of the 1970s and 1980s. Their work also appears in compilations like *Red, Hot and Latin*, a compact disc that also features American singer Laurie Anderson, and soundtracks of movies, such as *Star Maps*.

Echeverri has made a musical statement in her native country, where a rich musical heritage has been recently besieged by facile repetitiveness. Such is the case of groups and interpreters like Alkimia, Charlie Zaa, and Carlos Vives, artists who are internationally known and whose success stems from remakings of the famous Cuban group Sonora Matancera, Olimpo Cárdenas, and the *vallenatos* (typical Colombian music from the area of the Atlantic, more specifically from the Valle de Upar). The other option for young Colombian (and Latin American) artists (such as Shakira and Ricky Martin) has been the employment of formulaic packages (clothes, lyrics, sounds, advertisements) like those promoted by the Gloria and Emilio Estefan consortium, which presents musical crossover and standardization as the ultimate goal for success in the United States.

Echeverri's irreverent look, the sagacity of her lyrics, and her honest opinions attest to her uniqueness on the Latin American musical scene. Although sometimes she recycles traditional genres of music such as *vallenato, cumbia,* and bolero, her music subverts the hegemonic notions of culture. Furthermore, Echeverri's revisionistic approach allows a new kind of relationship between local and regional traditions, and between old and new traditions. It also bears witness to the fact that there are no boundaries for women who generate infinite forms of creativeness.

Further Reading

"Andrea Echeverri de los Aterciopelados." Interview with Bernardo Golinger and Eva Golinger. *Broadsheet* (January–March 1999). http://www.quintaraza.com/Aterciopelados.html

Aterciopelados. Interview with Larry La Fountain-Stokes. *Claridad* (San Juan), November 17, 1997, 22–23.

Echeverri, Andrea. Interview with Lola Salcedo Castañeda. *Mujer* (Santafé de Bogotá), December 1997–January 1998): 42–46.

Suárez, Juana. "Florecitas rockeras: ¿Hay un espacio para la mujer en el *Rock en español*?" *Latin American Cultural Transformations,* edited by Mary Jo Dudley. Ithaca, N.Y.: Cornell University Press, forthcoming.

Juana Suárez

DIAMELA ELTIT

(August 24, 1949–)

Chile: Author

Born in Santiago, Chile, Diamela Eltit has been recognized as one of the most innovative Latin American writers of her generation. Her experimental style is transgressive and iconoclastic, Eltit is well known for her keen exploration of marginal and subaltern subject positions. In six major books, written between 1983 and 1998, some of which have been translated into English and French, Eltit's experimentation with various literary forms questioned the novel as a genre and allowed her to develop a distinct feminist voice. Since receiving her bachelor's degree from the University of Chile, Eltit has taught literature in various universities in Chile and the United States. Her literary and scholarly work has been supported by international awards including a Guggenheim in 1985, a Woodrow Wilson International Center for Scholars fellowship in 1988, and a Social Science Research Council scholarship in 1988. Between 1990 and 1993, Eltit was Chile's cultural attaché in Mexico for the first democratically elected government since Augusto Pinochet's dictatorship. After her return to Chile, Eltit resumed her academic career at the Metropolitan Technology University in Santiago. In 1995, her novel *Los vigilantes* (The Watchmen) received the José Nuez Martín prize for the best Chilean novel published in 1993–1994.

Eltit's work has made a significant contribution to the growing discussion that began in the 1980s concerning the significance of women's writing in Latin America. Eltit's exploration of the voices of marginal subjects such as the urban poor, the mentally ill, and women seeks to challenge the commonsense discourse imposed by authoritarianism and the consumer society in the modern capitalist market. In the case of women's marginality, the author finds the feminine in a specific historical and political context that cannot be understood in biological terms. In her novels, the feminine is characterized by an overflow of desire and eroticism that questions traditional norms of gender and sexuality. For Eltit, terms such as "feminine literature," "women's writing," or "feminist literature" are not unique to the social and biological bodies of women. Strongly influenced by the poststructuralist writings of Michel

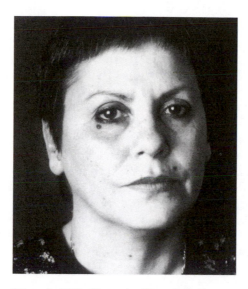

Diamela Eltit. Photo by Francisco Zegers.
Courtesy of Diamela Eltit.

Foucault, Roland Barthes, and Gilles Deleuze, her novels emphasize that language itself embodies society's oppressive structures and therefore is not a trustworthy instrument to represent the past. By consciously violating established rhetorical and grammatical conventions, Eltit underscores the complicity of language in the construction of official histories.

Eltit's experimentation with language was influenced by her interaction with painters and performance and video artists during the early 1980s. Together with the poet Raúl Zurita and the artist Lotty Rosenfeld, she founded the Collective of Art Actions (CADA), a group whose self-defined objective was to rescue Chilean culture during the military dictatorship. Although they were criticized for their avant-garde inscrutability, CADA gained some notoriety for making daring public art performances that questioned the authoritarianism and paternalism of the Pinochet regime. CADA's radical experimentation stood in sharp contrast to the exotic primitivist aesthetic, laden with images of an authentic and pure pre-Columbian past, of much of the antiauthoritarian arts and literature of the period. CADA's publishing house, Ornitorrinco (Platypus), enabled many young writers, including Eltit, to publish their first novels.

Eltit's first novel, *Lumpérica*, a neologism that alludes to Latin America's marginal subcultures, was published in 1983 and translated into English in 1997 as *E. Iluminata*. This text's mix of poetry, fragments of a screenplay, and what might be described as written performance art forgoes the plot or character conventions of the traditional novel. The crucial first chapter is organized around three scenes which take place in a public square in Santiago, where a woman, referred to by the name of L. Iluminada, interacts with a group of street people referred to as Los Pálidos (the pale ones). L. Iluminada, who initially occupies the center of the square and is illuminated by a neon sign, is observed by Los Pálidos from the corners of the square. As an extended metaphor of literature, L. Iluminada struggles unsuccessfully to capture the malleable identities of her marginal subjects. Through a series of commentaries, stage directions, and criticism of each scene, the narrator emphasizes the cinematic construction of the text. Much of the human interaction in this novel seems to be permeated by the inquisitive and destructive power of an authoritarian society. In the second chapter, a series of police-like questioning destined to get at the "truth" of the events taking place in the public square seems to undermine any kind of communal or social interaction. In the following chapters, the text becomes progressively fragmented, and its main subject is literary tradition and language itself.

In 1986 Eltit published her second novel, *Por la patria* (For the Country), a neo-epic text in which Eltit defines communal space as essentially feminine. The protagonist is a woman whose name, Coya, a reference to the practice of Inca emperors of marrying their own sisters, embodies the tensions in Latin American history from the colonial period until the present. At a later point in the narrative, Coya changes her name to Coa, a reference to the street argot spoken by criminals in urban Chile, indicating a dramatic shift in the novel's historical and linguistic referents. As with the Inca's sister/wife, women in this novel exhibit a paradoxical centrality because their bodies serve as instruments that generate, mediate, and perpetuate a male-dominated national history. By exploring the historical origins of her mother tongue and contrasting it with marginal or minor languages, Eltit returns to the theme of language and power, particularly the role played by such key institutions as the state and the family in the production and circulation of meaning.

In the novel *El cuarto mundo* (The Fourth World, 1988), Eltit abandons the epic voice and returns to the private space of family relations, incest, and adultery. While the novel exhibits a more conventional narrative and less linguistic experimentation than her earlier novels, it continues to question language's ability to represent reality. The first part is narrated by María Chipia, a young boy who begins his story while he is in his mother's womb. The fetus struggles to understand the relationship between his own body and what of his twin sister and mother. As an adolescent, María Chipia desires a masculine space outside the home dominated by his mother, but later in the novel he realizes that such a space is impossible to obtain. The first part of the novel ends with a family crisis centered on the mother's adultery. The second part, narrated by the twin sister, who is identified at the end of the novel by the name (in lower case) diamela eltit, describes her incestuous relationship with María Chipia which results in the birth of a new child.

Vaca sagrada (Sacred Cow, 1991) was Eltit's first novel after the end of the military dictatorship in Chile. As in her first works, an attempt to reconstruct the plot of this novel is futile as the narrative is structured around a series of characters who desperately seek an identity and a relationship with the past. Manuel, Sergio, Ana, Francisca, and the narrator wander about a city where want, pain, abandonment, and chaos create a space laden with obstacles that prevent them from establishing any kind of connection with the past and themselves. Manuel, for instance, yearns for the "south," a utopian space charged with visions of communitarian life and harmony with nature. In contrast, the narrator defines herself as urban, yet the city is for her a fragile territory characterized by incoherence and abnormality. Francisca also has an urban identity, but it is shaped by factories, urban slums, poverty, and unemployment. The novel makes it clear, however, that searching for an identity in the past or in old social utopias may not liberate its characters. For instance, regarding the struggle of the factory workers, the narrator concludes, "Las trabajadoras estaban infiltradas desde sus propios cerebros. No habría entendimiento. Habría solo una abortada danza, el maquillaje, la parodia verbal" (The workers were infiltrated from within their own brains. There wouldn't be an understanding. There would only be an aborted dance, makeup, verbal parody; author's translation).

In 1994 Eltit published *Los vigilantes*, a novel structured around the exchange of letters between a woman and a former lover who is the father of her son. Although we only read the woman's letters, the man's presence in her writing is overwhelming. Through her letters, the reader learns that the father is continually questioning the woman's authority over her life, ranging from her child-rearing practices to her own writing. As a result of his controlling vigilance, the woman's language becomes self-conscious. It is only toward the end of the novel, when the woman leaves her home, that she is able to escape the strictures of the man's language and to develop an alliance with her son's free and playful use of language. Here Eltit indirectly refers us to the work of Roland Barthes who emphasizes the joyous pleasure of writing and challenges the psychoanalytical tradition that places women outside the symbolic order. As in her other novels, women are to recover the languages condemned to disappear in a city coping with the remnants of a military dictatorship and the homogenizing nature of modernization.

With the publication of *Vaca sagrada*, the image of the dictator, always present in her earlier novels, is replaced by the coercion of a market that dominates the production of meaning in Latin America's new democracies. Eltit's most recent novel, *Los trabajadores de la muerte* (The Workers of Death, 1998), can be read as a feminist allegory of resistance to new discourses of modernization that condemn the majority to poverty and unemployment. In one key chapter, a young mutilated girl is confronted by a man who urges her to interpret an epic dream that recounts the death of an authoritarian leader. The girl refuses to do so under his terms asserting her right to decipher her own vision of the future. In this novel, Eltit returns to the city and its public spaces (a street, a shelter, a bar) where children, street vendors, invalids, and the homeless struggle to negotiate the anarchic space of the streets taken over by violence, uncertainty, and death.

In addition to these major works, Eltit has published two interdisciplinary texts that explore the discourse of madness. In *El padre mío* (My Father, 1989), she transcribes the rambling and increasingly incomprehensible testimony of a homeless man, thus challenging the conventions of the testimonial genre that assume that the subject speaks for the community. It has been argued that *El padre mío* parodies Pinochet's authoritarian and paternalistic rhetoric, therefore underscoring the unbridgeable gap between what the regime said and what its citizens experienced (Pratt 1996, 154). Following this approach, Eltit's *El infarto del alma* (Soul Attack, 1994), in a collaborative effort with photographer Paz Errazuriz, explores love and relationships among patients in a psychiatric hospital outside Santiago. The text superimposes the sentimental discourse of Spanish medieval poetry on the sick and abandoned bodies of the patients, thus breaking the barrier between high and low culture. The *amor loco* (crazy love) of educated and aristocratic poetry is intertwined with the marginal voices of the poor and mentally ill to create a text that documents emotional survival in one of the most vulnerable spaces in society.

Eltit's work has been recognized for her response to the dictatorial rhetoric of the Pinochet regime and Latin America's cultural and political institutions. By using several strategies, such as parody, irony, and allegory, her transgressive and irreverent fiction helps dismantle the culture of fear built during the dictatorship and represents a radical attempt to create a feminist discourse. By allying herself with those living on the margins of society, Eltit seeks to redefine the boundaries between public and private space. The urban streets and plazas, haunted by beggars, invalids, and madmen, become the sites of a complex reconfiguration of citizenship and community in relation to authoritarianism and the market. Eltit also questions and redefines the private norms that govern love, eroticism, and the family. Although the sometimes abstract imagery and the radical experimentation with language make her work elusive, Eltit's ideological and aesthetic project is one of the most compelling examples of Latin American fiction of the end of the twentieth century.

Further Reading

Kadir, Djelal. *The Other Writing: Postcolonial Essays in Latin America's Writing Culture*. West Lafayette, Ind.: Purdue University Press, 1993.

Pratt, Mary Louise. "Overwriting Pinochet: Undoing the Culture of Fear in Chile." *Modern Language Quarterly* 57, no. 2 (June 1996): 151–63.

Williams, Raymond L. *The Postmodern Novel in Latin America: Politics, Culture and the Crisis of Truth*. New York: St. Martin's Press, 1995.

Sandra Garabano

MARÍA FÉLIX
(May 4, 1914–   )

Mexico: Actress

A mythic actress who portrayed strong Mexican women in nontraditional roles, María de los Angeles Güereña is believed to have been born on May 4, 1914, in Álamos, a little town in the Mexican state of Sonora. Her parents, Bernardo Félix and Josefa Güereña, belonged to the middle class, and she was the next to the last of sixteen children. In her autobiography *María Félix. Todas mis guerras* (1993), she explains how, as a child, she used to play a dangerous game with her brother Pablo, which consisted of riding their horses standing and exchanging them at the same time. The feeling of freedom and competition with a boy that she experienced during this game would guide her throughout her life. At the end of Enrique Krauze's prologue to her autobiography, he insinuates incestuous feelings toward this brother (who died in military school), which could explain her personality.

The Félixes moved to Guadalajara, where María Félix became queen of the Carnival in 1930. According to Carmen Barajas Sandoval, Félix's boyfriend opposed the honor bestowed on her, so she broke up with him. Some time later she married a cosmetics salesman, Enrique Alvarez Alatorre, a man so jealous that he did not allow her to go out because men might pay her compliments. When Félix learned that her husband had gonorrhea, she decided to leave him, but Enrique managed to keep their son, Enrique Alvarez Félix. She had an affair with Francisco Vázquez Cuéllar, a man who according to Félix had the same yellow eyes as her brother Pablo. She moved to the capital to work with a plastic surgeon who used her as publicity, claiming to have operated on her

María Félix. Courtesy of Photofest.

nose, chin, breasts, and waist. As she states in her autobiography, she wanted to study, learn, and explore the world (Félix 1993, 53).

An engineer, Fernando Palacios, noticed her beauty one day and offered to make her an actress. In 1942 she signed a contract with Producciones Grovas S. A. to perform in her first film, *El peñón de las ánimas* (The Peak of the Spirits, 1943), along with Mexican idol, Jorge Negrete. She had several obstacles to overcome: her stammer and Negrete's opposition to her participation in the film. During the filming she met singer Raúl Prado, with whom she would have a short-lived marriage. Félix's father considered acting an indecent occupation for a woman, and he forced all his children to sign a paper stating that their sister was a "lost woman" and a disgrace to the family. This action hurt her feelings, but at the same time it was a liberation that gave her "a license to fly" (Félix 1993, 65). The movie was a success and she signed a contract for her second one, *María Eugenia* (1942). In this film there is a scene in which she appears in a white bathing suit, and a photographer manipulated the still to show her naked, which was published by many newspapers and magazines. She later married singer Agustín Lara, who dedicated twelve songs to her. Together they planned to kidnap her child in Ajijic, Jalisco, after the boy had sent a letter saying that his father wanted to send him to a boarding school. Ironically, she later sent him to a boarding school in Canada.

In 1943 Félix starred in *Doña Bárbara* (Miss Barbara), a film based on the homonymous novel written by Rómulo Gallegos. She played a character that would give her national recognition: a strong woman in command of her own life, who used men, through witchcraft, for her own profit. After making this motion picture she was referred to as La Doña. Most of the roles in her other movies were modeled after this "devourer of men," as can be concluded from the following titles: *La mujer sin alma* (The Woman Without a Soul, 1944), *La monja alférez* (The Lieutenant Nun, 1944), *La devoradora* (The Devourer, 1946), *La mujer de todos* (Every Man's Woman, 1946), *Doña Diabla* (Miss Devil, 1948), *Mesalina* (1951), *La bandida* (The Bandit, 1963), and *La generala* (The General's Wife, 1970). Félix found a project for her own life in the literary model of Doña Bárbara (Taibó 1985, 32).

Félix divorced Lara six years after they were married and had an affair with millionaire Jorge Pasquel. She started her European career acting alongside such stars as Fernando Rey and Vittorio Gassmann. She starred in the Spanish films *Mare Nostrum* (1948), *Una mujer cualquiera* (A Loose Woman, 1949), *La noche del sábado* (Saturday Night, 1950), and *La corona negra* (The Black Crown, 1951). In Italy she filmed *Mesalina* (1951) and *Incantésimo trágico* (Tragic Enchantment, 1951). Her next motion picture, *La pasión desnuda* (Naked Passion, 1952), was filmed in Argentina under the direction of Luis César Amadori. In Argentina she became friends with **Eva María Duarte de Peron** in 1951 and almost married actor Carlos Thompson. Instead, after returning to Mexico, she married Jorge Negrete in 1952, but he died a year later. She was roundly criticized when she wore pants to the wake. After making the films *Camelia* (1953), *Reportaje* (News Report, 1953), *El rapto* (The Kidnapping, 1953), and *La bella Otero* (The Beautiful Otero Woman, 1954), she acted in Jean Renoir's *French-CanCan* (1954) and in *Les Héros sont fatigués* (The Heroes Are Exhausted, 1955). According to Barajas Sandoval, she had several affairs with famous men, including Spanish bullfighter Luis Miguel Domínguín, and in 1956 she married her fifth husband, French businessman Alex Berger. By this time she was internationally famous.

In 1957 she returned to Spain to participate in her last European movie, *Faustina* (1957). Two years later, she performed in Spanish director Luis Buñuel's *Los ambiciosos* (The Ambitious, 1959). In 1970 she played the role of a soldier in the last of her forty-seven films, *La generala*. According to her biographer, Félix did not work in Hollywood because she did not want to (Taibó 1985, 38). Félix was not highly regarded by film critics but she was awarded four Ariels (the Mexican equivalent of the Oscar). Moreover, according to one scholar, she was identified as a myth by Octavio Paz in the prologue to *María Félix*, in *Sapogonia*, a novel written by Anna Castillo, and in *Diálogos* (Dialogues), by Salvador Novo (Cantú 1996, 6). Mexican novelist Carlos Fuentes wrote about Félix in *Orquídeas a la luz de la luna* (Orchids in the Moonlight, 1982) and *Zona* sagrada

(Holy Place, 1967), where she was portrayed as a detached mother (Cantú, 6). In *Zona sagrada*, her son Enrique is depicted as a sexually frustrated character who suffers from an Oedipus complex. There is even a cross-dressing scene in which the son puts on his mother's clothes and paints his mother's famous mole on his face. Félix was painted by her friend, Mexican muralist Diego Rivera, and by José Orozco, Lenore Carrington, and Antoine Tzapoff.

From the beginning of her autobiography she details her "wars" to keep her freedom and admits that on certain occasions she had to hurt men to stop them from subjugating her (Félix 1993, 18). Though she does not view her life as a paradigm for anyone else, Félix is proud of her contribution to the liberation of Mexican women (19). She wants Mexican women to consider different alternatives to being a "domestic slave": "I would be satisfied if any female reader, motivated by my words, struggled a little harder than she is used to" (217). Paradoxically, the prologue by Enrique Krauze to her autobiography is entitled "Heart of a Man," with all its implicit connotations. Félix defends herself from multiple accusations made throughout her life, such as killing her secretary, stealing an emerald necklace, marrying for money and publicity, lesbianism, and even drug addiction. When she was a child, her mother gave her some words to live by: "Better number one than number two." To achieve this, she had to fight stereotypes; the jealousy of other women, including her sisters (one of whom tried to kill her by pushing her into a well); and the sexual harassment of a priest, Father Mireles, who tried to kiss her when she was ten. She explains that when she is pushed to fight she is not afraid of anything (18).

In her acting career, Félix played in roles different from the traditional ones of Mexican women of her time. The same could be said of her private life, where she challenged men and could not be subdued by the established moral prejudice of her society.

Further Reading

Barajas Sandoval, Carmen. *Una mujer llamada María Félix*. México, D. F.: Edamex, 1992.

Cantú, Rosalinda. "The María Félix Myth: Emergent Feminist Ideology in a Public and Private Life." Master's thesis, University of Michigan, 1996.

Félix, María. *María Félix. Todas mis guerras*. México, D. F.: Clío, 1993.

Taibó I, Paco Ignacio. *María Félix. 47 pasos por el cine*. México, D. F.: Joaquín Mortiz/Planeta, 1985.

Ignacio López-Calvo

ROSARIO FERRÉ

(?, 1938–   )

Puerto Rico: Author

Rosario Ferré is known for her corrosive literary parodies of sexism, racism, and socioeconomic exploitation in Puerto Rico. She began writing poetry and short stories for a literary magazine in 1970 and has since published children's literature, criticism, essays on feminism, historical books, and novels.

Ferré was born in Ponce, Puerto Rico, into a wealthy and politically powerful family. Her father, Luis A. Ferré, founded the Partido Nuevo Progresista (New Progressive party) and served as governor of the island from 1968 to 1972. He owned the conservative daily *El día* (The Day), one of Puerto Rico's main newspapers, which he sold to Rosario's brother, Antonio Luis Ferré, who then named it *El neuvo día* (The New Day).

Ferré majored in French and English at Manhattanville College (a school directed by nuns in Westchester County, New York) and married in 1960, shortly after graduating. She grew dissatisfied with her role as a traditional wife and mother and pursued graduate studies in literature at the University of Puerto Rico in Río Piedras. During this time she studied with Peruvian novelist Mario Vargas Llosa and literary critic Angel Rama.

When her mother died in 1970, she bequeathed Rosario a considerable inheritance, granting her the financial freedom to divorce her husband in 1972 and support her three children independently. These events, coupled with the fact that she had joined Luis Muñoz Marín's Partido Popular Democrático (Popular Democratic party), alienated her from her family. In 1983 Ferré moved to Washington, D.C., with her second husband, whom she soon divorced. She later earned a Ph.D. at the University of Maryland, where she defended her doctoral dissertation on the short fiction of the Argentine writer Julio Cortázar in 1987.

In 1970, while studying Latin American literature at the University of Puerto Rico, Ferré founded and edited a literary magazine called *Zona de carga y descarga* (Loading and Unloading Zone) with a number of her fellow students (Olga Nolla, Yvonne Ochard, and Manuel Ramos Otero) and professors (Mercedes López Baralt, Luce López Baralt, and Angel

Rama). The purpose of this magazine was to publish young and un-known writers who, at the time, had no other venue through which to disseminate their work in Puerto Rico. Although *Zona de carga y descarga* was a student-run and student-edited magazine that received no external funding, it quickly became one of the most important journals on the island. Its shocking content and creative visual layout symbolized the social, political, and cultural turmoil of the 1960s and 1970s. Ferré wrote for each issue and in this way began to discover her identity as a writer. The denunciation of patriarchal, class-based, colonial and neocolonial subordination remains a constant throughout Ferré's literary work. Sexually explicit language; the grotesque, carnivalistic celebrations of the lower-class black Caribbean culture; and irreverent parodies of upper-class hypocrisy are the trademarks of her fiction.

Ferré's first short story, "La muñeca menor" (The Youngest Doll), which appeared in the magazine's first issue, remains one of Ferré's most frequently anthologized texts. The story combines a fantastic occurrence with the symbolic metaphor (woman-as-doll) constituting a feminist cri-tique of Puerto Rican society. In 1972 Ferré published "Cuando las mu-jeres quieren a los hombres" (When Women Love Men), also published in *Zona de carga y descarga*. The story's language and plot, in which a rich widow and prostitute meet to discuss their dead ex-lover/ex-husband, was considered so scandalous that the magazine was burned in protest.

Ferré's early experimental writing shows the influence of writers such as Julio Cortázar, José Donoso, and Manuel Puig. Her fragmented non-linear texts demand an active reader, dedicated to decoding a literary puzzle that, in the end, resists any single or definitive interpretation. In 1976 Ferré published her first book, *Papeles de pandora* (Pandora's Papers), which includes many of the short stories and narrative poems that she had written for *Zona de carga y descarga*. One particularly unconventional story, "La bella durmiente" (Sleeping Beauty), comprises a number of diverse and seemingly unconnected texts: letters, newspaper clippings, photo album captions, baby-shower ideas, a birth announcement, dance scenes, and enigmatic, unpunctuated fragments of stream of conscious-ness. "La bella durmiente" is a highly ironic text that severely criticizes the patronizing domination of women by men in Puerto Rican high so-ciety. Other books of short fiction and poetry include *Las dos Venecias* (The Two Venices, 1990) and *La batalla de las vírgenes* (The Battle of the Virgins, 1993). She published a book of poetry, *Fábulas de la garza desan-grada* (Fables of the Bled Swan), in 1982.

Ferré's first book of criticism, *Sitio a Eros: Trece ensayos literarios* (The Seige of Eros: Thirteen Literary Essays, 1980), is a collection of feminist essays comparing the exploration of identity between nineteenth- and twentieth-century women writers such as Virginia Woolf, Simone de Beauvoir, Anaïs Nin, **Julia de Burgos**, and Lillian Hellman. Ferré has read feminist critical theory extensively, including writers from the French tradition (Hélène Cixous, Luce Irigaray, and Julia Kristeva) and North American feminists (such as Gloria Steinem). In her well-known essay "La cocina de la escritura" (The Writer's Kitchen), Ferré explores the origins of her own writing. In another essay, "La autenticidad de la mujer en el arte" (The Authenticity of Women in Art), Ferré argues that women should resort to writing to come to know themselves. Ferré has written one more book of essays devoted to women and writing, *El árbol de sus sombras* (The Tree and Its Shadows, 1989). In the essay from which the book takes its name, Ferré explores the creative process and the relationship between writers, fiction, and literary criticism. She has published two other books of literary criticism, *El acomodador: Una lectura fantástica de Felisberto* (The Usher: A Fantastic Reading of Filisbert, 1986) and *Cortázar, el romántico en su observatorio* (Cortázar, the Romantic in His Observatory, 1990).

In 1990 she published *El coloquio de las perras* (The Bitches' Colloquy), evoking Miguel de Cervantes's classic exemplary novel, *The Dialogue of the Dogs*, in the context of contemporary Latin America. In Ferré's text, two female dogs named Fina and Franca discuss literature, particularly the canonical male authors of the so-called Boom of the 1960s and early 1970s and issues affecting Puerto Rican women writers.

Although Ferré is completely bilingual, she has, until recently, always written first in Spanish and then insisted on translating her own work into English. However, based on *Sweet Diamond Dust* (1988), the translation of *Maldito amor* (1986), a highly fragmented novel that explores the concealed racism of Puerto Rican society within the context of the island's political transition from landed aristocracy to a neocolonial industrialized territory, some critics assert that her English renditions do not attain the same level of intensity as her books written in Spanish.

An overview of Ferré's literary corpus reveals a sustained effort to experiment with a variety of literary genres, including children's literature and historical books, such as a book about her father titled *Luis A. Ferré: Memorias de Ponce* (Luis A. Ferré: Memoirs of Ponce, 1992).

In 1995 Ferré published *The House on the Lagoon* originally in English, to give her access to a larger reading audience. The 407-page saga alternates back and forth between the perspectives of a wife and her husband. An important commercial success, *The House on the Lagoon* was a finalist for the National Book Award in 1995. Ferré's most recent book, *Eccentric Neighborhoods* (1998), a fictionalized memoir about her mother, critiques the abuse of social and political power in Puerto Rico.

Further Reading

Castillo, Debra A. "Surfacing: Rosario Ferré and Julieta Campos, with Rosario Castellanos." In *Talking Back: Toward a Latin American Feminist Literary Criticism*. Ithaca, N.Y.: Cornell University Press, 1992. 137–84.

Franco, Jean. "Self-destructing Heroines." *Minnesota Review* 22 (1984): 105–15.

Hintz, Susan S. *Rosario Ferré, A Search for Identity*. New York: Peter Lang, 1995.

Jaffe, Janice A. "Translation and Prostitution: Rosario Ferré's *Maldito amor* and *Sweet Diamond Dust*." *Latin American Literary Review* 23, no. 46 (1995): 66–82.

Perry, Donna Marie. Interview with Rosario Ferré in *Backtalk: Women Writers Speak Out: Interviews*, 83–104. New Brunswick, N.J.: Rutgers University Press, 1993.

Robert Neustadt

BENITA GALEANA
(1904?–April 17, 1995)

Mexico: Political Activist

Benita Galeana, a Mexican Communist party activist, was born in San Jerónimo de Juárez, Guerrero, a small town about eighty kilometers from Acapulco. Her year of her birth has been variously recorded as 1904, 1907, and even as late as 1910, but the date that makes the best sense in terms of understanding key moments in her life story is 1904. This is also the date that Galeana herself consistently maintained to be the correct one. Galeana's father, Genaro Galeana Lacunza, was a landowner who, by the time of his daughter's childhood, had lost control of his property to other family members. The early deaths of her parents (her mother died when Benita was two years old, and her father when she was six) left Benita and her other young siblings in the care of their oldest sister, Camila. The family was poor, and Galeana was forced to work in her sister's household from an early age, assisting in the everyday tasks of milking the cows, preparing food for sale, making cheese, working in the fields, and caring for Camila's children. Each year the family went to the coast to work on the rice plantations, a typical way for peasants in Guerrero to earn some cash income. In spite of an intense desire to learn to read and write, Galeana was not allowed to attend school during her childhood, and the lack of literacy was one of many obstacles that

Benita Galeana. Photo by Javier Aspe. Courtesy of Latin
American Literary Review Press.

she struggled to overcome during her entire lifetime. Possessed of a
strong determination to leave San Jerónimo and her sister's harsh tutelage in order to migrate to Mexico City, Galeana moved to Acapulco in
about 1920, where she had a child, Lilia, whom she raised as a single
parent.

In roughly 1924 Galeana realized her dream of moving to Mexico City,
where she spent most of her adult life. Once there, her youth and her
lack of education and marketable skills left her with few options other
than domestic work or employment at one of the capital city's many
dance halls. She tried her hand at both of these marginalized and ex-
ploitative lines of work before entering into a relationship with a taxi
cab driver who was also a member of the Mexican Communist party
(founded in 1919). Through her partner, Galeana began to have contact
with other party members and to learn about the principles of social and
economic justice upon which the movement was founded. The conditions of her first arrest at a Communist party rally and the subsequent
time spent in jail became a turning point in her life because they forced
her to experience, in a new and direct way, the injustice of a system that
exploited the poor and suppressed the public expression of political
views that challenged the status quo. Galeana was attracted to the Mex-

ican Communist party and its platform of workers' rights, the eight-hour day, women's rights, and redistribution of land. These ideals she continued to support during her long life as a political and labor activist.

Galeana joined the party in about 1929, during the presidency of Emilio Portes Gil (1928–1930). Portes Gil and his successor, Pascual Ortiz Rubio, declared the Mexican Communist party to be illegal, which forced its operations underground until 1936, when Lázaro Cárdenas lifted the prohibition and legalized the party again. In the first years of Galeana's party affiliation and activism, she was subjected to the government's repressive and violent tactics as it persecuted Communist leaders and suppressed their activities. During the period of clandestinity, they continued to produce and distribute the party newspaper, *El machete* (The Machete), founded in 1924 and supported by leading Mexican artists and intellectuals, including Diego Rivera, David Alfaro Siqueiros, and Xavier Guerrero. The party also held rallies, posted antigovernment propaganda, supported anarchists Nicola Sacco and Bartolomeo Vanzetti who were on trial in the United States, spoke out against fascism in Mexico and abroad, and tried to organize factory workers into unions. Those caught participating in these activities were subject to arrest and jail sentences, and Galeana, who sold *El machete* and was a popular speaker at public meetings, was arrested and incarcerated more than fifty times.

In 1939 Galeana wrote an autobiographical narrative that was published in 1940 under the title *Benita*. Although she was unable to read, she had taught herself the alphabet, and she managed to use a typewriter to record her life story by sounding out the words and typing them phonetically. She gave the manuscript to a fellow party activist, a journalist and her future husband Mario Gil (also spelled Gill), who corrected the spelling and provided needed punctuation and chapter breaks. Imprenta Mels, a Communist party print shop, published the book in 1940, illustrated with woodcuts made by artists belonging to the Taller de Gráfica Popular (People's Graphics Workshop). *Benita* recounts the harsh conditions of Galena's childhood in San Jerónimo and her early years in Mexico City before focusing on her political militancy of the late 1920s and early 1930s. A preface by Mario Gil attests to the authentic nature of the document as the product of Galeana's hand. In the final chapter, Galeana states that she wrote her autobiography to demonstrate the transforming power of her commitment to socialist ideals and as a call to other poor Mexicans, especially to poor Mexican women, to join the struggle. Galeana also wrote and published a second manuscript entitled *El peso mocho* (The Damaged Coin, 1979), which is a collection of short narratives based on life in San Jerónimo. In spite of her extremely limited literacy skills, Galeana showed a strong vocation for writing and an understanding of the importance of recording the experiences of the common people as a counterdiscourse to official history. Throughout her life, she was dependent on others to evaluate her writing and put it into publishable form, a process that resulted in the loss of a third manuscript that treated her views on politics and contemporary events.

Benita Galeana and Mario Gil were married for more than thirty years until he died in the 1970s. Her daughter, Lilia, died in her late twenties, and over the years Benita and her husband raised six other girls who were in need of a home. Galeana's home in the Periodistas neighborhood of Mexico City was purchased by the Federal District government in 1993 under an agreement to catalogue and preserve her archives and her husband's library and to create a women's center to be called La Casa de la Mujer Benita Galeana (Benita Galeana Women's House). This resource center would be a tribute to her lifelong dedication to improving the condition of women in Mexico, starting with the struggle for suffrage and including such issues as day care and employment. In an interview published in the magazine *fem* [sic] in 1993, Galeana spoke in favor of abortion rights, and she expressed her acceptance and respect for lesbians, maintaining her position at the cutting edge of Mexican feminism.

Starting in the 1940s and until she reached retirement age, Galeana worked for the post office and then for the social security administration. In the post office she served as a union delegate. Galeana's commitment to the international Communist movement was unwavering, and in her later years she remained a visible and active figure in movements for social justice in Mexico City and nationwide. She worked on behalf of the railroad workers' strike in 1958, helping to organize the women to meet their basic needs during the work stoppage. In 1968 she supported the student movement, and after the massacre in the Plaza de las Tres Culturas on October 2, 1968, she visited the students in jail, bringing them food and medicine and helping them make contact with family members. After the 1985 earthquake in Mexico City, she gave away many of her possessions to those who had lost everything in the disaster. An outspoken critic of the government, Galeana gave many newspaper interviews throughout the years in which she denounced the ruling Partido Revolucionario Institucional (PRI, the Institutional Revolutionary Party), presidential politics, and Mexico's relationship with the United States. In October 1988, she visited Cuba by invitation of the Federación de Mujeres Cubanas (Federation of Cuban Women), and in 1989 she traveled to Panama to receive a medal of honor from leader Manuel Noriega. An admirer of the Ejército Zapatista de Liberación Nacional (EZLN, or the Zapatista Army of National Liberation), which represented the insurgency of indigenous men and women, she visited Chiapas in August 1994 in a gesture of solidarity with their demands. Galeana's long life is an example of the human capacity to overcome hardship and adversity through both individual determination and participation in a collective struggle. Her dedication to socialist principles of economic justice and to women's rights was unwavering, and her courage in overcoming obstacles to her goals was unflinching.

Further Reading

Galeana, Benita. *Benita*, translated by Amy Diane Prince. Pittsburgh: Latin American Literary Review Press, 1994.

Beth E. Jörgensen

ELENA GARRO
(December 11, 1916–August 22, 1998)

Mexico: Author, Playwright, Journalist, Screenwriter

Elena Garro was a playwright, novelist, choreographer, journalist, screenwriter, poet, and political activist. Garro was born in Puebla, Mexico, to a Spanish father, José Antonio Garro Melendreras, and a Mexican mother, Esperanza Navarro Benítez. She spent much of her childhood in Iguala, in the state of Guerrero. This was the setting for her political novel *Los recuerdos del porvenir* (Recollections of Things to Come, 1963).

In 1936 Garro attended the National University of Mexico, where she choreographed for the university theater. In June 1937, she married poet Octavio Paz, who did not allow her to continue her studies. This was the beginning of Garro's struggle to find her literary and political identity against a domineering husband and a patriarchal society.

Two weeks after their marriage and in spite of the raging civil war, Garro and Paz traveled to Spain because his poem "No pasarán" (They Shall Not Pass) led to an invitation to the Congress of Antifascist writers. The couple went to Paris and returned to Mexico, where their daughter, Helena Paz, was born on December 12, 1939. In 1943 Paz received a Guggenheim scholarship, and they traveled to the United States.

Two years later, Paz accepted a diplomatic post as secretary of the Mexican consulate in Paris. Garro's novella, *Primer amor* (First Love, 1996), recreates the post–World War II period as the characters encounter German prisoners.

From 1946 to 1951, Garro and Paz lived in Paris in close contact with French surrealists, such as André Breton, and well-known Latin American writers. During this period, Garro wrote poems but never attempted

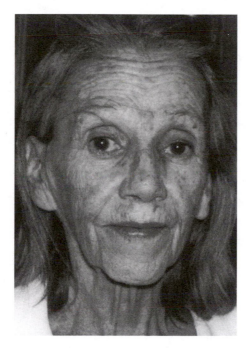

Elena Garro. Courtesy of Rhina Toruño.

to publish them. In 1952 Octavio Paz went to Japan as chief of the Mexican diplomatic delegation, and he took his family with him.

In 1953 they went to Berne, Switzerland, where, hospitalized, Garro wrote *Los recuerdos del porvenir* (1963), which won the Xavier Villaurrutia Prize (1963). Garro's book acknowledges the small town of Iguala, Guerrero, Mexico, and many persons there whom she had greatly admired ever since her childhood. The historical framework of this novel refers to the Cristeros revolt, a counterrevolutionary Catholic movement centered in southwestern Mexico. This novel perhaps influenced Gabriel García Márquez's *One Hundred Years of Solitude*, which was published four years later (Alegría 1986, 277).

Addressing the issue of why the novel was not among the so-called Boom novels of the 1960s, Garro stated, "[Because] I am a woman and the novel was considered 'religious' for referring to the Cristeros Revolt" (personal interview, 1997).

At the end of 1953, the family returned to Mexico where Garro began research on General Felipe Angeles, a forgotten hero of the Mexican Revolution who had been condemned by the government against the will of his people. Though the documentary drama was finished by 1954, it was not published until 1967.

During the 1950s Garro become very active and successful as a screen-writer, political activist, and journalist. She wrote many movie scripts, including *De noche vienes* (You Come at Night), *Las señoritas Vivanco* (The Vivanco Ladies), and *La escondida* (The Hidden Woman), starring **María Félix**, and she published *Un hogar sólido* (A Solid Home), a collection of twelve plays in 1958.

Garro expressed her support for the struggle of the downtrodden In-dians through journalism. Being vocal about her political engagement led to her exile when President Adolfo López Mateos asked Octavio Paz in 1959 to take his wife out of the country. Paz sent her to New York. Later they moved to Paris where Paz was the cultural attaché of the Mexican embassy.

Garro returned to Mexico in 1963. She received the Villaurrutia Prize for *Los recuerdos del porvenir*, and she published a collection of short sto-ries titled *La semana de colores* (The Week of Colors) that year.

By September 1968 the student movement was very active throughout Mexico. A badly injured student leader, left for dead in front of Garro's house, became part of her political novel, *Y Matarazo no llamó . . .* (And Matarazo Never Called, 1991). After the October 2, 1968, Tlatelolco mas-sacre, Garro was branded by the government as a radical leftist, an in-stigator of the student revolt. Garro inadvertently alienated herself by naming the intellectuals who were involved in the movement. Isolation led Garro and her daughter to move to the United States in 1972. Their experience is depicted in the black humor of *Andamos huyendo, Lola* (We Are Fleeing Lola, 1980).

In 1974, after eighteen months in New York City, the two Elenas fled to Spain, the land of Garro's father, where their legal problems regarding their citizenship status surfaced, as portrayed in *Testimonios sobre Mariana* (Testimonies about Mariana, 1981) and *Reencuentro de personajes* (Re-encounter of Characters, 1981). Garro's relatives in Spain avoided her because the press labeled her a Communist. This frustrating experience is reflected in her autobiographical novel *La casa junto al río* (The House by the River, 1982). Though the Garroses had lived in Spain since 1974, they were asked to leave the country in 1980 because Octavio Paz re-quested their removal as a condition to his acceptance of the Miguel Cervantes Prize.

In Paris, mother and daughter reenacted their experiences as illegal immigrants. Garros's daughter, Elena, contacted Paz who provided some money and helped her get a job in the Mexican consulate in Paris, where she worked until they returned to Mexico in 1993.

During this period Garro published her so-called autobiographical novel: *Testimonios sobre Mariana* (1981), about her life with Octavio Paz in Paris. This novel, coinciding with *La casa junto al río*, deploys a lyrical magical realist style. Their ending is similar too: the heroines both find a solution beyond this life.

In 1982 Garro published *Reencuentro de personajes,* an experimental novel, originally written in 1965, about a Mexican woman, who leaves husband and country to go to Europe with her lover only to discover he is a wealthy psychopathic homosexual and a criminal.

In 1993 Garro's self-imposed exile ended, and she and her daughter settled in Cuernavaca. Garro passed away on August 22, 1998. During this period, Helena Paz had several of her mother's manuscripts published. In 1995 *Inés* appeared and in 1996 *Un traje rojo para un duelo* (A Red Dress for a Mourning), *Un corazón en un bote de basura* (A Heart in a Trash Can), and, as a collection, two short novels, *Busca mi esquela* (Look for My Death Note) and *Primer amor* (First Love). These two short novels won the International Prize Sor Juana Inés de La Cruz in 1996. In 1997 two short story books came out: *El accidente y otros cuentos inéditos* (The Accident and Other Unpublished Stories) and *La vida empieza a las tres. Hoy es jueves. La feria o De noche vienes* (Life Begins at Three. Today is Thursday. The Fair or You Come at Night).

Among Garro's later works, the most meaningful is *Un traje rojo para un duelo,* an autobiographical novel in which the narrator is Helena Paz and her paternal grandmother, Doña Pili, is the evil character. Though Garro did not want it published, they published it because of their dire economic condition. After this publication, her contact with Octavio Paz ended. *Mi hermanita Magdalena* (My Little Sister Magdalena), a novel that had been in storage for at least twenty years, was posthumously published in December 1998.

Today Garro figures among the best-known, contemporary Latin American writers with García Márquez, Carlos Fuentes, and Alejo Carpentier. Garro mastered the magical-realist technique of developing themes within cyclical time. Garro also wrote drama in the classical style. *Felipe Angeles* (1979) follows Aristotelian conventions. Some of her short stories, plays, and novels, such as *Los recuerdos del porvenir,* have been made into movies.

Garro's work as a whole reflects a deep sense of social realism. Her mythical, magical, and mysterious style is at its best when she articulates the horrors of the oppression of Mexican society.

Further Reading

Alegría, Fernando. *Nueva historia de la literatura hispanoamericana.* 4th ed. Hanover, NH: Del Norte, 1986.

Cypess, Sandra Messinger. "Visual and Verbal Distances in the Mexican Theater: The Plays of Elena Garro." In *Woman as Myth and Metaphor in Latin American Literature,* edited by Carmelo Virgilio and Naomi Lindstrom, 44–62. Columbia: University of Missouri Press, 1985.

Fox-Lockert, Lucía. "Elena Garro." In *Woman Novelists in Spain and Spanish America*, 228–40. Metuchen, N.J.: Scarecrow Press, 1979.

Hardin, Michael. "Inscribing and Incorporating the Marginal: (P)Recreating the Female Artist in Elena Garro's *Recollections of Things to Come*." *Hispanic Journal* 16, no. 1 (1995): 147–59.

Larson, Catherine. "Recollections of Plays to Come: Echoes and Foreshadowing in the Theatre of Elena Garro." *Latin American Theatre Review* 22, no. 2 (1989): 31–36.

Rosser, Harry Enrique. "Form and Content in Elena Garro's *Los recuerdos del porvenir*." *Revista canadiense de estudios hispánicos* 2, no. 3 (Spring 1978): 282–94.

Stall, Anita K., ed. *A Different Reality; Studies on the Work of Elena Garro*. Lewisburg, Pa.: Bucknell University Press, 1990.

Winkler, Julie Ann. "Insiders, Outsiders, and the Slippery Center: Marginality in *Los recuerdos del porvenir*." *Indiana Journal of Hispanic Literatures* 8 (1996): 177–95.

Rhina Toruño

IVONE GEBARA
(December 9, 1944–   )
Brazil: Theologian, Author, Educator

Ivone Gebara, a feminist theologian who uses her interest in ecology to improve the social conditions of women and the disadvantaged, was born in São Paulo, Brazil. Even though her parents were not especially religious, she was strongly interested in religion from childhood, perhaps as a result of having studied at a Catholic school along with her two sisters. Her interest in religion came as a "mixture of attraction and fear, as if the universe with which she was confronted was full of secrets, challenges and special powers" (personal communication, May 1999). This interest in religious issues had always been connected to the poor. From an early age she realized that the situation of misery and discrimination that encompassed a large portion of Latin America was terribly unjust, and, as a result, she questioned the establishment. The numerous questions that this situation raised influenced her career and her research.

As a young woman Gebara had to overcome her first and possibly most difficult challenge: her parents' disapproval of her becoming a nun. She used firm resolve to overcome this difficulty and became a sister of the Augustinian Congregation of Sisters of Our Lady in 1967. Later she was faced with another challenge: the hierarchy of the Catholic Church, as observed in the growing strength of the conservative right wing while progressive alternative trends (such as liberation theology) weakened.

Gebara's intellectual curiosity, social consciousness, and community spirit led her to continue her studies at the Pontifícia Catholic University of São Paulo (PUC-SP), where she completed a doctorate in philosophy in 1975. In 1998 she completed a second doctorate, this time in religious sciences, at the Catholic University of Louvain in Belgium.

Gebara has also been active as a professor and researcher. She taught at Auburn Theological Seminary and Union Theological Seminary in New York for six months in 1994. She was a philosophy and theology professor for seventeen years at the Theological Institute of Recife in northeastern Brazil until it was closed by the Vatican in 1989. She also worked for twelve years at the Department of Research and Assistance, an interdisciplinary organization specializing in the theological training of alternative, grassroots ministries. The general focus of her research has been feminist theology in Latin America, encompassing a broad spectrum of issues, such as the place of religion today, deconstruction in feminist theology, the problems facing modern women, and feminist hermeneutics (the interpretation of the Holy Scriptures from a female perspective). Her current studies are focused on ecofeminism, that is, feminism applied to ecological issues. The main objective of her research is on the poor and oppressed, one of the fundamentals of liberation theology.

Since 1973 Gebara has lived in the state of Pernambuco, in northeastern Brazil, in a lower-income community, and she regularly provides assistance to the poor. Although she does not belong to a specific group, Gebara is frequently called upon by several church organizations to give workshops and social assistance.

Among the people who have influenced Gebara's work are José Comblin, a Belgian theologian who has lived in Brazil for many years (and Gebara's professor at the university), her colleagues at the Theological Institute of Recife, D. Helder Câmara through his political views, and some of the feminist theologians in the United States and Germany, including Dorothé Solle, Rosemary Radford Ruether, and Elisabeth Fiorenza. The writings of Peruvian theologian Gustavo Gutiérrez have also left their imprint on her work.

Gebara's research includes eleven books and numerous articles published and translated in different countries, such as Brazil, Spain, France, and the United States. Her books, on occasion written with coauthor Maria Clara Bingemer, have had widespread repercussions, and her works, both on liberation theology and ecofeminism, are among the most relevant studies on the subject.

The main features of Gebara's work are her analytical ability, innovative character, and concern for social issues. Her writing is based on the reality of Latin America, specifically northeastern Brazil. Among her most recent works are *Teologia ecofeminista: Ensaio para repensar o conhecimento e a Religião* (Ecofeminist Theology: Rethinking Knowledge and Religion, 1997), *Le Mal au Féminin: Réflexions Théologiques à partir du Féminisme* (The Female Evil: Theological Reflections based on Feminism, 1999)—her doctoral dissertation at the Catholic University of Louvain published by L'Harmattan), and *Longing for Running Waters* (1999). *Teologia ecofeminista* is an excellent example of her work and current interest in the field of ecofeminism. In her previous book, *Teologia a ritmo de mulher* (Theology for Women, 1995), she referred to the problem of feminist hermeneutics in relation to the Bible by developing nine characteristics that, in her opinion, make up feminist hermeneutics.

Gebara's ecofeminist perspective emerges in her publications as a result of her experience in working with women of lower income of northeastern Brazil and in working with the poor of inner-city communities. This perspective reflects an effort to combine the theories of feminist theology with her concern about ecology in such a way that humanity would be able to establish a better relationship with the universe. In this sense, Gebara has been able to blend three topics that are hard to combine—feminism, ecology, and theology—based on trends of the last three decades in which theological discourse is closely related to social justice and economic and political issues. Also, this concern with feminism for the future of planet earth can be established by a direct relationship between humankind's destiny and the destiny of the physical world. On the other hand, she believes that social justice cannot be separated from an awareness of ecology and, as a result, the Church should pay attention to this issue. Ecofeminism is a line of thought as well as a social movement whose priorities include defending the ecosystem and women. It relates to women through nature, since both are being exploited within a patriarchal hierarchy.

One of Gebara's strengths is that she not only makes her observations, but presents practical guidelines for action. For her, ecofeminist politics has to be analytical and active, and it has to be related to the antiracist, antisexist, and antielitist struggle, since most women, children, African Americans, and indigenous peoples tend to be the first victims of the deterioration of the ecosystem. In this sense, she establishes a relationship among race, gender, and social class with an ecological awareness.

Since 1990 Gebara has taught several courses and directed workshops at many community service centers and universities. She has participated in conferences not only in Brazil, but also in Austria, Germany, Belgium, and France, and she has traveled extensively to Canada, the United States, and several Latin American countries, including Chile, Argentina, Nicaragua, and Guatemala.

Gebara is a member of the Teólogos(as) do Terceiro Mundo (Theologians of the Third World) of the Núcleo de Estudos da Mulher e Relações de Gênero, or NEMGE (Center for Studies on Women and Gender Issues), and she is a consultant for several different grassroots organizations, including the Serviço à Mulher Marginalizada (Services for Marginalized Women), A Casa da Mulher do Nordeste (Women's Home of the Northeast), Centro Ecumênico de Serviços à Educação Popular (Ecumenical Service Center for Popular Education), and the Sindicato das Domésticas de Pernambuco (Pernambuco Union of Maids). During the past two years she has been heard on Brazilian radio stations such as CBN and Radio Olinda.

Gebara's current goals are to continue with international consulting and to dedicate time to the support of women's issues, especially those of lower-income women in Recife and nearby cities. Ultimately her goal is to continue writing.

Further Reading

Gebara, Ivone. "Cosmic Theology: Ecofeminism and Panentheism." In *Readings in Ecology and Feminist Theology*, edited by Mary Heather Mackinnon and Moni McIntyre, 208–13. Kansas City: Sheed & Ward, 1995.

———. "A Cry for Life from Latin America: Spirituality of the Poor." In *Spirituality of the Third World*, edited by K. C. Abraham and Bernadette Mbuy-Beya, 109–18. Maryknoll, N.Y.: Orbis Books, 1994.

———. *Longing for Running Waters*. Minneapolis: Fortress Press, 1999.

———. "Mary." In *Mysterium Liberationis: Fundamental Concepts of Liberation Theology*, edited by Ignacio Ellacuría and Jon Sobrino and translated by Dinah Livingstone, 482–95. Maryknoll, N.Y.: Orbis Books, 1993.

———. "The Trinity and Human Experience: An Ecofeminist Approach." In *Women Healing Earth: Third World Women on Ecology, Feminism, and Religion*, edited by Rosemary Radford Ruether and translated by David Molineaux, 13–23. Maryknoll, N.Y.: Orbis Books, 1996.

———. "What Sacred Scriptures Are Sacred Authority? Ambiguities of the Bible in the Lives of Latin American Women." In *Women's Sacred Scriptures*, edited by Pui-Lan Kwok and Elisabeth Schüssler Fiorenza and translated by Paul Burns, 7–19. Maryknoll, N.Y.: Orbis Books, 1998.

———. "Women Doing Theology in Latin America." In *Through Her Eyes*, edited by Elsa Tamez and translated by Phillip Berryman, 125–34. Maryknoll, N.Y.: Orbis Books, 1989.

Gebara, Ivone, and Maria Clara Bingemer. *Mary, Mother of God, Mother of the Poor*. Maryknoll, N.Y.: Orbis Books, 1989.

Lizbeth Souza Fuertes

TERESA GISBERT CARBONELL DE MESA
(November 11, 1926–   )

Bolivia: Architect, Educator, Historian

Architect, historian, and art historian, Teresa Gisbert Carbonell was born into a family of Spanish emigrants; her mother was from Barcelona and her father from Valencia. Gisbert had a comfortable childhood and was educated in a private Catholic school, Santa Ana in La Paz. Gisbert studied at the Major University of San Andrés in La Paz. In 1950 she obtained her bachelor's degree in architecture and urbanism. After finishing her studies, she married José de Mesa, and together they went to Spain to complete their graduate studies in art history. During 1952 and 1953 she worked as a researcher at the Laboratory of Art of the University of Seville and at the Diego Velázquez Art Institute, which is part of the Superior Council of Scientific Investigations. After their return from Spain, Gisbert and her husband had a difficult time obtaining jobs as architects, and both worked as professors of art history. Her first published book (written jointly with her husband) was *Holguín y la pintura virreinal en Bolivia* (Holguín and Viceregal Bolivian Painting, 1977). Gisbert and her husband have four children: Carlos, Andrés, Isabel, and Teresa.

Gisbert obtained numerous national and international awards for her innovative research in art, architecture, and history. In 1959 and in 1968 she received a Guggenheim fellowship, and during 1990–1991 and 1993–1994 she was a visiting scholar at the Getty Research Institute for the History of Art and the Humanities, Los Angeles.

Teaching has also been a significant component of Gisbert's activities. For sixteen years (1954–1970) she taught Bolivian culture and art history in the faculty of humanities at the University of San Andrés. During 1972 and 1975 she was a professor of American art in the faculty of architecture at the same institution. In 1987 and 1993 she taught a seminar called Andean Myth and Art in the School of Higher Social Education at the University of Paris. She gave the same seminar at the Culture Institute in Ecuador in 1992. In 1991 Gisbert taught a course called Systems of Representation and Identity in the Andes, a graduate course at FLACSO (Facultad Latinoamericana de Ciencias Sociales) Bolivia, for the superior diploma in Andean studies. In 1995 she gave a seminar called Survival of the Indigenous

Teresa Gisbert Carbonell de Mesa. Photo by Fabiola Fernández
Salek. Courtesy of Teresa Gisbert.

Culture in Latin America at the Interamerican University in Puerto Rico.
Currently, she is a professor at the University of Our Lady of La Paz, a
private institution in La Paz. She has also given several conferences about
viceregal art at different cultural and academic institutions.

During her career, she has held several important positions in the cultural world. From 1970 until 1976 she was the director of the National
Art Museum in La Paz. From 1983 to 1984 she was the president of the
Bolivian Society for History, and from 1985 to 1989 she was the director
of the Bolivian Cultural Institute. For seven years (1986–1992), she was
the president of the International Council on Monuments and Sites (ICO-
MOS) in Bolivia.

Gisbert is also a member of numerous professional organizations,
namely the College of Architects of Bolivia, the Bolivian Academy of
History, the National Academy of Sciences (Bolivia), the Bolivarian Architect Society (Caracas), and the Chilean Academy of History. Among
other distinguished activities, she is a correspondent of the Spanish
Royal Academy of History, the San Fernando Royal Academy of Arts,
and the Academy of Fine Arts in Seville, and she is a member of the
Editorial Advisory Board of the *Colonial Latin American Review*.

She has received numerous awards for her research in history and
architecture. In 1957 she received the second Literature Award, and in

1965 she was declared woman of the year in La Paz. Gisbert also won a cultural award from the Vicente Ballivián Foundation in 1984. She was granted the Medal of Merit by the Spanish government and also the Order of Isabel the Catholic, conferred by the king of Spain. In 1987 she received the Order of the Condor of the Andes, the most important recognition awarded by the Bolivian government, and two years later she was recognized by the French government for her many years of remarkable contributions to culture. In 1995 she was awarded the National Cultural Award in Bolivia.

Gisbert has said that one of her greatest satisfactions was achieved during the 1980s when she started to produce her intellectual work independent of her husband (personal interview, December 1998). One of her major accomplishments was *Iconografía y mitos indígenas en el arte* (Indigenous Iconography and Myths in Art, 1980), original research that signaled Gisbert's intellectual independence.

Gisbert had to overcome a significant obstacle during her years at the university in the early 1940s: sexism. One of only a few women students at the university, she had to deal with numerous prejudices. Fortunately, her family was very supportive and allowed her a freedom that most women in Bolivia at that time did not enjoy. At the university, her classmates turned off the lights when she entered the room and made obscene comments in front of her. However, as time went by, her classmates got accustomed to her presence and she became just another student.

Gisbert needed great inner strength to pursue further studies. She had to do things considered improper for a woman at that time. She was sometimes out of the house until late at night finishing projects, and she occasionally went out to eat with her professors and classmates, mostly men, which at that time was considered scandalous.

During her career, she has found herself faced with a difficulty faced by every researcher in Bolivia: lack of financial resources and support from the government and from the private sector as well. Researchers in less-developed nations not only have to meet the challenge of their profession (original contributions) but also obtain the necessary resources to publish their research. Despite these difficulties she has managed to write and cowrite several books.

Most of the time, researchers have to finance their books personally. When they can obtain a publisher, earnings range from $1 to $5 per book. Considering the reduced markets in Bolivia, it is not very much. At present, support for research has slightly improved, and some institutions, such as the University of San Andrés, the National Academy of Sciences, and the Institute of Education, provide funds for original work. Nonetheless, private support is still the best option for financing research for established and well-known scholars such as Gisbert.

Gisbert and her husband have built a private library specializing in the colonial period of the Andes, which has enormously facilitated their access to bibliography, something generally very challenging in Bolivia. Additionally, working with colonial art requires travel to areas that are often hard to reach, increasing the difficulty of making a topographical survey (measurements) and the cost of taking pictures. The transportation infrastructure in the Andean region is very poor, and every trip is an adventure. As if all that were not enough, access to some of the buildings, for example churches, requires special permits.

Gisbert considers her most important work to be *Arquitectura andina* (Andean Architecture, 1997) and *Historia de la pintura cuzqueña* (History of Painting in Cuzco, 1962), both written with José de Mesa. Among her most important independent research are *Iconografía y mitos indígenas en el arte* and a book that is currently in print provisionally entitled *El otro* (The Other), which concerns the vision that seventeenth-century Bolivians had of the Turkish, Chinese, Jews, and others. Other significant independent works are *Arte textil y mundo andino* (Textile Art and the Andean World, 1987) and *Historia de la vivienda y asentamientos humanos* (History of Human Homes and Settlements, 1988). In history, Gisbert has coauthored *Historia de Bolivia* (History of Bolivia, 1997) and *Manual de historia de Bolivia* (Handbook of Bolivian History, 1994), two prominent, as well as pioneering, history books that have had several printings to date (personal interview, December 1998).

Two main influences in her life have been Hugo Iñígez and Marco Dorsa (Gisbert's art professors in Spain), who encouraged her to specialize in the Andean region, rather than in Spanish art, Gisbert's initial inclination. Iñígez and Dorsa argued that a lot of research had already been done in Europe, but the Andean region offered a new world to discover. Since Gisbert undertook the study of the colonial period of the Andes, she has never left it.

As a researcher, she spends at least three hours a day writing, and her normal pace is from four to five hours a day, with a tendency to increase now that she has retired from her other activities. It was not until after about twenty years of research and data collecting in Peru and Bolivia that Gisbert and Mesa began their first theorizing about mestizo architecture, indigenous influence, and vision of the "other."

Gisbert thinks that a woman needs to acquire two major qualities to succeed: a high educational background and support from the household. She is socially conscious of the problems presented to women in a sexist society, and she is very concerned about the lack of improvement in the standards of living and the situation of women, especially in the lower stratums of society and in the rural areas, where the rate of illiteracy is alarmingly high (personal interview, December 1998).

Gisbert has managed to overcome the challenge of being a woman studying in the 1940s and 1950s, and moreover, she has succeeded in establishing herself as a cultural icon and as one of the most important researchers in history and architecture. Gisbert is one of the very few women in Bolivia who has achieved such a high level of recognition as a result of her professional contributions. Most women famous in Bolivia have begun their careers in the political arena.

Further Reading

Gisbert, Teresa. *Iconografía y mitos indígenas en el arte*, 9–10. La Paz: Don Bosco, 1980.

Mesa, José de, and Teresa Gisbert. *Historia de la pintura cuzqueña*, edited by the Fundación Augusto Wiese and Gillermo Lohman Villena, 10–15. Lima: Fundación Augusto Wiese, 1982.

Fabiola Fernández Salek

MARGO GLANTZ
(January 28, 1930–   )
Mexico: Author, Critic

Margo Glantz is a tireless author and literary critic who has earned recognition in her native Mexico as well as abroad. She was born in Mexico City, the daughter of Jewish immigrants who arrived at the port of Veracruz in 1925 from Russia. She grew up in the environment of the Ashkenazi community in Mexico City, of which she writes extensively in her book *Las genealogías* (The Family Tree, 1981).

Glantz received a master's degree in literature from the National Autonomous University of Mexico (UNAM), where she also studied art history and theater. She later earned a doctorate in literature from the University of Paris. As a professor, she has held a teaching position at the UNAM and has likewise been a visiting professor at a number of universities in the United States, including Yale. In 1982–1983 she was the director of publications for the Secretaría de Educación Pública (Ministry of Public Education) and from 1983 to 1986 Glantz was the director of literature at the Instituto Nacional de Bellas Artes (National Institute of Fine Arts). She founded the journal *Punto de partida* (Starting Point) and serves on the editorial board of several other well-known periodical publications. In addition to these high-profile positions within Mexico, Glantz served as the cultural attaché to the Mexican embassy in London from 1983 to 1986.

As a literary critic, Glantz is recognized for her work in the area of colonial Latin American literature, an area in which she has conducted extensive research. Her research focuses on such authors as Sor Juana Inés de la Cruz (1648–1695), the famous seventeenth-century nun who is much acclaimed as the first feminist of the Americas, as well as on Bernal Díaz del Castillo (1492–1580?) and Alvar Núñez Cabeza de Vaca (1490?–1564?).

As an author, Glantz has penned a variety of innovative and highly imaginative works. She won the Magda Donato prize in 1982 for *Las genealogías* and the prestigious Javier Villaurrutia prize for *Síndrome de naufragios* (Syndrome of Shipwrecks, 1984). Her works often contain a good deal of humor, which she tends to use as a weapon to confront established norms and criticize the patriarchal institutions of Mexico. Among works of this type are *Las mil y una calorías (una novela dietética)* (One Thousand and One Calories [a Dietetic Novel], 1978), *Doscientas ballenas azules* (Two Hundred Blue Whales, 1979), and *Síndrome de naufragios*. Also worthy of mention are her ingenious essays collected in *De la amorosa inclinación a enredarse en cabellos* (On the Loving Inclination to Tangle with Tresses, 1984) and *La lengua en la mano* (Tongue in Hand, 1983). *De la amorosa* showcases the author's talent of combining myth, popular culture, literature, and religious tradition into an informative and entertaining amalgam of critical cultural inquiry. *La lengua*, a collection of essays on literature from Latin America and Europe, focuses on representations of the female body. The title of the book is a tongue-in-cheek play on words that infers the different meanings of tongue: as object, as language/speech, and as interpreter. With insightful observations, Glantz ties the essays in the volume to the unique history of Mexico, specifically the figures of Jerónimo de Aguilar, a Spaniard who lived among the Maya on the island of Cozumel, and Doña Marina or La Malinche (the woman the Spanish explorer Hernán Cortés used as a *lengua*, or interpreters, in his conquest of the Aztecs. *La lengua en la mano* takes its title from the double meaning of "tongue" as the organ of speech and eating as well as language.

Glantz's literary and interpretive writings comprise topics, influences, and sources that cover such diverse areas as ancient mythology; the Bible; popular culture; literatures of France, the United States, and Latin America; theater and film; and a recurring preoccupation with the human body, the erotic, and the natural world. Perhaps the most overriding and apparent influence of Glantz's cultural formation is that of the role of literature—more specifically the power of the written word—as being a constant and active participant in all her endeavors. In this regard, it is fairly easy to see that she is very much the product of her environment, having come of age within the cosmopolitan environment afforded by her Russian-speaking, intellectual, Jewish parents and their friends within the hegemonic confines of Hispano-Catholic Mexican society. Glantz's life and works have been very much about crossing borders and .

Margo Glantz. Photo by Alina López Cámara y
Glantz. Courtesy of Alina López Cámara y
Glantz.

transgressing boundaries, as she herself has made clear on several different occasions.

Glantz has also shown a profound concern for uncovering origins, and she does so in a most intimate way in her 1981 autobiographical pseudo-novel *Las genealogías*. The text, narrated as a search for family history, is built around a series of anecdotes and information gleaned from taped interviews with her parents. From the beginning, the reader is given a glimpse of the author's hybrid cultural identity and is invited to accompany Glantz on her sojourn through the family tree. After listing a variety of objects that can be found in her home (a shofar, a menorah, popular Catholic saints, pre-Hispanic idols, and even a Christmas tree), she states, "My brother-in-law says I don't seem Jewish, because Jews, like our first cousins the Arabs, hate images. So everything is mine and yet it isn't, and I look Jewish and I don't and that is why I am writing this—my family history, the story of my own family tree" (Glantz 1991, 4). This brief anecdote sets the tone for the rest of the text and makes it clear that not only her identity but the mere concept of identity is not a simple one.

Glantz's father, a Yiddish poet, was well-known in Mexico, and he was a central figure in the intellectual milieu of the Ashkenazic community in Mexico City, as well as the larger non-Jewish artistic community. In fact, the book often reads as a sort of "who's who" of Mexican culture. Her text is replete with stories of her father's literary meetings, his contemporaries, his activities, and how her environment shaped her as a child. She also speaks of her mother's strong influence and her intelligence and capacity for business (she was the owner and operator of a bakery/café that became a gathering place). The book narrates the family history in multiple voices, and the narration is interspersed with facsimiles of letters, documents, and, most significantly, photographs. The pictorial narration is secondary to the written, but not less important. With the inclusion of the photographs, Glantz adds another dimension to her text, one that lends an image of authenticity to her story. As the reader experiences the story as told by the narrator(s), that story is brought to life by the accompanying photos of marriages, anniversaries, and other special occasions as well as portraits of her family members. Perhaps two of the most significant photos are the portraits of her father: one a profile of the Jewish intellectual, poet, and father and the other a view of Jacobo Glantz in traditional Mexican garb (wide-brimmed sombrero and serape) with a caption that reads, "Father Mexicanised." These photos are indicative of Glantz's narrative project: to meld the two distinct aspects of her identity into one. This project is undertaken by the majority of Jewish writers in Mexico (most of whom are women), but *Las genealogías* is by far the work that has received the most critical attention. It is an excellent example of feminine autobiography, as a hybrid text, and as an extraordinary contribution to the growing body of Latin American Jewish literature.

Glantz has been able to overcome the inherent machismo of Mexican society in many ways to become one of the leading cultural and literary figures of the country. She has forged a space not only for Mexican women, but also for Jewish culture. As she has constructed her own identity from the many diverse facets of her life, she has also helped to construct a model for a viable Mexican-Jewish identity.

Further Reading

García Pinto, Magdalena. "Margo Glantz." In *Women Writers of Latin America: Intimate Histories*, translated by Trudy Blach and Magdalena García Pinto, 105–22. Austin: University of Texas Press, 1991.

Glantz, Margo. *Las genealogías*. Mexico, D.F.: Martin Casillas Editores, 1981.

———. *The Family Tree: An Illustrated Novel*, translated by Susan Bassnet. London: Serpent's Tail, 1991.

Glickman, Nora. "Margo Glantz." In *Tradition and Innovation. Reflections on Latin American Jewish Writing*, edited by Robert DiAntonio and Nora Glickman, 18–20. Albany: State University of New York Press, 1993.

Jörgensen, Beth E. "Margo Glantz, Tongue in Hand." In *Reinterpreting the Spanish American Essay: Women Writers of the 19th and 20th Centuries*, edited by Doris Meyer, 188–96. Austin: University of Texas Press, 1995.

Oropesa, Salvador. "Glantz, Margo." In *Jewish Writers of Latin America: A Dictionary*, edited by Darrell B. Lockhart, 213–17. New York: Garland, 1997.

Darrell B. Lockhart

CHIQUINHA GONZAGA (BIRTHNAME: FRANCISCA EDWIGES NEVES GONZAGA)

(October 17, 1847–February 28, 1935)

Brazil: Composer, Musician

Born in Rio de Janeiro, Chiquinha Gonzaga was a pioneer in both her professional and social lives as the first female composer, conductor, performer, music teacher, and writer in Brazil to utilize her own work to ensure her personal survival. She was involved in many important changes that swept through Brazilian society at the turn of the century. She had to struggle in order to assert herself as an accomplished musician within a male-dominated environment; in the same way, she worked for the end of slavery and the opening of a republican society. She questioned social rules and traditional female roles throughout her life and established and lived under an order she forged for herself.

Gonzaga's mother, Rosa María de Lima, was a mestiza (of mixed European and indigenous blood) who had Francisca, her first child, while still single. Her father, Lieutenant José Basileu Neves Gonzaga, recognized Francisca Gonzaga's paternity eight months later and formed a family with Lima. His action was highly unusual for that time. His family did not approve of the marriage because of Lima's social position, the circumstances of the marriage, and racial prejudice. Nevertheless, Francisca Gonzaga had a family, siblings, and access to an adequate education. A priest instructed her in writing, reading, mathematics, and religion and provided her with an introduction to foreign languages. A conductor, Lobo, and an uncle, Antonio Eliseu, were responsible for her musical formation.

Gonzaga was married at the age of sixteen to Jacinto Ribeiro do Amaral, a businessman chosen by her family, with whom she had three children. Problems in their marriage, including her husband's forbidding her to play the piano and guitar, led Gonzaga to leave him. The ensuing scandal was crucial for her career and future attitudes. In line with prevailing societal attitudes, her parents disapproved of her behavior and did not allow her to return home. To support herself, she began to play the piano professionally in ensembles and created a family of other musicians. She met an engineer, João Batista de Carvalho Júnior, with whom

Chiquinha Gonzaga, circa 1865. Photo by
Modesto   Photographo.   Courtesy   of
Edinha Diniz.

she lived. Their union produced a daughter but, in approximately 1875,
Gonzaga left both of them. Again, she was met with a social condem-
nation that worsened her already tarnished reputation.

At the same time she faced social sanctions for her dismissal of traditional female roles, she achieved professional success. She played at
pastry shops and cabarets and composed a hit in 1877, the polka
"Atraente" (Attractive). Taking advantage of the flourishing popularity
of musical theater, she began to write songs and even lyrics for musical
plays, a principal source of her growing importance in popular music.
While living in a poor neighborhood, she observed the popularity of
street festivals and celebrations. This inspired her to compose the first
written carnival march, "Ó abre alas" (Make Way, composed between
1897 and 1899), which is still popular today. During this period, she
worked not only in Brazil but also in Portugal, and there are records of
her visits to that country in 1902 and 1904, with a longer stay from 1906
to 1909. Meanwhile, she met a Portuguese musician, João Batista Fernandes Lage, thirty-six years her junior, and took him as her lover. Chiquinha Gonzaga, now a mature woman, foresaw another scandal in the
making. Thus, in 1902, she introduced João Batista as her son and, with
this pretense, they lived together until her death in 1935.

Her philosophy toward life and her desire to break down social barriers and flout conventions fuel the lyrics of her still popular carnival march, "Ó abre alas": "Make way / I want to pass through / Rosa de Ouro [a carnival group] is going to win / Throw open your wings / I want to pass through / I am a bohemian / that I cannot deny."

This composition, set against the background of carnival, can be considered a statement of self-affirmation and independence. The emphasis on the first-person pronoun, placed in a carnival march, produces a dialectical meaning. The self-affirmation of Gonzaga, as a composer, is underscored by the first-person pronoun as both singular and female. However, its performance assumes a collective character because it is sung by a large group of people who are having fun in the carnival crowd. When her music was played and sung during carnival by the population, which was part of a thoroughly male-oriented society at that time, a new order is invoked as Gonzaga and other Brazilian women abandon their passivity to take an active new role. This is made clear when she asserts her undeniable bohemian behavior, a behavior restricted to men at that time. There is also a sense of profanity and mockery because she employs the march, originally a "serious" musical form used in solemn situations such as military parades and funeral processions, in a carnival context. Therefore, a conventionally rigid and ordered form is used in a context of extreme flexibility and disorder. Furthermore, Gonzaga indirectly criticizes society, the military life, and her family, especially on her father's side—all of them bound by strict rules that, in turn, they tried to impose on her.

Ultimately, "Ó abre alas" has as its main characteristic the striking display of paradox in order to challenge it. The dualities of male and female, individual and collective, passive and active, rigid and flexible are all being challenged, as well as seriousness and joy and discipline and insubordination. "Ó abre alas" questions the rules of society and gender. It transforms the social axis from male to female. Through the pairing of rhyming verbs, Gonzaga turned negation into victory and denied the status quo in favor of a new kind of consciousness, the realization of female freedom.

Gonzaga, however, was not just concerned with gender. Other important contributions to Brazilian popular music were songs Gonzaga composed for the *burleta Forrobodó* (1912) by Luiz Peixoto and Carlos Bettencourt. This play, a huge success, was performed more than 1,500 times in Brazil. The *burleta* is a particular musical theater genre adapted to Brazilian taste. It comes from operetta and has its roots in the Italian opera buffa or comic opera. *Forrobodó* was the name of a suburban nightclub attended mainly by Afro-Brazilians and lower-income people. The performance shows the audience the types of people found in Brazil: the *mulata* (dark-skinned woman), the *mulato* (dark-skinned man), the *malandro* (the idler), the Portuguese immigrant, and the French prostitute. The variety of characters mirrored the spectrum of Brazilian people, the mixture of races and colors, which the audience enthusiastically accepted. It is considered the first time that daily life and the common idiom were performed on a Brazilian stage. Gonzaga composed songs that, if analyzed in their function, demonstrate the specificities of this Brazilian musical theater genre. *Forrobodó* has danceable musical numbers that express the peculiarities or stereotypes of its characters, such as the sensuality of the *mulata* or the social maneuverability of the *malandro*, through a wide use of syncopations and rhythmic variations that, in conjunction with the lyrics, allow for a better portrayal and profile of the character.

Gonzaga also employed an ample variety of rhythmic styles, well known and popular in Brazil at that time, such as the waltz, polka, *modinha* (a type of ballad), carnival march, *quadrilha* (quadrille), and *desafio* (challenge). This mixture of foreign rhythms with ones nationalized or created in Brazil is very common in Brazilian popular music and has always played a fundamental role in Brazilian musicianship. Gonzaga was sensitive to this inherent eclecticism, and this was her main musical characteristic—a whole and unbiased approach to Brazilian music that celebrated its diversity.

In 1914 Gonzaga's instrumental composition written in 1895 and called "O corta-jaca" (a type of dance step) or "Gaúcho" (cowboy) with a *maxixe* rhythm (a precursor of the samba) was performed on the guitar at an official party held at the government palace. This was a double scandal in Brazilian society because the type of the music played was associated with lower-class society; moreover, the instrument used, the guitar, was related to bohemians and drunkards. Furthermore, it was a markedly popular song written by a woman of questionable reputation. However, this tune became so famous that Darius Milhaud quoted it in his experimental polytonal medley *Le Boeuf sur le toit* (The Ox on the Rooftop, 1919–1920). Obviously, there was recognition of Brazilian popular music and Gonzaga's work.

Gonzaga's innovations went beyond music to policy and the legal rights of writers. For example, in 1917, she founded the first association for theatrical authors' copyrights (SBAT) to protect people who write plays and music for the theater. She was attacking a system of exploitation of the authors by publishers, a system of which Gonzaga was one of many victims. This association is still active, and its headquarters, in Rio de Janeiro, maintains Gonzaga's archive with all the material that she produced. Unfortunately, most manuscripts have not been well preserved.

Gonzaga's last work was composed in 1933, for the operetta *Maria*, when she was eighty-five years old. The playscript was by Viriato Corrêa, an accomplished Brazilian author of romance who was not very familiar with theatrical writing. Throughout the play Gonzaga made corrections and adjustments to Corrêa's lyrics, often recycling her old material.

Gonzaga's works include waltzes, mazurkas, polkas, *habaneras*, Brazilian tangos, *modinhas*, *choros* (literally, laments), *maxixes*, carnival marches, and many other popular genres as well as religious pieces. She wrote for piano, band, vocal, orchestra, and chamber ensembles. Through her work, she engaged in social and political arenas, selling her manuscripts to raise money to free a slave musician or participating in meetings to change the political regime. In every case, she demonstrated a unique personal and determined reaction to the problems posed to her, constantly risking misunderstanding and scandal, but also creating opportunities for her sometimes revolutionary ideas. Her work contributed substantially to her vision and critique of society. Her actions and way of life made opinions concrete, which, in turn, opened up new horizons for Brazilian women.

Further Reading

Cohen, Aaron I. "Chiquinha Gonzaga." In *International Encyclopedia of Women Composers*, 2d ed. New York: Books & Music, 1987.
Fernandes, Adriana. "Chiquinha Gonzaga." In *The Feminist Encyclopedia of Latin American Literature*. Westport, Conn.: Greenwood Press, forthcoming.
Magaldi, Cristina. "Chiquinha Gonzaga." In *The Norton/Grove Dictionary of Women Composers*, edited by Julie Anne Sadie and Rhian Samuel. New York: W. W. Norton, 1995.

Adriana Fernandes

BEATRIZ GONZÁLEZ
(November 16, 1938–   )

Colombia: Artist

Beatriz González is a painter whose work constitutes a social critique of daily life in her native Colombia and a testimony of the way Latin American artists see their art and their being on the periphery of the art world. Her work always has an iconoclastic touch in it, and it is often misinterpreted as anecdotal, of interest only on a local level. It has often been described as a late pop, and she as a kitschy artist. Ironic, irreverent, and controversial, her paintings can be seen as about taste, or at least the lack of it. Her work is a continuous process of reconciling opposites: the particular with the universal, high with popular art, and European classics with a provincial style. Being on the periphery is very familiar to the artist. Born in 1938 in the provincial capital of Bucaramanga, she nonetheless became quickly acquainted with the inner circles of art while studying at the University of the Andes in Bogotá. It is here, after graduating, that she began to leave her mark and stand out among her contemporaries.

Influenced by the works of the abstract expressionists, she began a series of abstractions in the style of seventeenth century Dutch painter Jan Vermeer. These paintings, *Las encajeras* (The Lacemakers) of the early 1960s, form a body of work that has clearly marked differences with American abstraction, with which she was quickly paired. Her work does not center on the subconscious but is a series of references to local culture and the myths and geography of her country rather than a universal (European) source of inspiration. This is González's way of rebelling against the dictates from Paris and New York that had been blindly followed up to then by Latin American artists. By obsessively working and reworking the same theme over a period of two years, *Las encajeras* were transformed into an image often seen in Colombian popular culture: the ever popular and cheaply printed card with the image of saints, sports people, and other popular imagery that is so popular among Colombian peasants. In turn, kitsch makes her work subversive, through what she calls "the happiness of underdevelopment" (Ponce de León 1988, 15). In 1965 she started a new stage of her work with *Los suicidas de Sisga I* (The Sisga Suicides I), for which she obtained a first prize in the XVII Annual Salon of National artists. Incorporating a yellow-press photograph of a couple who had a suicide pact, she constructed a work that comments on a society marked by sentimentalism and the lack of cultural sophistication. From then on, she constantly used newspaper clippings as a graphic source, which provided her with two advantages: she had ready access to flat images that easily adapted to her style, and she had at her disposal a constant stream of images of the daily life of Colombian society.

When newspaper clippings and popular image cards had become a permanent graphic source for her work, she manipulated and reinterpreted all sorts of popular (and some sacred) imagery. Her work emphasized the changes that images suffer in the process of being mass-produced with the rudimentary printing methods so commonplace in the South American market of the 1960s (Traba 1977, 66). Popular image cards are a good source of graphic material, but newspaper clippings are even better for González, for they are full of images related to the beliefs and even superstitions of Colombians. In Colombia the newspapers are intrinsically aligned with a particular political point of view, whether it be the right of the Conservative party or the center of the Liberal party. Newspapers are just another front for attack and indoctrination by political rulers, and as such they hold great power over all structures of Colombian society. This is the source that González used so extensively during the late 1960s in an attempt to subvert and ridicule the message sent by the big press interests. Thus, in this way, newspaper clippings of beauty queens and political leaders are mixed up with holy cards and photos of victims of crimes of passion in a series entitled Historia Extensa de Colombia (Extended history of Colombia).

At the same time that González was completing her Extended History, she expanded her repertoire beyond Colombian borders. She once again appropriated images from the great masters of European art or the great actors of Western life. Images of John F. Kennedy, the paintings of Edward Manet and Sandro Botticelli, photos of Pope John Paul or Carlos Gardel, and Da Vinci's *Last Supper* all became part of her imagery, but with a twist very typical of her. All have been transformed into kitschy objects more closely related to a humble Colombian reality than to the glamorous world of the glossy magazines. Beginning in 1967, following intuition and chance, she began painting 3-D objects. By painting images such as a fallen Christ on a coffee table or a Last Supper on a Metal Bed, she brought down so-called high art to the level of domestic life. At the same time, her furniture lost none of its functionality.

Her concern with daily life in Colombia has led her to create a series completely devoted to the political events in her country. The decade of the 1980s saw the nation under attack by drug cartels and the terrorist actions of guerrilla movements. As a response to these attacks, the extreme right in the country banded together to form their own paramilitary groups. These groups killed many left-wing leaders as well as any dissident voice within the traditional parties. These events recalled the period known as La Violencia (The Violence) of the 1940s and 1950s when an undeclared civil war left more than 200,000 dead. It is this state of violence and disarray that González represents in her work of the late 1980s and during the 1990s. The vast stream of photographs published by the mass media were her graphic source of material: forced disappearances, kidnappings, car bombings, assassinations, murder of political figures, and the daily presence of the violence that has left a deep mark on Colombia. One of the events that she portrayed during this period was an action of the military that left more than 150 people dead in a single night. After the leftist guerrilla group M-19 seized and held hostage the nation's Supreme Court in November 1985, the top commanders of the nation's military forces ordered an attack that left the building engulfed in a fire that lasted all night. It is still not known for sure how many disappeared. González's response was to create two versions of the same pastel drawing: "Mr. President, What an Honor To Be with You at This Historical Moment" (1986). In both versions, President Belisario Betancur and his cabinet are seated around a table. In the first version, there is a vase of flowers at the center of the table; in the second version, the flowers have been replaced by a charred figure that symbolizes the burning and disappearance of some of the bodies of the guerrillas and their hostages. The flat use of pigment and the almost childlike quality of the drawing used by the artist leaves the viewer with an uncertain feeling, as absurd and surreal as the political climate of the country at that moment. This treatment is repeated over and over again in the many paintings in which she depicts the violence so commonplace in the country from then on: the massacres from both sides represented in *Apocalipsis camuflado* (Camouflaged Apocalypse, 1989), *Tapen, tapen* (Cover, Cover, 1994), or the series called *Madres de Las Delicias* (Mothers of Las Delicias, 1996).

The latest series is based on press photographs of the mothers of sixty soldiers kidnapped by the guerrillas and used as pawns by both the government and the insurrectionists. With this series, she became even more personally involved and set out to represent the drama of the individual rather than that of society.

Underdevelopment and bad taste are the two elements that help one to understand her work more clearly. Instead of centering on her condition as a Colombian or a provincial, conditions that refer only to a fixed time and social environment, one must look beyond that. And the only way to understand her work is by focusing on the visual rather than on the thematic in the new means of representation that González has developed. By looking beyond any immediate reference that will soon be outdated, one will find a whole new philosophy of art and a body of work that will last past its own chronological references.

González has represented Colombia in different art biennials. Her work has traveled extensively around the world. It has been featured by the Museo del Barrio (Barrio Museum) in New York City in 1988 and 1997, and in the National Museum of Women in the Arts, Washington, D.C., in 1996. González has been working as curator of the art and history collections at the Museo Nacional de Bogotá (National Museum of Bogotá) since 1993.

Further Reading

Ardila, Jaime, and Beatriz González. *Apuntes para la historia extensa*. Bogotá, Colombia: Editorial Tercer Mundo, 1974– .

Cobo Borda, Juan Gustavo, et al. *Reportajes a Beatriz González*. Bogotá, Colombia: Impresores Colombianos, 1981.

Ponce de León, Carolina. "Beatriz González in situ." In *Beatriz González: Una pintora de provincia*, edited by Marta Calderón et al., 12–29. Bogotá, Colombia: Carlos Valencia Editores, 1988.

Traba, Marta. *Los muebles de Beatriz González*. Bogotá, Colombia: Museo de Arte Moderno de Bogotá, 1977.

Rubén D. Durán

ASTRID HADAD

(?, 1958–)

Mexico: Performance Artist, Singer

Astrid Hadad, a contemporary Mexican, lesbian performance artist and singer, has, within the past decade, negotiated a very particular space inside the homophobic arena of Mexican culture. Hadad, who has Lebanese ancestors, was born in Chetumal, Quintana Roo (in the deep south of Mexico). She studied theater in Mexico City at the University Theater Center, and after a short career as an actress she decided to dedicate her life to singing *rancheras* and boleros, both popular Mexican musical genres. She has worked, almost since the beginning of her career, with a group of musicians called Los Tarzanes (the Tarzans).

Hadad began her cabaret shows in a cantina in downtown Mexico City, El Bar Cristal (the Crystal Bar), a bar-cabaret from the 1930s. Even in these first productions, it was possible to see one of her most significant characteristics: involving the public with her presentation, sometimes challenging or disturbing the spectator to provoke consciousness regarding some cultural problem. From the very beginning, Hadad established a rapport with the audience. The audience quickly grasps the rules of the game. Mexico's rich cultural history allows performance art- · ists to restore to life the dynamic of cabaret.

Two elements should be mentioned before Hadad's performance art is analyzed. The first is that marginality has found a way of expressing itself in the history of Mexico. In the chronicles of popular life in the nineteenth and twentieth centuries there is always a carnivalesque spirit. The city routinely holds big festivities in the neighborhoods, family parties, uncountable cabarets, innumerable cantinas, and splendid theaters. The theater of the musical review, tent theater, and later films have brought together Mexicans from different social classes. The modern imaginary of the city started at that moment, specifically with *la carpa* (the tent). The imaginary—halfway between a mental image, a concept, and a psychological reality—is the relation that holds together the different elements that collectively constitute the identity of the city's people. *La carpa* allowed theatrical space for the marginalized: leprous, hairless *nacos* (rustics, especially of indigenous extraction); all of them legendary characters that produced figures such as Cantinflas, Tin Tan, Pedro Infante, and Ninon Sevilla. It is not by chance that performance artists like Jesusa Rodríguez and Astrid Hadad have tried to recapture this historical moment. *La carpa* consists basically of a scenic space in which the circus and the *teatro frívolo* (literally, frivolous theater) are mixed; it is the theater of the marginal review of the 1920s and 1930s in Mexico City. In *la carpa*, unlike in the *teatro de revista* (Musical theater), chance, the obscene, eschatology, and cursing are used generously. Often attacked by the censors, *la carpa* is a school of double meanings. Despite the distance from its origin to the revista, there is always a certain imitation in *la carpa*: sopranos dressed in *china poblana* (literally, little Chinese girl from Puebla; the reference is to a Chinese woman from the 1800s who in dressing mixed traditions of China and Puebla; now her "look" is the typical Puebla outfit), tap dancers, comedians, and choruses of women in scanty clothing. In this kind of genre there is drama, comedy, and operetta. Ingenuity is found in the way in which the audience pretends to have never before heard the tired jokes being repeated by the performer and agrees to react sentimentally even to poorly performed tear-jerking lyrics about the misfortunes of cruel love. It is in these two ways that this type of performance exemplifies a decadent art, to the extent that it relies on the absence of originality and artistic perfection.

One can see how Astrid Hadad's performances are specifically related to the figure of the diva of the 1940s who performed in cabarets and musical reviews during the early period of the emergence of modern urban culture in Mexico City. Divas have an ambiguous symbolic status in the imaginary of Mexico City. The divas demanded sexual and professional autonomy. Since the divas created an "autonomous" sexual behavior, Hadad recovers this space as a queer space. Queer is understood here as a term that condenses her work as part of the struggle against the compulsory heterosexuality of Mexican culture. The divas were models for all classes because they broke with convention and found spaces for behaviors and ways of living previously inconceivable for women in Mexico. At the same time, since the divas' space did not challenge the life of the bourgeois family, which found a way to remain untouchable, the divas confirmed the patriarchal structure. What is important for Hadad is that the divas negotiated a new space for Mexican women. The divas created a space by simultaneously using frantic movement and the stillness of a statue-like body in a trance of hysteria and a facial expression that was the equivalent of adultery and the loss of reason (Monsiváis 1981, 24).

Hadad's spectacles, and specifically the lyrics of her songs, demand this trance of hysteria. A clear example of this is found in the beginning of her musical production ¡Ay! (the paradigmatic exclamation in Spanish), in which the singer appears to be drowning (in one photograph, she is shown with water up to her neck), while she screams.

Hadad's presence on the stage, her costumes, voice, and choreography,

Astrid Hadad. Photo by Pancho Gilardi. Courtesy of Astrid Hadad.

all add up to a lascivious style that points to a melodramatic imperson-
ation of the life of a diva, such as that of María Conesa or Celia Mon-
talván. Hadad combines the elements previously mentioned with a
bellicose contact with the audience. This new factor establishes a distance
from the middle-class image of the divas of the 1930s in Mexico. Hadad
wants to take a new, historical step for the figure of the diva. She wants
to change this autonomous space into a nonmasculine or antistraight
space. Hadad's performance reflects a desire to recover lesbian historical
figures, such as Chavela Vargas and Lucha Reyes, and also elements of
traditional Mexican culture. She seeks to resignify and to situate these
icons, myths, and real women within a new sociocultural history. In
Corazón sangrante (Bleeding Heart), a video performance, the "discourse
of power" is visually situated on a strong female body—a body whose
sensuality Hadad emphasizes and takes pleasure in, although in Mexico,
it is a body that all structures of society attempt to regulate.

By wearing a moustache or spurs, Hadad symbolically appropriates
the masculine power that dominates all official discourse in Mexico, be

it religious, social, or political, and thus visually represents the arbitrary and theatrical aspects of gender construction in her culture. By using hysteria as a masculine representation of women, Hadad redefines a visibility within different parameters. In *Corazón sangrante*, Hadad seems literally to be eating her heart. By using the graphical representation of the song's lyrics, she unmasks the ideological violence implied by the traditional romantic song. In this way, the hilarity is a strategy to awaken the consciousness and to produce complicity between Hadad and the spectator. This affinity enhances the solidarity among the various groups represented in the audience, as she becomes the iconic referent of the national symbols by interpreting, to the letter, the songs that Mexicans usually listen to with great pleasure.

In this way, Hadad moves toward disrupting the male gaze. She attempts to make the spectator aware of her or his position as a voyeur and as an accomplice in the systems being criticized. Yet, this controlled ambiguity presents an ideological problem. Her use of the visibility of the female body and the use of history as a strategy of consciousness can be seen as a reinscription of woman as an object for male pleasure. But Hadad demands her right to enjoy her body and her sexuality, and she offers them for enjoyment to others—men or women. She claims that women can enjoy other women, even if they are heterosexual.

Hadad's artistic body is more the body of a *copera* (the tough-as-nails cantina waitress who may also occasionally double as a prostitute) who challenges the public with her flesh, in contrast to the divas who, at the beginning of the 1930s, became very refined bourgeois artists. The *coperas* of the beginning of the century (1911–1913) come from the frivolous theater, before the genre of musical theater was established with its splendor and before it was socially accepted in the 1920s. In this theater, the audience was part of the show, confronting actresses and actors, changing the dialogue so that it was impossible to have two identical performances.

Hadad's dramatization of the female body proposes to deconstruct the sexual and gender categories established in Mexican culture. At the same time, she gives the spectator the sense that these categories need to be considered as representations of political and cultural circumstances. Hadad's body is strategically and artistically reconstructed. It would seem that the nature of artistic work is to widen language's social limits toward other human body shapes and social permissiveness. This strategy is a trick, an artifice of the representation of herself, of her fragmented identity, as are the hundreds of fragmented Hadads that drop from the sky dressed like *monjas coronadas* (garlanded nuns) in her video *Corazón sangrante*. What Hadad finally tells us with her performance is that her body, as everybody's, is a body with a history that started before she was born. Religious objects and practices inscribed her childhood.

Hadad understands herself as the consciousness of her histories and of her sexual and political dissidence. She thinks performance and game are synonymous. She plays with her histories in the same way history plays with us, which is analogous to how language functions. We are inserted into language; it has the possibility of being activated by what can be colloquially called motives. Therefore, although language is unmotivated, it is not capricious. In the same way we are inserted into a history, and without intent, we "make our own." We provide meaning within language, body, and history; we critique intentions within them; we play with them through signification as well as reference; and then we leave history, body, and language, as much without intent, for the use of others after our deaths. The history of Hadad's female body is the history of a queer body narrated through the hysteria of a Mexican woman, which is strategically visible through her performance.

Urban life, as a cultural structure, develops many ways of representation in a citizen's body. Every day the city itself becomes a gigantic spectator, and the citizens turn into actors of an unwritten play, performers of the urban collective imaginary. The cast, natives of the city as stage, daily creates and re-creates the imaginary. For these reasons, the city is not only a physical phenomenon, a way to occupy the space, but also a place where personal expressiveness occurs in tension with the social order. Hadad's cultural production is a way to explore a different, alternative gender construction vis-à-vis contemporary Mexican show business in the urban space. In the case of Hadad, this analysis is from the perspective of an artist who reflects upon her own culture and tries to re-create a body and a dissident sexuality by finding its roots in the underground queer Mexican tradition. She also manifests universal cultural influences in order to question the official construction of gender, politics, and history.

Further Reading

Costantino, Roselyn. "Through Their Eyes and Bodies: Mexican Women Performance Artists, Feminism, and Mexican Astrid Hadad." In *Latinas on Stage*, edited by Alicia Arrizón and Lillian Manzor-Coats. Berkeley, Calif.: Third Woman Press, forthcoming.

Debroise, Olivier, et al. *The Bleeding Heart/El corazón sangrante*. Boston: Institute of Contemporary Art, 1991.

Monsiváis, Carlos. *Escenas de pudor y liviandad*. México, D. F.: Gijalbo, 1981. 23–45.

———. "Los espacios marginales." *Debate femenino* 17 (1998): 20–38.

———. "Ortodoxia y heterodoxia en las alcobas." *Debate feminista* 6, no. 2 (1995): 183–210.

Orozco, José Clemente. *Autobiografía*. México, D. F.: Ediciones Era, 1970.

Gastón A. Alzate

ANGELA HERNÁNDEZ NUÑEZ
(May 6, 1954–)
Dominican Republic: Author, Poet

Angela Hernández Nuñez, who was born in Jarabacoa, Dominican Republic, stands out as one of the most prominent women authors of her country today. Even though she went on to graduate with honors in chemical engineering at the Autonomous University of Santo Domingo, she started writing as a teenager. Since 1989 Hernández has been a member of the Comité de Intelectuales de Apoyo of the Universidad Autónoma de Santo Domingo (Committee of Intellectuals in Support of the Autonomous University of Santo Domingo), a member of the Dominican Chapter of Criticism for Latin America, and the Director of Ce-Mujer, the Centro Nacional de Ayuda y Estudio de la Mujer (National Center for Assistance and Study of Woman). These positions show the extensive recognition Hernández has achieved for her literary production and feminist endeavors. Despite having four children, Hernández has traveled extensively on speaking engagements throughout the Caribbean, Central and South America, Europe, China, and the United States. At a local level, Hernández frequently collaborates in the organization of events such as La Mujer en la Canción y en la Poesía (Women Singers and Poets, 1982), Homage to Aída Cartagena Portalatín (1983), Conference on Women and Writing (1989), and the Centennial Celebration of Salomé Ureña's Death (1997). During the 1980s Hernández participated in the most productive groups of women poets in the Dominican Republic. In 1983 she was an active member of Círculo de Mujeres Poetas (Circle of Women Poets), an organization founded by Sherazada Chiqui Vicioso. In 1987 Hernández delivered the inaugural speech at the Grupo de Mujeres Creadoras (Group of Creative Women). Since then, Hernández has participated in every event organized by these two major groups. Along with Chiqui Vicioso, she is one of the most active and inspiring authors of the new generation of twelve poets whose writing charts a new female territory.

Her collections of essays, *Emergencia del silencio* (Emerging from Silence, 1985) and *De críticos y creadores* (Critics and Creators, 1988), show a keen insight for literary criticism and an energetic and promising feminist voice. Hernández has published several collections of poetry, in-

Angela Hernández Nuñez. Courtesy of
Fernando Acevedo.

cluding *Tizne y cristal* (Soot and Crystal, 1985), *Desafío* (Challenge, 1985),
Edades de asombro (Ages of Amazement, 1985), *Arca espejada* (Mirrored
Ark, 1994), and *Telar de rebeldía* (Loom of Defiance, 1998). Her short stories have been collected in the following books: *Alótropos* (Allotropies,
1989), *Masticar una rosa* (To Chew a Rose, 1993), and *Piedra de sacrificio*
(Sacrificial Stone, 1999), the winner of the 1998 Premio Nacional de Cuentos (National Short Story Prize). Hernández is equally well known as a
poet, a writer of ground-breaking short stories, and feminist essays. A
selective overview of her work demonstrates the diverse ways in which
she has interpreted the realities of Dominican women at the end of the
millennium.

In her essays, Hernández asserts that, at this particular juncture,
women should not hold on to conventions but rather cut themselves free
from their moorings. They are to view the panorama from the sea, feeling
the shiver of doubt and solitude but ready to be reborn, through memory
and enlightenment (Hernández 1991, xii). Hernández's becoming unmoored is a new locus of enunciation, a space in between, without roots,
a place where the feminine silenced subculture and certain elements of
the patriarchal imaginary can be negotiated. The conflictive politics of
sexual difference is to be rearticulated through memory. While their mar-

ginal position in literary history determines the predicament of Dominican women writers, Hernández's poems focus on this place in between that appears as a mutating map presented from a wandering point of view, from an "inter-space" resulting from having become unmoored. This unexpected positionality diffuses the borders of the map. This is a land written on clouds, transparencies, moving and shapeless spots, from a point of enunciation alien to conventional loci and paradigms.

In her poems, Hernández explores diverse itineraries to reach her own map, enunciated from her feminine body. In the attempt, she discovers an enriching and disturbing fact: "Soy extranjera en mis propias raíces" (I am a foreigner in my own roots), a line from her book *Arca espejada* (1994). The poetic voice of *Arca espejada* calls for a liberation through poetry. Hernández's text gives rise to a new poetics of women's writing. The interaction between verse fragmentation and the multifaceted complexity of metaphor results in poems akin to puzzles, in that they offer multiple solutions. Moreover, each poem is a multitextured work in which the surface of language does not remain static but shifts continually.

Hernández's intense short stories are carefully crafted. Her feminist approach, which embodies a dissident perspective on the literary status quo of her country, is a crucial dimension of both her poetry and her fiction. These stories explode the limits set by maps and the body, and the author undermines assumptions and rewrites the official history. In other words, she transforms the imaginary and rearticulates the politics of difference from these new loci of enunciation. Her poetry and her short stories are demanding, for the reader is to imagine an alternative hybrid culture. Hernández seeks a new place of enunciation where women can be subjects rather than fragments dispersed by an unavoidable historic wind (1991, xiii). Both Hernández and the women writers from the aforementioned literary circles stress the need to become identifiable subjects in the reconstruction of an identity, which is not limited to the personal, the national, or the Caribbean.

Finally, Hernández's work has raised the expectations of numerous critics both in her country and abroad. Some of her readers have praised her complex poetry, which develops the profound meaning of contemporary issues through an intricate labyrinth of fragments. In the aesthetic space created in her works, literature by and about women in the Dominican Republic comes into its own.

Hernández's work offers a new challenge. Her effective and coherent provocation is all the more powerful when one considers the impact of colonization, governmental repression in dictatorial regimes, and the patriarchal literary forces that have shaped and continue to shape the Dominican Republic.

Further Reading

Gimbernat González, Ester. "Poetas dominicanas de hoy: Coreografía de la imagen." *Letras femeninas* 22, nos. 1–2 (1996): 143–63.
Hernández, Angela. *Arca espejada*. Santo Domingo: Editora Búho, 1994.
———. *Libertad, creación e identidad*. Santo Domingo: Editora Universitaria, 1991.

Ester Gimbernat González

ROSARIO IBARRA DE PIEDRA
(February 24, 1927–   )
Mexico: Political Activist

Rosario Ibarra was a middle-class mother of four whose love for her son transformed her into a political activist and Mexico's premier defender of human rights and first woman candidate for president. She humbly claims that her only political qualification is her status as the mother of a missing son, but it was through her personal conviction and moral force that she became a symbol of change and hope in Mexico. Although she is a physically slight woman, her demeanor is commanding and intense.

Rosario Ibarra was born in Saltillo, in the northern state of Coahuila, Mexico. Her middle-class family had roots in social activism. Her maternal grandmother, Aída Villareal, fought for women's suffrage, and her agronomist father supported the 1910 revolution. When she was young, the family moved to Chihuahua and later settled in Monterrey. While attending the Monterrey Civil College, she met a teacher, Jesús Piedra Rosales, who would later become her husband. She completed her secondary education and considered going on to study law, but her marriage precluded this possibility. The couple had four children: Maria del Rosario, Jesús, Claudia, and Carlos. Her husband, a doctor by profession, was a member of the Mexican Communist party. Ibarra planned to live out her life comfortably in Monterrey, but these plans were irrevocably changed in 1975.

In the early 1970s, a number of armed revolutionary movements appeared in Mexico. Ibarra's son Jesús was a medical student who had almost finished his training when he joined an urban guerrilla group to fight for the dispossessed. He went underground in November 1974 and disappeared on April 18, 1975. After her son's abduction, presumably by

Rosario Ibarra de Piedra. Courtesy of Melissa M. Forbis.

the state, the family moved to Mexico City for what Ibarra thought would be a brief and successful search for Jesús. She still lives there.

It was this tragic event that led her to find other mothers with missing children and, ultimately, to the political awakening that would make her a tireless activist for human rights. She believes that it is shameful that she has been forced to fight against her own government because she has been unable to get justice. She looked for justice but found an arbitrary, terrible injustice. Her years of political activism have broken the silence, making this injustice a national and international issue.

In April 1977, Ibarra and the other mothers formed the Committee for the Defense of Political Prisoners, Exiles, Fugitives, and Disappeared Persons of Mexico. In June 1977, they held their first demonstration to demand the release of the missing and distributed a poster with five photographs, including Ibarra's son Jesús. The poster encouraged people to send in photos of their missing loved ones, and soon hundreds arrived. When the committee formed there were no other human rights organizations in Mexico. They defend all persons who have disappeared and political prisoners regardless of affiliation or ideology. The presence of the committee created a space for the creation of other human rights organizations in Mexico.

On August 28, 1978, eighty-three mothers from the group staged a hunger strike in the Metropolitan Cathedral in Mexico City to demand the return of the missing and to ask for a general amnesty for political prisoners and exiles. On September 1, 1978, President José López Portillo gave in to their demands and decreed a general law of amnesty. At the time, 481 people had disappeared. Although the government never officially admitted that it had illegally detained people, those who were released testified to the committee about the conditions in the military camps and clandestine prisons and about the status of the others they had seen. The committee later added the Greek word Eureka! (I have found it) in honor of the 148 persons "found" by the committee.

Ibarra participated in seven hunger strikes, from relatively short ones to the longest of twenty-six days. The hunger strikes were only one of the inventive tactics used by the committee to bring their issues to public attention. Upon his release, one man the committee had fought to liberate came to Ibarra with a message. He told her that the hope of those being held incommunicado would last as long as she and the rest of the committee continued their struggle. Ibarra promised him that she would not give up. She has kept that promise.

The work of the committee has taken Ibarra to many parts of Mexico, where she has spoken to people in factories, peasant cooperatives, and universities. She had journeyed to the United States, Canada, and Europe to talk about the struggle in Mexico. She first went to the United States in 1978 to denounce the disappearances of persons and repression in front of the United Nations. She has also traveled to other parts of Latin America to meet family members of the missing and representatives of human rights organizations. During this time, her efforts were met with skepticism by many of the same people who later would champion her cause. She was told that Mexico could never be seen in the same light as Chile and Argentina. She did not become bitter, but instead she forged ahead believing that whoever thinks there is a democracy in Mexico does not know the truth and that she must speak that truth.

Ibarra viewed this fight not just as an isolated problem, but as one that needed to be part of a national political struggle. To further this coalition, she formed the National Front Against Repression in 1979 with fifty-four organizations around Mexico. The pressure this larger group exerted on the government resulted in more liberations. The front, which included unions and peasant groups, existed thirteen years.

Ibarra has also participated in electoral politics at a national level. Recognizing her ongoing work for human rights, the Partido Revolucionario de Trabajo (Revolutionary Worker's Party, or PRT) asked Ibarra to be their candidate for the presidency in 1982. She was the first woman ever to appear on the ballot in Mexico. Although she knew she would not win, she spent six months traveling around the country using the opportunity to denounce the policies of the ruling Partido Revolucionario

Institucional (Institutional Revolutionary party, or PRI) and to bring more attention to the campaign for human rights in Mexico.

Though she belongs to no political party, she was elected federal deputy for the PRT in 1985. She believes that any citizen has the right to be heard, but she was pragmatic enough to see that as a deputy her words had more resonance, especially outside of Mexico. When people from other countries realized that this federal deputy was the same woman who had spoken to them about the repression in Mexico, she seemed more credible. She also became more of a target. She and her family have received more than forty death threats. Her elected post, however, offered a certain protection from the threat of violence.

Ibarra was nominated as a candidate for the Nobel Peace Prize in 1986, 1987, and 1989. She never believed that she would be chosen for the prize, but once again, her public recognition put pressure on the Mexican government, resulting in the release of more of the people who had disappeared.

She ran again for president on behalf of the PRT in 1988. Although Ibarra never received more than 2 percent of the vote, her belief that human rights are an integral part of democracy brought a greater awareness of these issues to a wider spectrum of society. In 1994 she was again elected federal deputy, this time for the Partido Revolucionario Democrático (Revolutionary Democratic party, or PRD). She currently works as an advisor on human rights to the mayor of Mexico City.

A recent but strong influence on Ibarra has been the Ejército Zapatista de Liberación Nacional (Zapatista National Liberation Army, or EZLN), which is fighting for indigenous autonomy in Chiapas. She was sad that her husband was not alive to see the birth of this movement, which she regards as a continuation of their son's struggle. The uprising in Chiapas on January 1, 1994, injected new life into Mexico's Left and the work of the committee. In honor of their efforts, mothers of the committee were invited to spend Mother's Day 1998 with the EZLN in La Realidad. During their visit, the primary school of that indigenous village was inaugurated and given the name of Ibarra's son Jesús.

In 1998 she was among 300 human rights defenders invited to a ceremony held in Paris to honor the fiftieth anniversary of the Universal Declaration of Human Rights. While there, she was asked by the EZLN to coordinate the *Consulta*, the Zapatista plebiscite, which was aimed at publicizing their demand for indigenous autonomy. She accepted and spent the next six months organizing and promoting the *Consulta*.

She is currently director of the Foundation Rosario Ibarra for Democracy, Justice, and Freedom, which was created to give juridical status to the committee's work and publish the magazine *Insumisa*. The foundation was established on August 28, 1998, the twentieth anniversary of the hunger strike held in the Mexico City cathedral.

Ibarra believes that saving even only one life was worth her twenty years of struggle even if that one person was not her own son. Like the mothers of the Plaza de Mayo in Argentina, the mothers of Eureka! have been called *locas*, crazies. Ibarra is dismissed by the government as an idealist who is out of touch with reality. But for Ibarra this insanity is the insanity of love and of hope. She refuses to renounce what others call crazy because it is intimately linked with the connections to, and convictions of, their children. She believes that as long as the children are not free, the mothers will remain in their place in the struggle. If those who have disappeared are found, then as mother and child they will struggle together.

Further Reading

De Palma, Anthony. "Mexico City Journal: Among the Ruins of the Left, a Pillar Stands." *New York Times*, October 5, 1994, A4.
Epstein, Nadine. "Mexico's First Woman for Prez." *Ms.*, March 1988, 68.
López, Robert J. "Activist Tells of Struggle in Mexico." *Los Angeles Times*, January 24, 1999, B3.
Poniatowska, Elena. *Fuerte es el silencio*. México, D.F.: Ediciones Era, 1982.
Riding, Alan. "Profile of Rosario Ibarra de Piedra." *New York Times*, July 27, 1978, 2.

Melissa M. Forbis

CAROLINA MARIA DE JESUS
(date unknown, 1914/1921?–1977)
Brazil: Author

Author Carolina Maria de Jesus was able to bring to a wide audience an eyewitness account of what the life of recently freed slaves in nineteenth-century Brazil was like, and, with her diaries, she can be counted among those few Brazilians who have given a daily testimony of the legacy of slavery well into the twentieth century. Her diaries, proverbs, and memoirs detail her life since childhood, the wisdom she developed through much suffering, and her acute political thinking. Her poems, recently collected under the title *Antologia Pessoal* (1996), reveal her knowledge of Brazilian folklore and popular rhythms.

Carolina Maria de Jesus was born in the town of Sacramento, in the

state of Minas Gerais, and she died on a small farm in the interior of the
state of São Paulo. In spite of the great success—and scandal—provoked
by her first book (*Quarto de despejo*, 1960, translated as *Child of the Dark*
in 1963) and in spite of the three other books she published during her
lifetime (*Casa de Alvenaria*, 1961, translated as *I'm Going to Have a Little
House*, 1997; *Provérbios*, 1963; and *Pedaços da fome* [Piece of Hunger], 1963),
she died as poor as she always had lived.

Her first book, *Quarto de despejo*, consists of excerpts of the diaries she
wrote between July 15, 1955, and January 1, 1960. At the time, she
worked collecting paper and scrap metal in the streets. She had three
children (each with a different father) and lived in the São Paulo slum
called Canindé. Throughout the diary, she comments on the political
events of the day, the situation of her fellow slum dwellers, and repeated
instances of racism and discrimination against her and others who were
as poor and as black as she.

It is surprising that a woman who attended only two years of school,
who was a single black mother, and who lived in a slum could have
ever written such a diary. A combination of chance and perseverance
was responsible for its publication. As she says in the diary, she collected
the notebooks she wrote in from the garbage, sometimes sewing together
loose sheets to make a notebook. One day, when some adults were about
to break the swings in a recently opened playground for the children of
the slum, de Jesus told them to let the children play and threatened to
put their names in "her book." A reporter for a local newspaper, Audálio
Dantas, overheard her and asked to see her book. After some time, he
gained her confidence and she showed him what she had written: stories,
poems, and the diary. After reading some of the material, Dantas dis-
carded the stories and poems as childish but began to publish excerpts
of the diaries in the newspaper. At the same time, he secured a publication in the form of a book.

The book, *Quarto de despejo*, brought de Jesus immediate fame, some
money, the possibility of finally moving to the brick house she always
had dreamed of. The book also gained her the enmity of the other slum
dwellers, who threw stones at the truck that was taking away her belongings from the shack where she had lived in Canindé. When she
settled in a clean neighborhood, she found out that there too she could
not be happy. The neighbors avoided her, and her children were out-
casts. She bought some land near the city of São Paulo and went to live
there with her three children.

Unfortunately, neither the crops nor the little roadside grocery store
she opened proved successful. Sources disagree about whether she returned to the streets to collect paper and scrap metal. What seems clear,
however, is that she became profoundly disenchanted with Brazilian
journalists and politicians and decided to have nothing else to do with

them. It is not surprising, therefore, that she gave the manuscript of *Diário de Bitita*, a memoir of her childhood, to some French journalists who came to interview her on the farm. The book was first published in France, and only years later did it appear in Brazil. It has recently been translated in the United States as *Bitita's Diary* (1998).

The importance of this memoir cannot be emphasized enough. Even though it does not have the immediacy of either *Quarto de despejo* or *Casa de alvenaria*, *Diário de Bitita* can be seen as de Jesus's legacy to the history of the struggle of Brazilian blacks. In this book, de Jesus relates not only her own personal struggle to overcome extreme poverty, discrimination, and persecution, but also the suffering of those who, like her own maternal grandfather, lived through the inequities and injustices visited upon the newly freed slaves and the blacks who were trying to find their space in the Brazilian order of the early twentieth century.

Her grandfather was the protector of the whole family and a man who commanded respect for his wisdom and kindness, even though he was illiterate. Her mother, Cota, born after the signing of the *ventre livre* (free womb law), signed in 1871, declaring that all children of slaves born from that date on would be free, was also illiterate. De Jesus was the product of an affair with a man from another town, referred to as "a poet." Because she demonstrated great intelligence since her earliest years, her mother accepted the suggestion of a local teacher and enrolled the girl in elementary school. Although de Jesus at first did not want to attend school because the other children taunted her, she learned to read and write and developed a great love for school and for reading. Her school years were short lived: after two years, her mother and stepfather moved the family to a farm that belonged to Wanderley de Andrade. The owner allowed them to plant subsistence crops while they worked for him.

On this farm, Carolina discovered her love for planting and watching things grow, which undoubtedly influenced her later decision to buy a little farm for herself. It was also during this period that she was first cheated by an employer, the wife of the owner of the farm, who refused to pay her any salary after she had worked as a maid for six months. This same woman, according to de Jesus, raised three little orphaned black girls who would later take on the housework, perpetuating the slave work blacks had allegedly been freed from in 1888. After some time, the farmer expelled the family, saying that they did not work. They returned to Sacramento, poorer than they had left.

From this point on, de Jesus's life became a succession of horrors. Once, when she developed sores on her legs, she decided to go to another city in search of treatment. She looked for an aunt, but the woman, who was white, refused to help her or even to give her any food. After days wandering through the streets, she found shelter with the nuns of a hospital. Since she could not stay there indefinitely, she looked for a job as a maid. Finally, when the sores on her legs healed, she returned to Sacramento, to be closer to her mother.

Her mother could not help her either or even protect her from the tyrants of the town, who once threw both of them in a cell because de Jesus had criticized the mayor. Mother and daughter were in prison for five days during which time they were whipped, forced to clean the grass in front of the prison, and not given any food.

This time of her life influenced de Jesus's later writings in profound ways. She learned literally through her own flesh the weight of racism and the danger of speaking up. From a child whose intelligence was praised, she became a young adult whose same intelligence turned into a dangerous shortcoming and a reason for harsh punishment.

Yet, it is the same sharp intelligence that she demonstrates both in *Child of the Dark* and *I'm Going to Have a Little House*. In both of these diaries, de Jesus does not spare politicians, priests, or her neighbors when she thinks that they are wrong or hypocritical. With her writings, always done in longhand, de Jesus gives the reader a clear idea of what it meant for her, as well as for other poor people like her, to live in a country where the much touted "racial democracy" was an empty formula or one more way to cover the great injustices done to those who could not defend themselves, like the poor black man executed by the police in Sacramento, and mulatto girls transformed into prostitutes and killed by syphilis before they turned eighteen.

Recently, professors José Carlos Sebe Bom Meihy and Robert M. Levine republished de Jesus's diary without editing it. This book, *Meu estranho diário* (My Strange Diary, 1996), still not available in English, contains her reflections about the nature of fame and about her relationship with the literati of her time (who mostly looked at her as an outcast). The same professors have started an internet home-page that deals exclusively with de Jesus's work to bring her legacy not just to Afro-Brazilians, but to the whole world.

Further Reading

Fox, Patricia D. "The Diary of Carolina Maria de Jesus: A Paradoxical Enunciation." *Proceedings of the Black Image in Latin American Culture Conference.* Slippery Rock, Pa.: Slippery Rock University, 1989. 241–51.

Jesus, Carolina Maria de. *Bitita's Diary. The Childhood of Carolina Maria de Jesus,* translated by Emmanuelle Oliveira and Beth Joan Vinkler. Armonk, N.Y.: Sharpe, 1998.

———. *Child of the Dark,* translated by David St. Clair. New York: Penguin Books, 1963.

————. *I'm Going to Have a Little House: The Second Diary of Carolina Maria de Jesus*, translated by Melvin Arrigton, Jr., and Robert Levine. Lincoln: University of Nebraska Press, 1997.

Meihy, José Carlos Bom, and Robert M. Levine. *The Life and Death of Carolina Maria de Jesus*. Albuquerque: University of New Mexico Press, 1995.

Eva Paulino Bueno

CLEMENTINA DE JESUS
(?, 1901/1902?–1987)
Brazil: Singer

Clementina de Jesus was an Afro-Brazilian singer whose songs were considered the last link in Brazil to the native music of nineteenth-century Africa.

Poverty in any country is an affliction to the mind and body. Being poor in the Third World is a much greater burden. Old age and poverty in underdeveloped countries are especially oppressive. As if this were not enough, add to all of these the disadvantages of being a woman in a male-dominated culture. Now, to ensure a full measure of misery, consider the consequences of being black in a society where dark skin is often a lifelong sentence to oblivion. This is a reflection on the life of Clementina de Jesus and her days of glory on the musical stages of Brazil.

Clementina de Jesus was born at the beginning of the century in the interior of the state of Rio de Janeiro. She grew up singing *jongos, corimas, modas, chulas*, and other types of traditional Brazilian songs taught to her by her mother. While working as a family maid for many years, she sang these songs as she cooked, washed, and cleaned the house. At the age of sixty-one she was "discovered" by Herminio Bello de Carvalho and invited to participate in a stage production showcasing varieties of popular music. Her success was instantaneous. The impact of her personality and intense depth of feeling impressed both the critics and the public.

Above all, Clementina's music was rich and unconventional, as was her voice. Her songs mixed long forgotten, traditional African melodies (sometimes sung in native dialects) with the music of Terreiros—Afro-Brazilian spiritualist ritual temples—with Christian hymns learned at the local Catholic Church and traditional samba music. Her musical style, characterized by a coarse voice, an oratorical delivery, and an interaction

Clementina de Jesus. Photo by Madalena
Schwartz. Courtesy of Acervo Fotográfico
do Instituto Moreira Salles.

of body and song, captivated stage and television audiences. After her
initial success, she recorded samba and popular music with many of
Brazil's most famous composers, including Caetano Veloso and Paulinho
da Viola. At the age of sixty-eight, she recorded the first of nine albums.
Although she died in poverty in 1987, she left behind a legacy that tran-
scends her few short years in the spotlight. Although she was popular
on the stage because of her personality and the exotic timber of her voice,
her records sold poorly and today are hard to find.

Was she fortunate to have been loved and respected for over two decades? Was she blessed by having the opportunity to work with Brazil's
greatest artists and represent her country abroad? Or were the late recognition, the brevity of her musical career, and poor remuneration for
her work just other misfortunes in the life of a poor, old, black woman?
The answer is yes to all of the above.

Her talent brought her fame, but not fortune. Had she been a middle-
class woman, or from a younger generation, or if her skin had been
lighter, it is very possible that her success would have been achieved
earlier in life and the monetary rewards would have been more significant and enduring.

Through her music and personality, de Jesus was a symbol of African
heritage and culture. She was unique because her Africanness was nat-

ural, not discovered. The fact that she could sing the African songs of her ancestors in their native dialects confirms the closeness of that link. Those songs might have been learned at the feet of her grandmother, possibly among the last of the slaves brought to Brazil prior to 1851, when foreign pressure, British warships, and growing public opposition effectively banned the horrendous practice.

No other black musician in Brazil of her time was as closely associated with traditional African culture as she was. She was the last living link to the days of slavery. To be sure, other black performers were becoming more vocal about their blackness and the problems facing Afro-Brazilians. However, theirs was a political blackness of a discovered social identity that for the most part followed the footpaths of the American civil rights movement of the 1960s. Her blackness was deeper, rooted in native traditions and songs handed down through generations.

Perhaps it is unfair to compare de Jesus with other black Brazilian artists of the 1970s. Most of them were of a new generation, born into a world of television, mass communications, and social consciousness. Although they are black, they are also one or two generations farther removed from the harsh labor of the sugarcane fields and the cruel life of slavery and even farther from the green forests of Mother Africa. She was born in 1902. Hers was the generation of Ary Barroso and Mário de Andrade, of the *samba-canção* (a cool, softened samba that emphasizes melody over rhythm, having more sophisticated lyrics, usually tied to sentimental themes) and the modern art movement of the 1920s and 1930s, when the rigid social standards incarcerated blacks at the bottom of society. Save for a scattering of mulatto and black intellectuals, black cultural consciousness in the first half of the century existed in a meager theatrical and literary limbo.

This was the period of "racial democracy," a theory identifying Brazil as the promised land, where all races lived in peace and harmony. The attitude of the ruling class and the offical propaganda transmitted to the Brazilian people was that a slow and "intelligent" assimilation of Indians and Afro-Brazilians would take place, imposing a European standard while incorporating "certain values of general interest or artistic importance" from the subcultures (Freyre 1966, 137).

For better or worse, this was the environment into which de Jesus was born and raised. It was not only her Brazil, but also that of Cartola, Ismael Silva, Donga, and Pixinguinha, black composers and musicians whose success served to substantiate the "racial democracy" ideology. They were black, but they were more *sambistas* than black artists. Their work and talents were the "certain values" selected to be assimilated. Like jazz in the United States, samba was considered a safe vehicle for black expression, which could be appreciated and incorporated into white culture without undue risk.

After a half century, black intellectuals realized that the promise of emancipation, achieved in 1889, had not produced the social or material progress they had hoped for. Slowly, beginning in the 1940s, a few brave pioneers began to publish periodicals and use the theater to explore the concept of "blackness" in Brazil. By the time de Jesus appeared in the music halls of Rio de Janeiro, a new vision of black consciousness and values had been born. She embodied a multicultural heritage rich in African and European traditions. From the chants in African dialects learned from her mother to the Catholic hymns sung in the church choir; from the temples of *candomblé* and the samba recitals to the most important stages of Brazil, de Jesus reflected the totality of the black experience.

Perhaps the most fitting eulogy for de Jesus are the words of one of her greatest hits, "Sonho meu" (My Dream), in which she despondently expresses conflicting emotions of hope and melancholy. As a stranger in a far land, yearning for freedom, yet conscious that her guiding light—and that of her people—had been lost, she resigns herself to the cold morning gloom of an unfulfilled dream. Even so, for every line expressing despair and pessimism, there is also a consequent "my dream" refrain, expressed in a powerful rhythm that brings hope and refuses to die.

As in the song, her life and work convey melancholy. She lived both triumph and tragedy. Although her career was short, she is considered one of Brazil's most important musical personalities of this century. Had things been different, she might have achieved more, but then she would not have been Clementina.

Further Reading

Efegê, Jota. *Figuras e Coisas da Música Popular Brasileira*. Rio de Janeiro, Brazil: Funarte, 1980.

Freyre, Gilberto. *New World in the Tropics: The Culture of Modern Brazil*. New York: Knopf, 1966.

McGowan, Chris, and Ricardo Pessanha. *The Billboard Book of Brazilian Music*. New York: Watson-Guptill Publications, 1991.

Clarice Deal

FRIDA KAHLO

(July 6, 1907–July 13, 1954)

Mexico: Artist

Frida Kahlo was one of the few women in the early to mid-1900s who openly addressed certain cultural issues and tendencies that were not readily dealt with in the artistic world. Her art is still daring. Her 150 or so extraordinary paintings admirably chronicle her experiences and the pains she endured throughout her life. Kahlo was Mexican, primitive, bound to her indigenous roots, and at the same time an embodiment of the most contemporary currents of art. In French surrealist André Bretón's words, "The art of Frida Kahlo is a ribbon around the bomb" (Kettenmann 1992, 36), and he recognized her as a fellow surrealist. Her art is at once extremely seductive, feminine, personal, and universal.

Magdalena Carmen Frida Kahlo was born in Coyoacán, Mexico, a suburb of Mexico City, to a Mexican mother of Spanish and Indian descent and a Hungarian Jewish father, a photographer. Kahlo later changed her birthday to July 7, 1910, although the reasons remain unclear. Perhaps it might have had something to do with her identification with the birth of modern Mexico. Kahlo liked to call herself a "daughter of the Mexican Revolution" (the Mexican revolution took place between 1910 and 1920) (Grimberg 1993/94, 45).

Frida Kahlo experienced a series of tragedies that shaped her life. At the age of seven she contracted polio which left her with a deformed leg, the object of ridicule of her peers. In 1925 she was in a serious trolley car accident in Mexico City. Her boyfriend at the time, Gómez Arias, who was with her in the tram, is quoted as saying, "The trolley's metal handrail . . . entered her lower body on the left side and exited through her vagina, tearing its left lip" (Collins 1995, 185). This accident caused Kahlo serious pain during the remainder of her life.

Kahlo was fifteen and attending the National Preparatory School when she fell in love with the famous muralist Diego Rivera, who was then thirty-six years of age. Around 1927 Kahlo and Rivera began an affair and married two years later. To Kahlo, Rivera was "as irresistible as he was ugly . . . a boy frog standing on his hind legs" (Zamora 1990, 185).

Through the influence of the quintessentially Mexican Rivera, Kahlo began "painting works influenced by indigenous Mexican art [and]

Frida Kahlo. Courtesy of Photofest.

dressing in the colorful, feminine costumes of the Tehuantepec peninsula" (Collins 1995, 185). While she embraced Mexican culture, traditions, and folklore, she also wrote about and painted her feelings toward the marginalized members of society, feminists, lesbians, gays, Chicanos.

Politically she professed Trotskyism and Leninism. Her political life and her personal life merged when she became the lover of Leon Trotsky, whom the couple had invited to live with them in their house in Coyoacán in 1937, to spite Rivera, who was also having affairs. In her portrait dedicated to Leon Trotsky she depicted herself holding a letter that reads, "For Leon Trotsky with love, I dedicate the painting, November 7, 1937" (Lowe 1995, 5). When Trotsky was assassinated, both Kahlo and Rivera were under suspicion.

Some of Kahlo's masterpieces were painted between 1932 and 1954. During the early 1930s, Kahlo traveled with Diego to San Francisco, Detroit, and New York while he worked for American capitalists on large commissions with leftist themes (Collins 1995, 186). In *Henry Ford Hos-*

pital (1932), Kahlo painted her bloody body, a fetus, a broken pelvis, and injured genitalia lying on a hospital bed as if in a nightmare following one of her miscarriages. In 1937, when she painted *The Deceased Dimas*, Kahlo followed an ancient Mexican tradition of painting the recently dead in a state of repose. *The Two Fridas* (1939), painted after her divorce from Rivera, shows Kahlo with her heart painfully broken and her hand holding surgical pincers to cut the vein leading to her heart. In *Self-Portrait* (1940), Kahlo appears with a symbolic necklace of thorns. The colors are bright, reddish purple, warm green, yellow, cobalt blue, navy blue, and bloody magenta. Kahlo confesses in her letters, "My paintings are well-painted, not nimbly but patiently. My painting contains in it the message of pain" (Zamora 1990, 157).

In *The Deceased Dimas* (1937), as in other paintings, Kahlo seems very close to the Mexican spirit: Catholic celebrations are mixed with popular, indigenous, and pagan rituals in which people offer gifts, and expensive food is presented to the dead. This is particularly noticeable in her depiction of the famous annual celebration of the Day of the Dead. References to indigenous beliefs appear in *The Little Deer* (1946), where the deer, with Kahlo's face, presents her bloody body pierced by arrows. It has been noted that "in Aztec belief the deer was the sign for the right foot" (Herrera 1991, 190), thus perhaps depicting Kahlo's deformed foot. The painting also reflects the suffering caused by the continuous infidelities of Diego Rivera, particularly in the horns of cuckoldry. Through her paintings, Kahlo found a way to make art from her suffering both in her personal and psychological life. In *The Love Embrace of the Universe* (1949), the Mother Nature figure represents the glorification of Kahlo's Mexican roots with the mountain goddess embracing her and nurturing her while she carries a baby in her arms, Rivera. *Self-Portrait with the Portrait of Doctor Farill* (1951) is Kahlo's version of a *retablo*, typically a humble *ex-voto* painted on wood or metal alluding to a loss and thanking the Virgin or the saints for deliverance.

In *Moses* (1945), Kahlo reflects upon her Jewish background. In her letter "Moses" from 1945, Kahlo wrote how she organized the space in the picture to include Zeus, Jehovah, Apollo, and Meso-American deities Coatlicue and Tlaloc: "I had space for [the gods] in their respective heavens, I wanted to divide the celestial world of imagination and poetry from the terrestrial world of fear of death" (Zamora 1990, 122). The idea of different gods, religions, and races contributes to a very complex painting in which reality and inner life create the circle of life and death, construction and destruction. "*Moses* reveals Kahlo's urge to encompass all time and all space in one vision" (Herrera 1991, 328).

Although not religious in the traditional sense, Kahlo and Rivera defended the faith of her ancestors against discrimination. At a hotel in Detroit that would not register Jews, Rivera shouted defiantly, "But Frida and I have Jewish blood! We are going to have to leave!" Anxious to keep their business, a hotel official offered to lower the rate (Herrera 1991, 134). Another racial episode took place at the home of automaker Henry Ford, a well-known anti-Semite: "At the dining room table Kahlo turned to Henry Ford, and asked, 'Mr. Ford, are you Jewish?' " (135).

In a panel painted by Rivera, *Detroit Industry* (1932), Kahlo painted herself as a pretty mechanical doll on a little motorized pedestal, holding the Mexican flag. In 1933 she painted the famous *My Dress Hangs There*, an ironic view comparing life in the United States to life in Mexico. The canvas is densely crowded with gasoline pumps, skyscrapers, industrial smokestacks, and other symbols of North American capitalism. In *Marxism Will Give Health to the Sick* (1954), a hand projects from Marx's head and strangles an American eagle, thus linking Kahlo's pain with her hope in the future. Kahlo went to a public demonstration against the Central Intelligence Agency eleven days before her death.

Kahlo's last painting, *Long Live Life* (1954), was completed only eight days before her death, which probably was suicide by drug overdose. She had attempted to end her life several times previously. At the time of her death, Kahlo was deeply depressed following the amputation of her leg. In *Long Live Life*, a sliced watermelon shows the eternal duality between life and death. Kahlo's life ended on July 13, 1954; on the same day, she was cremated in front of a handful of spectators. Popular tradition has it that the fire was so hot that the crematorium's doors burst open, only to display Kahlo upright with her hair in a halo of fire and with the appearance of a smile on her face. In one of the last entries in her journal, she had written, "I hope the leaving is joyful—and I hope never to return" (Kahlo, 1995, 285). Although she has been dead for nearly half a century, her artistic legacy not only endures, it grows.

Further Reading

Burrus, Christina. *Diego Rivera, Frida Kahlo*. Martigny, Switzerland: Foundation Pierre Gianadda, 1998.

Collins, Amy Fine. "Diary of a Mad Artist." *Vanity Fear* 58, no. 9 (1995): 175–88, 227–29.

Cruz, Barbara. *Portrait of a Mexican Painter*. Springfield, N.J.: Enslow, 1996.

Drucker, Malka. *Frida Kahlo*. Albuquerque: University of New Mexico Press, 1991.

Grimberg, Salomon. Review of *Frida Kahlo*, by Raqurl Tibol; *Frida Kahlo*, by Sarah Lowe; *Frida Kahlo, 1907–1954: Pain and Passion*, by Andrea Ketterman; and *Frida Kahlo: Torment and Triumph in Her Life and Art*, by Martha Zamora. *Women's Art Journal* 14, no. 2 (1993/1994): 45–48.

Herrera, Hayden. *Frida Kahlo, The Paintings*. New York: Harper Collins, 1991.

Kahlo, Frida. *The Diary of Frida Kahlo: An Intimate Self-Portrait*, translated by Barbara Crow de Toledo and Ricardo Pohlenz with introduction by Carlos Fuentes. New York: Harry Abrams, 1995.

Kettenmann, Andrea. *Frida Kahlo, 1907–1954. Pain and Passion.* Cologne, Germany: Benedikt Taschen, 1992.

Lowe, Sarah. *The Diary of Frida Kahlo: An Intimate Self-Portrait.* New York: Harry Adams, 1995.

Milner, Frank. *Frida Kahlo.* London: Bisow Books, 1995.

Poniatowska, Elena. *Frida Kahlo: The Camera Seduced.* San Francisco: Chronicle Books, 1992.

Richmond, Robin. *Frida Kahlo.* Boston: Little, Brown, 1993.

Turner, Robyn Montana. *Frida Kahlo: Mexico.* San Francisco: Pomegranate Artbooks, 1994.

Zamora, Martha. *Frida Kahlo: The Brush of Anguish.* San Francisco: Chronicle Books, 1990.

———. *The Letters of Frida Kahlo. Cartas Apasionadas.* San Francisco: Chronicle Books, 1995.

Raquel Jacobs

JULIETA KIRKWOOD
(April 5, 1936–April 8, 1985)

Chile: Sociologist, Researcher, Educator, Feminist Activist

Julieta Kirkwood, Chilean sociologist, researcher, teacher, political activist, and advocate of women's rights, was a leading figure in contemporary Latin-American feminism. Kirkwood's work and ideas were a central force behind the women's movements in Chile during the 1980s under the military regime. Her clear analyses of authoritarianism, feminism, and the relationship between women's groups and political parties are a major contribution to the intellectual history of Latin America.

María Julieta Kirkwood Bañados was born in Santiago de Chile. Her father, Johnny Kirkwood, was an accountant who traveled extensively with his wife and four children from the mining camps of the Atacama Desert in the north, to the southern city of Concepción. Her mother, Julieta Bañados, taught Julieta and her sister Elizabeth how to sew, knit, and perform other domestic responsibilities. Kirkwood learned from the age of seven that women's work was different from that of men.

Kirkwood, who was a brilliant student, completed her high school education in Santiago in the early 1950s. At the end of the 1950s, she entered the University of Chile to study public administration but later switched to sociology. During her studies, she married and had a son. By the time Kirkwood graduated from the university in 1968, her marriage was over. In 1969 Kirkwood completed a second degree in political science. After graduating, she worked as a researcher for the Sociology Department at the University of Chile for three years. In 1970 she married Rodrigo Baños, a sociologist at FLACSO, a non-governmental organization for research in the social sciences, and had the second of her two sons.

In 1972 Kirkwood began her work as a teacher and researcher at FLACSO. A year later, the coup led by General Augusto Pinochet on September 11, 1973, transformed her life forever. The violent destruction of Salvador Allende's government meant an end to the hope of achieving a more just socioeconomic order, a project that Kirkwood, as a Socialist, supported. The repressive regime installed by the junta sought to "cleanse" the nation of the ideology of Marxism and socialism. Moreover, Pinochet's patriarchal stance sought to depoliticize women through a rigid separation between the masculine/public and the feminine/private spheres of influence. Paradoxically, the exacerbation of sexism and patriarchy had rendered the traditional authoritarian order of Chilean society even more visible. Kirkwood, already aware of this fact, based on her personal experiences and her reading of the works of Simone de Beauvoir and Sheila Rowbotham, decided to challenge the dictatorship.

Four years after the coup, other women in Santiago met regularly with Kirkwood to exchange ideas about women's issues. They focused on women from the lowest economic sectors, who had been hit the hardest by repression and the new economic policies. In May 1979, they formed the Círculo de Estudios de la Mujer (Women's Studies Circle) to deliberate about women's reality; to promote dialogue and action among women of different backgrounds and ideologies; to raise consciousness about issues that affect women, and to promote research on those issues. As an opposition group, it was supported by the Academia de Humanismo Cristiano (Academy of Christian Humanism), "an umbrella organization instituted by the Church to provide a safe 'space' for alternative research centers, political expression, and the articulation of dissent" (Chuchryck 1994, 77). One of their first activities was a presentation, in July 1979, titled "El trabajo de la mujer" (Woman's Work), a collection of testimonies by women forced to earn a living as a result of the acute poverty brought about by the new economic model. In October 1979, Kirkwood, Irma Arriagada, Rosa Bravo, and María Isabel Cruzat published this document as the first article of the circle. In addition, Kirkwood led and organized workshops enthusiastically received on "Women and Work," "Women and Health," and "Politics and History: The Formation of a Feminine Conscience."

Kirkwood often drove her small, red Volkswagen Beetle to the poorest shantytowns on the outskirts of Santiago to talk to women who could not leave their homes and children. Her ideas created enormous interest. Although she was physically small and delicate, with shoulder-length, curly dark hair, her conviction, irreverence, sense of humor, and intelligence engaged and captivated her listeners. She found friendship and support in people of many economic levels, but especially among poor working women who knew firsthand of the brutality of machismo both in and out of their homes. Alongside the positive reactions to her work in 1979, Kirkwood faced a devastating personal issue: she had breast cancer. She was told she had five years to live.

While still working at FLACSO, Kirkwood began to participate more actively in the circle. She attended their meetings on Mondays, listening to the discussions while knitting, which provided her with the metaphor of the "knot" that she was to use in her essay "The Knots of Feminist Knowledge" (1983). Based on French philosopher and historian Michel Foucault's concept of *savoir/pouvoir* (knowledge/power), Kirkwood developed the image of social knots formed by threads of knowledge and power. She distinguished between dominant patriarchal knots and feminist knots. Authoritarianism, Kirkwood argued, a thread forming the dominant knots, always sought to eliminate dialogue when confronted with opposition. Feminism, Kirkwood maintained, should try to unravel and separate the threads forming the social fabric to understand their twists and readjust them. Unraveling knots was a prerequisite to recuperating power and elaborating new knowledge. It meant understanding the contradictions between the dominant social values and concrete, daily human experiences. It also constituted an active critical resistance to a system of socioeconomic exclusions, particularly damaging to women. Inspired by the lively discussions of the circle and the need to elaborate the new knowledge derived from them, Kirkwood created, in 1980, the *Boletín del Círculo de Estudios de la Mujer* (Bulletin of the Women's Studies Circle), which appeared until 1983.

In 1981, as a member of a collective of socialist feminist women, the Federación de Mujeres Socialistas (Federation of Socialist Women), Kirkwood created the journal *Furia* (Fury), which appeared six times until 1984. The journal's name reflected women's anger toward the dominant sociopolitical system. She wrote five of its six editorials under the pseudonym Adela H. In the first issue of March 1981, Kirkwood, aware of the Left's traditional view of women, stated, "We believe that at the risk of losing its own integrity, the Socialist project cannot exclude the demands of any discriminated group within a capitalist society, either because of political beliefs, economic level, ethnicity, gender, or age."

In the winter of 1982, there was a heated public debate about divorce in Santiago that originated from a statement made by Pinochet's wife, Lucía Hiriart, who favored divorce as a means of protecting women powerless to otherwise confront abusive husbands. An article published in *Revista HOY* (Journal TODAY) compared the opinions of feminists of the circle with those of the bishops of Santiago and Valparaíso. The bishops deplored the "nightmare" of the divorce issue. Since the topic was too hot to handle, the regime's reaction was to silence the ensuing debate. As a response, Kirkwood wrote an editorial for the *Boletín* in September 1982 entitled, "El divorcio ¿también en receso?" (Divorce, Another Issue Adjourned?), in which she argued for an amendment of the law prohibiting divorce. Her opinion clashed with the Catholic Church's position on the matter. A second editorial, titled "La ley del eterno divorcio" (The Law of Eternal Divorce), was the catalyst for the split between the circle and the Academy of Christian Humanism. They were expelled from the Church organization in November 1983. After the expulsion, Kirkwood, Rosalba Todaro, Patricia Crispi, and María Antonieta Saá, among others, saw an urgent need to establish two independent centers for feminist research and action. The first was a site for political activity: the Casa de la Mujer La Morada (La Morada Women's House), a center of analysis and information on the status of women. Kirkwood suggested the name La Morada from the double meaning of the Spanish adjective *morado* (the color purple, associated with feminism) and the noun *morada* (dwelling or home). The second site was named Centro de Estudios de la Mujer (Center for the Studies of Woman), which would develop the theoretical material derived from the activities of La Morada.

In May 1983, Kirkwood proposed the establishment of the Chilean Feminist Movement from the tower of a church in Santiago during a meeting of the then still existing circle. Its motto, Kirkwood argued, should be "democracy for the nation and the home" (*Boletín*, 1). It became a central slogan for the political campaigns to restore democracy in Chile. Kirkwood then led the formation of MEMCH83, Movimiento Pro Emancipacion de la Mujer Chilena (Movement for the Emancipation of the Chilean Woman), an opposition organization that coordinated the activities of both feminist and nonfeminist groups. The group's name was derived from the original MEMCH formed in 1935, a result of Kirkwood's major task to recover what she called the invisible, nonwritten history of women's efforts to politicize their demands. The movement adopted the name in recognition of the efforts of the 1935 MEMCH members to achieve equal rights.

In July 1983, Kirkwood went to Lima, Peru, to the Second Latin American and Caribbean Feminist Conference. Witnessing how women of different nationalities and ethnicities brought into the political arena issues considered private and nonpolitical reenergized her. In her article "Fiesta en Lima" (Celebration in Lima), Kirkwood wrote, "Everywhere women are transforming themselves into *subjects*, women are starting to speak, they are converging in workshops, groups, and conferences in the city and the country, organizing through politics" (Kirkwood 1987, 63). In Lima she met Peruvian sociologist Virginia Vargas, the founder of the Centro de la Mujer Peruana Flora Tristán (Peruvian Women's Center Flora Tristán). In September 1983, Kirkwood gave a presentation in Mexico City at the 11th Latin American Studies Association (LASA) titled "El feminismo como negación del autoritarismo" (Feminism as a Negation of Authoritarianism).

Her last article, an editorial for *Furia* titled "Hay que tener niñas bonitas" (We Should Have Pretty Girls), appeared in November 1984. At that time, Pinochet's regime, faced with public unrest caused by a strong economic recession that especially affected poor women, had ordered a state of siege. In the editorial, Kirkwood accused conservative Chilean women of complicity with the regime in condemning poorer women's mobilizations: "You honeycomb lady, smiling, but hard as a rock will say you do not want women in the streets so, persecute them! In the office or the factory so, close them! No marches to produce chaos, jail them!"

During the first months of 1985, Kirkwood underwent intensive chemotherapy for breast cancer. Too weak to write, she dictated to a friend, Vicky Quevedo. Her last thoughts included in the introduction of *Ser política en Chile* (Being Female and Political in Chile) were directed at Pinochet, "While you ridiculous patriarch, spitting and coughing, vociferate your power in serial decrees, I organize my papers" (Kirkwood 1987, 17). In March 1985, as a last resort, her doctor suggested a treatment available in the United States. While preparing for that trip, her condition rapidly deteriorated, and she was taken to the intensive care unit of a clinic in Santiago. On one of her last days, when she briefly took off her oxygen mask, she discovered that no women doctors worked at the clinic. She commented, "Soon there will be many" (Kirkwood 1987, 17). Kirkwood died on the morning of April 8, at the age of forty-nine. Respecting her declared atheism, the funeral wake was held at La Morada. The dwelling was full of friends, colleagues, and students. Her friends remembered her love of classical music and played Tommasso Albinoni's *Adaggio* that evening. Her casket was covered by a purple sheet and surrounded by fresh flowers. At the cemetery, her coffin was carried to the grave by a group of women friends while singing "La cigarra" (The Cicada), a song about rebirth written by Argentine singer Mercedes Sosa. Her family placed on the tombstone the name Julieta Kirkwood and the symbol of womanhood.

In 1986 FLACSO published *Ser política en Chile. Las feministas y los partidos* (Being Female and Political in Chile. The Feminists and the Parties), which included the documents for discussion that Kirkwood had written for FLACSO. In 1987 two compilations of her articles were published as books. *Tejiendo rebeldías* (Weaving Rebellions) is the work of Patricia Crispi, who assembled thirty articles and essays that had appeared in *Furia* and the *Boletín* between 1979 and 1984. *Feminarios* (a neologism, something like "feminaries") is a compilation of Kirkwood's writings put together by Sonia Montecino. In 1990, five years after her death, *Ser política en Chile* was reedited as *Ser política en Chile. Los nudos de la sabiduría feminista* (Being Female and Political in Chile. The Nodes of Feminist Wisdom).

Further Reading

Agosín, Marjorie, and Doris Meyer. "Julieta Kirkwood." In *Re-reading the Spanish American Essay. Translations of 19th and 20th Century Women's Essays,* edited by Doris Meyer, 263–75. Austin: University of Texas Press, 1995.

Boletín del Círculo de la Mujer de la Academia de Humanismo Cristiano 1 (April 1980): 1.

Chuchryck, Patricia. "Feminist Anti-Authoritarian Politics: The Role of Women's Organizations in the Chilean Transition to Democracy." In *The Women's Movement in Latin America. Feminism and the Transition to Democracy,* edited by Jane S. Jaquette, 149–84. Boulder, Colo.: Westview Press, 1991.

———. "From Dictatorship to Democracy: The Women's Movement in Chile." In *The Women's Movement in Latin America. Participation and Democracy,* edited by Jane S. Jaquette, 65–107. 2d ed. Boulder, Colo.: Westview Press, 1994.

Kirkwood, Julieta. *Ser política en Chile: Las feministas y los partidos.* Santiago, Chile: Facultad Latinoamericana de Ciencias Sociales, 1986.

———. *Tejiendo rebeldías. Escritos feministas de Julieta Kirkwood Hilvanados por Patricia Crispi,* edited by Patricia Crispi. Santiago, Chile: Centro de Estudios de la Mujer and Casa de la Mujer La Morada, 1987.

———. "Women and Politics in Chile." *International Social Science Journal* 35 (1983): 625–37.

Cecilia Ojeda

CLAUDIA LARS
(December 20, 1899–July 22, 1974)

El Salvador: Author, Poet

Claudia Lars is one of the leading voices in twentieth-century Salvadoran literature. Creator of an exquisite and rigorously wrought lyric poetry, she achieved recognition and prominence in a male-dominated literary environment. She also authored a book of memoirs and several hundred uncollected articles and essays. Less known is her role as a cultural promoter late in her life.

Claudia Lars, who was baptized Margarita del Carmen Brannon Vega, was born in Armenia, a middle-sized town in the western Salvadoran department of Sonsonate. Armenia, at the time known as San Silvestre Guaymoco, is located on the slopes of the Cordillera del Bálsamo, a region originally populated by Pipil Indians but in process of rapid change as a result of coffee growth. Lars's mother, Manuela Vega Zelayandía, came from a locally respected family who claimed descent from the Spanish conquistadores and counted among its ancestors participants in the independence movement of the early nineteenth century. Lars's mother married an American of Irish descent, Peter Patrick Brannon, an engineer who had traveled through many Latin American countries and established himself in El Salvador, perhaps attracted by the prosperity generated in the golden years of coffee. Don Patricio, as Armenians called Peter Patrick, was not a common adventurer in search of rapid fortune. He was an educated and cultured man who, early in his life, had been attracted by socialist ideals. By the time of the birth of his daughter, however, he was primarily interested in the Theosophical movement initiated by Madame Helena Petrovna Blavatsky, which sought to integrate the wisdom of Eastern religions (especially Buddhism and Hinduism) into Western thought. It is said that he had met the famous Madame Blavatsky on a trip to London, and he was the founder of the first Theosophical club in El Salvador. Don Patricio's literary and religious inclinations, as well as his relationships with Salvadoran intellectuals, influenced his daughter's career.

Lars was sent to La Asunción, a religious school run by French nuns in Santa Ana, El Salvador's second largest city and then known as the coffee capital. La Asunción was an institution designed to make pious and virtuous mothers of young women from the elite. It provided, nonetheless, the basics of a literary culture to Lars, who had manifested literary talents since early in her life.

In 1919 Lars met, through family friends, Salomón de la Selva, a young Nicaraguan poet who encouraged her to further her literary career. De la Selva sent some of her poems to Joaquín García Monge, a Costa Rican writer and editor of *Repertorio americano* (American Repertoire), a prestigious weekly literary magazine that had collaborators and subscribers from all of Latin America. Lars published her first poems signed with her real name, Carmen Brannon. Thus began a long relationship with *Repertorio americano*.

After finishing school, Lars was sent to Long Island, New York, to improve her English. First, she stayed with paternal relatives, but shortly afterward she moved to New York City, outside of her relatives' surveillance. There, Lars met LeRoy Beers, a young middle-class New Yorker. They married in 1923.

Thanks to Don Patricio's influences with El Salvador's American community, Beers was designated counsel general of the United States in El Salvador. The young couple settled in San Salvador, where Lars's only son, LeRoy, was born in 1927. Beers got involved in the navigation business and finally resigned his diplomatic post, and the family moved to Costa Rica. In San José, Lars found a more stimulating climate for her writing. Through *Repertorio americano*, she published her first book in 1934, *Estrellas en el pozo* (Stars in the Well), a collection of poems she published under the name of Claudia Lars, which to her had Nordic connotations. During these years her marriage with Beers failed. At the time of her separation, Lars became emotionally involved with José Basileo Acuña, a Catholic priest who became the impossible love of some of her most beautiful poems.

Lars took charge of the upbringing of her son. Her life was difficult. She changed residence many times, back to El Salvador, to the United States, and to Mexico trying to make a living. This assertion of her independence was the subject of criticism by the traditionally conservative and intolerant Salvadoran respectable society. Nevertheless, Lars managed to develop a literary career and to find a place among Salvadoran intellectuals. She was very close to a group of artists with whom she shared aesthetic, religious, and political ideas. Among them were Alberto Guerra Trigueros, Serafín Quiteño, and Salarrué, a respected painter and writer who was one of her dearest friends. A second volume of poetry, *Canción redonda* (Round Song, 1937) was dedicated to him. Although Lars was never directly involved in Salvadoran politics, she was sensitive to social injustices and critical of the military rule. Her poetry is mostly lyrical and very intimate in tone, but in many occasions she wrote more overtly political poetry to protest the abuses of power. Some of these poems were collected in *Romances de norte y sur* (Ballads of North and South, 1946).

After fifteen years of separation, Lars divorced Beers to marry, in 1949, Salvador Samayoa Chinchilla, a prestigious Guatemalan writer. They had intellectual affinities, but the marriage did not last long. In 1955 Lars began to collaborate with official cultural institutions in El Salvador, institutions that had been recently established during the rule of Oscar Osorio, an enlightened and moderate colonel who was trying to modernize the country.

From 1959 to 1970, Claudia Lars was the editor of *Cultura*, a literary journal under the auspices of the Ministry of Education. Her dedication to this cultural enterprise was outstanding. Lars encouraged many young writers to follow literary careers, among them some that had been labeled as Communists and therefore banned, such as Roque Dalton, Manlio Argueta, and Roberto Armijo.

Lars published, during her life, the following volumes of poetry: *Estrellas en el pozo* (1934), *Canción Redonda* (1937), *La casa de vidrio* (The Glass

House, 1942), *Romances de norte y sur* (1946), *Sonetos* (Sonnets, 1947), *Ciudad bajo mi voz* (City Beneath My Voice, 1947), *Fábula de una verdad* (Fable of a Truth, 1959), *Sobre el ángel y el hombre* (Of the Angel and Man, 1963), *Del fino amanecer* (On the Fine Dawning, 1966), and *Nuestro pulsante mundo* (Our Pulsing World, 1969). Several uncollected works (among them "Cartas escritas cuando crece la noche" [Letters Written When the Night Deepens]) appear in *Obras escogidas* (Collected Works), a collection of Lars's poetry prepared by Matilde Elena López and published by Editorial Universitaria in 1974. In 1959 Lars published *Memorias de infancia* (Memoirs of Childhood), a lyrical narrative of her childhood in Armenia.

Claudia Lars died after losing a long and painful battle with cancer. She was seventy-four years old.

Further Reading

Escobar, Francisco Andrés. "Primera lectura de Claudia Lars." In Claudia Lars, *Tierra de infancia*, 5–31. San Salvador, El Salvador: UCA Editores, 1987.

González Huguet, Carmen. "Prólogo." In Claudia Lars, *Poesía completa*, 1.19–62. San Salvador, El Salvador: Dirección de Publicaciones e Impresos, 1999.

López, Matilde. "Prólogo." In Claudia Lars, *Obras escogidas*, xi–xii. San Salvador, El Salvador: Editorial Universitaria, 1974.

Ricardo Roque Baldovinos

LOLITA LEBRÓN
(1919–   )

Puerto Rico: Political Activist

Born in Lares, Puerto Rico, Lolita Lebrón, a political activist who resorted to violence to try to free Puerto Rico from U.S. dominance, currently lives in Trujillo Alto. In 1949, when she was twenty-one, Lebrón immigrated to New York City to work in a clothing factory, leaving her son, Félix, and her newborn daughter, Gladys, in the care of her family. She became involved in union leadership activities in the New York factories she worked in and later joined the Puerto Rican Nationalist party, under the direction of Pedro Albizu Campos. By joining the National party, Lebrón reaffirmed her "divine mission" to achieve independence for Puerto Rico.

The Puerto Rican Nationalist party was founded in 1922 with the purpose of attacking growing U.S. imperialism on the island. North Americans were expropriating the old agricultural installations and their belongings and converting the former owners into *peones* (unskilled laborers) of the invaders' new capital. Pedro Albizu Campos created an archetypical nationalist program which promoted the need to defend the nation from the newcomers' exploitation. Albizu Campos represented the radicalism of a social class that had attained a precarious social condition caused by North American imperialism. It caused an isolation among Puerto Rican laborers, a recurrence of the syndrome of single-person leadership, a massive imperialistic repression directed at nationalist militants, and the eventual dissolution of the National party as a political force within Puerto Rican society. The party proposed the national sovereignty of the island as a synonym of individual freedom. Albizu Campos believed that violence of the classes against each other is the classic means to find liberty, as exemplified in other great nineteenth-century social revolutions (Parker Harson 1957, 77). Thus, the struggle against the ambitious colonizer, the United States, reflects, for the rest of Latin America, the thought of Albizu Campos, who regarded the North American empire as the classical enemy of Hispanic culture for its limitless ambition in favor of the materialistic aspects of North America (Parker Harson 1957, 78).

The work of Albizu Campos inspired a portion of the generations of the 1930s until his death in 1965. Consequently, the majority of the new generation, Lolita Lebrón among them, were victims of poverty, workers' oppression in the New York factories, and second-class citizenship, and they found in Albizu Campos's patriotism inspiration to struggle for freedom and independence for Puerto Rico as a national republic.

On March 1, 1954, opening day of the Tenth Conference of Inter-American Issues in Caracas, Venezuela, Lebrón, together with Rafael Cancel Miranda, Andrés Figueroa Cordero, and Irvin Flores, attacked the gallery of the House of Representatives of the United States with a 38-caliber pistol and injured five congressmen. This act of violence was carried out as an explicit protest against the occupation of Puerto Rico by the United States. The protagonists sought to embarrass the United States in its role in the conference by getting the attention of the international press. On June 16, 1954, in the Federal Court of Washington, D.C., Lebrón was sentenced to fifty-seven years in prison. In the 1950s, the United States was caught up in the Cold War, and the act of this nationalist leader could be defined only as a terrorist act or an act of insanity. Subsequently, Lebrón was taken from prison to Saint Elizabeth Hospital in New York for mental illness, where the famous poet Ezra Pound was also confined. Throughout the intervening years, Puerto Ricans who advocate independence for the island have considered Lebrón a "brave woman and a fighter for the freedom" (Ojito 1998, 1).

Lebrón was offered house arrest in exchange for imprisonment, but she refused it and insisted that President Jimmy Carter grant her full release. In 1979 the U.S. government freed Lebrón, and she returned to Puerto Rico, where she serves as an advisor to leftist groups fighting for the independence of the island. In her view, the struggle is not over, but now it had to be carried out in a more peaceful manner. Likewise, Lebrón is quite concerned about the culture of the island and the Puerto Rican family, as well as the problem of the destruction of the environment caused by American industries, which are exempt from federal taxes.

The death of her daughter, Gladys Méndez, and her granddaughter, Irene Vilar, have added an extra dimension of pain and suffering to the family. In 1996 her granddaughter, Irene Vilar, published a book, *A Message from God in the Atomic Age*, while under psychiatric treatment in Syracuse, New York. The book deals with Lebrón's family history, as well as the causes of Vilar's mental depression which led her to attempt suicide after her mother's death. The book was attacked by Lebrón, who claimed it to be full of lies about her daughter, Gladys Méndez, who, according to Vilar, probably committed suicide. Lebrón affirms that her daughter did not kill herself but was the victim of a car accident in 1978. Irene Vilar, on the other hand, claims that her book was not intended to debunk the almost mythical and charismatic figure of her grandmother, but simply to evoke the memory of her mother.

In addition to her work as a political activist, Lebrón is a poet, and in 1976 she published *Sándalo en la celda* (Sandalwood in the Cell), which she wrote in prison. One of the most important aspects of this book is the theme of forgiveness extended by one of the victims from the confines of prison to her North American oppressors. *Sandalwood* symbolizes the piety of a woman privileged by the emotions of love. For Francisco Matos Paolí, the Puerto Rican National Laureate, Lebrón's poems combine political commitment with lyrical aspects represented by the mystical joys of Virgin Mary. It is as though this poetry constituted a heroic song to Puerto Rican national independence (Matos Paoli 1977, 3).

As a lover of literature, Lebrón reads and enjoys classical works of literature. Her favorite is Miguel de Cervantes's *Don Quixote*. According to her granddaughter, Lebrón knows by heart specific episodes and precise details of the book, which she describes as a doctrinary discourse with great imagination and a sense of freedom (Vilar 1996, 269). Vilar stated in an interview that appears in her book (258–74) that Lebrón and Don Quixote live and walk together.

Today, Lebrón's activities extend to philanthropic work, visiting and assisting patients in the hospital, meditating, and following the mystical life, as she calls it. After her years in prison, the nationalistic leader felt the call of Jesus Christ when she heard a voice that said to her, "Because of the spiritual impoverishment of the earth many shall succumb" (Vilar

1996, 261). It is thus that Lebrón will remain eternally in the history of Puerto Rico and Latin America, as the champion of a tireless struggle to realize her ideals: liberty and sovereignty for Puerto Rico and Latin America and the freedom of Latin America from U.S. cultural, political, and economical rule.

Further Reading

Gil de Lamadrid Navarro, Antonio. *Los indómitos*. Río Piedras, Puerto Rico: Editorial Edil, 1981.

Maldonado-Denis, Manuel. "Aproximación crítica al fenómeno nacionalista en Puerto Rico." In *Puerto Rico, una crisis histórica*, 138–71. México, D.F.: Editorial Nuestro Tiempo, 1979.

Matos Paoli, Francisco. "Yo oigo un rumor celestial." In Lolita Lebrón, *Sándalo en la celda*, 1–7. Cataño, Puerto Rico: Editorial Betances, 1977.

Ojito, Mirta. "Shots Pursue Three Generations." *New York Times*, June 1, 1998, p. 1.

Parker Harson, Earl. *Transformación: El moderno Puerto Rico*, translated by Victoriano Pérez. México, D.F.: Editorial Intercontinental, 1957.

Vilar, Irene. *A Message from God in the Atomic Age*, translated by Gregory Rabassa. New York: Pantheon Books, 1996.

Carlos Manuel Rivera

CLARICE LISPECTOR
(December 19, 1920–December 9, 1977)
Brazil: Author

One of Brazil's most eminent writers of experimental fiction and the country's first woman reporter, Clarice Lispector was born in Tchetchelnik, the Ukraine, while her parents, Pedro and Marieta Lispector, and her two sisters, Elisa and Tânia, were leaving Russia to escape anti-Semitic persecution brought about by the Russian Revolution of 1917. The Lispectors continued their voyage to Brazil after Lispector was born. They arrived in Maceió (Alagoas), where they had relatives, in February 1921.

Because Maceió was then a little town, they moved to Recife, Pernambuco. Lispector completed elementary school there at the Grupo Escolar João Barbalho and started secondary school at the Ginásio Pernambucano. While she was still in elementary school, Lispector showed an interest in fiction. She is reported to have written several stories and to have sent them to a local newspaper, the *Diário de Pernambuco* (Pernambuco Daily), which published children's stories in the "O 'Diário' das Crianças" (Children's Diary) section. None of them was ever published. Before finishing her third school year at the Ginásio Pernambucano, her family moved to Rio de Janeiro in search of a better life. In the capital, Lispector completed her secondary school education at the Colégio Sílvio Leite.

In Rio de Janeiro, Lispector discovered the world of books and developed an insatiable desire for reading. While browsing in local bookstores, she discovered, quite by accident, the works of novelists Graciliano Ramos, José de Alencar, Machado de Assis, Mário de Andrade, Rachel de Queiroz, Fyodor Dostoyevski, Hermann Hesse, and Julien Green. Hesse's *Steppenwolf* (1927) purportedly made such a great impression on her that she started to think about writing novels.

Lispector completed a two-year preparatory course for law school and enrolled in the National Faculty of Law in 1940. However, after her father's death that same year, she started to work to support herself while continuing in school. She tutored students in mathematics and Portuguese. She also translated scientific documents for a local laboratory. Later, she became a copy editor for the Agência Nacional, the national news agency. In 1942 a job at *A noite* (the Evening News) made her the first woman reporter. Sometime after securing this permanent job, Lispector chanced upon Katherine Mansfield's novel *Bliss* (1920). After discovering that Mansfield was a famous writer, Lispector knew that she also wanted to become an author. With the support of friends at the newspaper, she published her first novel, *Perto do coração selvagem* (Near to the Wild Heart, 1944), which received very positive reviews and the Graça Aranha prize a few years later.

Before graduating from law school in 1944, she married Maury Gurgel Valente, a classmate who was preparing for foreign service. After passing the entrance exam for Itamaraty, Brazil's Ministry of Foreign Relations, Gurgel Valente and Lispector prepared to leave for Naples, Italy, where he served as a diplomat during World War II. While volunteering at a local hospital for wounded Brazilian soldiers, Lispector finished writing her second novel, *O lustre* (The Chandelier, 1946), which she had started in Brazil. In 1946 Valente was posted to Berne, Switzerland, where Lispector gave birth to her first son, Pedro. While performing the duties of a diplomat's wife and mother, she managed to write her third novel, *A cidade sitiada* (The Besieged City, 1949).

In 1952 Maury and Lispector moved to the United States, where their second son, Paulo, was born. Domestic responsibilities made writing her fourth novel difficult. It is during this time that her son Paulo, who was then three years old, asked Lispector to write a story for him. She wrote *O mistério do coelho pensante* (The Mystery of the Thinking Rabbit) around 1957, but it was not published until 1967. In 1959 she finally completed, with some difficulty, *A maça no escuro* (The Apple in the Dark, 1961), which won the Cármen Dolores Barbosa Prize. In 1959, before leaving the United States to return permanently to Brazil, Lispector put together a collection of short stories entitled *Laços de família* (Family Ties, 1960). Ironically, at the same time, she decided to get a divorce. Lispector would finally be free to devote herself to her children and her writing.

Since Lispector could not make a living solely from the sale of her books and the alimony she received from Valente, she wrote short stories for the magazine *Senhor* (Mister). In 1959 she wrote short stories about an encounter with the Other ("A menor mulher do mundo" [The Smallest Woman in the World]), about expiation ("O crime do professor de matemática" [The Crime of the Math Professor]), hate ("O bufalo" [The Buffalo]), and the snares of family relationships ("Feliz aniversário" [Happy Birthday]). At the same time, she started to write a column for the *Correio da manhá* (Morning Courier) and the *Diário da noite* (Evening Newspaper). In these columns, she gave readers makeup, fashion, and decorating tips. In the late 1960s and early 1970s, she interviewed celebrities for the magazines *Manchete* (Headline) and *Fatos & fotos* (Facts and Photos). From 1967 to 1973, she wrote weekly articles for the *Jornal do Brasil* (Journal of Brazil). In spite of the financially unfavorable circumstances that surrounded the publication of these pieces, Lispector liked working for newspapers.

In 1964 Lispector began the most productive years of her literary career with the publication of her fifth novel, *A paixão segundo G. H.* (The Passion According to G. H.), and a compilation of short stories, *A legião estrangeira* (The Foreign Legion). In both works, Lispector continues to explore the relationship between language and existence. *The Foreign Legion*, in particular, expresses a particular preoccupation with literary creativity.

After writing *Uma aprendizagem; ou, o livro dos prazeres* (An Apprenticeship; or, The Book of Pleasures, 1969), an unusual dialogue between a man (Ulisses) and a woman (Lóri) on how to attain true love, Lispector pursued an increasing interest in the short story form with the publication of two collections. *Felicidade clandestina* (Clandestine Happiness, 1971) contains several unpublished stories, some of which deal with the desires of a poor young girl ("Felicidade clandestina," "Restos de carnaval" [Remains of Carnival], and "Cem anos de perdão" [One Hundred Years of Forgiveness]). Others—"O ovo e a galinha" (The Egg and the Chicken) and "Macacos" (Monkeys)—are tied thematically to the subject of rivalry among children and animals. *A imitação da rosa* (The Imitation of the Rose, 1973) reprises a number of previously published stories, such as "A imitação da rosa," "A menor mulher do mundo," "O crime do professor de matemática," and "Feliz aniversário." With her sixth novel, *Água viva* (The Stream of Life, 1973), Lispector returned to her introspective narrative technique. This time she explores, through the medium of a confessional letter, a (female) narrator's analysis of a failing love affair. As the title suggests, water is a metaphor for the fluidity of life and the freedom the narrator desires. In the following year, she published two volumes of darkly humorous stories. One was a compilation of mythological, philosophical, and psychological pieces (*Onde estivestes de noite* [Where Were You Last Night, 1974]), and the other was a collection of stories based on erotic and sexual themes (*A via crucis do corpo* [The Via Crucis of the Body, 1974]). In 1974 Lispector also wrote a children's story about the day-to-day life of a married farm chicken named Laura entitled *A vida íntima de Laura* (The Intimate Life of Laura, 1974).

In her last novel, *A hora da estrela* (The Hour of the Star, 1977), Lispector exposes through the perspective of a self-conscious narrator the plight of a Brazilian girl (Macabéa) who leaves the northeast for the big city. Instead of finding a better life, the heroine ends up being struck and killed by a yellow Mercedes-Benz. Affected by his protagonist's fatal accident, the narrator dies of grief. Coincidentally, Lispector, the author, also dies after a short-lived fight with cancer of the uterus.

After Lispector's death, a series of events have attested to an enduring interest in the Brazilian writer's work. Her closest friend, Olga de Borelli, put together and published *Um sopro de vida* (A Breath of Life, 1978), a semiautobiographical novel Lispector completed the year before her death. Lispector's son Paulo published an anthology of *crônicas* (newspaper articles) Lispector wrote for the *Jornal do Brasil* from 1967 to 1973, which he entitled *A descoberta do mundo* (The Discovery of the World, 1984). In 1986 Suzana Amaral made a film of *A hora da estrela* starring Marcella Cartaxo in the role of Macabéa. Two years ago, the National Library of Rio de Janeiro commemorated the twentieth anniversary of Lispector's death with an exposition of a private collection of paintings the author painted around 1975: "Explosao" (Explosion), "Sem título" (Untitled), "Medo" (Fear), "Luta sangrenta pela paz" (Bloody Struggle for Peace), and "Tentativa de ser alegre" (Attempt to Be Happy).

In retrospect, Lispector modernized Brazilian fiction which, at the time she wrote her first novel, was dominated by regionalistic themes. With the publication of *Perto do coração selvagem*, Lispector proved that a Brazilian psychological novel was possible. The introspective narrative style that brought together language, identity, and reality revolutionized Brazilian literature of the 1940s and 1950s. Moreover, her female characters' phenomenological quests for authentic identities amidst a male-dominated society place Lispector as one of the first Brazilian feminists. It was indeed Lispector's particular portrayal of women's psychological and social experience, coupled with her penchant for subversion of logic, closure, and patriarchal discourse, that led Algerian French writer Hélène Cixous to develop a keen interest in the Lispectorian fiction, where she claims to have located an exemplary site of *écriture féminine*. Because of her innovative work, Lispector is today one of the most widely read foreign authors in the United States and Europe.

Lispector was also Brazil's first woman reporter, an excellent short story writer, *cronista* (chronicler), and an amateur painter. Her journalistic experience apparently had a beneficial effect on her writing by keeping her close to the social problems that preoccupied and continue to preoccupy the minds of Brazilian men and women. Although she was not born in Brazil, one can assuredly say that she truly was Brazilian.

Further Reading

Cixous, Hélène. "Clarice Lispector: The Approach, Letting Oneself (Be) Read (by) Clarice Lispector. The Passion According to C. L." In *"Coming to Writing" and Other Essays*, edited by Deborah Jenson and translated by Sarah Cornell, Deborah Jenson, Ann Liddle, and Susan Sellers, 59–77. Cambridge, Mass.: Harvard University Press, 1991.

———. "Reaching the Point of Wheat, or a Portrait of the Artist as a Maturing Woman." *New Literary History* 19, no. 1 (1987): 1–21.

Fitz, Earl E. *Clarice Lispector*. Boston: Twayne, 1985.

Marting, Diane E. *Clarice Lispector: A Bio-Bibliography*. Westport, Conn.: Greenwood Press, 1993.

Levilson C. Reis

DULCE MARÍA LOYNAZ
(December 10, 1902–April 27, 1997)
Cuba: Poet

Prize-winning Cuban poet Dulce María Loynaz was born in Havana, Cuba, and died, a blind victim of liver cancer, at the age of ninety-four. Her body was buried to the sounds of the "Himno invasor" (Invader Hymn), a political hymn of the Cuban independentists written by her father. Baptized María Mercedes, she was called Loynaz at an early age. Her ancestors were British and Basque. Her father's family came from the town of San Sebastián, in Spain, and arrived in Cuba in the eighteenth century. At that time the last name was written Loinaz, but at the end of the nineteenth century the spelling changed to Loynaz.

José Antonio Loinaz y Sobremonte married Ana de Vergara y Miranda, who was directly related to Vasco Porcallo de Figueroa. The Galician bloodline (through the Figueroas), the Asturian bloodline (through the Mirandas), and the Basque bloodline from the Loinazes joined the Indian bloodline provided by Vasco Porcallo. Through the years, the Loinaz family were related to some of the most prestigious families on the island: the Agüeros, the Armenteros, the Varonas, the Arteagas, and the Betancourts. All of these names became well known through their involvement in Cuban letters or their status as important historical figures. The first Loinaz came to live in Puerto Príncipe, Cuba, in 1608. As an army general, Loynaz's father fought for independence during the Cuban emancipation from Spain. He was a well-educated man and wrote his own memoirs, *Memorias de la guerra* (Memories of War, 1839), edited in 1989 by Loynaz.

Loynaz's mother, who came from Havana, loved painting, reading, and embroidery. Loynaz was the oldest child. She had two brothers—Enrique (1904–1966) and Carlos Manuel (1906–1977)—and one sister, Flor (1908–1986). All the siblings loved art and literature. Carlos Manuel was a famous poet and composer until he became mentally ill in the 1930s when he was still young; he was a good friend of Spanish playwright Federico García Lorca.

About Loynaz's childhood, British critic Verity Smith stated, "Loynaz told me of the pain caused in her childhood by her parents' divorce, something that created scandal and grief granted both the period in which the event took place (around 1910) together with the fact that theirs was a distinguished family of practicing Catholics" (1991, 149).

She began to write her own autobiography, entitled *Jardín* (Garden) in 1928 at the age of twenty-six, and she finished it in 1935 when she was thirty-three years old, although the volume was not published until 1951. The family lived in a nice neighborhood of Havana, El Vedado, in a solid, large house surrounded by tropical plants. The house was first destroyed during Castro's revolution and then transformed into a homeless shelter. After the revolution it was filmed to illustrate the decadence of the Cuban bourgeoisie. Later on in her life, Loynaz lived in a different house in the same neighborhood. Her mother wanted each of her children to have a university degree. Because Loynaz did not know what to select as a career, her mother decided on law. At the age of twenty-four, in 1927, Loynaz graduated from the University of Havana with a doctoral degree in civil law. She became a real estate lawyer, and she had a successful practice until 1961, when she retired. Although she liked the study of law, she did not enjoy practicing it. By her own account, having to talk in front of the magistrates made her nervous. Nevertheless, due to her professionalism as a lawyer, in 1944, she received the Orden González Lanuza prize.

Loynaz married twice but never had any children. At the age of thirty-five, in 1937, she first married her cousin, Enrique Quesada y Loynaz, whom she later divorced in 1943 because he could not tolerate either her commitment to poetry or her fame. She married a second time, in 1946, a journalist from the Canary Islands, Pablo Alvarez de Cañas, who decided to leave Cuba in 1961 for political reasons; when he returned in 1972 he was ill and died in 1974. Loynaz never agreed with his reasons for leaving the island, and she remained in Cuba during and after Castro's revolution, even though she did not necessarily agree with all of the principles of the revolution. According to her, the daughter of a liberator will never have a good reason to leave the motherland. Her own sense of patriotism was very much embedded in her family's involvement in Cuban history.

She loved to travel, and she had the chance to visit Turkey, Syria, Libya, Palestine, and Egypt. While in Egypt in 1929, she was impressed by Luxor's beauty and wrote a long poem, "Carta de amor a Tut-Ank-Amon" (Love letter to Tut-Ank-Amon), in which she expressed all her passion for knowledge and her love of history and culture. In 1937 she visited the United States and Mexico, and during 1946–1947 she traveled through South America. Loynaz was aware of her privileged social condition compared to other women in Cuba. According to one source, "In 1903, 70% of the women's population were servants. In 1907, among all the professionals, only 12 were women. In 1919, 50% of the women workers were servants; 33% worked in the tobacco industry; 10% in other services, and 5% in agricultural jobs" (Randall 1971, 6).

Loynaz took advantage of her social position in order to become a poet. She forged her own personal and ethical values and challenged any established rules and social patterns. As Bárbara, her alter ego in *Jardín* indicates, she aimed to unfold herself infinitely without breaking, without losing herself in the middle. As was the case for many other literary women of her time, being privileged did not mean overcoming the rule of a patriarchal society: miscommunication and solitude represented some of the main obstacles she had to deal with during her life. She fought against those problems in her writing by elaborating a system of metaphors that illuminated her own understanding of women's restrictive position in society. According to her, women articulate for themselves a kind of mysticism that allows them to fight patriarchal rigidity through the fluidity of water that infuses nature as well as one's own imagination. Thus, Loynaz anticipated some of French philosopher Luce Irigaray's theories concerning feminine writing. Her poems in *Juegos de agua* (Water Games, 1947) represent these ideas. Among her poetic productions, a long poem entitled "Canto a la mujer estéril" (Song to the Sterile Woman, 1937) stands out. Her collections of poetry include *Versos*

(Verses, 1938), *poemas sin nombre* (Poems without a Name, 1955), *Ultimos días de una casa* (Last Days of a House, 1958), and *Poemas náufragos* (Castaway Poems, 1993).

Loynaz is a complex figure—an intellectual, a woman searching for her own liberation from dictatorships and upper-class conventions, and someone deeply rooted in the ethical values of her ancestral identity. Loynaz was recognized in Cuba and Spain during the years previous to the 1959 revolution with numerous awards for her own poetry. In 1947 she received the Alfonso X El Sabio cross from the Spanish minister of culture in Madrid. In 1948 Cuban President Ramón Grau San Martín awarded her the Carlos Manuel Céspedes cross and bestowed on her the Mariana Grajales prize, one of the most prestigious prizes given to female benefactors on the island. Even the Vatican recognized Alvarez de Cañas and Loynaz for their work in favor of the Salesian order. The same year, an homage was organized in her honor at the University of Havana, and in Rome she was elected honorary member of the Poetry International Society. In 1950 she became an honorary member of the Institute of Hispanic Culture in Madrid. In 1951 she was recognized as the "adopted daughter" of the city of Tenerife in the Canary Islands. In 1956, at the age of fifty-four, she was elected to the National Academy of Arts and Letters of Havana. Spanish professor of Latin American literature and prominent literary historian Federico de Onís invited her in 1952 to give a scholarly talk and read her poetry at Columbia University. In 1959 she was elected a member of the Cuban Academy of Language. During the following years, Loynaz remained culturally active in Cuba, writing and giving lectures. In 1968 she was chosen to be a member of the Spanish Academy of Language. Fidel Castro's government named her president of the Cuban Academy of Language, and the organization was housed in her personal residence.

Loynaz maintained a friendship with many important literary figures, among them Gabriela Mistral, Teresa de la Parra, and **Lydia Cabrera**. The Spanish poets Federico García Lorca and Juan Ramón Jiménez stayed in her home when they traveled to Havana.

Loynaz also wrote *Un verano en Tenerife* (A Summer in Tenerife, 1958) and several essays compiled in *Ensayos* (Essays, 1996), *Confesiones de Dulce María Loynaz* (Confessions, 1993), *Fe de vida* (Testimony of My Life, 1994), and *Cartas que no se extraviaron* (Unlost Letters, 1997). She was a regular contributor to the Spanish newspaper *ABC*, as well as to several Cuban and Mexican newspapers: *El Diario de la Marina* (Navy newspaper), *Social* (Social), *Grafos* (Graphos), *Revista cubana* (Cuban Review), *Revista bimestre cubana* (Cuban Bimestrial Review), *Orígenes* (Origins), and *Excélsior* (Excelsior). In 1987 she was awarded the Cuban National Prize for Literature. In 1984 she was nominated for the Cervantes Prize, an honor she later received in 1992.

Further Reading

Araujo, N. "Nature and Imagination: The Bestiary of Dulce María Loynaz." In *The Reordering of Culture: Latin America, the Caribbean and Canada in the Hood*, edited by Alvina Ruprecht, 187–98. Ottawa: Carleton University Press, 1995.

Behar, Ruth. "Dulce María Loynaz: A Woman Who No Longer Exists." *Michigan Quarterly Review* 36, no. 4 (1997): 529–37.

Horno-Delgado, Asunción. *Margen acuático: Dulce María Loynaz*. Madrid: Júcar, 1998.

Randall, Margaret. *Mujeres en revolución*. Havana, Cuba: Ciencias Sociales, 1971.

Rodríguez, Ileana. "Dulce María Loynaz: Garden/Nation—*Parva Domus: Magna Quies*." In *House/Garden/Nation*, 88–107. Durham: Duke University Press, 1994.

Smith, Verity. "Dwarfed by Snow White: Feminist Revisions of Fairy Tale Discourse in the Narrative of Luisa María Bombal and Dulce María Loynaz." In *Feminist Readings on Spanish and Latin-American Literature*, edited by L. P. Condé and S. M. Hart, 137–49. Lewiston, N.Y.: Edwin Mellen Press, 1991.

West, Alan. "Dulce María Loynaz: The House Where the Nation Dreams." In *Tropics of History: Cuba Imagined*, 85–105. Westport, Conn.: Bergin & Garvey, 1997.

Asunción Horno-Delgado

ROSA LUNA
(June 20, 1937–June 13, 1993)
Uruguay: Dancer

Rosa Amelia Luna, who in later years would become not only a popular artist dedicated to the dance of the *candombe*, but also a cultural icon of the Uruguayan people, was born in Montevideo, Uruguay, in a *conventillo*, or tenement house called Medio Mundo (Half-World).

She was the second daughter of a single woman, Ceferina Luna, known as La Chunga, a laundrywoman who with her low-paying job tried to feed her children, but seven of them died of malnutrition and its effects. Luna survived and grew up in the small room without amenities that housed her large family. In the tenement houses in Montevideo lived poor people, especially blacks and immigrants. The *conventillo* had a large, open central yard where at night the drums—*tamboriles*—were played and people danced to the rhythm of the Afro-Uruguayan *candombe*.

Rosa Luna. Photo by Diario El País. Courtesy of
Aída Gelbtrunk and María Cristina Burgueño.

Luna's schooling was brief but long enough for her to suffer racism
when the mother of a classmate protested her daughter having to sit
next to a black girl. At the age of nine, her stepfather sent her to work
as a maid in rich households where she was exploited and subjected to
sexual harassment. Racial discrimination in Uruguay, a country where 5
percent of the population has African roots, was widespread but fell
short of segregation. When Luna was born in 1937, the magazine *Nuestra
raza* (Our Race) published an article stating, "It is written in the constitution and other laws that racial equality for all citizens is a right . . . [but
there is] a group formed by free men who are marginalized by society
through prejudice, denying them even education" (Pereda Valdés 1965,
189).

A myth of Uruguayan identity, expressed through the *candombe*,
started to bud when Luna, still under twenty, began performing as a
vedette dancer in the Uruguayan carnival, the most popular celebration
in the country. Her debut was with the group Los Zorros Negros (The
Black Foxes). Then she joined another group called *Palán Palán*, and she
finally became a member of a *comparsa*, or group, named Fantasía Negra
(Black Fantasy). Years later she had her own *candombe* group, Comparsa

Afro Oriental (Afro-Uruguayan Group), and she founded several others (Luna and Abirad 1988, 40).

Candombe, the Afro-Uruguayan music and dance, is one of the few real folk expressions of Uruguay. Integral to the *candombe* are the *comparsas* or *sociedades de negros* (black societies), groups of dancers and drummers. The *comparsas* include both black and white people, known as *lubolos* because they paint their faces black. The group includes drums, several colonial personages, and the *vedette* (a product of the French influence in Uruguay), which was added in the 1950s to the *comparsa*. Luna was the most popular of them.

The *llamadas* (literally "calls")—a parade of *comparsas*—are the most important, sensual, and colorful manifestation of African culture in Uruguay. They are held during carnivals in a neighborhood called Barrio Reus al Sur. They attract crowds of all ethnicities and social classes. It is in this context that Luna's definition of herself as a *candombera* (*candombe* performer) should be viewed. It is more than a dance: "To be a *candombera* you have to live, sleep, and smile, and cry. You have to love the people, be clear, sincere. And feel what you do. If not you are not a *candombera*" (Luna and Abirad 1988, 106). In this definition, it is possible to find most of the elements that made Luna a cultural icon and a symbol of Uruguayan identity. Luna embodies the fact that the masses, no matter what their ethnicity, despite poverty and without access to education, continue to fight to maintain a dream of a happiness that seems to be impossible.

Luna defined herself by expressing her feelings of sympathy and love to the people, and she transmitted vital strength from her big smile and her large body, with its energy and sensuality, as she danced. By being herself and taking her place in the *comparsa* among the blacks and the poor people, she became a figure in which the popular classes could recognize themselves and where they found moments of pleasurable respite. Luna commented, "Through dancing I relieve myself from the chains of sorrow, necessity, and oppression" (Luna and Abirad 1988, 47).

In her youth she grew from *carnavalera* (woman of the carnival) to "woman of the night." In fending off an attacking man, Luna killed him with a knife at the Café Antequera. She was not jailed, because of the circumstances of the incident, but she was afraid of how she would be received and did not perform in the carnival for some time. However, she could not resist her temperament and she began to dance again, not as an artist but as an ordinary person, in a *comparsa* that was participating in a *corso*, a type of eclectic carnival parade. There is something very engaging about a person who can face adversity and be able to laugh in the worst of circumstances. That capacity was evident in Luna who, despite her tragedy, found a medium to give joy to others and gratify herself through dance. Perhaps this was one of the reasons why many people have said that "she did represent us all."

Luna continued dancing in the carnival and overcoming other obstacles, and her popularity among the people grew until she was transformed into a living myth. She understood and accepted the phenomenon naturally: "They see me like the goddess I am not. And they offer me love, which I return" (Luna and Abirad 1988, 55).

She also took part in a radio program dedicated to the carnival, performed in theater productions and café concerts, wrote articles in newspapers about a large variety of themes, authored poems, and with her husband as a coauthor wrote an autobiography entitled colloquially *Sin tanga y sin tongo* (Without G-string and Without Lies, 1988).

Many years after her failed first marriage, she married Raúl Abirad, although he was twenty-four years younger than she was and white. The differences between them extended to religion, because Luna practiced a personal and private one, praying to a God whom she envisioned as "very poor" and "full of wisdom, kind, full of charity, and at the same time, human" (Luna and Abirad 1988, 62). They had an adopted child whom they affectionately called Rulito (Little Curl). Luna was thus a housewife and a mother, like any ordinary woman. She even traveled— somewhat against her will—because her artistic activity took her to Canada, Australia, the United States, and various countries in South America. It was in Canada, while performing, that she suffered a fatal heart attack on June 13, 1993, one week short of fifty-six.

A body can be a metaphor for social realities, feelings, necessities, desires, and their fulfillment. Luna's body was an exemplary symbol and metaphor. She had a dark black color. She was more than six feet tall, but her high heels and her *vedette*'s crown of feathers made her almost seven feet tall. All this made her "touch the outer layers of the atmosphere," as someone remarked who saw her fleetingly in his twenties, feeling, as never before, the banality of the ground on which he stood (personal interview with Demasi).

Luna gave that impression because her body had, like a prehistoric Venus, an eroticism that was based not solely on sexuality itself, but was linked to nature through its vitality, joy, and generosity. She had "enormous, unbelievable breasts" (Dubra 1997, 164), she had an ample mouth full of brilliant white teeth which was often posed in a scintillating smile, and she had an "elegant air," a heritage from her father, as she often proudly said.

Many stories about her can be found among the Uruguayan people. One story describes her performing in a very modest neighborhood. Many people waited to see her, but not many could afford the entrance fee. However, she produced a "miracle" when, after her performance at the club, she danced in the street for the neighborhood. She had a truck's headlights turned on, surrounded herself with her drums, and started a celebration for the poor people who loved carnival but could not afford to buy tickets. She gave them her beauty, her marvelous rhythm and movement, and she invited them to dance with her, weaving one by one the invisible strands that expanded the colorful tapestry of her legend (Escuder).

From her humble roots, Luna rose to a mythological status, of which she was well aware: "Do I represent a mystic or a tradition of ordinary Uruguayans? Or is my dance the expression of the dreams of freedom of the blacks, that all Uruguayans have embraced?" (Luna and Abirad 1988, 47). The myth took on different names or epithets: she was called Queen Luna, Asphalt Vedette, African Queen, Living Myth, Nocturnal Queen, African Goddess, and of the People.

At her death a crowd of over 300,000 accompanied her casket through the streets of Montevideo. Luna, as nobody else, managed to keep the unanimous love and respect of others, despite varied opinions and perspectives. Luna, with her greatness of character, was the first woman to emerge in Uruguayan society from the margins of poverty and blackness. She contributed to the acknowledgement of and respect for the African elements of Uruguayan culture and identity. Moreover, she opened this path for the marginalized people she represented, who had never before been accepted by the cultivated elite, by rising above cultural barriers and prejudices.

Further Reading

Bonilla, Oscar. "Candombe: Un ritmo ancestral." *Revista Américas* 47 (November-December 1995): 45–49.

Demasi, Carlos. Personal interview. September 10, 1998.

Dubra, Adela. "Rosa Luna. Vivir a lo loco." In *Mujeres uruguayas. El lado femenino de nuestra historia*. Montevideo, Uruguay: Fundacion Banco de Boston y Alfaguaro, 1997.

Escuder, Leonor. "Rosa Luna en la fraternidad." Unpublished short story.

Galloza, Rubén. "A modo de prólogo . . ." In *El candombe: Sus orígenes, su historia, sus proyecciones*, edited by Tomás Olivera Chirimini and Juan Antonio Varese. Montevideo, Uruguay: El Galeón, 1992.

Luna, Rosa, and Raúl Abirad. *Sin tanga y sin tongo*. Montevideo, Uruguay: Proyección del Taller ed., 1988.

Olivera Chirimini, Tomás, and Juan Antonio Varese, eds. *El candombe: Sus orígenes, su historia, sus proyecciones*. Montevideo, Uruguay: El Galeón.

Pereda Valdés, Aldenfonso. *El negro en el Uruguay: Pasado y presente*. Montevideo: Revista del Instituto Histórico y Geográfico del Uruguay, 1965.

María Cristina Burgueño

MAE MENININHA DA GANTOIS. *See* Maria Escolástica da Conceição Nazaré.

RIGOBERTA MENCHÚ TUM
(January 4, 1959–   )
Guatemala: Human Rights Activist

Rigoberta Menchú Tum is a Guatemalan Maya-Quiché Indian whose dauntless crusade to end the human rights violations perpetrated against the indigenous people of her country has led her on a trajectory from peasant to national symbol to international campaigner for peace and spokesperson for the human rights of all oppressed peoples of the world. Her diligent activism earned her the Nobel Peace Prize in 1992 (the first indigenous person and the youngest person ever to receive this award), and she played an instrumental role in the signing of the 1996 Guatemalan Peace Accord which ended thirty-six years of internal armed conflict between military and guerrilla forces.

The sixth of the nine children of Vicente Menchú Pérez and Juana Tum K'otojá, Rigoberta was born in Chimel, a village in the highland region of Guatemala's northwest. Virtually unknown outside this altiplano region, Rigoberta achieved symbolic notoriety on January 31, 1980, when her father, a founding member of the indigenous and Ladino Committee for Peasant Unity (Comité de Unidad Campesina, or CUC), and twenty-seven others protesting human rights violations at the Spanish embassy in Guatemala were burned to death by the Guatemalan army. ("Ladino" means here any individual, whether indigenous or of mixed white and Indian extraction or mestizo, who renounces Mayan heritage to assimilate to dominant culture). Fearing for her own life, Rigoberta fled to Mexico, where she began more than a decade of self-imposed exile, yet continued, from abroad, to organize Guatemala's indigenous peasantry and advocate for their rights.

Herself a member of the CUC, early in 1982 Menchú joined a delegation of other Guatemalans likewise exiled in Mexico who journeyed throughout Europe and the United States to draw attention to the plight of Guatemala's peasants. It was during her stay in Paris that Arturo Taracena Arriola, then a representative of Guatemala's opposition movement in Europe, introduced Menchú to Elisabeth Burgos-Debray, a Vene-

Rigoberta Menchú Tum. Courtesy of Fundación Rigoberta Menchú Tum.

zuelan ethnographer to whom Menchú recounted the story of her life during a week-long series of interviews. Articulated in rudimentary Spanish—a language Menchú professed to have spoken for only three years (Burgos-Debray 1984, xi)—Menchú's account verbalized, in a direct and compelling manner, her family's existence against the inauspicious backdrop of economic, social, and political prejudice endured by Guatemala's indigenous people, in essence surviving conquest since 1492. Especially since the CIA-backed overthrow of populist-supported president Jacobo Arbenz Guzmán in 1954, Guatemala's history had been characterized by military commanded governmental oppression, political violence, human rights violations, and an increasing level of confrontation between the government and armed opposition groups.

In the course of narrating her life to Elisabeth Burgos, Menchú intertwined two distinct voices. One voice reflects at length upon her people's religious customs and cultural protocol. Menchú's other voice articulates centuries of exploitation. Often the two voices intersect, as when Menchú recounts her family's agricultural subsistence. In Chimel and its surroundings, her family cultivated corn, a staple of the indigenous diet and a principal player in their nature-embedded rituals and Mayan creation myths. However, unable to make a living solely on their altiplano crops, every year the family had to travel, sometimes for "two nights and a day," in a tarpaulin-covered truck that took "about forty people," together with their dogs, chickens, and cats, to a coffee-growing plantation on the Pacific coast. "By the end of the journey, the smell—the filth of people and animals—was unbearable" (Menchú 1984, 21; hereafter all quotes come from this source). Like most Maya, Menchú began working as a coffee picker when she was eight; two years later, she was picking seventy pounds a day and working "like an adult" (34–35): "I never had a childhood." On the plantation, Menchú became aware of her family's plight: "That's when my consciousness was born" (34).

Menchú also discovered prejudice and inequality in the reputedly modern Guatemala City where, not yet thirteen years old, she went to work as a maid, hoping to find better working conditions and to learn Spanish. When she returned to Chimel, she became a catechist instructing others about a Catholic religion tinged with Mayan beliefs and shaped by their political struggle. Her community had come into contact with missionaries of Catholic Action who promoted the teachings of the Bible in Guatemala's highlands. Menchú and her community identified themselves with Moses, Judith, and David, who fought unjust circumstances and despotic regimes. Menchú declared that her community embraced Catholic doctrines discriminately, forgoing beliefs that "taught us to be passive, to be a dormant people" (121).

Menchú explained to Burgos that her community's problems with the government began with Ladino landowners. For over twenty years, Vicente Menchú fought in the capital to retain his land legally; however, landowners and government Ladinos "had made a deal to take the peasants' land away from them" (103), commissioning military soldiers to throw the peasants out of their homes. Army henchmen—oftentimes "Ladinized" Indians themselves—looted or destroyed the peasants' belongings and killed their loved animals and pets. Ultimately, according to Menchú, her people organized into unions, learned Spanish, informed themselves about politics, joined forces with their poor Ladino counterparts, and began to demand and defend their human rights. They all realized "that the root of our problems lay in the ownership of the land" (166).

In 1977 the CUC was born, and the persecution of the Menchú family began as a backlash of their active participation in the union. Labeled Communists by the government, the Menchús felt hunted in their own Chimel. Rigoberta's father was kidnapped, imprisoned, and tortured several times. Petrocinio, her teenage brother, was betrayed for fifteen quetzales (which in 1979 equalled U.S. $15) by a member of the community and kidnapped as well. After torturing him for sixteen days, army soldiers lined up Petrocinio with other tortured people in the plaza of the village of Chajul and "poured petrol on them; and then the soldiers set fire to each one of them" (179). Four months later, Vicente Menchú died at the Spanish embassy. Shortly thereafter, Rigoberta's mother Juana, a peasant organizer herself, was kidnapped, repeatedly raped, and tortured by provincial high-ranking army officers. She was left to die on a hillside, and her body was consumed by buzzards and wild dogs.

The year after relating her life to Burgos, Menchú's twenty-four hours of tape-recorded conversations, transcribed and edited, were presented by the ethnographer in manuscript form as an entry to Cuba's Casa de las Américas (House of the Americas) literary contest; the text won in the category of best testimonial narrative. That year, Menchú's account was published in book form, summoning international attention to Guatemala's gruesome civil war and commanding respect abroad for Menchú's voice. By the turn of the decade, *I, Rigoberta Menchú* was fundamental to the multicultural canon, and its English version was adopted as a core textbook in campuses across North America and taught in courses transversing the spectrum of the humanities. To date, Menchú's testimony has been translated into more than ten languages and has sold over 500,000 copies worldwide. In *Crossing Borders* (1998), Menchú explains her active involvement in the Unitary Representation of the Guatemalan Opposition (RUOG) and its lobbying of the United Nations. In the original Spanish edition—*Rigoberta: La nieta de los mayas* (Rigoberta, Granddaughter of the Mayas)—the collaboration of Dante Liano, a Guatemalan writer and longtime friend of Menchú, and Gianni Minna, an Italian journalist, is explicitly credited on the cover as well as in her acknowledgements. Verso's English edition (1998), however, expunges altogether the collaborators' role—and Menchú's acknowledgments of it—in what has been labeled by Guatemalan author Arturo Arias an "act of piracy" and "intellectual theft" (personal communication, 2000).

Menchú's work at the United Nations led to the UN's recognition of the Working Group on Indigenous Peoples (which Menchú coordinated), the formation of the Sub-Commission on the Prevention of Discrimination and Protection of Ethnic Minorities, and the declaration of 1993 as International Year of the World's Indigenous People. On the Guatemalan front, Menchú cooperated with the activities of Guatemalan peasant, women, Maya, and human rights organizations and was a presiding participant in the Second Continental Congress, 500 Years of Indigenous, Black, and Popular Resistance, held in Quezaltenango in 1991.

Rigoberta Menchú's activism has been acknowledged by the West. Her supporters have conferred upon her multiple honorary doctorate degrees and humanitarian awards—including France's Legion of Honor and UNESCO's Education for Peace prize—and she has served as a goodwill ambassador to both UNESCO and the UN. In 1992 the Nobel Peace Prize was awarded to Menchú in recognition of her "work for social justice and ethnocultural reconciliation based on respect for the rights of indigenous peoples."

With the proceeds from the Nobel Peace Prize and the support of numerous international institutions and several foreign governments, the Nobel laureate established the Rigoberta Menchú Tum Foundation. Its mission is "the defense and promotion of human rights, particularly the rights of Indigenous Peoples; the active support of the struggle for peace and the promotion of the rights and values of Indigenous Peoples" (Rigoberta Menchú Foundation 1999). The foundation has carried out hundreds of projects in the areas of human and civil rights, education, health care, and community development, including housing, urban planning, and agricultural production. In May 1993, Menchú convened the First International Indigenous Summit in Chimaltenango, Guatemala; over 100 leaders and representatives of indigenous organizations across the world were present. On December 4, 1996, in Oslo City Hall—the same building where she received the Nobel Peace Prize in 1992—Menchú witnessed the realization of a long-held dream: the signing of a peace accord that established a truce between Guatemala's military and rebel forces, and the UN's appointment of a Historical Clarification Commission (CEH) to investigate the human rights violations that took place during the thirty-six-year-old armed conflict between the nation's military and rebel forces.

Menchú also has detractors in the West. Some have found her controversial, chiefly the result—her supporters affirm—of efforts made by the Guatemalan government to discredit her by linking her to the National Revolutionary Unity of Guatemala (URNG), although Menchú repeatedly has denied being a guerrilla. In the early 1990s, her most vocal U.S. foe, Stanford University professor Dinesh D'Souza, formulated his defamatory campaign of Menchú in *Illiberal Education: The Politics of Race and Sex on Campus* (1991). His best-selling book brands Menchú as a "socialist" and a "Marxist," belittles significant episodes of her narrative, and contests the prominence given her book by the multicultural canon. Menchú's latest adverse critic is David Stoll, who studied anthropology at Stanford when the requirement of Menchú's text in humanities courses was being challenged. His 1999 book, *Rigoberta Menchú and the Story of All Poor Guatemalans*, disputes the veracity of significant portions of Menchú's book, suggests links between Marxist guerrillas and Menchú, and contends that her book served the Guerrilla Army of the Poor (EGP) to promote abroad the cause of the Guatemalan left. Stoll's challenge has been described as a debate between historical truth and narrative truth. Latin Americanists identify Menchú's text as a testimony (Jara and Vidal, 1986), drawn by the urgency of a situation: war, oppression, and revolution (Yúdice 1991, 17). Testimonial writing is a weapon of resistance.

In Guatemala's case, resistance became a necessity for the survival of the Maya people. The United Nations CEH report, released in February 1999, recorded 669 massacres and concluded that more than 200,000 people had died or disappeared as a result of counterinsurgency operations executed between 1981 and 1983.

Currently, in addition to her work at the foundation, Menchú heads the Indigenous Initiative for Peace, an international network of indigenous leaders.

Further Reading

Burgos-Debray, Elisabeth. "Introduction." *I, Rigoberta Menchú: An Indian Woman in Guatemala*, edited by Elisabeth Burgos-Debray and translated by Ann Wright, xi–xxi. London: Verso, 1984.

Carey-Webb, Allen, and Stephen Benz, eds. *Teaching and Testimony: Rigoberta Menchú and the North American Classroom*. Albany: State University of New York Press, 1996.

Jara, René, and Hernán Vidal. "Prólogo." In *Testimonio y literatura*, 1–5. Minneapolis, Minn.: Institute for the Study of Ideologies and Literature, 1986.

Lovell, W. George. "Surviving Conquest: The Maya of Guatemala in Historical Perspective." *Latin American Research Review* 23, no. 2 (1988): 25–37.

Menchú Tum, Rigoberta. *Crossing Borders*, translated by Ann Wright. London: Verso, 1998.

———. *I, Rigoberta Menchú: An Indian Woman in Guatemala*, edited by Elisabeth Burgos-Debray and translated by Ann Wright. London: Verso, 1984.

Rigoberta Menchú Foundation. http://ourworld.compuserve/homepages/rmtpaz/Menu_eng.htm. August 14, 1999.

United Nations Commission for Historical Clarification. "Guatemala Memory of Silence (Tz'inil Na'tab'al): Report of the Commission for Historical Clarification—Conclusions and Recommendations." http://hrdata.aaas.org/ceh/report/english/toc.html. American Association for the Advancement of Science and Human Rights Program. February 24, 2000.

Yúdice, George. "*Testimonio* and Postmodernism: Whom Does Testimonial Writing Represent?" *Latin American Perspectives* 18, no. 3 (Summer 1991): 15–31.

Zimmerman, Marc. *Literature and Resistance in Guatemala: Textual Modes and Cultural Politics from El Señor Presidente to Rigoberta Menchú*. Vols. 1 and 2. Athens: Ohio University Center for International Studies, 1995.

Rose McEwen

FANNY MIKEY

(December 26, 1931–   )

Argentina/Colombia: Actress

Fanny Mikey, a well-known actress in Spanish American artistic circles, was born in Argentina and eventually became a Colombian citizen. She has lived in Colombia since 1959, where she has worked not only as an actress, but also as a theatrical manager, promoting the performing arts in Colombia and abroad.

When World War II ended, postwar drama written and performed in Europe was reaching the stage in Argentina. Two types of theater could be found: the commercial type, represented in the theater district on Corrientes Avenue, and the independent theater. Thanks to the so-called Argentine independent theater, American playwrights such as Arthur Miller and Eugene O'Neill became available to the Southern Cone audiences.

As a child, Mikey's father used to read novels and short stories to her. When she was nine years old, he took her to watch the great comic actor Pepe Arias. From that moment on, theater and life became one for her. At the age of fifteen, she became a member of a prominent Jewish club. Lectures were given there, and important personalities from all over the world were invited. Cinema, shows of various kinds, and theater were all a part of the club's vast cultural activity. The first time director Leo Fiber saw Mikey, he invited her onto the stage to improvise. After Mikey improvised a scene in which she represented a woman in pain, looking for a job, and crying for her children, Fiber asked the fifteen-year-old to stay with the group. He invited her to perform in a William Saroyan play, and she accepted. Soon the young actress decided to study dramatic arts formally at the Argentine Hebrew Society, while continuing to perform with the group. Mikey attended classes taught by Heidy Crilla and Emilio Satanovsky. Crilla, a professional who trained Norma Aleandro and Cipe Lincovsky, gave Mikey yet another opportunity to act when she offered her a role in her version of Alejandro Casona's *La dama del alba* (The Lady of the Dawn). Mikey also worked under director Reynaldo D'Amore at a time when many great actors and directors were at the society, including Roberto Durán, Juan Carlos Gené, and Pedro I. Martínez.

When the society banned one of D'Amore's plays, Mikey considered making a trip to Peru to seek better fortune. Instead, she married Gastón Djian, the man who would finally force her to decide between marriage and acting. She chose marriage and subsisted for two years as a housewife. When the situation became unbearable, she made the painful decision to leave her husband. Mikey left home to go back to what she most wanted in life: to be on stage.

After an audition at the Odeón in Buenos Aires, she played the title role in Federico García Lorca's *Yerma*. For ten months, she worked as an actress at night and worked at a plastic factory during the day. Around that time, she was finally able to begin to dedicate herself full-time to acting. It was then that she encountered her old friend Pedro I. Martínez once again. Martínez was visiting Argentina while working for the new national television in Colombia. They fell in love, but he had to return to Colombia. One year later, Mikey boarded a ship in Valparaíso and landed in Buenaventura, a Colombian port on the Pacific Coast.

In Cali, along with Martínez and director Enrique Buenaventura, Mikey focused all her energy and efficacy on promoting cultural activities in the city. By that time, she was acting and helping to coordinate events. She started her professional activities in Colombia with the Cali Experimental Theater (TEC). In the early 1960s, the Art Festival in Cali, the most important event in Colombia, featured music, dance, and the plastic arts, but the performances by the TEC, directed by Buenaventura, were undoubtedly the festival's highlight. Mikey's work with the TEC was of great importance for her personal life, as well as for the numerous plays performed by the group. During her time in Cali, she played a tragic character in García Lorca's *La casa de Bernarda Alba* (The House of Bernarda Alba) and a character from the Colombian picaresque in *A la diestra de Dios Padre* (At the Right Hand of God the Father) by Tomás Carrasquilla. She went back to Argentina in 1967, although one year later she returned to Colombia.

During the 1970s, she joined the Bogotá Popular Theater (TPB) and helped build one of the first professional theatrical groups in Colombia. In Bogotá, theater director and actor Jorge Alí Triana, who was working in a Carlo Goldoni play, invited Mikey to be the protagonist. She accepted, and once again she found herself working toward establishing the TPB as one of today's most important Colombian groups. With Goldoni, Mikey was able to keep the play running for months, in Bogotá and in other major cities. From the 1970s, there has been a proliferation of groups, festivals, and different theatrical companies in Colombia. Mikey remained a part of the movement until she finally grew tired of the politics involved in theatrical circles.

After the TPB, she decided it was time for a new project. This time she chose a different genre: the *café concierto* (a type of variety program).

Mikey is the founder of La Gata Caliente (Hot Cat), the first Colombian *café concert*. On a small stage she mounted *Mamá Colombia* (Momma Colombia), a work that re-creates the political situation affecting the country. During her frequent visits to Buenos Aires, she had been able to see what artists like Nacha Guevara and Cipe Lincovsky were performing, and she brought back new material that she performed as a solo act. The result was a play called *Óiganme* (Hear Me), a collage of humor, political satire, and poetry. This time, Mikey was in charge of everything from planning the spectacle to performing what she had created. This was also one of the happiest periods of her life. In addition to being in charge of everything, she was free to perform anywhere in the country. After four years, however, she realized that she could not continue forever as a *café concert* performer.

During the 1980s, with new ideas and ambitions, Mikey set her sights elsewhere. The foundation of the National Theater (1978) was her idea, and today, more than twenty years later, it has three locations in Bogotá. In 1978 she proposed to a group of friends the idea of rebuilding an old, forgotten movie theater. Eventually, it was transformed into a modern stage theater. In December 1981, the first play to be performed was *El rehén* (The Hostage) by Brendan Beham. Mikey had finally achieved her goal: the creation of a setting where she could be in control, free from aesthetic and political discussions, where actors could be independent and earn a salary according to their efforts and hard work. In 1982 a first performance in Colombia of Edward Albee's *¿Quién le teme a Virginia Woolf* (Who's Afraid of Virginia Woolf) was staged. The performance, a major triumph, played to a full house for seven months. Both critics and audiences came to recognize the quality of the acting as well as the setting. The performances drew to a close when Mikey's health began to deteriorate. The bitterness of the role had finally affected her will and her heart. Her cardiac spasms prevented the play from continuing. From then on, the repertoire at the National Theater has included modern stage plays, as well as dramas written in Colombia.

Once again, Mikey would seek a new challenge, this time taking on the creation of the Bogotá Latin American Theater Festival, a major cultural event that attracts theater groups from all over the world, not only from Spain and Latin America. Companies from over thirty countries and five continents have participated in the festival, including such luminaries as the Royal Shakespeare Company, El Piccolo Teatro from Milan, and the Canadian group Carbono 14. The festival features theatrical representations, seminars, and workshops, and it has taken place every other year since 1988. Today it is recognized as one of the most important cultural events of its kind.

In 1994 Mikey joined forces with Jorge Alí Triana and Tomás Darío

Zapata to form the Grupo Colombia Ltda., a film production company whose credits include *Edipo alcalde* (Oedipus the Mayor).

Mikey is also responsible for initiating numerous spectacles on a large scale, such as inviting the Italian tenor Luciano Pavarotti to sing at the largest stadium in Bogotá. She has participated as an actress, producer, director, juror, and special guest in such festivals as the World Festival in Paris, the International Festival of Drama in Caracas, the Grand Mexico City Festival, and the Avignon Festival. As a director, she has worked in Madrid, Cadiz, Maribor, Buenos Aires, and at the Odéon in Paris. Her efforts to improve cultural activities in Colombia are numerous. She was in charge of the TEC's administration, directed five versions of the Cali Art Festival, and encouraged the creation of cultural weeks in different Colombian cities. She was also the executive director for the Bogotá Popular for seven years. Mikey remains one of the most outstanding figures in Colombian theater today.

Further Reading

Fundación Teatro Nacional. *Cincuenta años de vida artística*. Santafé de Bogotá: Fundación Teatro Nacional, 1996.

Villamil, María Elvira. "VI Festival Iberoamericano de Teatro de Bogotá." *Hispania* 81, no. 3 (1998): 647–48.

María Elvira Villamil and Steven Torres

PATRIA, MINERVA, AND MARÍA TERESA MIRABAL

(Patria, February 27, 1924–November 25, 1960; Minerva, March 13, 1926–November 25, 1960; María Teresa, October 15, 1935–November 25, 1960)

Dominican Republic: Political Activists

Founders of a resistance movement against a repressive regime in the Dominican Republic, Patria, Minerva, and María Teresa Mirabal Reyes, with their sister Bélgica Mirabal (Dedé), were the daughters of Enrique Mirabal and Mercedes (Chea) Reyes. They lived most of their lives in Ojo de Agua in the Dominican Republic. Rafael Leonidas Trujillo's government caused their death on November 25, 1960, six months before Trujillo was assassinated, which ended the Trujillo Era.

Enrique and Chea Mirabal married in 1923. At that time the United States was controlling the Dominican Republic as part of a program, imposed by President Theodore Roosevelt, that justified military intervention in Latin American countries where political instability would impede the payment of their international debts. The intervention in the Dominican Republic, which lasted eight years, from 1916 to 1924, created favorable conditions for the expansion of the U.S. sugar industry. Trujillo became part of the military police of the occupying forces.

In 1929 the Caribbean region was economically affected by the Great Depression in the United States. On the island, Dominicans were discontent with the economic situation, and the government of President Horacio Vásquez was overthrown. This coup was organized by Trujillo and his followers, who helped him become president in 1930.

It is under this political and economical crisis that the Mirabal sisters were born. Because Enrique Mirabal and his family were businessmen, their companies and properties were affected by the U.S. intervention on the island. From early childhood the sisters were exposed to the political resistance discussed constantly at home by family members and close friends.

Trujillo guaranteed the United States at the outset of his regime the same benefits they had received from the island during the occupation, and in so doing he won total support from the U.S. government. Later, Trujillo convinced the United States to let the Dominicans administer their own customhouse. When the petition was granted, commerce became favorable for Trujillo's personal wealth. Trujillo is notorious for his accumulation of an enormous fortune for himself and his family. His family influenced all commerce, industry, and transportation. To become so powerful, Trujillo oppressed the Dominicans, and his regime became known for its cruelty and the boldness of the process by which oppression was implemented.

The Mirabal sisters attended a private Catholic school where they met girls from other parts of the island and heard all kinds of horror stories about Trujillo and his military police. In 1936, when Minerva was ten years old, she heard from a friend, Daisy Ariza, how her father was tortured and killed by Trujillo for conspiring against his government. It was at this moment that Minerva started hating Trujillo's regime and everything he represented.

The Mirabal family witnessed the massacre against Haitians in October 1937. Many Haitians lived in the border zone having been hired by the Dominican government to work in the sugarcane fields. Historians give different reasons for the genocide, but all agree on Trujillo's need for control and his desire to create a whiter nation. More than 20,000 native and ethnic Haitians were killed. This episode adversely affected Trujillo politically in the Dominican Republic and internationally.

During World War II, Trujillo supported the United States and, in the meantime, continued to make himself rich with export profits. Don Enrique Mirabal's business also flourished, and his daughter Dedé left school to help him with the extra work. Patria also left school to marry Pedro González, who opposed Trujillo's regime and became part of the resistance movement. During the 1940s Minerva, equipped with a powerful radio, kept herself informed of the world's political events through news from Cuba and Venezuela. She also learned facts about the Dominican Republic that the citizens of the island did not know because of the strong censorship imposed on the country.

During the Cold War, Trujillo used the fear of international communism to increase his oppression of the Dominican people. It was then that a huge military apparatus, the Military Intelligence Service, was created. On the other hand, Trujillo felt international pressure to construct a more democratic nation. In 1945 the United Nations sent a delegation to the island to investigate the alleged elimination of civil rights. Trujillo was forced to make some concessions to appease international criticism, but two frustrated invasions, intended to overthrow him, made him return to his old tactics of repression and torture.

Trujillo was known not only for his cruelty and greediness, but also for his insatiable womanizing. He organized fancy parties where he would force young women to be his sexual partners. Usually, the women were very young virgins who could not reject him without fearing for their lives and those of their families. In October 1949, the Mirabal family received an invitation to attend one of these parties. Trujillo demanded their presence, especially Minerva's. The party was a dance held at Casa Borinquen in San Cristóbal, where orchestras playing Dominican music, *merengue*, entertained the select group.

The Mirabals attended the party, and Minerva danced with the dictator, all the while rejecting his sexual advances. In so doing, she provoked Trujillo's wrath. Sensing the unsettling events developing from this confrontation, the Mirabals left hurriedly, without Trujillo's consent, aggravating the situation. Even though Enrique Mirabal wrote a letter to Trujillo apologizing for the inappropriate way they had left the party, two days later he, his wife, and Minerva were taken prisoners. The imprisonment and release of members of the Mirabal family were part of the police tactics that resulted in the family's living in constant terror. Eventually, they were isolated and economically ruined. Enrique Mirabal's health deteriorated seriously in prison, and he died in 1953 after having been released.

Trujillo continued to harass Minerva. In 1952 she was accepted as a student by the law school, but the next year her application was rejected.

Patria, Minerva, and María Teresa Mirabal. Courtesy of Dedé Mirabal.

In order to be accepted again, she wrote and read a speech praising Trujillo's regime. Although she received her law degree with honors, the government refused to issue the license required for her to practice as a lawyer. At the university, Minerva met her future husband, Manuel Ta-várez Justo (Manolo), who later fought and died for a democratic Dominican Republic.

Cuba's revolution was a very influential event among the younger generations in Latin America, especially in the Dominican Republic. Minerva and María Teresa and their husbands, Manolo and José Leandro Guzmán Rodriguez, organized a resistance movement against Trujillo. This movement, later known as 14 de mayo (May 14), was based on a democratic ideology. María Teresa and Leandro trained new volunteers in the movement. Patria and Pedro's house was used as a meeting place, and Manolo was the leader of the organization. In January 1960, information about the movement was leaked to the government and all were arrested, except Patria. The women were released, incarcerated, and released again. Among the women arrested, only Sina Cabral was tortured, but it caused such an uproar that it helped prevent future torture of women. Men, however, continued to be tortured and were kept in isolation. They were finally released after Trujillo's death.

Trujillo's government was receiving an incredible amount of pressure from other countries to cease the oppression, and he was becoming an embarrassment to the United States. The Dominican Catholic Church promulgated a Pastoral Letter denouncing the regime's atrocities. Rómulo Betancourt, Venezuela's president, summoned the Latin American countries to unite in condemning Trujillo's government. Trujillo was so enraged that he ordered Betancourt's assassination. The assassination attempt, a failure, brought more pressure to bear against the dictatorship.

Trujillo believed that the Mirabal family was at least partly to blame for what was happening. He started to plan the sisters' assassination, but he wanted it to look like an accident. He ordered the husbands—at this time all three were in jail—moved to a prison in Puerto de Plata. To visit their husbands, the sisters had to traverse a solitary and poorly paved road. All their friends and family knew about the scheme, but nothing could deter the sisters from their weekly visit to their husbands. On November 25, 1960, Patria, Minerva, María Teresa, and their chauffeur, Rufino de la Cruz, were killed in an accident. The bodies showed evidence of torture and strangulation.

The assassination of the Mirabal sisters was the last blow to the Trujillo regime. In May 1961, Trujillo was assassinated. In July 1960, Manolo, Leandro, and Pedro were released, and it was only then that they could verify the rumors they had heard in prison about their wives' deaths. Dedé, the only surviving sister, and Chea, her mother, raised all the children of Patria, Minerva, and María Teresa.

Further Reading

Alvarez, Julia. *In the Time of the Butterflies*. Chapel Hill, N.C.: Algonquin Books, 1994.

Aquino García, Miguel. *Tres heroínas y un tirano*. Santo Domingo, Dominican Republic: Editora Corripio, 1996.

Ferreras, Ramón Alberto. *Las Mirabal*. Santo Domingo, Dominican Republic: Editora Cosmos, 1976.

Galván, William. *Minerva Mirabal: La historia de una heroína*. Santo Domingo, Dominican Republic: Editorial de la UASD, 1982.

Heidi Ann García

CARMEN MIRANDA
(February 9, 1909–August 5, 1955)

Brazil: Actress, Singer

Actress and singer Carmen Miranda is one of the great myths of Brazilian and American popular culture. In the 1940s, Miranda took Hollywood by storm and became one of its best paid stars and most recognizable figures. She was an exuberant, glamorous, and seductive performer. Her outrageous costumes, featuring towering hats of fruit, gave her the name "the Lady in the Tutti-Frutti Hat." A street-smart, witty, and savvy businesswoman, she had a Cinderella-like career until her tragic death from a massive heart attack, induced by a drug overdose, in 1955. Miranda's impact on popular culture has transcended national boundaries. She has become a figure that embodies an exoticized image of the Latin American "other."

Miranda was born Maria Do Carmo Miranda da Cunha in the province of Porto, Portugal. Her uncle, seeing in the newborn a certain Spanish flair, named her Carmen, after the famous protagonist of Georges Bizet's opera. She was born into the family of a strict barber, José Maria Pinto da Cunha, and a hard-working seamstress, Dona Maria Emília Miranda da Cunha. The difficult economic conditions endured by the family in Portugal led them to dream of a better life in the Americas. A few months after Carmen's birth, her father migrated to Rio de Janeiro. A year later, he sent for the rest of the family.

Economic hardship was not easy to leave behind. In Rio, Miranda's mother opened a boarding house in the business section of town to supplement the family's income. Dona Maria served hefty meals for little money to singers, dancers, and poets. Shortly after its opening, the pension became a favorite hangout for struggling artists.

When the Mirandas arrived in Rio, the city was heralded as progressive and cosmopolitan. The crowded boulevards and magnificent beachside neighborhoods of Copacabana and Ipanema made Rio one of the most captivating cities on the continent. On its outskirts rose the precarious houses of immigrant laborers from the struggling northern regions, seeking in the metropolis a chance to make a living. Samba, the popular musical form that would produce some of Brazil's most celebrated singers and songwriters, developed on these hillsides. The young Carmen, seduced by their music and poetry, loved to circulate around the tables in her mother's boarding house listening to their stories and songs.

The Mirandas' economic situation worsened when Olinda, Carmen's eldest sister, caught tuberculosis. At the age of fifteen Miranda took a steady-paying job in a hat store. She became popular among the clientele for her charm and her abilities as an entertainer. She often modeled the latest fashions for the wealthy customers while singing and dancing to popular songs. Miranda gave most of her earnings to her parents, and the little money she kept she used to sustain her addiction to the movies. Her abilities as a singer soon became well known in her neighborhood, and Miranda was routinely asked to sing at parties. Tango had become very popular in Rio, and she interpreted with great style the legendary songs of Argentine superstar Carlos Gardel.

Her father disapproved of the idea of a career in show business. However, economic opportunities for women were very limited at the time, and, in 1928 when Carmen got her first break, she took it and never looked back. That year, Carmen Miranda was introduced to Josué de

Carmen Miranda. Courtesy of Photofest.

Barros, a guitar player and songwriter from the northeastern city of Bahia, who was enchanted by her. Barros is credited for being the first to recognize Miranda's potential to bring samba to the general public. In 1929 Miranda recorded two songs by Barros: "Não va sim bora" (Don't Go Away) and "Se o samba e moda" (If Samba Is Fashionable).

From the beginning, Miranda seemed destined for fame. In her first year as a professional singer, she recorded forty different titles, and within a decade, she had recorded 281 songs in many different musical styles. Miranda's success is a testimony to the golden age of samba, which had achieved considerable market value in a growing economy. Although her voice was not of a wide range, her rhythm and playfulness were irresistible. In the 1930s, radio, which had become common in Brazilian households, spread the samba craze and Miranda's name throughout the country. Miranda became known as the Queen of Samba. The legend of the humble immigrant achieving a life of fame and wealth seemed to have come true: a daughter of Portuguese immigrants had risen to become one of Brazil's most prominent artists, embodying the rhythms that had descended from the shantytowns of Rio and fighting for acceptance among a rising middle class. In 1932, at the crest of her success in Brazil, Miranda embarked on her first international tour, visiting Argentina and Uruguay. She was received by hundreds of fans. On one of her many visits, Miranda met a struggling young actress by the name of Eva Duarte (Evita), the future wife of Argentine leader Juan Domingo Perón (*See* Eva María Duarte de Perón).

By 1935 Miranda was the highest paid singer in Brazil, and she had amassed a small fortune. The increased popularity of samba was further fueled by President Getulio Vargas's cultural politics, centered around Brazil's ethnic identity. Vargas, who rose to power in the Revolution of 1930, proposed a greater acceptance of black and mestizo cultural expressions. Miranda seemed to suit this new national identity as she dressed in the clothes of the bahiana, the African woman carrying fruits to the market, which was a highly charged national symbol. It was this image that Miranda learned to exploit in film. In the 1930s, she made six films; one of them, *Banana da terra* (Brazilian Banana), showed her wearing the Bahiana costume and singing her smash hit, Dorival Caimmi's "O que é que a bahiana tem?" (What Does a Girl from Bahia Have?).

In 1939, during a show at the Cassino da Urca nightclub, the singer was discovered by a Broadway impresario who hired her to star in *The Streets of Paris*. Miranda accepted, but not before insisting that she take her own band in order not to betray the authenticity of her music. The comedy team of Bud Abbott and Lou Costello and the French singer Jean Sablon also starred in the Broadway show *The Streets of Paris*. The comedians and singers were accompanied by chorus girls who gave the show a vaudeville atmosphere. Miranda came on stage with her celebrated bahiana outfit and seduced her audience with her singing and dancing. Miranda made the show a big success, and it continued to run for six months, later touring Pittsburgh, Philadelphia, Baltimore, and Washington, D.C. The Brazilian star was an instant success. Her foreign accent was considered delightful, as were her costumes and sensual dance moves. Six months after arriving in the United States, she had become the highest paid actress in the country and the hardest working woman in show business.

In July of the same year, however, an incident took place that forever tarnished her relationship with Brazilian fans. Miranda returned to her country to what many thought would be a glorious welcome home. In the Cassino da Urca, Miranda greeted her audience in English and proceeded to sing "South American Way" in English. Her audience reacted coldly, and a distraught Miranda sensed that many thought she had become assimilated to American culture. Some critics accused her of selling out to U.S. imperialism and submitting to the stereotype of a wild, exotic, sexually charged Latin American female.

Miranda's career in the United States developed along the lines of the Good Neighbor policy, an attempt to restore employment, consumption, and prosperity in the domestic market by expanding exports to Latin America and other regions of the world. The policy instigated the expansion of U.S. cultural horizons by generating propaganda that would convince the public to accept the exotic cultures represented by foreign artists. Many have argued that Miranda became the muse of the Good Neighbor policy. Her defenders argued that she was conscious of the mechanics of power and playfully bent the rules to advance the culture of her country. The interest of the United States in Latin America was reflected on the screen and especially in Miranda's opportunities as an actress. She made fourteen films in the United States. Among her most famous are *Down Argentine Way* (1940); *The Gang's All Here* (1943), a wartime musical; *Weekend in Havana* (1941), a musical travel adventure; and *That Night in Rio* (1941). Miranda kept an exhausting schedule, working in Broadway shows, restaurants, and nightclubs and on radio and television shows. Sometimes she rushed from the theaters to the nightclubs a few times a night in order to keep up with her engagements. Her income allowed her to buy a luxurious house in Beverly Hills and to send for her mother and sister to live with her.

At the end of War World II impresarios in Hollywood felt that the novelty of the Brazilian singer had worn off. Hollywood's sponsorship of the Good Neighbor policy had come to an end. In 1946 a picture taken of Miranda swinging in the arms of actor Cesar Romero exposed her without underwear, which caused a scandal during the McCarthy era. Shortly thereafter, Fox canceled her contract. Her marriage to David Sebastian in 1947, a Hollywood producer, was also on the rocks. Rumors of domestic violence started to spread. That same year, Miranda became pregnant and made a vow to stop working. But after a show in New York honoring those who had entertained troops during the war, she had a miscarriage. She fell into a depression and started taking pills. On August 5, 1955, after appearing on the Jimmy Durante television show, Miranda collapsed in front of a live audience. That was the last image of Carmen Miranda. She died at her home that night at the age of forty-six. Her funeral in Beverly Hills was attended by many Hollywood celebrities, but it was Rio de Janeiro, the city that saw her rise to stardom, that gave her remains a hero's rest. Her casket, covered with a flag, was paraded down the avenues of Rio accompanied by multitudes.

Further Reading

Carmen Miranda: Bananas Is My Business. Directed by Helena Solberg and David Meyer. Fox Lorber Home Video, A WinStar Company, 1994.

Gil-Montero, Martha. *Brazilian Bombshell: The Biography of Carmen Miranda.* New York: DIF, 1989.

López, Ana M. "Are All Latins from Manhattan?: Hollywood, Ethnography and Cultural Colonialism." In *Mediating Two Worlds: Cinematic Encounters in the Americas,* edited by John King, Ana M. López, and Manuel Alvarado, 67–80. London: BFI, 1993.

Tomás F. Taraborrelli

CARMEN NARANJO
(January 30, 1928–)
Costa Rica: Author, Government Administrator

Carmen Naranjo is one of Central America's most important female cultural figures, not only as a prolific writer, who has produced technically sophisticated novels and short stories, but also as an accomplished poet, essayist, and playwright. Her literary achievements have been widely recognized with multiple awards: the National Prize Aquileo Echeverría in 1966, for her novel *Los perros no ladraron* (The Dogs Did Not Bark, 1966); and the 1967 and 1968 Central American Floral Games, respectively, for *Camino al mediodía* (Road at Noon, 1968) and *Responso por el niño Juan Manuel* (Responsory for Juan Manuel, 1971), one of her most ambitious works. *Diário de una multitud* (A Multitude's Diary, 1965), which critics have characterized as one of the most important novels of contemporary Costa Rican and Central American literature, received the Premio Educa in 1974. Her short fiction has not been wanting for recognition: *Hoy es un largo día* (It's a Long Day Today, 1974) was awarded the Editorial Costa Rica Prize in 1973, and *Ondina* (1985), a collection of short stories, received the EDUCA Prize in 1982.

Naranjo's contributions to Costa Rican and Central American culture and society transcend the literary arena. She completed her degree in philosophy and letters at the University of Costa Rica but, instead of pursuing a career in teaching, she joined the Welfare Department in 1954, when her country was rapidly developing the social services sector. Naranjo became the highest ranking female civil servant in Costa Rican history when she was promoted to serve as the first female undersecretary of the social security system in 1961, and its first woman top administrative officer in 1971. She was appointed ambassador to Israel in 1972 (where she coincided with **Rosario Castellanos**), a significant diplomatic assignment given the economic and intellectual influence of the Costa Rican Jewish community. During her tenure as ambassador, she published numerous articles on Israel in the Costa Rican press in an effort to promote a better understanding between the two nations. These pieces were later collected in *Por Israel y las páginas de la Biblia* (Through Israel and the Bible's Pages, 1976). President Daniel Oduber recalled her in 1974 to invite her to join his cabinet as minister of culture, youth and sports. She thus became the politically most influential woman in Costa Rica. In 1982 she became director of the Museum of Costa Rican Art, and in 1984 she became director of EDUCA, the Central American University publishing house. Her civil service, however, extends beyond Costa Rican borders: she served as technical assistant for social security planning at the Organization of American States headquarters in Washington, D.C., and participated in UNICEF's program for the protection of childhood. In keeping with her concern for human rights, Naranjo presided over the Central American commission of aid to the families of "disappeared" students and teachers.

Naranjo's policies as minister of culture were progressive, and she placed cultural development at the center of the government's social and economic planning. Her *Cultura: La acción cultural en Latinoamérica. Estudio sobre la planificación cultural* (Cultural Activity in Latin America. A Study on Planning, 1978), which she published after leaving her post in the ministry, outlines the cultural agenda she attempted to develop during her tenure as minister. The book is applicable not only to Costa Rica's economic and social development, but also to other countries in Spanish America.

The core of her proposal is that cultural development is essential, and it is the key to economic development and social improvement. Economic growth should be responsive to the needs of the population at large and not primarily to the interests of a privileged minority. In Naranjo's vision, the inclusion of geographically, economically, and socially marginalized groups—the vast majority of Costa Rica's nonurban population—is central to any project of democratization. According to Naranjo, economic development and social advancement should not be imposed on these groups, but they should rather evolve from their needs and rights. In her thinking, economic integration of marginal social sectors is essential for the development of the country; such integration, however, should be accompanied by cultural integration, "the creation of new markets, and the economic restructuring of the regions" (Naranjo 1978, 26).

Naranjo's cultural policies sought to subvert the traditional Latin American elitist view, whereby culture is seen as a luxury that exists for the consumption and pleasure of an educated few. On the contrary, artistic creation is, in her mind, the result of a unique combination of both intellectual and manual abilities. More important, however, she believes in the centrality of culture and in its nonelitist development as a means of resistance to the negative effects of numbing advertising, empty slo-

Carmen Naranjo. Courtesy of Ardis L.
Nelson.

gans, and infinite consumerism promoted by the market. In an attempt
to promote cultural activity, and to make it accessible to the masses, she
founded the National Theater Company, the Symphonic Orchestra of
Costa Rica, and the Costa Rican Film Institute, which has become an
important instrument in attaining her goals, cognizant as she is of the
communicative power of both film and television images. She has ad-
vocated the production of videos destined primarily for television, as an
option to the mostly U.S. films and television series prevalent in Costa
Rica.

Conservative political sectors, feeling threatened by the implementa-
tion of her cultural agenda, have firmly opposed her proposals for cultural democratization. Naranjo became the main target of their attacks,
which resulted in her resignation in 1976. The immediate cause for her
stepping down from the ministry, apart from the realization that it
would not be possible to implement her policies, was a documentary
series made for television by the Costa Rican Film Institute. The series
focused on various critical points of Costa Rican society and economic
development: the indiscriminate exploitation of Costa Rica's rain forests
by both indigenous and foreign interests, the existence of widespread
malnutrition among Costa Rican children, the high rate of alcoholism
among the adult population, and prostitution as a means of economic
survival for a vast sector of poor women. The conservative sectors were

outraged at the image of Costa Rica portrayed by the films and accused Naranjo of social subversion. In her response to her accusers, she defended the objectivity of the films and her obligation as minister to address the economic and social problems affecting the country. The films made it patently clear that the widespread images of Costa Rica as an exception within Central America—ruled by solid democratic principles and inhabited by an ethnically homogenous population enjoying a high standard of living—were not entirely congruent with the experience of most Costa Ricans. Naranjo's films exposed what her literary works repeatedly denounce: Costa Rica's idyllic images are the product of a "history that has been a search for accommodation, for good appearances" (Naranjo 1965, 73). In her thinking, failing to recognize the mendacity of such notions contributes to a "hybrid system always favoring the privileged ones, the gentlemen of opportunity, in pursuit of the business deal, the easy money" (1965, 173).

Naranjo's criticism of the Costa Rican political and economic elite is coupled with a scathing characterization of Costa Rica's bureaucracy, which she intimately knows. *Los perros no ladraron* (1966) and segments of *Diario de una multitud* (1965), one of her most interesting and influential works, portray Costa Rican bureaucracy as unnecessarily hierarchical, inefficient, and stultifying. The tasks low- and middle-rank bureaucrats are required to perform are restrictive, boring, and repetitive. The atmosphere in the workplace is poor due to personal frustration and scarce opportunities for advancement. Petty bureaucrats spend most of their time plotting against each other in pursuit of favors from their bosses, higher placements, and improved remuneration. Worst of all, however, is the sense of helplessness and entrapment caused by limited opportunities, which force individuals to protect their positions by any means at their disposal: "The worst is to deny my right to being someone, to corner myself, so that no one can touch my job . . . that horrible job" (Naranjo 1978, 53). The idea that people's creativity and potential, despite the essential equality of human beings, is often hindered, even smothered, by economic, social, and personal circumstances in which every person develops pervades her work: "The tragedy of life is to be in a specific time and space, imbued with an energy that is meant for achieving deeper dimensions of being" (Naranjo 1985, 78).

Despite Naranjo's criticism of the national elite, which her work portrays as corrupt, opportunistic, immoral, and narcissistic in its responsibility in determining the livelihood of vast sectors of Costa Rican society, she does not exonerate the Don Nadie, the everyday person of personal failures. In "Cinco temas en busca de un pensador" (Five Topics in Search of a Thinker, 1976), Naranjo highlights specific negative features of most Costa Ricans. She analyzes five idioms pervasive in Costa Ricans' speech which reveal their attitudes toward life and the circumstances surrounding them. These expressions are: *ahí vamos* (there we go), *qué le vamos a hacer* (what is there to do), *a mí qué me importa* (I don't care), *de por sí* (in itself), and *idiay* (what a bother).

The expression *qué le vamos a hacer*, which she deems the "most common and telling of our language" (1976, 3), clearly connotes individual acceptance of a fatal destiny against which one feels impotent. Although Naranjo connects such acquiescence with the teachings of conservative Catholicism, which foster blind acceptance of fate, she does not exonerate the individual from such passive behavior. As the plural voice of *qué le vamos a hacer* and *ahí vamos* reveals, the accommodation is collective. Costa Ricans prefer to accept a given state of affairs rather than resist adversity and counteract it with action. Her fellow countrymen, according to Naranjo, find solace and justification for passiveness when they realize that individual problems are widespread. This "we" allows Costa Ricans to evade their lack of definition and identity and to avoid recognition of their individual failures.

Lack of drive and ambition are two other negative features she identifies in Costa Ricans: "Our people dream little, or hardly dream at all" (1976, 9); Costa Ricans are "a people without ideals, without goals in the culmination of a quiet day, hoping for an identical tomorrow" (9). Such lack of ambition makes Costa Ricans vulnerable to the schemes of corrupt politicians, greedy national interest groups, and the influence of foreign interests. In search for ways to fight their own boredom and to fill their own personal emptiness, Costa Ricans, according to Naranjo, are ready believers of the empty rhetoric of politicians, the designs of the business establishment, and the empty images and material objects invading their lives from abroad.

Despite her pessimism regarding Costa Ricans and Costa Rican society in general, Naranjo does not surrender the vision that guided her agenda as minister of culture: to build a country with a well-defined cultural identity responsive to the needs of the majority. Although most of her works, both fiction and poetry, present dystopic visions of Costa Rica, her individual, political, and cultural engagement are inspired by the conviction that it is possible to attain a society offering dignity, fraternity, and freedom to all its members. Naranjo is not only an outstanding figure of Costa Rican letters in particular, and Spanish American literature in general, but also a courageous public figure whose understanding of the ills and the potentials of her country and culture are applicable to Central and Latin America at large.

Further Reading

Martínez, Luz Ivette. *Carmen Naranjo y la narrativa femenina en Costa Rica*. San José, Costa Rica: Editorial Universitaria Centroamericana, 1987.

Naranjo, Carmen. "Cinco temas en busca de un pensador." *Repertorio americano* 2 (January–March 1976): 1–14.

———. *Cultura: La acción cultural en latinoamérica. Estudio sobre la planificación cultural.* San José, Costa Rica: ICAO, 1978.

———. *Diario de una multitud.* San José, Costa Rica: Editorial Universitaria Centroamericana, 1965.

———. *Memorias de un hombre palabra.* San José, Costa Rica: Editorial Costa Rica, 1978.

———. *Sobrepunto.* San José, Costa Rica: Editorial Universitaria Centroamericana, 1985.

Nelson, Ardis. "Carmen Naranjo and Costa Rican Literature." In *Reinterpreting the Spanish American Essay. Women Writers in the 19th and 20th Centuries,* edited by Doris Meyer, 177–87. Austin: University of Texas Press, 1995.

Rubio, Patricia. "Carmen Naranjo." In *Spanish American Women Writers. A Bio-Bibliographical Source Book,* edited by Diane Marting, 350–59. New York: Greenwood Press, 1984.

———. "Carmen Naranjo: From Poet to Minister." In *A Dream of Light and Shadow. Portraits of Latin American Women Writers,* edited by Marjorie Agosin, 195–206. Albuquerque: University of New Mexico Press, 1995.

Patricia Rubio

MARIA ESCOLÁSTICA DA CONCEIÇÃO NAZARÉ

(February 10, 1894–August 13, 1986)

Brazil: Spiritual Leader

Widely known as Mãe Menininha do Gantois, revered Brazilian spiritual leader Nazaré was born in Salvador, Bahia, Brazil, six years after the abolition of slavery. The daughter of Maria da Glória and Joaquim de Assunção, Mãe Menininha (literally, Mother Little Girl) was initiated into *candomblé* (Bahian term used to designate Afro-Brazilian religions) when she was just eight months old. In 1922, at the age of twenty-eight, she assumed the position of *iyalorixá* (mother-of-saint, a female spiritual leader) of Ilé Iya Omin Axé Iyamassê (House of the Mother of the Spiritual Force of Water and Mother of Xangô, the God of Father) of the *terreiro* (sacred space where *candomblé* ceremonies take place) of the Alto do Gantois, one of the oldest *terreiros* in Brazil, named for the French family who previously owned the property. The first *iyalorixá* was her

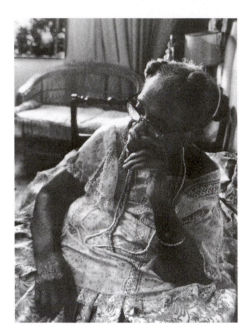

Maria Escolástica da Conceição Nazaré.
Photo by Madalena Schwartz. Courtesy of
Acervo Fotográfico do Instituto Moreira
Salles.

great-grandmother, Maria Júlia da Conceição Nazaré, followed by her
aunt, Pulquéria, and her own mother, Maria da Glória. According to
popular discourse, her whole family was of noble African lineage who
had family roots in Abeukutá in Nigeria.

It is said that in her sixty-four years as priestess, Mãe Menininha almost never left the *terreiro*, not even to visit her two daughters, Cleusa
and Carmen, both from her marriage to an attorney, Alvaro MacDowell
de Oliveira. In addition to her two biological daughters and her adopted
children, the *iyalorixá* had many grandchildren and great-grandchildren.

Popular discourse relates that Mãe Menininha's saint was Oxum, the
orixá of fresh water, wealth, and beauty, and that Mãe Menininha assumed the position of mother-of-saint because she was chosen directly
by the *orixás* (divinization of African ancestor or natural force) themselves, Oxóssi (*orixá* of the hunt), and Xangó (*orixá* of fire), not by another
mother-of-saint, as was the usual practice.

Candomblé, Mãe Menininha's religion, brought from Africa in the holds
of slave ships, was initially celebrated clandestinely because its practi-
tioners were persecuted by the police. The authorities passed a "law of
silence" that was directed only at *candomblé*: the *terreiros* were prohibited

from beating drums after 10:00 at night. In order to carry out this order, Pedro Azevedo Godilho, the feared Pedrito, chief of police of Salvador during the 1920s and 1930s, repeatedly invaded *terreiros*, violated sacred spaces, apprehended religious objects, and arrested mother- and father-of-saints. During this period of playing the strategical game of resistance and conciliation, she never rebelled against the institutions of power that supported the persecution of *candomblé*, the state or the Catholic Church, but she did not give up the practice of her religion either. Oral history relates that when the authorities prohibited the beating of drums after 10:00 at night, Mãe Menininha directed that the drums of her *terreiro* were to be made of dried gourds, an instrument permitted by the cult that produced a softer sound.

In 1937, just before the new election, Getúlio Vargas, the president of Brazil since 1930, sent in the military to close down the Congress and took complete control of the country. Vargas's new regime, called the Estado Novo (New State), banned political parties, imprisoned political opponents, and censored the press. At the same time, Vargas created one of the most powerful programs of national industrialization in Latin America which included a very progressive declaration of workers' rights. In 1945, at the end of World War II, at a time when Brazil was opening up and becoming more liberal, Mãe Menininha and Mãe Aninha were the first mother-of-saints to receive visits from artists, intellectuals, and politicians in their *terreiros*. This opening brought *candomblé* into view as one of the most important Brazilian manifestations of its cultural roots. With the renewed process of democratization in Brazil, the number of *candomblé terreiros* doubled in Salvador in just twenty years. Today approximately 1,300 *terreiros* are dispersed throughout the neighbor-hoods of Salvador.

The history of Mãe Menininha is interwoven with that of the people of Bahia. A descendant of African slaves, like so many other Bahians, she continued the traditions of her ancestors. In her way, she contributed to making Africa a part of Bahia, and she became one of the most charismatic figures that ever lived in the state. According to popular discourse, she defended her people and preserved the cult of the *orixás*. It is said that Mãe Menininha did not permit commercialization and thus the degradation of the *candomblé* that was practiced there, which happened in many other *terreiros*. Thus, the *terreiro* of Gantois is one of the most respected in the Afro-Brazilian culture for its fidelity to the true origins of *candomblé*.

In the game of sacred divining shells, Mãe Menininha was outstanding, and it is said that many important political decisions were made with them. She spiritually advised and helped anyone who sought her out. There was one thing she did not know how to do: evil.

This business of coming to me to unmarry or marry another's beloved is a waste of time. Even if I wanted to I couldn't do it because I don't know the secrets of those things. Now, to cure misfortunes or perturbations, I do everything that I can. I pray to the spirits, I work very hard. (Veloso et al. 1993, 5)

In February 1972, the fiftieth year anniversary of Mãe Menininha was celebrated. At the initiative of a committee composed of writers and artists—Carybé (Hector Júlio Paride Bernabó), Pierre Verger, James Amado, Waldeloir Rego, Mário Cravo, Dorival Caymmi, and Jorge Amado—a plaque was placed next to the entry door of the *candomblé* of Gantois with the following words:

In this house of Candomblé, headquarters of the Sociedade São Jorge do Gantois, Ilê Iya Omin Axé Iyamansê, located at the Largo de Pulquéria, at the Alto do Gantois, fifty years ago Dona Maria Escolástica Conceição Nazaré, Mother-of-Saint Menininha do Gantois, administers, in the high position of iyalorixá, with exemplary dedication and unceasing goodness, for the orixás and for the people of Bahia 1992—February—1972. (Amado 1986, 165)

The celebrations attracted Bahians, Brazilians, and foreigners from all walks of life: the governor, ex-governors, the mayor, senators, intellectuals, bankers, industrialists, dozens of daughter- and son-of-saints, and thousands of believers all came in reverence.

For the celebrations, Dorival Caymmi, a Bahian musician, composed a song that became one of his most popular, "Prayer to Mãe Menininha." For those residing outside of Bahia or who do not practice *candomblé*, Mãe Menininha became known by way of this paen, interpreted by Bahian singer Gal Costa. In this soft, simple, and prayerlike song, Dorival Caymmi celebrates the living image of Mãe Menininha, calling on her and describing her as the most brilliant star and the most beautiful Oxum.

Another recent poetic image describing Mãe Menininha is given by Jorge Amado:

A gown of lace, a flowered skirt, all in yellow tones, is the Oxum of Bahia, the face of goodness and the voice of experience. The table covered with a white towel, objects of silver, rituals, stones from the sea and the rivers, in the hand of Menininha, the sacred shells. The game begins, the mother-of-saint converses with the spirits, unravels the mystery, reveals the secret, removes the misdeeds. She knows of yesterday and of tomorrow. (Amado, 1986, 166)

Mãe Menininha died on August 13, 1986, after a prolonged illness. She suffered from elephantiasis and had to be hospitalized a number of times in 1986. According to the doctors, the cause of her death was the stoppage of her heart provoked by peritonitis.

The multitude of people who attended her burial, the speeches made by the representatives of power (politicians, industrial owners, artists), the firetruck that carried her body, and the governmental decree of three days of official mourning demonstrated her influence and prestige.

The successions of Gantois were always made according to bloodlines. It had been that way since her great-grandmother founded the *terreiro*. With the death of the most famous *ialorixá* of Bahia, Mãe Menininha, the role was passed to her daughter Cleusa Millet, who served as mother-of-saint until October 1998, when she died. The decision has yet to be made about who will take Mãe Cleusa's place.

Although Mãe Menininha died fourteen years ago, she is still present in Bahian culture in such celebrations and commemorations as the *Memorial for Menininha of Gantois* by Caetano Veloso, Jorge Amado, and others; and the Requiem for Mãe Menininha, composed and sung by Gilberto Gil as a tribute to her memory. Created to glorify the death of Mãe Menininha, this "requiem" piece with its funereal tone expresses the pain and sorrow felt after her death and the tears and profound longing that her disappearance has provoked in her people.

On February 10, 1994, for the centennial of the birth of Mãe Menininha, the Brazilian Mail and Telegraph Corporation paid her homage by placing her image on a stamp. She is remembered as a remarkable personality of Brazilian culture who sought to preserve the cultural identity of the Afro-Bahian people, resisting throughout her life the prejudice, intolerance, and racism of oppressive forces.

Further Reading

Amado, Jorge. *Bahia de Todos os Santos, guia de ruas e mistérios*. Rio de Janeiro, Brazil: Record, 1986.

———. *Jubiabá*. Translated by Margaret A. Neves. New York: Avon Books, 1984.

Carneiro, Edson. *Candomblés da Bahia*. Rio de Janeiro: Editora Civilização Brasileira, 1991.

Veloso, Caetano, et al., eds. *Memorial Mãe Menininha do Gantois*. Salvador, Brazil: Fundação Cultural do Estado da Bahia, 1993.

Jorge Vital Moreira

ANTONIA NOVELLO

(August 23, 1944–   )

Puerto Rico: Physician, Educator, Surgeon General

Former U.S. Surgeon General Antonia Coello Flores was born in Fajardo, Puerto Rico, daughter of Antonio Coello and Ana Delia Flores. Her parents divorced when she was three years old. Her mother then remarried. Her father died soon after. Fortunately she became fond of her stepfather. Her mother was a teacher and principal at the Yabucoa High School, a place far from home. Because of the distance, she saw her mother only on weekends. From an early age, Doña Ana Delia stressed the importance of education, and she gave her children a strong background in mathematics and science.

Novello was afflicted from birth with a chronic colon abnormality that necessitated long stays in hospitals. A poor public health system on her native island—then a U.S. territory until it reached commonwealth status in 1950—was responsible for putting off her much needed corrective surgery. Novello learned very early what it was like to be bedridden and helpless. The doctors and nurses treating her, in line with a tradition of humanitarian compassion, gave the ailing girl more than simple care. In fact, they became Novello's role models. Very soon she decided to become a doctor herself so that she could help other children and fight the neglect that she had suffered. In an interview about her mother's influence on her achievements, she said, "I went through a system of care that was not very keen, in a diseased state that makes you realize that there are good people and bad people in medicine, with a mother who said, 'I'm not going to let your disease be used for you not to succeed' " ("Antonia Novello, M.D., Profile").

Her recurring ailment did not prevent her from developing into an excellent student as well as a courageous and humorous adolescent. She was president of every club and a Girl Scout. At the age of fifteen she graduated from high school. In 1961, when she was eighteen years old, she underwent her first colon surgery, which relieved much of her pain. At the age of twenty she received a scholarship to study at the University of Puerto Rico in Río Piedras. In order to minimize the fact that she felt sick, she challenged herself by registering in the most difficult subjects, such as calculus, trigonometry, and quantitative chemistry. She successfully completed her Bachelor of Science degree in 1965. Afterward she was accepted at the medical school and she received her degree as a physician in 1970. Her colon ailment, which recurred when she was a medical student, was finally treated successfully at the Mayo Clinic. In spite of the long, painful convalescence that ensued, she continued her quest for excellence and achievement.

It was also during her stay at the medical school that she met Joseph Novello, a young U.S. Navy flight surgeon. They married in 1970 (the day after her graduation), and soon after they moved to Ann Arbor, Michigan, to continue their medical studies and training at the University of Michigan. Before becoming a doctor, Novello had hesitated between a career in pediatrics or in nephrology, but she decided to combine them. Between 1970 and 1973, she worked at the University of Michigan Hospital, where she treated children with kidney problems. In 1970, because of her skilled and caring treatment of patients, she was named Intern of the Year. She was the first woman—and, of course, the first Hispanic—to receive that award.

After five years in Michigan, the Novellos moved to Washington, D.C. There Novello continued to work in pediatric nephrology at Georgetown University Hospital, where she also studied other fields related to health. She opened her own pediatrics clinic in 1976. At that time the rates of infant death and morbidity were rather high in the D.C. area. Because of her humane approach and sensitivity, she suffered as much as the parents of the sick children, which caused her to renounce a career in practical pediatrics. Nevertheless, her social awareness and concern for children prompted her to apply in 1978 for a position in the U.S. Public Health Service, the government agency dealing with promoting preventive medicine. In 1979 she was also working with the National Institutes of Health in Bethesda, Maryland, where a few years later she became Deputy Director of the National Institute of Child Health and Human Development.

In 1982 she earned her master's degree in public health from the Johns Hopkins University in Baltimore, Maryland. While serving as professor of pediatrics at the Georgetown University Hospital, she was especially concerned with children that had been infected in utero with the AIDS virus. AIDS and its effect on the child population was always an especially important issue for her, and she calculated that in the year 2000 there would be an alarming number of children orphaned in the United States as a result of AIDS. Based on statistics, she proved that the number of AIDS-infected teenagers was larger than had been suspected, alerting the general population to its complacency amid the rampant disease.

In early 1988, she served on a congressional staff that offered advice to lawmakers about body organ donation and met with some of the largest beer and wine company representatives in order to convince them to eliminate advertising directed at young people. She also helped reinforce obligatory cigarette warning labels. In 1989 she had already earned a reputation as an expert on public health, demonstrated by her well-documented speeches and articles. She was especially conscious about the nation's serious problems concerning child mortality, AIDS-infected children, and alcohol and tobacco consumption among adolescents. In recognition of her deep commitment to public health and legal and medical issues, President George Bush nominated her to succeed C. Everett Koop as the surgeon general of the United States. The Senate swore her in on March 9, 1990. Because the surgeon general is also the head of the U.S. Public Health Service (an agency associated with the U.S. Navy), Novello now held the military rank of vice admiral. It was the first time that a Latin American, and moreover a Latin American woman, had been chosen for such a position.

Her first public speech as surgeon general was delivered with joy and pride in her native town of Fajardo. Afterward she addressed the most important forums in the United States and the world. She continued directing the nation's attention toward AIDS, focusing on the devastating effects of the epidemic on children and adolescents, visiting infected mothers, and creating support programs for families with AIDS while insisting on prevention. She also fought to eliminate tobacco and alcohol advertising in the mass media and stressed the need to understand and fight substance abuse among adolescents.

Novello also made the nation notice that health care among minorities was extremely poor. She saw specific problems among Hispanics, such as higher rates of kidney disease, lack of measles prevention, a higher number of deaths due to some kinds of cancer, and a disproportionate incidence of AIDS among Hispanic women and children. Because the office of the surgeon general is a sort of moral forum, she saw the time when she would deliver her message of "empowerment for women, children and minorities," as she said in an interview (Hawxhurst 1993, 22).

Antonia Novello is the recipient of numerous awards and honors. Other than over thirty honorary doctoral degrees, she is the recipient of the Surgeon General's Exemplary Service Medallion and Medal, the Legion of Merit Medal, the Congressional Hispanic Caucus Medal, and the Johns Hopkins Society of Scholars Award, among others. She is a member of Alpha Omega Alpha, the national honorary medical society.

Since leaving office, Novello has served as UNICEF's special representative for health and nutrition, concentrating her attention on smoking and substance abuse among children and adolescents. From that position, she has promoted global efforts to eliminate iodine and vitamin A deficiency disorders, and she has begun several programs of immunization.

Further Reading

"Antonia Novello, M.D., Profile." *Academy of Achievement*. http://www.achieve ment.org/frames.html.

Fernández, Mayra. *Antonia Novello, Doctor*. Cleveland, Ohio: Modern Curriculum Press, 1994.

Hawxhurst, Joan C. *Antonia Novello, U.S. Surgeon General*. Brookfield, Conn.: Mill-brook Press, 1993.

Novello, Antonia. *Antonia Novello*. Boston: Houghton Mifflin, 1997.

Stille, Darlene. *Extraordinary Women of Medicine*. New York: Children Press, 1997.

Manuel García Castellón

VICTORIA OCAMPO
(April 7, 1890–January 27, 1979)
Argentina: Author, Culture Promoter

Victoria Ocampo, a distinguished Argentinian writer and an advocate of cultural endeavors between Europe and the Americas, was born Victoria Ramona Rufina, the oldest of six girls born to an aristocratic family in Argentina with deep roots in the country's history. Her early years were spent under the tutelage of European governesses, learning French and English, and traveling to Europe where she spent months in Paris, London, Geneva, and Rome. Although her parents, Manuel Ocampo and Ramona Aguirre, believed that a good education was fundamental to their daughters' proper upbringing, they also believed that the daughters of prominent families had to be educated in the home. Ocampo had private instructors who taught her music, languages, history, religion, and basic math. Other subjects, such as classical languages and literature, the sciences, and philosophy, were reserved for boys. Ocampo later wrote extensively about the prejudices and obstacles that prevented women in Argentina from participating in the public sphere and limited their education: "[H]ow much I . . . suffered, how much the condition of women tortured me mentally, since my early adolescence! And this suffering was not gratuitous. I was wasting, I wasted so much time, and those lost years can never be regained" (Ocampo 1982, 85; author's translation).

From an early age, Ocampo showed a proclivity to literature. As a young adolescent she read the works of Sir Arthur Conan Doyle, Charles Dickens, Jules Verne, Guy de Maupassant, Edgar Allan Poe, and the Comtesse de Segur. Her literary heroes were not the writers, as they would be later in her life, but the characters they created, people who presented the conflicts that she was living as a young woman in early twentieth-century Argentina. They were the embodiment of the rash adventurer and the unyielding perfectionist, the willful and the disciplined. Throughout her life, these two aspects of her nature would surface again and again in her professional and personal relations.

In 1909, at the age of nineteen, Ocampo returned to Europe with her family. In Paris she decided to make up for the cultural isolation that she suffered in Buenos Aires. She was exposed to a vibrant city where art nouveau, modernism, and cubism were shaping art and literature. She enrolled at the Sorbonne, where she studied Greek literature and the works of Dante, Alighieri and Friedrich Nietzsche. This trip whetted her appetite for learning, but she was still under her parents' rule, and many limitations were placed on her. Marriage, she thought, would give her the freedom to explore the worlds of art and literature without limitations or restrictions. In 1912 back in Buenos Aires, she married Monaco Estrada, a young man from an aristocratic family, who, Ocampo thought, would be the door to freedom. However, she went from being "fathered" to being "husbanded." Victoria's insatiable thirst for knowledge and intellectual adventure were thwarted by the limitations placed on her by her status as a married woman, and she became estranged from her husband shortly after their wedding. They continued to live in the same house until 1922, when they officially separated.

Her interest in Dante, the thirteenth-century Italian poet, which was sparked during her year of study in France, became a constant literary interest, and the turmoil in her personal life moved her to write her first article for publication on his *Divine Comedy*. She eventually wrote more articles on Dante and a short book, *De Francesca a Beatrice* (From Francesca to Beatrice, 1924), which is a study of Dante's journey from physical passion to spiritual love. This book met with acerbic criticism from Paul Groussac, a respected critic of the time who suggested that she write about more feminine, personal matters. Ocampo did not follow this critic's suggestion but continued to write about literary and social issues in *La nación* (The Nation), one of Argentina's daily newspapers and later in her own literary review *Sur* (South), founded in 1931.

Between 1920 and 1930, Ocampo traveled extensively, meeting and nurturing friendships with writers, musicians, artists, and architects in Europe, the United States, and Argentina. In her travels she was continuously struck by the ignorance and misconceptions people across the Atlantic held about South America and Argentina in particular. The idea to link the Americas to Europe gave birth to *Sur*, a literary review that would serve as a vehicle to raise awareness about the literature and issues of both continents, a bridge that would bring them closer together. With the financial backing of Ocampo, the first issue of *Sur* was published in 1931. Among its contributors were Jorge Luis Borges, Waldo Frank, Eduardo Mallea, Guillermo de Torre, Alfonso Reyes, Drieu de la Rochelle, María Rosa Oliver, and Pedro Henriquez Ureña. Like many other of Ocampo's endeavors, *Sur* met with criticism. Some criticized its foreign contributions, others its elite readership, others its lack of political allegiance. The opposition did not subside as Ocampo continued to publish the review, introducing its readers to works by Thomas Mann, Aldous Huxley, Jean Piaget, Albert Camus, André Gide, André Breton, and T. S. Eliot and publishing whole issues devoted to the works of William Shakespeare and Mohandas Gandhi, or to topics such as the condition of women. In 1933 the literary review expanded in order to maximize profits and established a publishing house to publish books written by Spanish-speaking authors as well as translations of renowned foreign writers, such as André Malraux, Virginia Woolf, William Faulkner, Jean-Paul Sartre, and Vladimir Nabokov.

In spite of the opposition voiced by many authors and critics of *Sur*, they all agreed that the review played a crucial role in the diffusion of intellectual and literary works, and that its director, Ocampo, was a symbol of integrity and freedom of thought.

Among the issues that had troubled Ocampo since her youth was the condition of women. She was especially interested in women's education, the issue of *patria potestad*, the law that gave man ultimate legal control over his wife, children, and birth control. It is true that during Juan Perón's dictatorship, women gained political and social rights (the right to vote in 1947), but they also lost the right to divorce, which had been approved during the prior administration. In 1970, fifteen years after first suggesting it, Ocampo devoted three issues of *Sur* to the condition of women and the need for equality. She also published numerous essays on the subject of women vis-à-vis their social, political, and legal status, which have been collected in *Testimonios* (1935, 1941). Among her most influential essays on the subject are "La opinión judicial de la mujer como testigo" (Judicial Opinion Regarding Woman as a Witness); "El nombre de la mujer" (The Name of the Woman), in which Ocampo argues against the decree that prohibits a woman from assuming her maiden name again after separating from her husband; and "La mujer, sus derechos y sus responsabilidades" (Woman, Her Rights, and Her Responsibilities).

In spite of the gains made in the condition of women during Perón's regime, Ocampo remained an enemy of Perón and his wife, **Eva María Duarte de Perón**. The fact that Ocampo was considered an oligarch and a dissenting intellectual made her persona non grata during his years in power. Between 1946 and 1955, *Sur* continued to be published without interruption. It remained apolitical and concentrated on the literary issues of the intellectual elite. The international reputation of the review may have saved it from Perón's repression. Ocampo, however, did not survive his regime unscathed. In 1953, after the explosion of a bomb that nearly killed Perón, Ocampo was detained, interrogated, and incarcerated for twenty-six days in the prison of Buen Pastor. It is believed that she was set free as a result of pressure brought to bear by Chilean poet and educator Gabriela Mistral and Indian prime minister Jawaharlal Nehru. Ocampo believed that the days she spent in prison were a blessing in disguise. They allowed her to experience, perhaps for the first time in her life, the deprivation of material goods, of the comforts to which she was accustomed. She thought that it was during this period that she felt most free, that she was given the opportunity to live with other women of different economic and social classes, and to establish with them a bond, a sense of sisterhood and solidarity.

It was during Perón's rule that Ocampo began to write her autobiography, perhaps as a reaction to the regime's hostility toward the oligarchy and the elite to which she belonged. The six volumes of her autobiography are an attempt to place herself within a social and historical context. The first two volumes fuse the history of the family with the history of the country, highlighting their importance in the founding and development of Argentina. Later volumes emphasize her role in the development of Argentine culture through her work in *Sur*, as a cultural liaison between Argentina and the rest of the world, and as an outspoken advocate for women's rights. She avers that she was instrumental in the political, social, literary, and cultural development of the country.

Victoria Ocampo always had a mission. She chronicled in her essays critical issues of her time, the lives and works of distinguished citizens and writers, and the obstacles facing women. Because of her many accomplishments and her indisputable role as "cultural ambassador" of Argentina, she was elected to the Argentine Academy of Letters in 1977, becoming the first woman in Argentina to be granted this honor. During her acceptance speech she said, "After four hundred years . . . women are finally taking the place that they deserve in the world" (Meyer 1979, 238). During the next two years, her health began to fail, and she died on January 27, 1979, in the same house in San Isidro in which she had lived since she was two years old. In her essay "La mujer y su expresión" (Women and Their Literary Expression), Ocampo states, "Our own individual lives will not account to much, but all our lives, together, will affect our history to such an extent, that they will change its course" (Ocampo 1941, 283; author's translation). Ocampo's achievements and her steadfast commitment to justice and equal rights for women shaped the way in which Argentines approach world literature, art, and social and political issues. She was the bridge maker, not only between Europe and the Americas, but also between cultures and between the sexes.

Further Reading

King, John. *Sur: A Study of the Argentine Literary Journal and Its Role in the Development of a Culture*. Cambridge, England: Cambridge University Press, 1986.
Meyer, Doris. *Victoria Ocampo: Against the Wind and the Tide*. Austin: University of Texas Press, 1979.
Ocampo, Victoria. *Autobiografía II*. Buenos Aires: Sur, 1982.
———. *Testimonio*. Madrid: Revista de Occidente, 1935.
———. *Testimonio*. 2nd Series. Buenos Aires: Sur, 1941.

Adriana Rosman-Askot

ELIZABETH ODIO BENITO
(September 15, 1939–   )

Costa Rica: Attorney, Educator, Government Administrator

Elizabeth Odio Benito, an attorney and a political figure, is known and respected throughout Costa Rica as a strong-willed, highly principled individual, dedicated to the struggle for the rights of all human beings. In a recent conversation about her life experiences, the warm human quality of her personality came to the fore as she was speaking about her joys and musing about her many missions and the meaning of her life.

"My greatest joy? Oh, I have had so many joys in my life" (personal communication, 1999). She smiles as she remembers. Ever since her childhood, she has loved her contact with nature and the ocean. But above all, her family has given her countless joys. As a young student, she was elated when her parents praised her achievements, and she took immense pride in her father's professional successes. She recalls gratefully her first trip to her grandmother's Spain. In later years, she cherished her feeling of belonging to a blessed family when four nephews, a grandnephew, and a grandniece were born. Also, she appreciated the support her friends gave her on so many occasions, felt enthusiasm and satisfaction with her own successes after years of hard work at the University of Costa Rica, and experienced a deep sense of fulfillment after more than a decade of struggle working to defend and protect the rights of all human beings.

Born in Puntarenas on Costa Rica's Pacific Coast, Odio was raised in a family that believed in hard work and was committed to justice and to helping others. Her grandmother, Encarnación Ibáñez, who had emigrated from Spain, had to overcome incredible difficulties to raise eight children entirely on her own. Her grandmother's motto "Life is a struggle" was an early guide for Odio. Her father, Emiliano Odio Madrigal, a largely self-educated man who was motivated by the ideals of social service and justice, became a certified mathematics teacher, a scientist, and founder of the Colegio de Puntarenas, the first high school in the city. Her uncle, Ulysses Odio Santos, a distinguished judge and her father's brother, stimulated her to think, reason, inquire, and explore. Her mother, Esperanza Benito Ibañez, always supported her struggles and encouraged her to aim high.

After graduating with honors in 1956 from the Girls' Senior High School in San José, Odio entered the University of Costa Rica (UCR) and studied law. In 1964 she graduated as a lawyer and became a notary public in 1965. She continued in 1968 with graduate studies in social and economic development at the University of Buenos Aires and in 1969–1970 with teaching courses on the socioeconomic organization of Costa Rica, legal history, and civil law at the School of Social Service, a part of the law school at the University of Costa Rica.

In 1970 Odio established her own law practice, and in the years thereafter she pursued a "three-strand" career, being active, at times simultaneously, at times intermittently, in separate, but complementary settings, spread across Europe and the Americas, guided always by her commitment to social service and justice. The three "strands" of her career were her work in academics, in national politics, and in diverse functions related to the international concern with human rights, largely via organizations of the United Nations.

In the academic setting, Odio was involved for almost all those years in teaching, legal research, and academic administration. Her principal focus was her long-term association with UCR, where her career as the first woman professor at the law school culminated with a full professorship in 1986, which she held until her appointment in 1995 as Professor Emeritus. During her teaching career, she taught history of law, private law, labor law, family law, international human rights law, and the social and economic development of Costa Rica. She also conducted research and was the director of the Institute for Judicial Research and of the Institute for Social law. In addition, she served as administrator,

Elizabeth Odio Benito. Courtesy of José
Salazar.

including vice president, and for a short interim as president of the university.

She also taught and did research internationally in a wide variety of settings. In the 1970s, she served as a guest professor at the Fletcher School of Law in New York, where she taught courses on law and population. In the 1980s, through teaching and research, she began to focus on human rights in an international context. In that context, in 1982–1983 and 1990–1992, she taught an inter-American course on human rights at the Human Rights Institute in Costa Rica, which she had helped to establish. Also, from 1984 to 1987, she served with the Human Rights Subcommission of the United Nations in Geneva as rapporteur on discrimination and intolerance on account of religious beliefs. In 1986 and 1988, she taught about the inter-American system for the protection of human rights at the René Cassin Institute of the University of Strasbourg. In addition, in 1986–1987, she did postgraduate work in gender studies at the National Autonomous University in Heredia, Costa Rica.

In the 1990s, Odio returned to the Institute of Human Rights in Costa Rica and the inter-American course on human rights (1990, 1992, 1999). She also taught at the International School of Law of the University of Utrecht, the Netherlands (1995), the Military Academy and University of Zaragoza in Spain (1996), the University of Leiden in the Netherlands (1998), and the International Public Law School, University of Barcelona in Spain (1998).

Odio's second career, politics, represents the application of law and justice to public life. Her interest in politics began early. While still a student, she had run (though unsuccessfully) for political office as a candidate for *diputada*, or representative, in the Costa Rican legislature, intending to represent the National Liberation party, one of the two major political parties in Costa Rica. Later, Odio switched her affiliation to the Party of Social-Christian Unity (PUSC), the other major political party, which thereafter became the base for her remarkable career in national politics. This career began when party President Rodrigo Carazo Odio (1978–1982) named her his administration's minister of justice and clemency—the first woman to serve in this capacity—as well as to the post of attorney general of the Republic of Costa Rica.

In addition, during President Carazo's term, Odio became a member of the Subcommission for the Prevention of Discrimination and the Protection of Minorities of the United Nations' Commission of Human Rights (1980–1983). From 1983 to the present she has been the Latin American representative on the board of trustees of the United Nations Voluntary Fund for Victims of Torture. In the late 1980s, the Latin American Association for Human Rights awarded her the Monseñor Leónidas Proaño Award for Defenders of Peace, Justice, and Human Rights. In 1990 she was again named minister of justice and clemency, this time by President Angel Calderón Fournier for his 1990–1994 administration.

If during the 1980s Odio's concern with human rights—including her strong commitment to women's rights—had consistently increased, during the 1990s, her third career strand became truly dominant, particularly in connection with her second tenure as minister of justice and clemency. President Calderón proposed her name to the United Nations, and undoubtedly her academic qualifications enhanced her standing. In 1991 she became a member of the intergovernmental working group charged with developing an efficient international program with regard to crime and penal justice. From March to July 1993, she was ambassador before European organisms of the United Nations and then, from 1993 to 1998, she accepted her most important assignment. The only representative from Latin America, she was appointed as a judge at the International Criminal Tribunal for the former Yugoslavia at The Hague in the Netherlands, where she served as its vice president from 1993 to 1995. Finally, in 1998, she became president of the working group on an optional protocol for the International Convention against Torture.

Never before had she lived so intensely and for such a prolonged time in a foreign country, pursuing her profession in a foreign language. Moreover, the information on war crimes she had to deal with, the unbelievable violence human beings are capable of inflicting upon innocent fellow human beings, deeply affected and hurt her. It haunts her to this day (García H. 1999, 12A).

Just recently, as a further expression of appreciation for her work in international law and human rights, the Costa Rican Philip Jessup Association for International law honored Odio with the María de Peralta Award.

In 1998 Odio returned to her Costa Rican political career and was elected second vice president in the government of PUSC President Miguel Angel Rodríguez Echeverría (1998–2002). In addition, she took on the responsibilities of minister of the environment and energy. As such, she is particularly interested in promoting concern for the role of women as essential participants in environmental protection and regeneration.

In addition to her three-strand career, Odio has taken a lively interest in literature, literary criticism, and the arts, as her publications beyond the legal realm (most but not all in Spanish) demonstrate.

Where will Odio go in the future? Asked if she will run for president, she says, "I do not have that political ambition" (personal communication, 1999). Many Costa Ricans hope she will change her mind. Meanwhile, she does have other goals. She hopes to raise environmental consciousness in Costa Rica and make a sound environment the realistic ambition of every citizen and resident. Also, once she is no longer in an official position, she intends to write a book about her experiences as a judge with the UN Tribunal on War Crimes in the Former Yugoslavia.

Further Reading

García H., Roberto. "No habrá paz sin justicia." *La nación* 3, no. 3 (1999): 12A.
Zeledón Cartín, Elías. *Surcos de lucha. Libro biográfico, histórico y gráfico de la mujer costarricense*, 167–88. Heredia, Costa Rica: Instituto de Estudios de la Mujer, Facultad de Filosofía y Letras, Universidad Nacional, 1997.

Ilse Abshagen Leitinger

NINA PACARI

(October 9, 1961–   )

Ecuador: Politician

Nina Pacari rose from a marginalized childhood in a small Andean village in northern Ecuador to become a renowned leader of the country's
indigenous movement. With a strong connection to her native roots, Pacari developed a deep commitment to the well-being of the indigenous
peoples of Ecuador. She has given a voice to the oppressed and has
realized gains in the struggle to improve her community's socioeconomic
conditions. Pacari's solid indigenous ethnic identity and a strong bonding with her cultural roots have given her the strength and hope necessary to overcome the obstacles she has encountered.

Pacari grew up as María Estela Vega Cornejo in an acculturated family
living among mestizos (those of mixed European and indigenous heritage) in Cotacachi, a small town in the northern highland province of
Imbabura. She was the oldest in a family of eleven children, and her
hardworking, humble parents taught her the importance of striving for
a better future. Her father was a tradesman who, although of a quiet
nature, showed enthusiasm for financial and political affairs. He improved the family's economic situation through perseverance and hard
work. Pacari's mother, a kind, loving, and understanding woman who
was always committed to her children, demonstrated the significance of
honoring and preserving one's cultural values, customs, and traditions.
Through the influence of people such as her mother and grandmother,
Pacari discovered the strength and endurance that her Indian roots could
provide.

Pacari's childhood was filled with hard work and a daily struggle to
attain a better future. As an Indian girl living among mestizos, she experienced racism along with the temptation to shed her ethnic identity.
Others cut their hair, put on Western clothes, spoke Spanish, and entered
the mestizo world. Early in her life, Pacari underwent changes that led
her away from her indigenous traditions and toward the mainstream
culture. From the age of fourteen, however, Pacari began to depart on a
course independent from her home and community. Instead of marrying,
settling down, and raising a family, she violated social expectations and
left home to pursue an education. Her aspirations led her to become one
of the first Indians in Cotacachi to gain a higher education. She attended

Nina Pacari. Courtesy of Judy Hinojosa.

a Catholic secondary school where she became the best student. Racial discrimination, however, prevented her from participating in scholastic events. Nevertheless, she excelled in her studies and became the first Indian woman in Ecuador to earn a university degree in jurisprudence.

Pacari's political consciousness was awakened while she was studying for her law degree at the Central University in Quito. She became involved in student organizations and a cultural workshop that embraced indigenous values and heritage. As part of this trend, the students attempted to preserve the Quichua language that was starting to disappear, especially among young people. Meanwhile, these students were becoming aware that while they were regaining an ethnic consciousness, they still bore Spanish names. For this reason, at the age of twenty-four, María Estela Vega legally changed her name to Nina Pacari. Nina is a Quichua word that means fire, light, or heat; Pacari is the dawn. Her name indicates the dawning of a new consciousness.

With an education, many people in her position would have left the Indian world to advance their own economic and cultural interests; instead, she returned to her community to defend the rights of other Indians. Pacari underwent her early political formation through her work with the Federation of Indigenous and Country Peoples of Imbabura (FICI). Pacari is very critical of the long history of Western, neocolonial, and imperialist abuses of indigenous cultures: "For almost five centuries we have been the most exploited sector of society" (Pacari 1984, 116). Indian communities have suffered attacks on their land, culture, language, religion, and political structures. "They weren't able to destroy us," Pacari concluded, "because we are the fruit of a millenarian culture" (1984, 114).

After working with FICI, Pacari used her legal training to work with indigenous communities in the central highland province of Chimborazo. She helped them with a variety of problems involving land and labor rights, as well as other social problems. This work was fulfilling for her, and it also led to greater empowerment for the Indian masses in Ecuador. In the process, Pacari developed a more profound critique of indigenous society. Indians were not "ethnic minorities" but nationalities with their own language, history, territory, socioeconomic structure, and culture. Their struggle was to claim the rights associated with that status. Pacari began to press for legal reforms that would recognize indigenous nationalities, officially recognize the Quichua language, democratize access to political power, and provide Indians with land.

Pacari assumed a national presence in Ecuador in 1989 through her work as a legal advisor with the Confederation of Indigenous Nationalities of Ecuador (CONAIE). CONAIE had emerged in November 1986 in an attempt to organize all indigenous groups in Ecuador into one pan-Indian movement dedicated to working for social, political, and educational reforms that would benefit the indigenous nations. CONAIE erupted into the national consciousness in June 1990 when it led the largest, most powerful uprising for indigenous rights in Ecuador's history—an uprising that paralyzed the country for a week.

During the 1990 uprising, Pacari returned to Chimborazo to visit indigenous communities and encourage them to participate in the coordinated activities. Largely through the leadership of women, the Indians blocked roads with boulders and tree trunks. Through such mass actions, the Indians forced the government and the military to back down and enter into discussions with CONAIE. In Quito Pacari formed part of a legal commission that initiated a dialogue with the government. From that point forward, she has remained deeply involved in indigenous politics on a national level. Reflecting later on the 1990 uprising, Pacari saw it as a turning point in organizing indigenous efforts in Ecuador. It led to a reaffirmation of indigenous identity and a consolidation of organizational structures. More important, the uprising led Indians to articulate judicial claims aimed at constitutional revisions that would result in true equality for all peoples in Ecuador.

Land has historically been a principal demand of Ecuador's indigenous movement, and Pacari has long pressed for land rights for Indian communities. As in the rest of Latin America, over the last five centuries, a small group of wealthy landowners had taken almost all the land away from the Indians. The result was an extreme imbalance in land holdings that the Indians have long sought to correct. Whereas the white elite saw land as a commodity, indigenous peoples, Pacari states, "see land as an essential foundation for our culture, political organization and economic development, and of life itself" (Pacari 1996, 25). Without land, Indian communities and culture cannot survive.

The 1937 *Ley de Comunas* (Law of Communes) defended the Indians' right to hold land communally, but much of their land has been on steep mountain slopes. The elite controlled the fertile valley lands. In 1964 the Ecuadorian government expanded these rights with an agrarian reform law that granted some Indians titles to small plots of land on the haciendas where they worked. In 1994 conservative president Sixto Durán Ballén implemented a new agrarian development law drafted by large landowners. This law, part of the government's neoliberal structural adjustment program, would have eliminated the minor gains achieved by the Indian movement over the course of the twentieth century.

Pacari played a leading role in consulting with indigenous peoples and small farmers on this law, and she drafted a detailed alternative proposal to the government's law and defended the interests of indigenous peoples. In June 1994, indigenous organizations responded to the government's free-market reform and the undemocratic nature of its adaptation with an uprising that shut down the country for two weeks. The uprising forced the government to negotiate with the indigenous peoples. Pacari became the key leader in these negotiations. Although it was an uphill struggle against a colonialist mentality, racist assumptions about the Indians, and an already promulgated law, she helped force the government to concede to some of the indigenous movement's demands for a continuing process of agrarian reform and defense of communal lands.

Pacari's political career continued to flourish in the following years. In 1997 the National Assembly selected her as the national executive secretary for the planning and development of Indian and African groups. She actively participated in working for the well-being of both peoples. In the same year she served a one-year term as a representative from the province of Chimborazo in the National Constituent Assembly which wrote a new constitution that recognizes the pluricultural and multiethnic nature of the Ecuadorian state. In August 1998, she became the first Indian woman to win election to Ecuador's National Assembly. She was elected vice president of the assembly, and through this position she has gained a greater presence for all indigenous groups in Ecuador.

Pacari faces what she terms a triple discrimination: discrimination for being a woman, an Indian, and a female lawyer, a profession that traditionally belongs to men. Pacari notes that machismo is a European import; gender discrimination is largely missing within Indian communities. She believes that embracing traditional Indian values is a path toward human liberation. Today, Pacari continues to dress in the traditional indigenous costume of her community, and she speaks her native Quichua language.

Pacari continues today to work actively with Ecuador's Indian movement to defend Indian communities from the devastating consequences of neoliberal economic reforms and elite assimilationist attempts to suppress ethnic identities. She has consistently defended Indian rights for self-determination and the preservation of cultural identity, values, and language. Pacari has expressed that the key demand of Ecuador's indigenous movement is "the construction of a plurinational state that tolerates and encourages diversity among different groups in society" (Pacari 1996, 25). In struggling to achieve this goal, Nina Pacari has become a key player in Ecuador's Indian movement.

Further Reading

Pacari, Nina. "Las cultures nacionales en el estado multinacional ecuatoriano." *Antropolgía, cuadernos de investigación* 3 (November 1984): 113–22.

———. "Los indios y su lucha jurídico-política." *Revista ecuatoriana de pensamiento marxista* 12 (1989): 41–47.

———. "Levantamiento indígena." In *Sismo étnico en el Ecuador: Varias perspectivas*, edited by José Almeida et al., 169–86. Quito, Ecuador: CEDIME-Ediciones Abya-Yala, 1993.

———. "Taking on the Neoliberal Agenda." *NACLA Report on the Americas* 29, no. 5 (March-April 1996): 23–32.

Marc Becker and Judy Hinojosa

CRISTINA PERI ROSSI
(November 12, 1941–   )

Uruguay: Author, Political Activist

Cristina Peri Rossi's life and work as a writer and political activist stands as an example of the courage and determination that Latin American women have displayed in the face of overwhelming obstacles. She battled the rampant sexism of a society that almost prevented her from becoming a writer and discouraged her from pursuing other professional interests; she resisted homophobia on many occasions, most notably when she was forced to undergo therapy as a young woman to "cure"

Cristina Peri Rossi. Photo by Rosa Mar-
queta. Courtesy of *Quimera*.

her from her lesbianism (personal interview, July 7–8, 1993); she escaped
what was to become one of the most repressive Latin American dictatorships; and she made Spain, the country of her exile for thirteen years,
her new home, despite having experienced xenophobia. Against all these
odds, Peri Rossi has emerged as one of the most vibrant and daring
voices of contemporary Latin American literature.

Peri Rossi was born in Montevideo to a family of Italian immigrants.
Her father, Ambrosio Peri, was a textile worker. His early death does
not seem to have influenced his daughter's life. However, her mother,
Julieta Rossi, a schoolteacher who recognized her daughter's literary talents, has been a constant source of inspiration for Peri Rossi. Peri Rossi
studied biology for two years at the university and music privately, but
soon she transferred to the Artigas Institute, a selective teacher's college,
where she majored in comparative literature. Peri Rossi soon became
fascinated with language and writing: at six, she declared before her
extended family that she was going to become a writer. There was general laughter, but her mother believed her (Dejbord 1994–1995, 107).
Other family members opposed her literary inclinations. Her uncle, for
example, told her that "women don't write. And when they do, they
commit suicide" (Peri Rossi 1989, 25).

This was not the only sexist injunction Peri Rossi would have to face.
She soon found that everything she enjoyed most was considered unfem-

inine. Despite sexism and homophobia, Peri Rossi became an acclaimed and charismatic writer, journalist, and educator. In 1968 she was awarded two prestigious literary prizes. She received the Premio de los Jóvenes (Youth Prize) of *Arca* (Treasure Chest) magazine for a collection of short stories, *Los museos abandonados* (The Abandoned Museums), and in 1969 she obtained the Premio Marcha (March Prize) for her first novel, *El libro de mis primos* (My Cousin's Book). Uruguayan critic Angel Rama hailed Peri Rossi as one of the most important younger writers of her generation.

Peri Rossi ignored her family's disapproval of publishing her first book, *Viviendo* (Living, 1963), a collection of short stories. In addition to being a prolific writer and journalist, she defied homophobia by cohabiting with a female lover at the age of nineteen. When she and her first partner separated, Peri Rossi was urged to undergo psychoanalytic therapy, and her partner was institutionalized. After six months, Peri Rossi stopped the therapy because she realized that she was being manipulated into denying her lesbianism, which was intimately related to her writing (personal interview July 7–8, 1993). In 1971 she published a collection of erotic poems, *Evohé* (Greek), the call to the bacchanalia celebrating erotic passion and transgression, liberating the most hidden impulses, the most secret desires, in which the beloved is a female. This caused a stir, both within the left and the right. Peri Rossi had hoped that her leftist allies would accept her lesbianism because she had worked for progressive causes. Instead, the book provoked a "great scandal" (Peri Rossi, interview, 1995, 61). A more detailed explanation of Uruguay's political and social situation around the late 1960s will help illuminate the obstacles Peri Rossi faced because of her leftist ideology, her feminist ideals, and her open lesbianism.

From 1968 to 1973, Uruguay experienced a period of severe economic recession, civil unrest, and guerrilla activity. Increasingly conservative and repressive governments manipulated guerrilla threats to curtail citizens' civil rights and to impose a military dictatorship (1973–1985). A country that was once known and admired as "the Switzerland of South America" (Weinstein 1988, 23) suffered a regime "that was to be the most totalitarian on the continent" (45). Disheartened at what it saw as the impossibility of improving economic conditions and civil liberties in Uruguay through peaceful means, the MLN-Tupamaros guerrilla movement (Movimiento de Liberación Nacional, or National Liberation Movement) was formed in 1963 "around a nucleus of disenchanted members of the socialist party," and it became public in 1967 (39).

The 1971 elections saw a temporary cease-fire from the Tupamaros, who decided to support a new party, the Frente Amplio (Broad Front). An electoral coalition of left-wing parties (including the Communists and Socialists, but also some defectors from the two main parties, Blancos and Colorados), which ran under the legal designation of the Christian Democratic party, the Frente Amplio was formed in 1970. The coalition obtained an impressive 30 percent of the vote in Montevideo, turning the party into an uncomfortable opposition for the winning Colorado president, Juan María Bordaberry. From that moment on, all members of the Frente Amplio were persecuted. Soon, with the brutal escalation of guerrilla activity in April 1972, the government found the excuse it needed to declare "a state of internal war" and to justify kidnappings and tortures (Weinstein 1988, 46).

Although she never officially militated in either of the two main leftist parties—Socialist and Communist—Peri Rossi belonged to the Frente Amplio as an independent and was thus suspect. Peri Rossi also assiduously wrote for *Marcha*, a progressive publication that became the target of governmental persecution. At twenty-four, Peri Rossi was the youngest of a group composed mostly of fifty- and sixty-year-olds and one of very few women. She was responsible for many of the literary reviews of the publication. Furthermore, Peri Rossi routinely wrote for *El popular* (The People's Paper), the Communist party's newspaper. In addition, for three months, Peri Rossi harbored in her house a young, leftist student of hers who was associated with the Tupamaros.

On October 4, 1972, when her life was in danger, Peri Rossi reluctantly went into exile. Within twenty-four hours she had boarded an Italian ship and departed for Barcelona, Spain, where she has lived ever since. In exile, Peri Rossi became one of the most active and best-known organizers of the opposition to the military dictatorship, so much so that her identity as a writer was overshadowed by her identity as a political organizer. Despite her activist involvement, exile was such a horrific experience for her that she often considered suicide. Two things helped the young writer keep her sanity: "the fight against the dictatorship . . . and, in all justice . . . my relationship with Ana Basualdo, an Argentinian exiled in Barcelona who was, for ten years, my twin soul. . . . Her love, her trust in me, and, especially, her literary stimulus helped me recover part of what I had lost" (Peri Rossi, Letter, 1995).

In 1974 the Uruguayan dictatorship refused to renew Peri Rossi's passport. Because Spain was still under Francisco Franco's dictatorship, Spain did not give Peri Rossi any kind of protection; rather, it collaborated with the Uruguayan police. As a consequence, she fled to Paris with the help of Argentine writer Julio Cortázar. At the end of 1974, Peri Rossi managed to return to Spain with Spanish nationality, but she did not recover her Uruguayan nationality until the military dictatorship fell in 1985. Since then, she has held dual citizenship.

With the arrival of democracy in Uruguay, Peri Rossi suffered an identity crisis. After a soul-searching trip to Uruguay, she decided to remain in Spain. Peri Rossi insists that she does not feel comfortable in Spain, but she believes a writer needs to feel discomfort in order to write (Peri Rossi 1989, 24). Her latest novel, *El amor es una droga dura* (Love is a Hard Drug), appeared in 1999. She has produced an extensive body of works: four novels, six short story collections, eight books of poetry, a book of essays (*Fantasías eróticas* [Erotic Fantasies]), and numerous journalistic pieces in some of the most prestigious Spanish publications. She is often invited to lecture and to participate in roundtable discussions in Spain, Latin America, and the United States. This prolific production adds to her early publications in Uruguay, which include three short story collections, a novel, and a book of poems.

Peri Rossi's talent has been recognized not only in terms of successful sales for her books, but also with fellowships and literary awards. Most notably, in 1980, the Deutscher Akademischer Austatusschdients invited Peri Rossi to spend eight months in Berlin. There, she began her poetry collection *Europa después de la lluvia* (Europe after the Rain), with which she was a finalist for the Premio Extraordinario de Poesía Iberoamericana de la Fundación Banco de España (Extraordinary Ibero-American Poetry Prize granted by the Bank of Spain Foundation) in 1987. Among many other prestigious literary awards, in 1991 Peri Rossi received the Gran Premio Ciutat de Barcelona (Grand Prize of the City of Barcelona) for the best collection of poetry in Spanish for her book *Babel bárbara* (Barbarous Babel, 1991). Perhaps her best-known work is her novel *La nave de los locos* (Ship of Fools, 1984), an accomplished allegory of exile that goes beyond the strictly political implications of the theme to challenge notions of inclusion and exclusion at all levels of human experience, especially at the level of gender and sexual practices.

As a journalist and translator, Peri Rossi's contributions are numerous and important. During her earlier years of exile, Peri Rossi established ties with the leftist Catalonian intelligentsia which collaborated with, among other publications, the famous, now-defunct magazine *Triunfo* (Triumph). There, as had been the case in Uruguay with *Marcha*, she met older male intellectuals who mentored her. In Barcelona, she also established friendships with several Spanish women writers, including Ana María Moix, Montserrat Roig, and Esther Tusquets. As a translator, Peri Rossi has made available in Spanish works by such important women writers as Monique Wittig and **Clarice Lispector**.

Although now established as a fiction writer, poet, journalist, and translator, Peri Rossi's commitment to political activism has never faltered. She insists that writers maintain a social and political commitment that extends beyond narrow notions of the political to encompass, for example, sexual liberation (Peri Rossi 1989, 25). From a feminist perspective, Peri Rossi critiques the cultural, historical, and social mechanisms involved in the normalization of rigid gender categories and the imposition of heterosexual practices as the model for "proper" sexual behavior.

Further Reading

Dejbord, Parizad. "De rupturas y enfrentamientos: Una entrevista con Cristina
    Peri Rossi." *Antípodas* 6–7 (1994–1995): 95–109.
Peri Rossi, Cristina. "La escritura como acto de gracia." Interview with Luis
    Brano and Lauro Marauda. *Brecha*, January 13, 1989, 24–25.
———. "Extraterritorialidades marchen, y dos cafes." Interview with Tatiana
    Oroño. *La hora cultural*, February 4, 1988, 2–3.
———. Interview with Gema Pérez-Sánchez. *Hispamérica* 72 (1995): 59–72.
———. Letter to the author, September 14, 1995.
———. Personal interview, July 7–8, 1993.
Weinstein, Martin. *Uruguay: Democracy at the Crossroads*. Boulder, Colo.: West-
    view Press, 1988.

Gema P. Pérez-Sánchez

EVA MARÍA DUARTE DE PERÓN
(April 26, 1919–July 26, 1952)
Argentina: Actress, First Lady, Politician

Evita is, undoubtedly, one of the most controversial female figures in
twentieth-century Latin America, and probably the most powerful Latin
American woman of her time. Many Argentines idolized her; others de-
spised her. It would be difficult to deny, however, that her life changed
the face of Argentina. Born María Eva Ibarguren in a small town called
Los Toldos, near the Argentine pampas, she was the daughter of Juan
Duarte, a conservative rancher, and his mistress, Juana Ibarguren. The
stigma of illegitimacy haunted Evita throughout her life.

In 1908 Juan Duarte was named deputy justice of the peace, but Juan
Duarte lost his political influence and was forced to move to Quiroga
for a year after Radical party candidate Hipólito Yrigoyen won the presidential elections in 1916. Their economic situation did not improve
there, and the family decided to return to Los Toldos. In 1926 Juan
Duarte died in a car accident in Chivilcoy. Eva Duarte's family was hu-
miliated when they were not allowed to enter his lawful wife's house
for her father's funeral.

Since Juan was the only source of income, Eva's family struggled for
survival until her mother and older sisters, Elisa and Blanca, found jobs
as cooks in the homes of local rich people. In her autobiography *La razón*

Eva María Duarte de Perón. Courtesy of
Photofest.

de mi vida (The Reason for My Life, 1952), Eva Perón explains how she
became aware of social inequalities during this period. When she was
ten, the family moved to Junín, where Perón began to develop her artistic
vocation by reciting poetry. After performing a role in a school play, she
decided to become an actress. Her three sisters all married, but she
dreamed about independence. At the age of fifteen and with the help of
tango singer Agustín Magaldi, she left Junín in search of a career in the
capital, Buenos Aires.

Perón was successful as a radio and film actress. She joined the Com-
pañía Argentina de Comedias (Argentine Comedy Company), directed
by actress Eva France. She debuted on March 28, 1935, with a small role
in the vaudeville play *La Señora de los Pérez* (Mrs. Pérez). She continued
with the company until January 1936 and performed in *Cada casa es un
mundo* (Every Household Is a World), *Mme. San Gene*, and *La dama, el
caballero y el ladrón* (The Lady, the Gentleman, and the Thief). In May she
toured with a company and in December she joined Pablo Suero's Company in the play *Los inocentes* (The Innocents). She later joined the com-

pany of Armando Discépolo, and on March 5, 1937, she performed in *La nueva colonia* (The New Colony), a play written by Italian playwright Luigi Pirandello. In August she acted in the film *Segundos afuera* (Seconds Outside) and participated in the radio drama *Oro blanco* (White Gold).

Perón acted simultaneously in films, theater, and radio, and she also worked in the areas of publicity and graphic arts. From 1938 to 1940 she was with the companies of Perina Dealissi, Camila Quiroga, and Leopoldo Tomás Samari. She had small roles in the movies *La carga de los valientes* (The Charge of the Brave), *El más infeliz del pueblo* (The Unhappiest Man in Town), and *Una novia en apuros* (A Fiancée in Trouble). She received more important roles in the films *La cabalgata del circo* (The Ride of the Circus, 1944) and *La pródiga* (The Woman with a Past, 1945), a film that was never released. Perón worked in radio, and in 1939 she headed the Company of the Theater of the Air, along with Pascual Pelliciotta. Her programs were broadcast in Radio Argentina El Mundo (Radio Argentina the World), and in 1943 she began a series of biographies of illustrious women for Radio Belgrano, the beginning of her struggle for the emancipation of women. Despite her success, Perón did not forget her family. When her brother stole some money from the bank where he worked, Eva sold most of her possessions to bail him out of jail.

On June 4, 1943, President Ramón Castillo was ousted by a military coup led by General Pedro P. Ramírez. Colonel Juan Domingo Perón was appointed to the National Department of Labor, which he transformed into the Secretaría de Trabajo y Previsión (Secretariat of Labor and Welfare). Eva Perón had always been able to make the necessary connections to get better parts in the theater. When, on January 15, 1944, the city of San Juan was destroyed by an earthquake, Juan Perón invited several Argentine celebrities to participate in a fund-raising concert organized to help the victims. Among them was Eva Duarte. Despite their difference in age, they started an affair and she soon shared his apartment.

At the time, Eva Perón had three programs in Radio Belgrano: one that exalted the goals of the 1943 revolution, the drama *Tempest*, and *Queen of Kings*, in which she starred. On May 6, 1944, she was named president of the Agrupación Radial Argentina (Argentine Radio Association), a union she had created a year before. She now decided to take a politically active role beside Juan Perón. On October 13, 1945, he was arrested and imprisoned on the island Martín García. Four days later, Eva Perón organized a mass rally of workers and *descamisados* (shirtless ones) at the Plaza de Mayo to demand the return of their colonel. Juan Perón was released and that night he promised, from the balcony of the presidential Casa Rosada, to hold new elections. Juan Perón and Eva Duarte legitimized their relationship by marrying in a civil ceremony on October 22, 1945, and in a religious one on December 10. When Ramírez resigned, General Farrell named Juan Perón vice president of the republic. He was also named minister of war, and he kept his position in the Secretariat of Labor and Welfare. Worker support brought Juan Perón to power in 1946, 1952, and again in 1973, after eighteen years in exile. Perón, the candidate of the Labor party, beat the Democratic Union candidate Tamborini in February 1946. Hortensio Quijano, who used a train that he called *El descamisado* for his political campaign, was Perón's vice president.

For the first time in Argentine politics, a candidate's wife accompanied him and collaborated in the campaign. She became a fervent apostle, and her popularity was a political asset. On February 8, she organized a meeting of working women at Luna Park in Buenos Aires to show support for the Labor party. Since Perón was ill, Eva Perón tried to speak to the crowd, but she was repeatedly interrupted. A few months later, however, she was widely acclaimed after she made a distinction between Eva Perón, the first lady, and Evita, rejected by oligarchs, but loved by the disadvantaged. Evita became a bridge between the president and the people. She continued the good relations with the unions that her husband had established and created her Fundación Eva Perón (Eva Perón Foundation) which was eventually dismantled by a military coup in 1955. Her popularity increased with her visits to factories and poor neighborhoods, and with her struggle for social justice. She created *hogar-escuelas* (home-schools) and a workers' children tourism plan which took care of education, entertainment, and health care. The foundation built twelve hospitals for workers throughout the country, and a school of nursing. It provided food, social services, health care, pensions, and housing for the poor, senior citizens, and single women. The Eva Perón Hospital Train provided health care for people in remote areas. Finally, the foundation helped victims of catastrophes in Ecuador, Spain, Italy, Israel, Japan, Peru, and Bolivia.

Funding for these activities became controversial. The foundation claimed the funding came from the workers' unions and the Ministry of Social Welfare, but rumor had it that the donations were forced. Every worker was required to donate one day's pay per year, and businesses were also expected to donate money.

In August Eva Perón met with the Peronista leaders with the objective of fighting for women's suffrage, which was achieved on September 23, 1947. She had become the focus of international attention in June 1947, when she was officially invited to Spain by the government of the dictator Francisco Franco, who honored her with the Grand Cross of Isabel the Catholic. The goodwill tour continued in Italy, Portugal, France, Switzerland, Monaco, Brazil, and Uruguay, but the reception was not as warm as it had been in Spain, partly because she was regarded by some as a representative of fascism. In Italy she met Pope Pius XII, who gave her a gold rosary, but the visit lasted only twenty minutes. Finally, she felt frustrated because the British crown refused to invite her to Buckingham Palace (Navarro 1997, 179). In these countries she visited workers' neighborhoods where she learned about social action and gave several donations.

In 1949 Eva Duarte Perón became president of the Partido Peronista Femenino (Peronist Women's Party), which created *unidades básicas*, or basic units, which were both campaign headquarters and social work centers where women could get financial aid or learn a profession. The figure of Evita was influential in achieving the right to vote for women, but the success was the culmination of a process in which many feminist Argentine groups participated. In September 1947—on the initiative of Eva Perón—women received the right to vote. In the 1951 elections, almost four million women voted, and the Peronista party included women as candidates for election: twenty-three female deputies and six female senators were elected. However, in Evita's concept of feminism, women "should, for love, be united to the cause and doctrine of a man worthy of trust" (Evita Perón Historical Research Foundation 1999, 2.10). One critic indicates that, despite her charisma and untiring activism, Evita Perón fomented the immobility, and the paternal and authoritarian character of her husband's regime (Aguinis 1988, 736). Furthermore, her foundation promoted dependency and subjugated the trade unionists (135–37).

Eva Perón was criticized by the opposition, as well as by various sectors of Peronism. Juan Perón, who is thought to have admired Adolf Hitler and Benito Mussolini (Dujovne Ortiz 1996, 83), tried to eliminate any sort of opposition, and many Argentineans were forced to leave. Evita herself took revenge on enemies from her youth or from her acting career by putting them on a blacklist. One of them was the rival actor Libertad Lamarque. When the ladies of the Sociedad de Beneficencia (Ladies Aid Society) refused to name Evita their honorary president (as had been the tradition with first ladies), Eva Perón cut federal funding and used that money for her foundation.

In 1950 and 1951, Evita became very ill, and she was diagnosed with terminal uterine cancer. She had considered serving as her husband's vice president, but on August 31, 1951, pressured by the military, she renounced that goal. She accompanied Perón during his second inauguration, but that was her last public appearance. On July 26, 1952, she died at the age of thirty-three. Almost a million Argentines demonstrated their grief in the streets of Buenos Aires, and an estimated three million visited her coffin to pay their last respects. Thousands of appeals requested her canonization. Tomás Eloy Martínez's novel *Santa Evita* (1995) deals with the manipulation of her embalmed corpse by the military junta that overthrew Juan Perón in 1955. Evita is not only a myth, she is also considered a true saint.

Further Reading

Aguinis, Marcos. *Un país de novela; viaje hacia la mentalidad de los argentinos.* Buenos Aires: Planeta, 1988.

Chavez, Fermín. *Eva Perón, sin mitos.* Buenos Aires: Editorial Fraterna, 1990.

Dujovne Ortiz, Alicia. *Eva Perón,* translated by Shawn Fields. New York: St. Martin's Press, 1996.

Evita: An Intimate Portrait of Eva Perón, edited by Tomás de Elia and Juan Pablo Queiroz. New York: Rizolli International Publications, 1997.

Evita Perón Historical Research Foundation. *Biography,* Parts 1, 2. Translated by Dolane Larson. October 24, 1999. <http://www.evitaperon.org/biography/part1.html>

Fraser, Nicholas, and Marysa Navarro. *Evita Perón; The Real Life of Eva Perón.* 1980. New York: W. W. Norton, 1996.

Harbison, W. A. *Evita. Saint or Sinner.* New York: St. Martin's Press, 1996.

Martínez, Tomás Eloy. *Santa Evita,* translated by Helen Lane. New York: Random House, 1995.

Navarro, Marysa. *Evita.* Buenos Aires: Planeta, 1997.

Perón, Eva María Duarte. *Evita: In My Own Words,* translated by Laura Dail; introduction by Joseph A. Page. New York: New Press, 1996. Previously issued as *Evita by Evita: Eva Duarte de Perón Tells Her Own Story.* London: Proteus, 1980.

Ignacio López-Calvo

ALEJANDRA PIZARNIK
(April 29, 1936–September 26, 1977)
Argentina: Poet, Translator

An emotionally tortured poet, Flora Alejandra Pizarnik was born in Avellaneda, Buenos Aires. Her parents, Rejzla (Rosa) Bromiker and Elías I. Pizarnik, Russian Jews from the town of Rovne, Ukraine, immigrated to Argentina in 1934. According to her biographer, Cristina Piña, her father's original surname, Pozharnik, was altered upon arrival in Buenos Aires. A few years later, he was a well-established *cuéntenick* (door to door vendor) of jewelry. At this time, during the Holocaust, the remaining relatives living in the Soviet Union were killed. Elías Pizarnik and a brother, who lived in Paris, were the only survivors. These facts, never mentioned in the Alejandra Pizarnik's works, could represent, however, an emotional background that has significantly influenced her adult life as well as the direction of her literary creation.

After completing high school in Avellaneda, Alejandra Pizarnik studied philosophy and literature, and later journalism, at the Universidad de Buenos Aires. In 1955 she began to attend painting classes with famous Uruguayan Juan Battle Planas. Also, she began translating the works of Paul Eluard and surrealist poet André Breton from the French. During the same year, she published her first book of poems, *La tierra más ajena* (The Most Alien Land), a work she rejected later. In 1956 Pizarnik published another book of poems, *La última inocencia* (The Last Innocence), followed by *Las aventuras perdidas* (The Lost Adventures, 1958). At this time she belonged to the avant-garde poetry group Poesía de Buenos Aires (Buenos Aires poetry) with Elizabeth Azcona Cranwell, Edgar Bayley, Oliveiro Girondo, and Olga Orozco. In 1960 she settled in Paris for four years. *Arbol de Diana* (Diana's Tree, 1962), published by the prestigious publisher Sur of Buenos Aires with a prologue by Octavio Paz, and *Los trabajos y las noches* (The Labors and the Nights, 1965) are from this period. During her stay in France, Pizarnik collaborated with *Les Lettres nouvelles* (New Letters), *Nouvelle Révue française* (New French Review), *Mito* (Myth), the literary review from Spain *Papeles de Sons Armadans* (Papers of Sons Armadans), *Zona franca* (Free Zone), and many other European and Latin American journals. She translated the works of writers Antonin Artaud, Aimé Cesaire, Henri Michaux, Michel Leiris, and Leopold S. Senghor into Spanish. When Pizarnik returned to Argentina in 1965, she was already considered one of the more significant lyric voices of Latin America.

She published *Extracción de la piedra de la locura* (Extraction of the Madness Stone) in 1968, followed by *El infierno musical* (The Musical Hell, 1971), her last book of poems. In 1971 *La condesa sangrienta* (The Bloody Countess) appeared in Buenos Aires. It is the tale of the sadistic Hungarian countess Erzsébet Báthóry (1560–1614), written as poetic prose, which had been previously published in 1965 in the Mexican journal *Diálogos*. She also collaborated on the preparation of an anthology of her writings in which the inclusion of her critical essays was considered; it was finally edited in Spain as a posthumous work under the title of *El deseo de la palabra* (The Desire of Word, 1975). Short theater pieces of a satirical tone never published by the author and the play *Los poseídos entre lilas* (Possessed among Lilacs), along with her last poems, were gathered in 1982 by her friends Olga Orozco and Ana Becciú in the book *Textos de sombra y últimos poemas* (Texts of Shadow and Last Poems).

Pizarnik won the Buenos Aires First Prize for Poetry in 1966 and was

honored with a Guggenheim fellowship in 1968. She also received a Ful-
bright scholarship in 1972 but had to turn it down because she was
unable to leave Argentina due to her depression and illness. Tragically,
at a time when Pizarnik was obtaining increasing recognition of her literary talent in Argentina as well as abroad, she became more and more
unstable and unable to manage her anguish. After several attempts to
take her life, she was committed to a psychiatric clinic (Altamiranda
1994, 327).

After a breakdown, a tragic tone superseded the previously lyrical and
hopeful tone of her poetry. Her poetry has been classified into two periods: the first period ends with *Arbol de Diana* and *Los trabajos y las
noches*, the two books of highest poetic value. Her later poetry and plays
represent an extreme deconstruction of discourse based on a joyful and
obscene game of semantic and phonic elements, which can be seen as
embodying her inner turmoil. As a whole, however, Pizarnik's work presents a remarkable continuity around a few central themes that recur
throughout all her writings: death and silence, and the fear and the pleasure of embracing them. In *Extracción* and *El infierno musical*, words are
reduced to essentials, and the powerful image of silence as emptiness is
perceived like a mute demand. Her addressing herself as "other" reveals
a dramatic division of the self both identified as a mystical attitude and
a schizophrenic manifestation. One critic considers her fragmentation, as
well as her perception of being a foreigner, as a Jewish attitude which
he claims is common to many other Jewish writers (Senkman 1983, 337).

Her radical search for the absolute and her going toward the limits of
reality through an almost religious linguistic transparency make her poetry especially meaningful and provocative. Pizarnik's experimentation
with language also has its origins in surrealism, with which she became
familiar in the Paris of the 1960s.

During the period that she spent in France, Pizarnik's interest in painting linked her with artists who are both writers and painters. For instance, Pizarnik has naif, small drawings with numbers (published in the
Buenos Aires edition of *Extracción* and *Condesa*), which follow the illus-
tration pattern of Unica Zürn, the companion of the German painter
Hans Bellmer. Another significant connection to examine is the influence
of Valentine Boué Penrose, also a painter, from whom Pizarnik took the
Countess Bathóry's story, and many of Penrose's surrealist lesbian col-
lages (from *Dons des féminines* 1951) seem to materialize in some of Pizarnik's cryptic work.

Ambiguity of gender is another key point in Pizarnik's love poetry.
Words rarely show gender agreement. Even when Pizarnik uses the masculine form, for instance, in "amado" (loved), it appears both as an ad-
jectivation of "body" that allows for ambivalence, and as a rhetorical
formulation (Altamiranda 1994, 331–32). According to critics such as

Sylvia Molloy, this recurrent lack of gender marks point at what cannot be said, or the constantly invoked place of silence, characteristic of lesbian discourse.

La condesa sangrienta is a brief, lyrical narrative composed of eleven vignettes that gloss Valentine Penrose's historical novel *La Comtesse sanglante* (The Bloody Countess, 1957) on Countess Bathóry, who killed more than 600 virgins in sadistic and erotic rituals. Its publication was delayed in Buenos Aires, possibly as a way to protect the author from the rigid Argentine censorship of the time. Though within a climate of horror and aesthetic fascination, *Condesa* is the only Pizarnik text that openly shows lesbian desire. However, its prevailing images may be linked to Pizarnik's other writings. The shewolf, a metaphor for the countess, is a recurrent image in Pizarnik's poetry (Chávez Silverman 1995: 295–96). Similarly, the term *autómata* (automaton) for "La virgen de hierro" (The Iron Maiden)—a torture device described in one of the vignettes—is a word Pizarnik frequently uses to refer to herself. We can assume there is a link between the manipulation of peasant maidens in *Condesa* and the paraphernalia of dolls, in Pizarnik's imaginary, which includes the setting for her own death, since she was found lying among made-up dolls. In Pizarnik's book the key term is contemplation. We are privy to and become accomplices to the countess' contemplation of the bodies and the suffering of the maidens.

Shortly before Penrose's publication, Georges Bataille dedicated a few pages to the Hungarian countess in his *Larmes d'Eros* (Eros's Tears, 1956), which incoporated her into the iconography of French surrealism. The morbid history of the Eastern European countess also captivated Pizarnik because of its violence, which alludes to a dictatorial society, as it signals "the matching violence with which (sexuality) has been repressed" (Molloy 1997, 257).

Pizarnik's last bitter years were marked not only by emotional distress but by acute asthma and financial need. Pizarnik was marginalized as a Jew, a woman, and a lesbian. During a weekend leave from the clinic where she had been hospitalized for psychiatric treatment, she committed suicide by overdosing on drugs on September 25, 1972.

Further Reading

Altamiranda, Daniel. "Alejandra Pizarnik." In *Latin American Writers on Gay and Lesbian Themes*, edited by David W. Foster, 326–36. Westport, Conn.: Greenwood Press, 1994.

Borinsky, Alicia. "Alejandra Pizarnik: The Self and Its Impossible Landscapes." In *A Dream of Light and Shadow*, edited by Marjorie Agosín, 291–302. Albuquerque: New Mexico University Press, 1995.

Chávez Silverman, Suzanne. "The Look That Kills: The 'Unacceptable Beauty' of

Alejandra Pizarnik's *La condesa sangrienta.*" In *¿Entiendes?* edited by Emilie L. Bergmann and Paul J. Smith, 281–305. Durham, N.C.: Duke University Press, 1995.

Foster, David William. "The Representation of the Body in the Poetry of Alejandra Pizarnik." *Hispanic Review* 62, no. 3 (1994): 319–47.

Molloy, Sylvia. "From Sappho to Baffo." In *Sex and Sexuality in Latin America,* edited by Daniel Balderston et al., 250–58. Durham, N.C.: Duke University Press, 1997.

Piña, Cristina. *Alejandra Pizarnik.* Buenos Aires: Planeta, 1991.

Senkman, Leonardo. *La identidad judía en la literatura argentina.* Buenos Aires: Pardes, 1983.

M. Cristina Guzzo

JOSEFINA PLÁ
(January 9, 1909–January 11, 1999)

Paraguay: Journalist, Artist, Poet, Critic

Although she was born in the Canary Islands (Spain), Josefina Plá adopted Paraguay as her homeland and worked to promote its cultural, national, and social unity in an artistic career spanning more than seventy years. Plá penned more than fifty books during her lifetime and received national and international acclaim and distinctions. Remembered as a poet, playwright, essayist, ceramic artist, critic, and journalist, Plá's influence and contributions to Paraguay's avant-garde movement created lasting effects that still reverberate today.

Born María Josefina Plá Guerra Galvany, Plá spent the first three years of her life in Fuerteventura, Canary Islands, with her parents, Leopoldo Plá and Rafaela Guerra Galvani. Her father's position as a government employee required that the family move to Spain, and the family relocated frequently. Because of this, Plá spent the majority of her childhood and adolescent years in various cities within the Valencia and Andalusia regions of Spain. Plá's father greatly influenced his daughter's literary career with his private library full of history books and the works of such authors as Jean-Jacques Rousseau, Honoré de Balzac, Gustave Flaubert, and Benito Perez Galdós, along with nightly oral readings in their living room. When she was eleven, Plá began the Spanish equivalent of high school, and she published her first poems at age fourteen in the magazine *Donostia* (San Sebastian, 1923).

After receiving her high school education in commercial studies, she

Josefina Plá. Courtesy of Teresa Méndez-Faith.

was taking master's courses when she met her future husband, Andrés Campos Cervera, during a family vacation in Villajoyosa, in Alicante. The then thirty-five-year-old Paraguayan, perhaps best known by his pseudonym Julián de la Herrería, discovered his true artistic calling in Valencia and devoted himself completely to ceramics. According to Plá, Campos Cervera's grant ended six days after they met, and he had to return to Paraguay. Plá's father predicted failure and the disappearance of the so-called delinquent boyfriend, but twenty months later, when Campos Cervera asked for Plá's hand, her father consented to the marriage. Plá and Campos Cervera were married on December 17, 1926.

Plá arrived in Asunción, Paraguay, in 1927 to live with her husband. The couple devoted themselves to their respective artistic endeavors. While her husband taught classes at the Polytechnic Institute, Plá began her journalistic career as a contributor to *El orden* (Order), *La tribuna* (The Tribune), and *La nación* (Nation). In 1928 Plá became the Paraguayan correspondent for the Argentina-based magazine *Orientación* (Orientation). In 1929 she was the radio reporter for Paraguay's first radio station and hers was the first female voice broadcast in the country. She returned to Spain to help promote her husband's career, where she displayed her own ceramic works, under Cervera Campos's guidance, in a successful Madrid exposition in 1931. When the couple returned to Paraguay after three years, Plá was named editorial secretary of the newspaper *El liberal* (The Liberal). The newspaper paired Plá with actor and dramatist Roque Centurión Miranda; the team collaborated for three decades.

During the Chaco war (1932–1935), which affected all Paraguayans, Plá published her first book, *El precio de los sueños* (The Price of Dreams, 1934), a collection of poems written during her adolescent years. Later that same year, Plá and her husband returned to Valencia, Spain, where they both continued their artistic development in ceramics. One year later, when they decided to return to Paraguay, they found they were unable to return owing the Spanish Civil War. In 1937 the couple once again attempted to make the trip; this time they were detained by Campos Cervera's untimely death. The widowed Plá finally returned to Asunción in 1938. The Paraguayan government confined her to the city Clorinda out of suspicion for her artistic ties with the volatile Spanish Republic. Plá appealed the decision, citing her journalistic work in Paraguay during the war, and the government rescinded her confinement.

The return to Asunción inaugurated perhaps the most influential and artistic period of Plá's life. Along with other avant-garde artists, including Hérib Campos Cervera (her husband's nephew), Augusto Roa Bastos, and Julio Correa, Plá helped lead the important Paraguayan literary generation of the 1940s. Plá, under the auspices of this literary movement, wanted poetry to represent both intellectual and social development and to convey both social and psychoanalytic significance. In addition to her newspaper columns and theater pieces, Plá presented several radio segments addressing World War II, with Roa Bastos, entitled *Antes y después de la guerra* (Before and After the War). Plá's influence, along with that of Roa Bastos, continued well into the 1950s and 1960s. In 1946 Plá began her six-year position as director of ceramic classes at the Centro Cultural Paraguayo Americano (Paraguayan American Cultural Center). This position marks an important period when plastic arts expanded to include ceramics and Plá's importance in Paraguay's artistic development.

While the 1940s reflect Plá's emergence as both a leading artist and critic, the 1950s attest to her highly prolific career, and the 1960s and 1970s officially recognize her talent. Beginning with an exposition in Rio de Janeiro and including the numerous exhibitions that followed, Plá received several local awards, including Brazil's Diploma de Honor (1952), the Arno award (1957) for distinction in modern Paraguayan plastic arts, the Lavorel award (1964) celebrating her distinguished writing, a gold medal from Brazil's Department of Culture (1979), and Paraguay's Woman of the Year award in 1977. These awards honored Plá for her contributions to Paraguay's culture and artistic development, but she also received international distinctions from Italy, Spain, Venezuela, and the United States for her personal achievements.

These honors did not come without tremendous effort and an extraordinary production by Plá. In an era that expressed great hostility toward political and national sentimentalism, Plá worked to reincorporate national pride and renew aesthetic appreciation through various artistic representations. Thirty years after her first literary publication, Plá rejuvenated her poetic popularity in the 1960s with works such as *La raíz Y la aurora* (The Root and Dawn, 1960), *Rostros en el agua* (Faces in the Water, 1963), *Invención de la muerte* (Invention of Death, 1965), and *El polvo enamorado* (Enamored Dust, 1968). Although many poems found in these collections deal with the themes of love, death, and the torment and suffering associated with such intense emotions, Plá's poetry expresses personal grief and the politically turbulent years of her adopted country following the wars of the 1930s and 1940s. Plá collaborated with fellow artist and friend João Rossi on a theory of aesthetic principles entitled *Arte nuevo* (New Art, 1952). Her influence also manifests itself through the various artistic groups to which Plá contributed, including critics (Asociación Internacional de Críticos de Arte, or International Association of Art Critics), painters (Grupo Arte Nuevo, or New Art Group), writers (Generación del Cuarenta, or 1940s Generation), and playwrights (Teatro Debate El Galpón, or the Warehouse Theater Debate). Finally, Plá expanded her journalistic career with frequent columns in such periodicals as *Revista comunidad* (Community Review) and *La tribuna*.

Amazingly, the momentum of Plá's artistic career continued. In the 1970s, Plá not only served as coordinator of the literary magazine *Signos* (Signs) and editor of the *Suplemento cultural* (Culture Supplement), she also collaborated on a radio program entitled *Cinco minutos de cultura* (Five Minutes of Culture), a series that lasted until 1983, and she continued teaching ceramics and theater courses at various centers and universities. Perhaps the 1980s best demonstrate Plá's eclectic ingenuity and her talents as a critic, essayist, historian, and writer. Her poetic works, *Tiempo y tiniebla* (Time and Shadow, 1982) through *La llama y la arena* (Flame and Sand, 1987), enjoyed national and international success alongside her collections of short stories, including *El espejo y el canasto* (The Mirror and the Basket, 1981) and *La muralla robada* (The Stolen Wall, 1989). Surprisingly, Plá's greatest production in the 1980s did not come from her poetic and narrative voices, but rather from her critical voice. Among all her other publications, Plá also published *Voces femeninas en la poesía paraguaya* (Feminine Voices in Paraguayan Poetry, 1982), *La cultura paraguaya y el libro* (Paraguayan Culture and the Novel, 1983), *Españoles en la cultura del Paraguay* (Spaniards in Paraguayan Culture, 1985), and *En la piel de la mujer* (In Women's Skin, 1987). These works attest to Plá's prolificacy as a writer and demonstrate her dedication and affection for Paraguay.

National and international honors also followed Plá throughout the 1980s. Among others, Plá received an honorary doctorate degree from

Paraguay's National University and won an award for her collection of poems entitled *Los treinta mil ausentes* (The Thirty Thousand Absent Ones, 1985) and a Mottart Award for literature from the French Academy in 1987. She was named member of the Academia de Lengua Española del Paraguay (Spanish Language Academy of Paraguay), the Sociedad de Escritores del Paraguay (Society of Paraguayan Writers), and honored member of the Sociedad Argentina de Autores (Argentinean Society of Authors). With the ceramics, paintings, tape recordings, and other personal objects left behind after her husband's passing, she opened the Museo Julián de la Herrería (Julián de la Herrería Museum) in 1988 to celebrate his art and honor his memory. Plá herself was honored in 1989 with the dedication of the Josefina Plá Hall in Paraguay's Centro de Artes Visuales (Center of Visual Arts), and in 1991 she received the Sociedad International de Juristas (International Society of Jurists) award for her efforts advocating human rights.

When Plá passed away on January 11, 1999, she left a legacy that spanned over seventy years and changed the artistic climate of Paraguay. Although Plá's poetic, narrative, historical, and journalistic contributions have received national and international acclaim, her literary presence and artistic influences merit exceedingly more scholarly attention and appreciation.

Further Reading

Jones, W. Knapp. "Josefina Plá: A Paraguayan Dramatist." In *Actas de la IV Conferencia de Lenguas y Literatura Románicas*. Lexington: University of Kentucky, 1951.

Plá, Josefina. *The British in Paraguay: 1850–1870*, translated by Brian Charles MacDermot. Richmond, England: Richmond Publishing, 1976.

———. "Como me veo." *Alba de América: Revista Literaria* 13, nos. 24–25 (July 1995): 39–46.

Deborah Foote

ELENA PONIATOWSKA
(May 19, 1932–)

Mexico: Author, Journalist

The noted Mexican writer Elena Poniatowska was born in Paris, France, in 1932, where she lived until the age of ten. Her mother, Paula Amor

Elena Poniatowska. Photo by Deanna
Heikkinen. Courtesy of Nora Erro-Peralta.

de Poniatowski, is a Mexican who was born and raised in France, and
her father, Juan Evremont Sperry Poniatowska, was a Frenchman of Po-
lish origin. Both parents were of aristocratic background; her father traced
his ancestry to Stanislaus II, the last king of Poland before partition. In
1942 the family left France to take up permanent residence in Mexico,
where her maternal grandparents lived. In Mexico City the future writer
attended a private British-run academy called the Windsor School, and
she completed her high school education in the United States at the Sacred
Heart Convent outside of Philadelphia. Poniatowska did not go to college,
although her many outstanding achievements as a journalist and a writer
of fiction and nonfiction literature have earned her the honorary doctorate
of humane letters from the University of Sinaloa in Sinaloa, Mexico, the
New School for Social Research in New York, and Florida Atlantic University in Boca Raton, as well as visiting professorships at the University
of California at Davis, the Five Colleges in Massachusetts, and Florida
Atlantic University. In 1998 she was elected an honorary fellow of the
Modern Language Association, and she is a recipient of the Gabriela
Mistral Medal in Chile. Married to the Mexican astronomer Guillermo
Haro, who died in 1988, she is the mother of three children. Poniatowska
travels extensively to speaking engagements throughout Mexico, the
United States, Europe, and South America.
    Elena Poniatowska is equally well known as a journalist, a writer of

groundbreaking works of nonfictional literature, and a novelist. Some of her books cross the fluid boundaries between fiction and nonfiction by blending testimonial, documentary, and imaginative writing practices. She started her career in journalism in 1954 by conducting and publishing an interview every day for a full year for the Mexico City daily *Excélsior*. This intensive exposure to Mexican and foreign writers, artists, intellectuals, and politicians provided an education for her through immersion in the cultural milieu of the capital city, and it introduced Poniatowska as an energetic and irreverent young reporter. In 1955 she took a job with the daily newspaper *Novedades* (News), and over the years she has also contributed hundreds of interviews and articles to other important publications including *¡Siempre!* (Always!), *Vuelta* (Return), *Plural* (Plural), *fem*, and *La Jornada* (The Journey). She was a founding editor of the influential feminist magazine *fem* in 1976, and a feminist perspective is a crucial dimension of her writing, which embodies a dissident, even activist orientation vis-á-vis the status quo. She has contributed to the cultural life of her country through her participation in the founding of the publishing house Editorial Siglo Veintiuno and the Cineteca Nacional (national film library). For many years she had conducted a weekly writers' workshop in Tlacopac, and a number of the participants have published works that they created within the workshop. In 1978 Poniatowska received the National Journalism Prize for the interview genre, a prize never before awarded to a woman.

A selective overview of Poniatowska's published works must include the following ten titles that demonstrate the diverse ways in which she had interpreted Mexican society for over forty-five years as a writer. Poniatowska is known as a feminist and socially committed writer who pays particular attention to the experiences of Mexico's most marginalized citizens. *Palabras cruzadas* (Crossed Words, 1961) is a collection of her early interviews published in *Excélsior* and *Novedades*. These articles treat figures such as Diego Rivera, Lázaro Cárdenas, Juan Rulfo, and Alfonso Reyes with a combination of deference and irreverence, curiosity, insight, and naiveté that broke the established journalistic mold. Many contemporary journalists, particularly women in the field, credit Poniatowska with pioneering work that pushed the limits of newspaper writing in the 1950s and 1960s and introduced a new investigative approach and a critical perspective on the government and other institutions of power. Also in a journalistic vein, Poniatowska published a series of *costumbrista* (local-color) articles about the Sunday pastimes and leisure activities of the working poor in Mexico City in her 1963 book *Todo empezó el domingo* (It All Began on Sunday), reissued in 1997. Here in the urban milieu and popular culture are portrayed in sentimentalized terms that reflect the social distance between the writer or reader and the subject matter of the short sketches. Later works overcame that distance by inscribing the interview-based process that often informs her writing.

Hasta no verte Jesús mío (Here's to You, Sweet Jesus, 1969), one of Poniatowska's most celebrated texts, is a novel based on the oral testimony of an elderly woman living in a poor area on the periphery of the capital. The book's protagonist, Jesusa Palancares, experienced firsthand the Mexican revolution of 1910 and the many changes brought about by the tremendous growth and the increasing urbanization and industrialization of Mexico City. This testimonial novel has been heralded as a landmark work of Mexican literature for its innovative style and its representation of the voice and the experience of a poor, illiterate woman. The book won the Mazatlán Literary Prize in 1970.

La noche de Tlatelolco (Massacre in Mexico, 1971) is an oral history of the 1968 Mexican student movement. Its montage of the many voices of students, parents, and others involved in the movement offers an alternative and oppositional account of the student movement's goals and the government's repression of it during the summer and fall of 1968. This powerful testimony remains one of the best-selling books in Mexico almost thirty years after its publication. Upon its publication, it was awarded the prestigious Xavier Villarrutia Prize, but Poniatowska rejected the award in an open letter to President Luis Echeverría that expressed her protest against the previous regime's violent tactics and especially the October 2, 1968, massacre of students and other peaceful protesters in Mexico City's Plaza de las Tres Culturas (Plaza of the Three Cultures, also known as Tlatelolco).

Fuerte es el silencio (Silence Is Strong, 1980) is also an outstanding achievement in nonfiction writing. Its five chapters chronicle contemporary social movements and unrest including the 1968 student movement, a land recovery action, and a hunger strike undertaken by mothers of political prisoners who had "disappeared." A final significant testimonial work is the chronicle of the 1985 Mexico City earthquake, *Nada, nadie: Las voces del temblor* (Nothing, Nobody: Voices of the Mexico City Earthquake, 1988).

Among Poniatowska's many works of fiction are the short stories collected in 1979 in the book *De noche vienes* (The Night Visitor). These stories of upper-class privilege, gender difference, and popular class and ethnic discrimination include a reprinting of the narratives of *Lilus Kikus*, first published in 1954. *La "Flor de Lis"* (Fleur-de-lis, 1988), a feminine and feminist bildungsroman, explores the upbringing of a daughter of a wealthy, Eurocentric family in Mexico in the 1940s and 1950s and portrays the mother-daughter relationship with particular poignancy and insight. In focusing on the love and the tensions existing between a mother and daughter, this book also breaks new ground in Mexican literature. *Tinísima* (1992), also a winner of the Mazatlán Prize, crosses the boundaries between biography and novel to re-create in sympathetic terms a controversial figure in twentieth-century Mexican culture: the Italian-born photographer and Communist activist Tina Modotti. The book, based on a decade of archival research and extensive interviews with people who knew Modotti, portrays a complex, talented, and often misunderstood personality who broke with social conventions in her attempt to realize her artistic potential and her revolutionary aspirations.

Finally, Poniatowska frequently collaborates on photographic essays representing Mexican life, customs, and cultures. A well-known example is *Juchitán de las mujeres* (The Women of Juchitán, 1989). In this book, Poniatowska's essays accompany photographs taken by Graciela Iturbide of the indigenous women of the Juchitán on the Isthmus of Tehuantepec in the state of Oaxaca.

Poniatowska has long been one of the most important journalists and literary authors of contemporary Mexico. In a career that spans forty-five years of continuous production and innovation, she has inscribed in dozens of texts a commitment to celebrating and critiquing Mexican society and to creating an ever broader, more inclusive picture of the people and the experiences that constitute Mexican national life and culture. Her representations of women of all social classes have received particular acclaim, and in her interviews and in recent biographical essays she has also treated notable male intellectuals such as Nobel laureate author Octavio Paz. A hallmark of her writing and of her immense impact on Mexican letters is her ability to engage with the voices of the many others who make up a diverse community and to transform their stories creatively into literary texts of great honesty and integrity.

Further Reading

García Pinto, Magdalena. "Interview with Elena Poniatowska." In *Women Writers of Latin America: Intimate Histories,* translated by Trudy Balch and Magdalena García Pinto, 163–81. Austin: University of Texas Press, 1991.

Jörgensen, Beth E. *The Writing of Elena Poniatowska: Engaging Dialogues.* Austin: University of Texas Press, 1994.

Poniatowska, Elena. "A Question Mark Inscribed on My Eyelids." In *The Writer and Her Work,* edited by Janet Sternberg, 82–96. New York: W. W. Norton, 1991.

Price, Greg, ed. "Elena Poniatowska." In *Latin America: The Writer's Journey.* London: Hamish Hamilton, 1990.

Steele, Cynthia. *Politics, Gender, and the Mexican Novel, 1968–1988: Beyond the Pyramid.* Austin: University of Texas Press, 1992.

Beth E. Jörgensen

MAGDA PORTAL
(May 27, 1903–July 11, 1989)
Peru: Political Activist, Poet

A prize-winning poet and the author of political essays, short stories, and a novel, Magda Portal was a founding member of the American Popular Revolutionary Alliance (APRA) and lifelong political activist and advocate for social justice and women's rights. On the one hand, Portal has been hailed as the "first poetess of Peru" (Mariátegui 1988, 263) and the most important female political figure of the twentieth century in Peru (Villavicencio 1989, 17). On the other, she has suffered not only the political persecution common to leftist activists, but also the social and personal persecution of a patriarchal society, which came to include even the male leaders of her own political party, the APRA.

Portal was born into a working-class family in Barranco, a coastal suburb of Lima, Peru. Portal has stated that the poverty, misery, and social injustice she suffered as a child contributed to her ideological formation. Childhood experiences of sadness and solitude, marked by her family's poverty, especially after the death of her father when she was six and the death of her stepfather ten years later, influenced her politics and literary production. In an interview, she describes the moment in which her social thinking began to take shape:

I was seven years old when they took our house away and threw us out into the street. . . . My mother was a widow and life was sad and difficult. . . . It was the first injustice. That I will never forget; I carry it right here in my head. Because of that I have always been a social fighter and I will continue to be until I die. (Forgues 1991, 57–58)

Due to her family's economic problems, Portal worked and attended classes only informally at the University of San Marcos. There she participated in student political organizations, met her husband, Federico Bolaños, and, in 1923, won her first literary prize for poetry. Her marriage was unsuccessful, but her political affiliations, especially with Víctor Raúl Haya de la Torre and his followers, flourished.

Portal met and fell in love with her husband's brother, a poet known by the pen name, Serafín Delmar. They had a daughter, Gloria del Mar, and collaborated on political and literary projects, but the relationship was stormy.

Magda Portal's literary and political activities were not typical for women of this period. A very hierarchized society in terms of race and class, the socioeconomic and cultural structures of Peru were very rigid, and with a constant stream of conservative governments, the national climate for radical female action was repressive.

In 1925 Portal and Delmar left the hostile atmosphere of the Leguía regime for Bolivia where they participated in political journalism and published a book of revolutionary short stories, *El derecho de matar* (The Right to Kill, 1926). Their activities led the Bolivian government to demand their return to Peru.

In Lima, Portal befriended important Marxist thinker José Carlos Mariátegui and began to publish poetry and essays in his influential journal *Amauta* and to participate in the political and intellectual meetings of the Mariátegui group. Mariátegui praised Portal's poetry in his classic work *Seven Interpretive Essays on Peruvian Reality* (1978). She is, in fact, the only female writer he analyzes in the essays.

In 1927 Portal, Delmar, Mariátegui, and others were arrested as suspected Communists. Portal was first deported to Cuba and then to Mexico. There, together again with Delmar and Haya, she and eight or nine others founded the Mexican cell of the APRA movement. Portal was named secretary general of the executive committee. She was the only woman founder and leader.

Portal spent two years studying in Mexico and a year traveling through Central America and the Caribbean giving lectures and founding new APRA cells. Portal has commented on the surprise with which she was often met as she arrived on the political scene: it was unusual for a woman, especially a young and attractive one, to organize political groups and give anti-imperialist and anti-oligarchic speeches.

With the overthrow of Augusto Leguía in 1930, Portal and other exiles returned home and formed the Peruvian APRA party, the PAP. Named the leader of the women's section of the national executive committee, Portal began her travels throughout Peru to seek out new *compañeras* (comrades) and to start the political consciousness-raising process. At the First National Congress of the PAP held in 1931, Portal was fundamental in putting forth and passing the first women's national platform in Peruvian history.

A renewed climate of persecution led to Portal's living and working in hiding, but she was arrested in 1934 and given a sentence of 500 days in the women's prison of Santo Tomás in Lima.

Released in 1936 from prison, and once again working under repressive conditions, in 1939 Portal decided to leave Peru with her daughter, Gloria, for six years of exile. She spent most of her time in Chile where she worked in the Ministry of Education, became affiliated with the As-

Magda Portal. By permission of Kathleen
Weaver.

sociation of Socialist Women, and was honored for work on behalf of
women's rights and democratic causes.

Back in Peru in 1945, Portal had doubts about the direction in which
Aprista politics were headed, given Haya's apparent concessions to the
oligarchies and to the United States. In 1946 she organized the First National Congress of Aprista Women in Lima. Unfortunately, it was also
around this time, in early 1947, that Portal's daughter, Gloria, committed
suicide.

The Second National Congress of the PAP met in 1948 and, reversing
the platform of 1931, declared, "Women are not active members of the
party, they are simply companions, because they are not citizens." Portal's attempts to discuss the issue were silenced by the leaders. "Why
did we fight for twenty long years, if only to hear men taking all the
credit for our accomplishments? . . . [T]his was going to limit us in a way
I could not accept. So, I got up and left" (Andradi and Portugal 1978,
217).

After an armed revolt orchestrated by the APRA failed, Portal appeared before a military tribunal in 1950 because of her association with
the party. During the proceedings she declared, "I can't keep on like this,
because I'm against them. I've already told them that they betrayed the

movement!" (Andradi and Portugal 1978, 219). Portal was acquitted of the charges, and, with the publication of her accusatory essay, "¿Quiénes traicionaron al pueblo?" (Who Betrayed the People?, 1950), she broke all ties with the APRA.

Portal continued to write and participate in the intellectual life of Lima, and in 1956 she published a novel, *La trampa* (The Trap), which reflects her imprisonment and critiques the APRA. From 1958 to 1971, she was the director of Mexico's Fondo de Cultura Económica publishing house in Lima. In 1965 she published a collection of poems, *Constancia del ser* (Constancy of Being).

Portal became a member of one of the first Lima-based feminist groups, ALIMUPER (Action for the Liberation of Peruvian Women), now known as the Flora Tristán Center of Peruvian Women. In recent years, it has held a short story contest, the Magda Portal Short Story Contest.

In 1978 Portal again stepped into the political arena as a candidate of the Revolutionary Action Socialist party for the Constitutional Assembly. From 1982 to 1986, Portal was president of Peru's National Association of Writers and Artists. In 1981 she was honored as a writer and activist by the Inter-American Congress of Women Writers.

In 1983 she traveled to France for the First International Colloquium on Flora Tristán, one of her favorite "feminist precursors" since 1944 when Portal was first invited to write about her in Chile.

Magda Portal died on July 11, 1989, in Lima. The Lima daily, *La república* (The Republic) headlined the obituary, "Magda Portal, the Poet of the Poor Has Died" (Weaver 41).

As an intellectual worker—poet, writer, political activist, and woman—Magda Portal presents a paradigmatic case of the process of the realization of the female political and literary figure during the twentieth century. The obstacles she overcame in her struggle for social justice and the decision she made always to remain true to her revolutionary spirit and ideology—in spite of the storm of sociopolitical resistance, persecution, and personal attack she knew it would bring down on her—position her as an exemplary, heroic, and certainly notable woman of the twentieth century.

Further Reading

Andradi, Esther, and Ana María Portugal. *Ser mujer en el Perú*. Lima, Peru: Ediciones Mujer y Autonomía, 1978.

Forgues, Roland. *Palabra viva: Las poetas se desnudan*. Lima, Peru: Editorial El Quijote, 1991.

Mariátegui, José Carlos. *Seven Interpretative Essays on Peruvian Reality*, translated by Marjory Urquidi. Austin: University of Texas Press, 1988.

Miller, Francesca. *Latin American Women and the Search for Social Justice*. Hanover, N.H.: University Press of New England, 1991.

Reedy, Daniel R. "Aspects of the Feminist Movement in Peruvian Letters and Politics." In *The Place of Literature in Interdisciplinary Approaches*, edited by Eugene R. Huck, 53–64. Carrollton, Ga.: Tomasson, 1975.

———. "Magda Portal." In *Spanish American Women Writers: A Bio-bibliographical Sourcebook*, edited by Diane E. Marting, 483–92. Westport, Conn.: Greenwood Press, 1990.

Villavicencio, Maritza F. "Aprender a recordarte." *Viva* 4 (September 1989): 16–17.

Weaver, Kathleen. *Magda Portal, Peruvian Rebel: A Life and Poems*. New York: Teacher's College Press: forthcoming.

Catherine M. Bryan

COMMANDER RAMONA, MAJOR ANA MARÍA, AND THE WOMEN OF THE EJÉRCITO ZAPATISTA DE LIBERACIÓN NACIONAL (EZLN), OR ZAPATISTA ARMY OF NATIONAL LIBERATION
(true identities and birthdates unknown)

Mexico: Guerrilla Leaders

Commander Ramona and Major Ana María are in the forefront of the fight for indigenous rights in Mexico. Women have formed important parts of many revolutionary movements and guerrilla struggles throughout Latin America in this century. What was so striking about the appearance in Chiapas, Mexico, of the Ejército Zapatista de Liberación Nacional (Zapatista Army of National Liberation, or EZLN) in 1994 was the masked presence of indigenous men *and* women and a list of demands that included women's rights. On January 1, 1994, the EZLN took a number of cities of Chiapas, including San Cristóbal, Ocosingo, Comitan, and Altamiranda. The maximum military commander of the highland zone, Major Ana María, led the takeover of San Cristóbal. Commander Ramona was so courageous despite being so frail that she swayed public opinion not by appealing to reason but to our feelings.

Commander Ramona, a diminutive, monolingual Tzotzil woman, in her characteristic red and white woven and embroidered blouse (*huipil*), has become one of the most forceful symbols of the Zapatista uprising.

Commander Ramona. Courtesy of Melissa
M. Forbis.

Women like Ramona have shattered the traditional image of guerrilla movements as bearded men in fatigues in the mountains and have brought awareness to the oppression of indigenous and *campesina* (rural) women.

These two women are more than just token symbols. They represent thousands of women united behind them in a struggle for a life with dignity and justice. Each woman has a personal and unique story of how she came to that struggle, but there are elements that weave these stories together. These women leaders are the first to say that they are no different, no more or less than any other. They wear masks for security reasons and because anonymity makes personal stories matter less and collective histories more important.

Major Ana María, one of the first members of the EZLN, came from a family involved in pacifist struggles for land rights. Early on she saw that these struggles did not work and that the people were repressed for protesting. At the age of fourteen, she went to take up arms in the mountains. She was one of only two women, but because of their presence, other women began to join. In the mountains, there is an equality, and the work is the same for men and women. Like Ana María, who was twenty-six at the time of the uprising, most of the insurgents are young, between seventeen and twenty-six years old. She notes that, although it was hard at first for men to receive orders from a woman, they came to understand the necessity for women to participate in all aspects of the struggle (Lovera et al. 1997, 19).

She believes that women joined when they realized that they had no rights in their own communities. In some ways, it has been easier for the women in the mountains because of the forced equality. In the base-support communities of the EZLN, however, a macho ideology still exists. Commander Ramona represents the struggle at home where the difficult changes in everyday life are being forged and contested (personal interview, July 1998).

Commander Ramona comes from a small village in the highlands. Her family was also involved in pacifist struggles. As a young woman, she had to leave to look for work in the city; there was no other way for her family to survive. She was treated poorly, and she learned that, in general, indigenous people receive no respect and are not paid fairly for their merchandise. When she returned home hoping to change things, it was hard for her to gain recognition and a position of responsibility in her community. Men simply were not used to seeing women in public life. However, her work in organizing and defending the rights of women weavers got her named to the Clandestine Indigenous Revolutionary Committee (CCRI), the civilian structure made up of people from the base communities that regulates the military's (EZLN) actions.

Ramona first appeared publicly, carrying the Mexican flag captured in January, at the peace talks held with the federal government in San Cristóbal in February 1994. That year, serious illness took her away from public life for an extended period. In 1996 she was sent as a representative to the first National Indigenous Congress. She was the first Zapatista to arrive in Mexico City, where tens of thousands greeted her. While there, she received medical attention that would not have been possible to get in Chiapas. Ramona also inaugurated the first National Gathering of Indigenous Women, held in August 1997 in Oaxaca.

Commander Trinidad asked of the world, "Why don't they respect us if they say we're all equal?" The women of the EZLN are triply oppressed for being woman, indigenous, and *campesina*. Although Chiapas is resource-rich, the wealth is not shared among all its inhabitants. The state has one of the highest indices of poverty in Mexico, concentrated in the rural areas. More than two-thirds of residents live in malnutrition (CIACH 1997, 31). Almost half of all houses have no running water and indigenous-majority municipalities have little electric service. Over 117 of every 100,000 women in Chiapas are victims of maternal mortality each year, and the infant mortality rate is approximately 65 out of every

1,000 births. Overall illiteracy is 30.4 percent, but in indigenous areas this rises to more than half.

In areas where there is a scarcity of arable land for subsistence crops, women seek work on plantations, as domestics in cities, or those who can sell their traditional crafts. They are forced to deal with the racism of ladino society, which denigrates their indigenous identities. Women experience further shame for not speaking Spanish and for not being able to read or write. The women say that indigenous men suffer exploitation, but the women suffer more.

In addition, women have had to face sexism from men within their own communities. Rosa described the situation before the uprising as being like a chicken, locked up in the kitchen. Women typically wake at 3 A.M. to begin preparing food for their husbands who rise at 5 A.M., and although a man's labor might end in the afternoon, the woman continues to work into the night. Young girls are forced into marriage, and once married they have no say in the number of children they want to bear. Many women must ask permission from their husbands or in-laws to leave. They suffer a social acceptance of domestic violence and are frequently excluded from public life (personal interview, July 1998).

Since 1994 an additional difficulty has been the presence and threat of the Mexican Federal Army, which has stationed over 50,000 troops in the indigenous regions. The soldiers bring in alcohol and prostitution, and they sexually harass and intimidate the women of the communities.

Some women of the communities were involved in larger social movements and began to evaluate their own needs within these other struggles for justice and to organize. Ideas from the women's movement and activism in the Catholic Church nourished the EZLN long before the uprising started. According to Ramona, the struggle is nothing without the women, and the struggle of indigenous women did not begin with and will not end with the EZLN (Lovera et al. 1997, 37).

The women of the communities say that Ramona left her home to show them the way and pull them along. Women like Ramona and Ana María have been role models for others. They have gone to villages to talk about the changes in their lives and the struggle ahead (Rovira 1996, 377).

It was out of these discussions that the Revolutionary Law of Women emerged. Compiled by Commander Ramona and others, the law contains many important ideas. The first part of the law is a list of demands, including health care and education, aimed at the government. The rest is aimed internally: a life free from violence and free from forced marriage, with the ability to decide how many children one will have and when, and participation in community decision making at a higher level. Their organizing has led to a ban on alcohol, which may be implicated in domestic violence and poverty.

The law, approved by the EZLN in March 1993, has been referred to by Subcommander Marcos, an EZLN leader, as the "first uprising" (Rovira 1996, 113). The novelty of such a law and the frank discussion of women's rights and desires that it spawned speak to the strength and success of women's organizing in the EZLN. Indeed, a woman like Ramona could exist only in an organization that had already begun to evaluate women's participation and become more inclusive.

Community women have organized to combat the low-intensity warfare. One of the most striking photographic images from early 1998 is that of a group of women armed with nothing more than sticks, with babies on their backs, repelling invading soldiers from their villages. The government has tried to divide them by offering gifts to those who give up. One woman said, "As if they think so little of us women that we could be bought for a bag of corn, a sack of beans when it is freedom and justice we are demanding" (personal interview, March 1998).

The women have also been active outside of their communities. In September 1997, 1,111 Zapatistas marched on Mexico City. Two of the five main delegates were women. The *Consulta*, or Zapatista plebiscite, in March 1999, sent 5,000 Zapatistas to municipalities all over the state of Mexico; half were women.

Their struggle is a struggle in progress. Some early feminist hopes resulted in disappointment when faced with the reality of continued sexism and violence in the EZLN. The women of the EZLN have also experienced disappointment with their feminist sisters for giving up so easily on the small space that they have fought so hard to gain. No matter what the outcome of the conflict, for most of the women, there is no going back. They will continue to demand justice from all and for all. As Ramona has said, "Our hope is that one day our situation will change, that we women are treated with respect, justice, and democracy" (Lovera et al. 1997, 36).

Further Reading

CIACH (Centro de Información y Análisis de Chiapas), CONPAZ (Coordinación de Organismos No Gubernamentales por la Paz), and SIPRO (Servicios Informativos Procesados). *Para entender Chiapas: Chiapas en cifras*. Mexico City: CIACH, CONPAZ, SIPRO, and Impretei. 1997.

Clarke, Ben, and Clifton Ross, eds. *Voice of Fire: Communiqués and Interviews from the Zapatista National Liberation Army*. Berkeley, Calif.: New Earth Publications, 1994.

Harvey, Neil. *The Chiapas Rebellion: The Struggle for Land and Democracy*. Durham, N.C.: Duke University Press, 1998.

Holloway, John, and Eloina Pelaez, eds. *Zapatista! Reinventing Revolution in Mexico*. London: Pluto Press, 1998.

Kampwirth, Karen. *Feminism and Guerrilla Politics in Latin America*. University Park, Pa.: Penn State University Press, forthcoming.

Katzenberger, Elaine, ed. *First World, Ha Ha Ha. The Zapatista Challenge*. San Francisco: City Lights, 1995.

La Botz, Dan. *Democracy in Mexico: Peasant Rebellion and Political Reform.* Boston: South End Press, 1995.

Lovera, Sara, and Nellys Palomo, eds. *Las Alzadas.* Mexico, D.F.: Comunicación e Información de la Mujer, 1997.

Marcos, Subcomandante. *Shadows of Tender Fury: Letters and Communiqués of Subcomandante Marcos and the Zapatista Army of National Liberation.* New York: Monthly Review Books, 1995.

Ross, John. *Rebellion from the Roots: Indian Uprising in Chiapas.* Monroe, Maine: Common Courage Press, 1995.

Rovira, Guiomar. *Mujeres de maiz.* México: Ediciones Era, 1996.

Russell, Phillip L. *The Chiapas Rebellion.* Austin, Texas: Mexico Resource Center, 1995.

Stephen, Lynn. *Zapatistas! Documents of the New Mexican Revolution.* Brooklyn, N.Y.: Autonomedia, 1994.

Melissa M. Forbis

IRENE SÁEZ CONDE
(December 13, 1961–   )

Venezuela: Politician, Governor

A young politician with wide exposure and progressive policies, Irene Sáez Conde was born into a middle-class family in Caracas, Venezuela. She grew up and was educated during the 1970s when Venezuela was awash with petrodollars and public services, such as health care and the education system, functioned well. The youngest of six children, she developed a strong sense of independence and purpose at an early age. Her mother died of cancer when she was three years old, forcing her to accept responsibilities early in life.

Sáez first gained national attention in 1981 when she was a candidate in the Miss Venezuela beauty pageant. She won the Venezuelan pageant and competed in the Miss Universe contest in New York City. On July 20, 1981, Sáez was crowned Miss Universe at Carnegie Hall. Her victory opened a world of opportunities to her. During the following year, Sáez traveled around the world fulfilling the duties of Miss Universe, meeting world leaders and interacting with the press and the public. Rather than accept offers to model and act after her reign as Miss Universe ended, Sáez returned to Venezuela to attend the university. She earned a bachelor's degree in political science at the Central University of Venezuela in 1989 and later enrolled in the master's program in political science at the Simón Bolívar University, but she did not complete the second degree.

Sáez became the spokesperson for Banco Consolidado (Consolidated Bank) after finishing her B.A. This experience gave her widespread public exposure in Venezuela and experience in the business arena, both of which were very valuable to her political career. Because of her position with Banco Consolidado, Sáez's image entered people's homes daily in newspaper and television advertisements and commercials. Already a recognizable identity in Venezuela, her stature began to expand beyond that of an ex–beauty queen. She served as Venezuela's cultural representative at the United Nations in 1989 and 1991 and was head of the Dirección de Relaciones Institucionales (Board of Institutional Relations) of the Asociación de Damas Salesianas (Salesian Women's Association). In 1992 Sáez entered politics.

In 1992 Sáez entered the race for mayor of Chacao as the official candidate of both Acción Democrática (AD) and Comité de Organización Politica Electoral Independiente (Committee of Independent Electoral Political Organization, or COPEI). Chacao, a small, upscale suburb of Caracas, is home to the headquarters of a number of major corporations and diplomatic and consular offices. The municipality is unique in Venezuela because it contains only small pockets of poverty. Sáez won the mayoral race easily. In 1995, when she ran for reelection as the candidate for Integración, Renovación Nueva Esperanza (Integration, Renovation, New Hope, or IRENE), with the support of Acción Democrática and COPEI, she won 96 percent of the vote.

As soon as she entered office, Sáez began working to make local government more efficient and responsive to citizens. She focused her resources on issues that affected people's quality of life, ones that were solvable at the local level. She started by upgrading the police, ambulance, and sanitation services in Chacao. Sáez employed crews to work around the clock to keep the streets of Chacao clean. She also labored to improve culture in Chacao, organizing tai chi classes for the elderly in local plazas and establishing two orchestras and a school of ballet. As mayor, she encouraged citizens to contact her office with suggestions for improvements and to report problems. Unlike most politicians, Sáez acted upon people's reports.

Between 1989 and 1994, Venezuela weathered massive rioting, two coup attempts, and the impeachment of a sitting president, as well as internal schisms and splits in the traditional parties. At the same time traditional parties and politicians failed to address the problems facing ordinary Venezuelans, Sáez developed her reputation for good, clean, and efficient governance. Her success in Chacao, combined with her partisan independence, transformed her into a symbol of the antipolitics mood sweeping the country.

Sáez's success as mayor of Chacao attracted criticism as well as praise. She was accused of being an image with little substance, a creation of her handlers and the media. Critics argued that she did not have the experience to be president of the republic. They contended that, compared to governing the whole of Venezuela, governing Chacao was relatively easy given its wealth and limited problems. As the possibility of her candidacy for president increased, she began to face subtle sexism from various sectors of society, most obviously from the armed forces. Sáez refused to accept traditional gender roles and defined herself as a politician, not as a "female" politician.

Praise for her actions as mayor far exceeded the criticism. By 1996 she was popular enough in Chacao and throughout Venezuela for manufacturers to ask her to model for an "Irene" doll. She agreed, and the promotion slogan for the doll stated bluntly, "Irene is the truth." As her public persona grew, her private life attracted more attention. Her devotion to saints became widely known; small statues of different saints decorate her desk. Sáez has also been linked with various national and international personalities, including the former president of Banco Consolidado José Alvarez Stelling; Andrés Caldera, the son of a former president of Venezuela; and New York real estate developer Donald Trump. Recently she was engaged to the governor of Miranda (the state that borders Caracas), Enrique Mendoza, but the relationship collapsed as a result of their busy lives.

Though noncommittal in public to the possibility, her name began to be mentioned as a candidate for the presidency as early as 1995. In polls conducted in 1996, Sáez had the support of 35 percent of the respondents. Her nearest rival at the time, Henrique Salas Römer, had 11 percent, and Hugo Chávez was the choice of 10 percent of Venezuelans.

Sáez's popularity was a product of her successes in Chacao and her partisan independence—her unwillingness to engage in politics as usual. From the start of her candidacy, the Christian democratic COPEI courted her as its candidate, and Sáez became the official COPEI candidate in September 1998. Her decision to ally with COPEI—one of the two traditionally dominant parties in Venezuela—was risky. Much of her early support came from her partisan independence and her distance from COPEI and the social democratic Acción Democrática. By linking herself with COPEI, Sáez placed her support from the antipolitics bloc of voters in jeopardy.

Sáez attempted to bridge partisan boundaries and attract independents in her campaign for the presidency. Though she received support from COPEI and other smaller parties, she claimed that her political independence remained intact.

The policies Sáez proposed during her campaign were largely reform-ist and in stark contrast to the more radical proposals of Hugo Chávez. Politically, she supported reforms to revitalize Venezuelan democracy by accelerating institutional decentralization, making the congress more accountable and responsive to citizens, and guaranteeing the independence of the judicial branch. She supported reforms to permit the direct reelection of presidents, the introduction of referenda at the national level, and the popular election of judges. She opposed calls for the death penalty as a means for combating soaring crime rates. Her social program centered on improving the quality of government services, including health care, education, housing, and infrastructure. Sáez supported market economics and was generally friendly toward the business community. Addressing corruption in the Venezuelan state, Sáez said she would strengthen the tax collection agency and customs to reduce evasion and the importation of contraband. Drawing attention to differences between her background in local government and Chávez's experience as a coup plotter, Sáez regularly emphasized her commitment to liberty, tolerance, and social justice in democracy.

Though she was widely recognized and respected, her candidacy faltered throughout 1998. By the time she accepted the COPEI nomination, her support in the polls had fallen below 20 percent. Pressure increased for a common candidate to oppose Chávez in the December presidential election. COPEI, Acción Democrática, and Proyecto Venezuela met to forge a last-minute alliance. Sáez tried to position herself as the natural alliance candidate, but her downward trajectory in the polls undermined her position. Two weeks before the election, COPEI and Acción Democrática threw their support behind Salas Römer. Without COPEI, Sáez placed third in the presidential election winning only 3 percent of the vote.

After losing her bid for the presidency, Sáez immediately returned to the campaign trail. The governor of Nueva Esparta died months after winning reelection in November 1998. Sáez entered the special March 1999 election for governor. Nueva Esparta, in eastern Venezuela, comprises mostly Isla Margarita. Its economy is based primarily on tourism.

In her campaign for governor, Sáez accepted support from President Hugo Chávez's party Movimiento V República and from the Polo Patriótico (Patriotic Pole) coalition. She rejected overtures from COPEI and Acción Democrática. Sáez touched on the same themes in Nueva Esparta that she had addressed as a presidential candidate and as mayor of Chacao. She won the election for governor with 70 percent of the vote.

As governor, Sáez has generally supported President Chávez. She urged her supporters to support the convocation of a Constituent Assembly and agreed that many of the problems facing Venezuela could be addressed in a Constituent Assembly. Though she accepted Chávez's plan for change, she has continued to be an advocate for the issues that attracted her to politics in Chacao in 1992. She has reiterated her belief that state and local government are key to democratic renewal in Venezuela and should not be undermined by the assembly's actions. Similarly, she has called for the assembly to elicit opinions from a broad range of political actors, including independent politicians, civil society groups, and nongovernmental organizations.

Throughout her life, Irene Sáez has demonstrated an ability to achieve her goals even as conditions change. The political environment in Venezuela changed dramatically between 1992 and 1999. The traditional parties have practically disappeared, but Sáez continues to fight for clean and efficient government. She has championed these basic issues in Chacao, on the campaign trail for president, and now in Nueva Esparta. Due to her self-confidence and strong sense of purpose, Irene Sáez will probably be an active participant in Venezuelan politics in the future, independent of the changes implemented by President Chávez and the Constituent Assembly.

Further Reading

"Irene Sáez Conde." *Primer Plano*, October 25, 1998. http://www.etheron.net/PrimerPlano/curIrene-Saez.html

Lander, Mabel. "Interview with Irene Sáez." *Transporte Magazine*, October 1997. http://www.transporte.com/english/articles/October_Irene.html

"El machismo venezolano afectó a Irene Sáez." *El universal digital*, November 5, 1998. http://politica.eud.com/1998/11/09/051198c.html

Schemo, Diana Jean. "Caracas Journal: After Beauty Crown, Now Jewel of City Hall." *New York Times News Service*, May 6, 1996. http://205.134.250.194/life/05061car.html

"Señorita Presidente." *Semana*, September 15–22, 1997. http://semana.com.co/users/semana/sep15/senorita.html

Michael R. Kulisheck

HAYDÉE SANTAMARÍA
(December 30, 1922–July 26, 1980)
Cuba: Political Activist, Culture Promoter

Haydée Santamaría, who was born in Encrucijada, Cuba, has been portrayed in official iconography as the embodiment of sacrifice and passion for the Cuban revolution. In 1959, under the auspices of the Cuban government, she became the founder and director of Casa de las Américas (House of the Americas), the Latin American and Caribbean Arts Institute in Havana. She held the position until her death by suicide in 1980. As a unique promoter of Caribbean and Latin American culture, she was also a powerful force for intercultural exchange.

Santamaría, an autodidactic, had the equivalent of a seventh-grade formal education. She grew up on the sugar plantation Constancia, located in Las Villas Province. Ostensibly strengthened by political strife and death (she lost her brother, her fiancé, and several fellow conspirators in the fight against Cuban dictator Fulgencio Batista), she was a woman of great sensibility who possessed natural intelligence and political pragmatism. In January 1959, when Batista conceded defeat to Fidel Castro's guerrillas and fled the country, Santamaría was among those who had survived the conflict with the dictator's army and the cruelty of his military intelligence service. She had dedicated years of underground support to Castro in the effort to bring about Batista's downfall. After such militant devotion to the Cuban revolution, Santamaría became a cultural figurehead.

From a young age, Santamaría and her brother Abel showed interest in social issues and political activism. Early on, both brother and sister were participants in the underground resistance movement that fought to remove Batista from power. They were militant members of the Orthodox Youth party opposed to Batista's coup d'état (March 10, 1952) and they edited and mimeographed the clandestine anti-Batista magazine *Son los mismos* (They Are the Same Ones).

On July 26, 1953, Abel's and Haydée's destinies changed forever when they took part in Castro's assault on the military fortress Cuartel Moncada in Santiago de Cuba. On July 26, 1953, Batista's troops captured them during the failed takeover of the military barracks. Most of Castro's fellow guerrilla fighters were killed. Batista's men brutally tortured Abel (who was second in command to Castro), gouging out his eyes and presenting one of them to Haydée, hoping to shock her into providing information. Haydée refused to cooperate. After that incident, Abel Santamaría and Haydée's fiancé, Boris Luis Santa Coloma, both perished.

As a result of Batista's reprisals, all twenty-one men captured at the Saturnino Lora hospital near the barracks were killed; only Santamaría and Melba Hernández survived. Approximately seventy coconspirators died in the aftermath by means of military execution or under torture during interrogation. Batista's troops eventually caught Fidel Castro and his brother Raúl, who had escaped during the attack. They were released from the prison at the Isle of Pines on May 15, 1955, as part of a general amnesty.

As an active member of the clandestinely organized National Direc-

Haydée Santamaría. Courtesy of Casa de
las Américas.

torate of the 26th of July Movement (organized by Castro in 1955 shortly
after the Moncada fiasco), Santamaría went underground with the alias
María. She completed several risky missions, carrying information and
money to the Sierra Maestra, to Havana, and to Santiago de Cuba. A
significant activist, she was instrumental in the organization and execution of the planned insurrection at Santiago de Cuba (November 30,
1956). During the uprising, which was to coincide with the landing of
the yacht *Granma* (carrying Castro, mythic Argentine guerrilla member
Che Guevara, and more than eighty men) on the southern shores of
Oriente, Batista's troops trapped Santamaría and others in a building.
She managed to escape along with her husband, Armando Hart, and
fellow collaborators Frank País and Vilma Espín. A few days later, on
December 2, the yacht carrying Castro and his men crashed on the rocks
along the shore during a storm. Batista's army killed all but twelve of
the men. The few who survived fled to the Sierra Maestra Mountains to
continue the struggle against Batista.

Santamaría and Hart intensified their work in the underground. They
traveled around the island collaborating with Castro and others in the
26th of July Movement and wreaked havoc on Batista's government
(planned insurgencies, support for battles against Batista's troops, and
the systematic destruction of the country's infrastructure). While Hart
was leaving Santiago to go on a secret mission, Batista's troops caught

and imprisoned him. Soon after his capture, Santamaría left the country and went to Miami to galvanize support from the exiled community in the United States.

In 1959, when the revolutionary guerrillas finally defeated Batista and came to power, Santamaría was reunited with her husband. The couple moved to Havana to participate in the new revolutionary government. In July 1959, Santamaría became director of Casa de las Américas. During the 1960s, while serving as head administrator at Casa, she gave birth to two children, Abel and Celia. She held several political posts throughout her career and was engaged in constant political action on a local level. She also traveled to other countries in the Communist bloc for conferences and official activities. In 1965 she was elected a member of the National Direction of the Party of the Socialist Revolution (PURSC); in 1974, a member of the National Committee of Federation of Cuban Women (FMC); and in 1975, a member of the Central Committee of the Communist Party of Cuba (PCC). She published articles and interviews of political, cultural, and social nature in the journals *Juventud rebelde* (Rebel Youth), *Periódico Granma* (Granma Journal), *Revista Bohemia* (Bohemia Review), and *Revista Santiago* (Santiago Review).

As director of Casa de las Américas, she led one of Cuba's prominent cultural institutions to productive heights during Cuba's tumultuous 1960s and 1970s. Casa's popularity and influence in the 1960s were unquestionable; the journal of the same name became one of the major cultural magazines of Latin America.

As an institution, Casa was a center for the promotion and dissemination of Latin American and Caribbean culture. The organization awarded prestigious literary prizes; published thousands of books; and promoted sculpture, photography, crafts, painting, and literature of every genre from all over Latin America. Several celebrated Latin American and European intellectuals made up part of the journal's editorial board, and others such as Colombian writer Gabriel García Márquez and Uruguayan Mario Benedetti served as members of juries for prizes awarded by the institution. Casa also developed departments of music and theater and created art competitions and centers of research, such as the Center for Caribbean Studies, founded in 1979.

From 1960 to 1965, under the editorship of Antón Arrufat and Fausto Masó, the journal *Casa de las Américas* published some of the best Latin American writers of the boom. *Casa* also printed numerous critical articles written by such notable critics as Angel Rama, Edmundo Desnoes, and Calvert Casey. In 1965 Roberto Fernández Retamar became chief editor and shifted the contents of the journal toward a more "committed" orientation.

There was also conflict at Casa. Santamaría found herself at the center of the imbroglio over the Padilla affair. The controversy began when the

Writer's Union (UNEAC) awarded the young poet Heberto Padilla a literary prize for his controversial book of poems *Fuera del juego* (Out of the Game, 1969). He did not actually receive the prize because some Cuban critics suspected that the text was a veiled criticism of the regime and alleged that Padilla's "defeatist" poetics suggested an antirevolutionary stance. Apparently, at first, Santamaría defended the award, but when Cuba's Internal Security intercepted a letter that several Latin American intellectuals had composed and sent to her (they were appealing Padilla's case), she was criticized for collaborating with purported enemies of the revolution (Franqui 1988, 366). In the end, she reversed herself and did not oppose the official call to rescind the award. By 1969 Santamaría had become a literary apparatchik for the Castro government. She made it clear to the juries for literary awards that no artist could remain apolitical since that position was always inherently political (i.e., obviously antirevolutionary) in a place like Cuba.

Santamaría's role as director was challenging but rewarding. Cultural officials broke through the diplomatic ostracism imposed by the U.S. embargo and established a cultural exchange with most Latin American countries that had severed diplomatic ties with Cuba. Since the revolution, Casa, as a cultural bridge and publishing house for the promotion of the arts and literature, had represented a period of great interest in, and worldwide dissemination of, Latin American culture. Santamaría's role as promoter of culture and director of Casa for two decades is firmly established in the history of Latin American culture.

Apparently, Santamaría had two unfulfilled wishes in her adult life. One was her passionate desire to fight alongside Che Guevara in Bolivia; Castro did not allow her to go. The second was to be part of a new revolutionary front in another country, which she was not able to do either.

In the year of the Mariel exodus (250,000 Cubans fled the island in 1980), while Cuba was celebrating the annual commemoration of the 26th of July Movement, Santamaría committed suicide. Her death was as powerfully symbolic as her life had been. Her many struggles and sacrifices represented an unending dedication to the history and the culture of the island; what her death signified remains a subject of uneasy and tense debate. Notwithstanding, Santamaría was a significant figure and a personification of the Cuban revolution.

Further Reading

Franqui, Carlos. *Diary of the Cuban Revolution*. New York: Viking Press, 1979.
———. *Vida, aventuras y desastres de un hombre llamado Castro*. Barcelona, Spain: Editorial Planeta, 1988.
Menton, Seymour. *Prose Fiction of the Revolution*. Austin: University of Texas Press, 1975.

Santamaría, Haydée. *Moncada*, with introduction by Robert Taber. Secaucus, N.J.:
   Lyle Stuart, 1980.

Linda S. Howe

BEATRIZ SANTOS ARRASCAETA
(January 20, 1947–   )

Uruguay: Singer, Educator, Author

Beatriz Santos, a songwriter, vocalist, journalist, choreographer, teacher,
and writer, was born in Montevideo, Uruguay. The older of two children,
Santos still lives with her family in Montevideo in Barrio Buceo, where
she has lived since her birth. She is the niece of Juan Julio Arrascaeta,
the "Langston Hughes" of Afro-Uruguayan poetry.

   After completing high school, Santos, like many other black Uruguayan women, worked as a domestic servant. However, her strong will;
her direct, outspoken, bold, nurturing, and independent-minded personality; her natural leadership; and her musical talent led her to break
the stereotype so often associated with black Uruguayan women. Because of her own personal experiences with racial and class discrimination, she challenged the tendencies that perpetuate stereotypes,
exploitation, and the subjugation of Afro-Uruguayan citizens. Santos's
concern for racial justice and the social and economic advancement of
black Uruguayan citizens embarked her on a career as one of the most
widely known civil rights activists in Uruguay.

   In 1977, under the direction of theater directors Hugo Blandamuro,
Raúl Lómez, and Wilfredo Toamaran, Santos began a career in children's
theater. Several years later, she worked with the New York director Ellen
Stewart, singing love songs in a musical version of William Shakespeare's *Romeo and Juliet*. Her strong, impressive voice brought her increasing popularity. She joined the theater group Odín, where she
performed *candombe*, the music and dance that originated among the
slaves of Uruguay. While with the group, Santos began to spread the
musical history of Afro-Uruguay. Through her own sound, she brings
black Uruguayan traditions to a wider audience. Today, she is a noted
vocalist of Afro-Uruguayan oral traditions.

   Santos's life changed when she participated in her first workshop on
Black America conducted by a professor from Swarthmore College at the

United States Cultural Alliance in Montevideo in 1980. Thereafter, Santos began to lecture on the customs, history, and folklore of the black community.

The early 1980s spurred Santos's career as a radio commentator on Afro-Uruguayan culture. From 1982 to 1988, she produced a variety of radio shows, including "Sangre, Sudor, Tambor" (Blood, Sweat, and Drums) and "Negritud" (Negritude) for channels 4, 5, and 10. Breaking ground, she created additional shows on black art for the Portuguese radio and television network and performed her *candombe* shows on the Spanish radio and television network and for Danish radio. Radio and television became another vehicle for Santos to educate the masses and to build positive images of Afro-Uruguayan citizens.

Santos's work has brought her to the attention of both national and international leaders. In 1985 she was invited to serve as the mistress of ceremony for an international seminar on apartheid. Because of her work in opposition to apartheid, she was selected to serve as a member of the Uruguayan Committee against Apartheid. Later, Santos was appointed to work with Dorothy Watson, a representative of the National Association for the Advancement of Colored People (NAACP), to plan a special program commemorating civil rights leader Martin Luther King, Jr. In 1986 the governor of the Brazilian state of Santa Catarina named Santos the cultural exchange coordinator between Brazil and Uruguay.

As the 1980s ended, Santos continued to lecture and sing. She presented the first program on black Uruguayan women at the University of the Republic and was invited by the University of São Paulo to participate in an international conference on slavery (1988). She coordinated, in the same year, a month of activities commemorating 100 years since the abolition of slavery in Brazil for the Brazilian-Uruguayan Cultural Institute. Santos participated in an international dialogue with *Roots* author Alex Haley, sponsored by Worldnet, on race in Uruguay, Guatemala, and Venezuela. Santos also wrote articles and editorials for *Mundo afro* (Afro World), the newest black Uruguayan periodical.

Santos is the founder of the Centro Cultural por la Paz y la Integración (Cultural Center for Peace and Integration, or CECUPI), an organization created to combat discrimination and to eradicate the multiple oppressions experienced by black Uruguayans. Their main project is to battle drug abuse in the Afro-Uruguayan community. To draw attention to their efforts, the organization held its first conference in October 1990 on Identity and Education of Afro-Uruguayans. In 1991 Santos sponsored the first international conference on Afro-Uruguayan culture with the participation of such Afro-Hispanic studies authorities as Marvin A. Lewis, William Luis, and Carlos Guillermo Wilson.

During this period, Santos made her first trip to the United States. Invited in 1991 by the University of Missouri-Columbia, she presented the state of Afro-Uruguay to the first international research conference on Afro-Hispanic literatures and languages. Since 1991 Santos has also lectured in Brazil and Africa. Her fight against racism is supplemented by her service to the executive committee of the Association of Afro Latin American Research, the World Association of Women Journalists and Writers, the Institute of the Promotion of Uruguayan Social Economy (IPRU), Elderhostel, and the Uruguayan Cultural and Social Association (ACSU, 1941), the oldest black cultural center and organization in Uruguay.

In 1995 Santos starred in *El desalojo de la calle de los negros* (Blacks Out on the Street), written by black Uruguayan playwright Jorge Emilio Cardoso. The play focuses on the government's removal of poor black Uruguayans from the *conventillos*, or old colonial mansions, which serve as tenements. Performed in the open air among the ruins of the Ansina housing complex in Barrio Reus al Sur, Santos sang about the destruction of the cradle of Afro-Uruguayan culture.

Santos was nationally recognized in 1995 as an inspiration for black Uruguayan achievement. She is featured in *Uruguayos por su nombre: Sepa quién es quién* (Uruguayans by Name: A Who's Who). Santos was profiled by the *Miami Herald* in 1997. Santos comments on her attempt to run for political office in 1996, when the Colorado party invited her to run. Despite her efforts, she lost the election. There are still no black political officials in Uruguay.

In October 1988 Santos was invited to attend the conference "Vital Voices: Women in Democracy," an ongoing U.S. initiative cosponsored by the Inter-American Development Bank (IDB), which places women leaders at the center of foreign policy concerns.

Equally important as Santos's involvement in reform movements is her contribution to Afro-Uruguayan discourse. After writing radio scripts and articles for newspapers, Santos's poetry appeared in 1993 in the *Afro-Hispanic Review*. Since 1993, Santos has published three books and several short stories. The contradictions between black and white reality inspired Santos to write her first book, *Historias de vida: Negros en el Uruguay* (Life Stories: Blacks in Uruguay). Published in 1994 and coauthored with Teresa Porzecanski, *Historias de vida* presents ten factual and documentary accounts of black Uruguayan life.

One year later, Santos published *El negro en el Río de la Plata* (Africans in the River Plate), with Argentine writer, Nené Lorriaga, which revisits black Uruguayan history from slavery to the present. Santos's third book, *La herencia cultural africana en las Américas* (African Cultural Heritage in the Americas, 1998), is an anthology of essays on such issues as the black woman, racism, sexism, civil rights, Afro-Uruguayan art, theater, *candombe*, carnival, and blacks in the diaspora. The first five essays trace the role of the black woman in the Americas, including a discussion of such black Uruguayan women writers as María Pintos, Maruja Techera, Lucila Núñez Barrios, Amparo Aguirre Barrios, Celia Núñez Altamiranda, Myriam Tammara la Cruz, Cristina Rodríguez Cabral, and Martha Fermina Gularte. The book concludes with Santos's view of the future of black America in the new millennium.

As a civic leader and activist, Santos draws attention to black Uruguayans beyond the realms of carnival as she struggles for social, economic, and racial equality. Her music, her lectures, her teachings, and her writings broaden the definition of what it means to be a black Uruguayan.

Further Reading

Campodónico, Miguel Angel. *Uruguayos por su nombre: Sepa quién es quién*. Montevideo, Uruguay: Editorial Fin de Siglo, 1995.

Ellison, Katherine. "Political Power Eludes Blacks in Latin America." *Miami Herald*, April 6, 1997, pp. 1, 22.

Santos, Beatriz Arrascaeta. *La herencia cultural africana en las Américas*. Montevideo, Uruguay: Ediciones Populares para América Latina, 1998.

Santos, Beatriz Arrascaeta, and Nene Lorriaga. *El negro en el Río de la Plata*. Buenos Aires, Argentina: Editorial Amerindia, 1995.

Santos, Beatriz Arrascaeta, and Teresa Porzecanski. *Historias de vida: Negros en el Uruguay*. Montevideo, Uruguay: Ediciones Populares para América Latina, 1994.

Caroll Mills Young

BENEDITA DA SILVA
(March 11, 1942–   )

Brazil: Politician, Poet

A champion of Brazil's oppressed in her political life and poetry, Benedita da Silva was born in Praia do Pinto, a former shantytown of Rio de Janeiro. As a child she moved to Morro do Chapéu Mangueira, in Leme, where she still lives. Since her birth, Silva has lived with the difficulties and obstacles to survival common to the poor of Third World countries. During childhood she faced hunger and misery, including rape when she was seven years old. She began to work when she was very young, helping her mother with domestic chores, carrying cans of water on her head, and participating in the organization of activities for her mother's *umbanda terreiro* (temple for Afro-Brazilian religions). At age seven Silva worked selling candy, shining shoes, and carrying bundles in the marketplace.

As a young woman, she had many professions: domestic worker, street seller, door-to-door salesperson, and factory worker. Later, with great persistence and effort, her situation improved. First she got work as a cleaning woman at a school and later as a public servant for Detran (similar to the Department of Motor Vehicles) in Rio de Janeiro.

In 1979 she completed a course of study to become a nursing aid and began work at the Hospital Miguel Couto, and she passed the Exame de Madureza (the high school equivalency exam). In 1982 Silva entered the university in Rio de Janeiro, where she graduated with a double degree in social services and social studies.

Through the difficulties she experienced during these early years, Silva learned that the empowerment of the oppressed could come about only if they united. Thus, she began her social commitment to organize her people. As a teacher at a community school in the shantytown of Chapéu Mangueira, she used the pedagogical method of Paulo Freire to teach children and adults to read and write. She brought the women of Chapéu Mangueira together in the Women's Association of Chapéu Mangueira. She was the founder, also, of the Women's Department of the Federation of Shantytown Associations of the State of Rio de Janeiro (FAFERJ) and participated in the creation of the Center of Shantytown and Periphery Women (CEMUF).

Silva, married three times and twice widowed, has two biological children. Her first marriage, at age sixteen, was to Newton Aldano da Silva, with whom she had her two children. In 1981, after a vascular cerebral accident, he died. In 1983 Silva married Agnaldo Bezerra dos Santos, known as Bola, an outstanding Communist-Christian community leader, who was imprisoned by the military forces during the Brazilian dictatorship (1964–1986). According to Silva, Bola was one of the most important political influences of her life. Bola died at Christmas time in 1988.

Today, Silva is married to Antonio Luis Sampaio, known as Pitanga, an Afro-Brazilian actor preferred by filmmaker Glauber Rocha (founder of the Brazilian New Cinema). Pitanga is an active member of the Workers' party (PT) and one of the most popular town councillors of Rio de Janeiro. Currently, he is secretary of sports for the state of Rio de Janeiro.

At the beginning of the 1980s, when popular resistance began to weaken the power and repressive control of the dictatorship, the Worker's party was created. Silva joined the party and its leader, Luis Ignácio Lula da Silva. From the start, she was a remarkable member. Her political career took off surprisingly quickly and was marked, from the beginning, by initiatives that stemmed from her own life history as an Afro-Brazilian woman in the shantytowns.

In 1982 Silva was elected town councillor for the Workers' party and assumed the leadership of the party in the Municipal Chamber of Rio de Janeiro.

In 1986 she was elected federal constitutional representative to the Bureau of the National Constitutional Assembly. Silva actively participated in the Afro-Brazilian, Indigenous Populations and Minorities Subcommittee and later in the Social Order Committee and in the Men and Women's Rights and Guarantees Committee.

Several of her proposals, reflecting her commitment to social change for the oppressed, were incorporated into the current constitution. She is the coauthor of the amendment that proclaims racial prejudice to be a crime, 120-day maternity leave, prohibition of salary differences based on race or gender, the right to receive day care for children until they are six years old, and the right of female prisoners to keep their children during the lactation period. She is also the author of an amendment that recommended the breaking of diplomatic relations with South Africa during apartheid, which, unfortunately, was rejected—by just fifteen votes.

Silva was reelected to the Chamber of Federal Deputies in 1990 with the most votes of all of the Workers' party candidates in Rio de Janeiro. In 1992 she was a candidate for mayor of the city of Rio de Janeiro and won in the first round. In the second round, although she did not win, she received an amazing 1,326,678 votes. In 1994 she was elected senator of the republic, the first Afro-Brazilian woman elected to the Federal Senate. She won the first vacancy with the greatest number of votes, more than 2,200,000. In 1998, shortly before the completion of her term, Silva left her position as senator to become the vice governor of the current governor of Rio de Janeiro, Anthony Garotinho.

In her last term as a federal representative, Silva participated in the elaboration of the Child and Adolescent Code, one of the most advanced pieces of legislation with regard to children's rights. At the United Nations International Conference on the Environment and Development (known as Rio-Eco/92) held in Rio de Janeiro, Silva participated in a forum promoted by nongovernmental organizations that investigated the mass sterilization of women.

In the Chamber of Deputies, she contributed to the passage of the United Nations Convention regarding the elimination of all forms of discrimination against women and also contributed to the Hague Convention for international cooperation and protection of children and adolescents in the process of international adoption. Silva actively participated in four parliamentary commissions of inquiry (the CPI that investigated the extermination of children and adolescents; the CPI that investigated violence against women; the CPI of the mass sterilization of women in Brazil, of which she was the creator; and the CPI that shed light on child and adolescent prostitution).

Silva presented the following proposed bills now being examined by the senate: regulating the nursing profession, regulating domestic servants, dealing with family birth control planning, forbidding the demand of a sterilization certificate for job admittance, and declaring a national holiday on November 20 as Afro-Brazilian Consciousness Day. Silva was also the author of the following proposals: creating a Permanent Committee on Human Rights in the Chamber of Deputies; regulating the inclusion of Afro-Brazilians in television production, film, and publicity; including the discipline of the history and culture of Africa in academic curricula; and suggesting to the executive power the creation of the National Council to Fight Against Racial Prejudice.

Silva is the founder and vice president of the Parliamentary Groups, Senegal-Brazil and Brazil-South Africa. She was twice the head of External Committees of the Chamber of Deputies which traveled to South Africa in 1991 and 1994. As a member of the World Council of Churches, she takes part in the group dedicated to fight against international racial prejudice. She is a member of the North American Association of Parliamentarians for Global Action, which brings together parliamentarians from all over the world.

Silva is a poet and author of many books about crucial Brazilian problems, such as racial and social discrimination against Afro-Brazilians, indigenous people, lesbians and gays, and abandoned children; the systematic theft of indigenous land; the extermination of children; land reform; and violence against and sterilization of poor women. Silva has also written articles on these topics for several important Brazilian newspapers, including *Jornal do Brasil* (Journal of Brazil), *Folha de São Paulo* (Blade of São Paulo), and *Correio brasiliense* (Brazilian Courier).

In her only book published in the United States, her life story, one of Silva's poems reveals the problematic of her national, racial, and gender identity. In this poem, she describes herself as a black woman who must fight against a white society that has turned her into a white man and castrated her. But, in spite of what white society has done to her, she proclaims that she will shout, make her voice heard to free herself, and be a black woman.

Benedita da Silva's politics, poetry, and life express all her deep consciousness of being Afro-Brazilian, female, and oppressed in a society that, based on differences of gender, race, and social class, excludes the majority of its people from the benefits of economic and social development. Her dedication and work in the struggle to change this situation make her one of the most remarkable women of Latin America in the twentieth century.

Further Reading

Silva, Benedita da. *Benedita da Silva: An Afro-Brazilian Woman's Story of Politics and Love*, edited by Medea Benjamin and Maisa Mendonça. Oakland, Calif.: Institute for Food and Development Policy, 1997.

Jorge Vital Moreira

ARMONÍA SOMERS
(October 7, 1914–March 1, 1994)
Uruguay: Educator, Author

Armonía Somers achieved unprecedented recognition as a distinguished educator and as an audacious writer who became one of the principal voices in Uruguayan narrative during the latter half of the twentieth century. The eldest of three daughters, she was born Armonía Liropeya Etchepare Locino in Pando, Uruguay. Of her parents, Pedro Etchepare, a seeker of social utopias, and María Judith Locino, a devout Catholic, Somers writes,

If chaos is understood as having had a freethinker father and a Catholic mother, the situation could have been somewhat difficult. But as it happened I was fascinated by both. I would fly to a utopia with one, but when I returned from the heights due to some daily reality, and there certainly were those, I would find the loving matriarchal circus net waiting for me safely below. Chaos was nothing more than a delirious game that taught me to take risks, but without fear, such as I have done always in my controversial literature. (Cosse 1990, 248)

Somers did not inherit the faith of either of her parents, but she did inherit a nostalgia and desire for an earthly state of perfection, despite the cruelty and pathos of human life that she chronicles so ably in her short stories and novels.

At the age of thirteen, Somers began traveling alone to Montevideo to attend a teacher training program. She obtained her degree from the Normal Institute in 1933 and began teaching in a variety of schools in Montevideo, where she became an acute observer of class differences and their impact on education:

I work in places that teach me a great deal . . . because I am sent to schools in poor neighborhoods such as La Teja, where children come to school with their fingers in their mouths to warm them since they have slept in tin shacks, places where rats cross the classroom floor. (Cosse 1990, 251–52)

She also observes that, in the privileged neighborhoods, children learn rapidly because they are well rested and well fed.

In 1944 Somers produced the first of several educational works that were published in Uruguay, Mexico, and Rome. Her first work, on Helen Keller's teacher, is entitled *Ana Sullivan Macy: La forja en noche plena* (Ana Sullivan Macy: The Forge in the Darkest Night, 1944). In 1957 Somers became assistant director of the Library and Pedagogical Museum of Uruguay, and in 1961 she was named director of the Pedagogical Museum. From 1962 to 1971, Somers served as the director of the Uruguayan National Center for Pedagogical Documentation and Information. In 1964 and 1965 she traveled to Europe to complete her studies of pedagogical documentation in Paris, Dijon, Geneva, and Madrid for UNESCO. Somers, who had married Rodolfo Henestrosa in 1955, retired from her career in education in 1971 as Armonía Etchepare de Henestrosa. Somers had met her husband, the director of Talleres Gráficos Sur, a publishing enterprise, in 1953 when she took her book *El derrumbamiento* (The Collapse, 1953) to his establishment to be printed. She always kept her public, civil identity quite distinct from her private, literary identity as Armonía Somers. In an interview, she expressed her opinion about teaching and writing:

They are separate pursuits because they embody two personalities. I can feel where they part company. As a writer, I was never a teacher, but as a teacher I was a writer, and so my classes were very imaginative and stimulating. But as a writer I was never didactic because that would have been frightful. I write that way in my other profession, in pedagogical essays, not in the novel. (Garfield 1987, 39)

Somers kept her two public personas, teacher and writer, separate by using her two names. This survival strategy allowed her to protect her privacy while pursuing and succeeding in two professions simultaneously, despite the usual obstacles encountered by a woman of her place and time. Somers explains how, before the publication of her first novel *La mujer desnuda* (The Naked Woman, 1950), she chose the name Somers: "I liked it because it is the root of the word summer in English and German, and I have a great deal to do with summer, perhaps because I was conceived in summer" (Cosse 1990, 255).

An air of mystery and the secret of Somers's identity is central to the reception of her first novel in Uruguay. *La mujer desnuda* originally appeared as a double edition in the magazine *Clima* (Climate) in 1950. It was attributed to male Uruguayan writers, a group of literary collaborators, a degenerate, a learned German or English author, a homosexual writer, and an anonymous sex maniac who had deposited his manuscripts in the Uruguayan National Library. No one surmised it could have been written by an Uruguayan woman, despite the name Armonía. When the author's identity had been established, Montevidean society was scandalized not only by Armonía's fantastic, horrific, erotic subject matter and direct language, but also by her daring use of a nom de plume. The mysterious writer Armonía Somers became something of a legend in Uruguay. Somers made good use of the speculations about her to create the private spaces she needed to continue with the real duality in her life: her two demanding careers.

By chronology, Somers belongs to the Uruguayan literary generation of 1945, which includes such writers as Mario Arregui, Mario Benedetti, Amanda Berenguer, José Pedro Díaz, Carlos Martínez Moreno, María Inés Silva Vila, Idea Vilariño, and Ida Vitale. Somers, however, did not consider herself part of this generation:

I feel no ties with the generation I ought to be part of. I believe that apart from the usual generations, the literary ones are not only chronological but also imply a certain homogeneity of form, motivation, semantics, and even in ideology, that separates them from previous or future generations. In my case (not because I feel superior or inferior, but rather different), I do not consider myself to be part of the generation that they usually call mine. (Garfield 1987, 38)

Somers came to be considered an original writer, but this was not always the case: "At first critics could not understand how something original could occur to me. Now it seems that I *am* original, but in those days I was not" (38).

Critical efforts were also expended in seeking influences, such as Guy de Maupassant, in Somers's work but they were in vain, for no one discovered her real teachers: the skillful craftsman Marcel Proust and the questioning cynic August Strindberg. In her narrative works, Somers combines the lightness of the fantastic mode with a more austere focus on the cruel aspects of human life such as hatred, rape, revenge, mysogyny, violence, and death. This combination is what differentiates her from other Southern Cone authors of existential and psychological narratives of the same period: for example, Ernesto Sábato, Roberto Arlt, and Juan Carlos Onetti. She uses direct language within dense narrative structures to bring about her unusual amalgam of thematic and stylistic elements. She is also apt to bend or break grammatical rules, a practice that has brought critical questioning of her grasp of grammar and syntax, especially at the beginning of her career when her writing was described as being a difficult struggle with words. Somers, the rigorously trained schoolteacher, was simply fashioning something new out of the rules she knew only too well.

It is instructive to look at the reception of Somers's work by two major critics, Mario Benedetti and Angel Rama, in order to understand the attitudes and expectations that helped and hindered her literary career. Somers's disconcerting writing is often described as being difficult. According to Somers, "One person, who will remain nameless, even said that I was the product of reader indigestion" (Garfield 1987, 38). That person was Mario Benedetti, who attacked Somers's structure, style, and grammar in a highly denigratory 1953 review of *El derrumbamiento* in *Número* (Number). He accuses her of "a false assimilation of certain sensationalist tendencies of contemporary narrative," producing in the five stories of *El derrumbamiento* "an indigestible hodgepodge of textual influences that are as risky as they are seductive" (Benedetti 1953, 102). Furthermore, he says that she does not legitimately represent chaos, but rather allows chaos unfortunately to affect all aspects of her writing.

In his well-known, frequently quoted 1963 article in *Marcha* (March), Angel Rama, who was a great supporter of Somers, described the contradictory reactions aroused by her work: "Everything is uncanny, alien, disconcerting, repulsive, and yet incredibly fascinating in the most unusual narrative work known to our literary history" (Rama 1963, 30). Rama astutely examines what is so unsettling yet so compelling about Somers's writing:

Here is a literature where the pedal of horror and repugnance has been pressed down as far as it will go in order to mobilize an underworld of creatures and atmospheres of a highly imaginative kind, which are simultaneously anchored, on account of her style, in a hallucinatory reality. . . . The author violently shoves [the elements of horror] into our field of vision, obliges us to acknowledge their existence, rubs them up against our skin in order to try and contaminate us . . . and, by doing so, plunge us into an uneasy, insecure world, breaking apart our well-worn habits. Armonía Somers understood and had the imagination to face the full range of possibilities of human behavior. From her teacher training days forward, she developed the observational and technical skills necessary to make her readers understand also. Hence the fascination of her narrative. (Rama 1963, 30).

Further Reading

Benedetti, Mario. Review of *El derrumbamiento*, by Armonía Somers. *Número* 5 (1953): 102–3.

Cosse, Rómulo, ed. *Armonía Somers, papeles críticos: Cuarenta años de literatura.* Montevideo, Uruguay: Librería Linardi y Risso, 1990.

Garfield, Evelyn Picon. *Women's Voices from Latin America: Interviews with Six Contemporary Authors.* Detroit, Mich.: Wayne State University Press, 1987.

Kantaris, Elia Geoffrey. *The Subversive Psyche: Contemporary Women's Narrative from Argentina and Uruguay.* Oxford, England: Oxford University Press, 1995.

Rama, Ángel. "La Insólita literatura de Somers: La fascinación del horror." *Marcha* 1188 (1963): 30.

Linda I. Koski

MERCEDES SOSA

(July 9, 1935–)

Argentina: Singer

Known to many as Pachamama (the mother of the land) or Black Sosa, "the voice of hope and justice for South America," "the voice of those without voice," singer Mercedes Sosa was born in Tucumán on Argentina's independence day. Her paternal grandparents were indigenous (Quechua), and her maternal grandmother was French.

Sosa performed publicly for the first time on the radio program *Hoy canto yo* (I Sing Today) in Tucumán in 1950. She sang the zamba (traditional Chilean folk song) "Triste estoy" (I Am Sad) written by Margarita Palacios. Her performance won her the opportunity to sing on the program for two months. She continued to sing in Tucumán until 1957. Throughout this period, Sosa collaborated regularly with the Peronist movement, singing at the popular demonstrations and events they promoted.

In 1957 Sosa married Oscar Matus, also a musician. They had a son who was born the following year. In 1958 they left Tucumán to live in Buenos Aires, where Sosa worked temporarily in the Office of Social Work at the Ministry of Education. In 1961 Sosa recorded her first album, "Zamba de los humildes" (Zamba for the Poor), which was released the following year without fanfare. In 1963 she signed a recording contract and moved to Uruguay. She won widespread recognition for her first album produced in Uruguay, "La zambera" (The Zamba Dancer).

The year 1962 was important for Argentine music. Sosa joined with other musicians (Armando Tejada, Oscar Matus, Vito, Francia, and Sendero) to form the New Argentine Singers Movement in the Journalists' Circle in Mendoza; Sosa was the lead singer in the group. The musical movement's manifesto argued that music can be a vehicle to reach "the people." Sosa performed with the movement, including a recital in 1964

Mercedes Sosa. Photo by Gabriel Diaz. Courtesy
of David W. Foster.

with Armando Tejada and her husband Oscar Matus. However, Sosa
began gradually to separate herself from the group. Inspired by other
composers and poets, she released an album entitled *Canciones con fun-
damento* (Songs for a Good Reason). In 1965 Sosa separated from her
husband. The painful experience of breaking with Matus and surviving
on her own resulted in her album *Zamba para no morir* (Zamba to Stay
Alive) which she recorded in 1966.

Though she says that her professional debut as Sosa was in 1965 at
the Cosquín Folk Festival, the full impact of her launch was felt a year
later when *Zamba para no morir* debuted on the main radio station in
Argentina, Radio El Mundo (Radio the World). In this same year Sosa
met the man who became her second husband, Pocho. Building on her
musical success, Sosa went on her first tour of Germany, Belgium, Switzerland, and the Netherlands. Later, in 1967, she returned to Europe,
traveling to France, Rome, Poland, and the Soviet Union, and toured the
United States.

The year 1968 was a difficult one for Sosa. When she toured, she performed music that was committed to the folk heritage of Argentina, as

well as works by other Latin American poets who were equally committed to their own lands and people. Conservative sectors of society criticized her harshly for visiting and collaborating with Communist regimes in Eastern Europe. In this same year, she released the albums "Mujeres argentinas" (Argentine Women), "Homenaje a Violeta Parra" (Homage to Violeta Parra), and "Con sabor a Mercedes Sosa" (With the Flavor of Mercedes Sosa), which was an homage to many of the most revered composers in Latin America.

In the 1970s Sosa became famous by singing the classics composed by Argentines Atahualpa Yupanqui, Eduardo Falú, and Horacio Guarany, and Chileans Violeta Parra and Víctor Jara (Jara was later assassinated by the Chilean dictatorship in the 1973 coup). Her sensual voice, her poncho, and her *bombo leguero* (large indigenous drum) were now known internationally. Moreover, she dedicated herself to introducing her listeners to the rich variety of folk music from the region, including *bagualas, carnavalitos, milongas, zambas, chayas, malambos*, and other types of traditional songs. Her lyrics, which became more and more political, openly addressed such issues as agrarian reform, human rights, and democracy. During a concert in La Plata, government security forces arrested Sosa along with her son, her band, and members of the audience. Throughout 1978, she received bomb threats at her performances and was arrested repeatedly, although she was always freed soon thereafter. The military government in Buenos Aires finally released a decree prohibiting her from performing and made it impossible for her to continue working.

Sosa moved to Madrid in 1979 and began a three-year exile. Upon arriving in Spain, she bought a house and a car to make tours of Europe. This period was painful: She was separated from her country, and her husband was diagnosed with cancer.

Sosa's music and spirit have always been characterized by a search for new forms, and during her time in Spain, she began to sing songs written by Milton Nascimento, Chico Buarque, and other Brazilian masters of pop music. In 1979 she sang her first concert for Amnesty International at the Royal Albert Hall in London. She also performed in Israel and toured in Canada, Colombia, and Brazil, where she was offered permanent residence.

In 1982 Sosa returned to her own country, one year before the Argentine dictatorship ended. She gave three emotional concerts in Buenos Aires at the Ópera Theatre which were received enthusiastically. Songs such as "Canta la cigarra" (The Cicada Sings), "Todo cambia" (Everything Changes), and her version of Fito Páez's "Yo vengo a ofrecer mi corazón" (I Come to Offer My Heart) captured the spirit of reconciliation that defined Argentina at that moment. Sosa recorded these concerts and released them as an album entitled *Mercedes Sosa en vivo en la Argentina*

(Mercedes Sosa Live in Concert); the album sold hundreds of thousands of copies. Sosa had been converted into a folk heroine, a symbol of the fight for justice, the resistance, maternal bravery, and artistic and human integrity.

In 1986 Sosa sang with singer and composer León Gieco, and their duet of the song "Sólo le pido a Dios" (I Only Ask from God) became famous. Sosa began to perform works by such colleagues as Fito Páez, Teresa Parodi, Antonio Tárrago Ros, and Víctor Heredia. Her fans and supporters became more and more diverse as people of all ages, both in Argentina and around the world, responded to her music. In 1987 and 1988, Sosa gave concerts in the United States as part of the tour Mercedes Sosa en Concierto: La Original, La Auténtica (Mercedes Sosa in Concert: The Original, the Authentic One). She performed in formal venues such as Carnegie Hall in New York City, as well as on university campuses. In 1988 Sosa returned to Argentina to participate in an Amnesty International tour with Bruce Springsteen, Peter Gabriel, and Sting, who dedicated the song "They Dance Alone" to the Mothers of the Plaza de Mayo for their struggle to know the whereabouts of their missing children as well as to the thousands of people who had disappeared in Argentina.

In 1991 Sosa gave a series of wildly successful concerts as part of the show Sin fronteras (Without Borders) at Luna Park in Buenos Aires. As well as Sosa, this event included the participation of two Argentines, Teresa Parodi and Silvina Garre; a Colombian, Leonar González Mina; a Venezuelan, Lilia Vera; a Mexican, Amparo Ochoa; and a Brazilian, Beth Carvalho. In this same year, Sosa dedicated a memorable concert at the Club Ferrocarril del Oeste stadium to the Mothers of the Plaza de Mayo.

In 1995 Sosa presented her tour Gestos de Amor (Gestures of Love) in the United States and Canada with the help of her New York agent Néstor Rodríguez Lacorén, the author of an homage written in verse for Sosa titled La nueva mujer—poemas (The New Woman—Poems, 1989). She traveled with her son and administrator, Fabián, and her musicians, guitarist Nicolás Brizuela, pianist Gustavo Spatocco, drummer Ernesto Lobo, and bassist Carlos Genoni.

Sosa's years of work and performance were recognized at a ceremony held in Avery Fischer Hall at New York City's Lincoln Center. The director of the United Nations Development Fund (UNIFEM), Noeleen Heyzer, joined by First Lady Hillary Clinton, presented Sosa with the Anniversary Award and named her the United Nations Woman of the Year for 1995. Sosa has received numerous other awards including the Premio Konex in the Female Folk category (1995).

Throughout her career, Sosa has participated in numerous films, including El santo de la espada (The Saint of the Sword, 1970), Güemes (1971), and Verano del potro (Summer of the Colt, 1990). She also participated in the International Festival of Viña del Mar in 1992–1993, the Second Christmas Concert at the Sala Nervi at the Vatican (1993), the International Festival of the Mar del Plata (1995), and the Americano in Mendoza (1995). Recently she performed the Argentine composer Ariel Ramírez's *Misa criolla* (Folk Mass) with Italian tenor Luciano Pavarotti.

Sosa has released more than sixty albums and CDs to worldwide success. She completed her most recent recording, the album "Al despertar" (Upon Awakening, 1988), after conquering illness, depression, and the near loss of her voice. Commitment and solidarity with "the people" have been the constant theme in Sosa's music, as well as her conviction that good will prevail during even the most painful moments and circumstances. Sosa lives in a modest apartment in Buenos Aires on Avenue 9 de Julio, where she continues her work as an artist of great integrity.

Further Reading

Bach, Caleb. "Mercedes Sosa." *Song Without Boundaries* 48, no. 3 (1996): 40–47.
Rodríguez Lacorén, Néstor. *New Woman: A Tribute to Mercedes Sosa.* New York: Latin Culture Publishers, 1989.

María del Mar López-Cabrales

MARTA TRABA
(January 5, 1930–November 27, 1983)
Argentina/Colombia: Author, Critic

A literary figure and an art critic, Marta Traba was born in Buenos Aires during the so-called *Década Infame* (Infamous Decade). Traba began her long exile in 1950, when Peronism was at its peak, and she lived in Buenos Aires, Rome, Paris, Bogotá, Montevideo, Caracas, San Juan, Barcelona, Washington, D.C., and Paris, reflecting her restless life. *Las ceremonias del verano* (The Ceremonies of Summer, 1966), her first autobiographical novel, describes the first stage of this journey. "Nobody ever dies in his homeland" is a line from her second novel, *Los laberintos insolados* (Sunburned Labyrinths, 1967), which turned out to foreshadow her own fate.

Her life and work show the intertwining of art criticism and literature. Her first book, published in 1952, was a poetry collection, *La historia natural de la alegría* (The Natural History of Happiness). Criticism and

Marta Traba. Courtesy of the Estate of
Marta Traba.

fiction interface in *Los cuatro monstruos cardinales* (The Four Cardinal
Monsters), published in Mexico in 1964. This process recurred in her
essay "Hipótesis sobre una escritura diferente" (Hypothesis Concerning
a Different Writing, 1981) and *Arte de América Latina: 1900–1980* (Latin
American Art: 1900–1980), published posthumously in 1994. By 1982,
when Traba published "Hipótesis sobre una escritura diferente," she had
already published a considerable body of narrative. In 1966, thanks to
Las ceremonias del verano, she attained international recognition with the
Casa de las Américas (House of the Americas) award, one of the most
prestigious literary prizes at that time. Traba considered that *Las ceremonias del verano* was a late incursion of hers into literature (García Pinto
1984, 44). *Los laberintos insolados, Pasó así* (That's How It Happened, 1968),
and *La jugada del sexto día* (The Play on the Sixth Day, 1969) followed.

A gap in Traba's narrative production lasted a decade. Then she produced what, according to her, was the most important work she ever
wrote: *Homérica latina* (Latin Homerics, 1979). In an interview, she
admitted that this was a more serious approach to literature (Garfield
1987, 131–132). Although there is a high level of maturity in this work,
it is marked by a loss of intimacy.

Homérica latina and the other novels that followed, such as *Conversación
al Sur* (Conversation in the South, trans. as *Mothers and Shadows*, 1981)
and *En cualquier lugar* (In Any Place, 1984), marked an end to her second

and last narrative stage. The main topics of her last two novels are the abuse of power and the willingness to attain liberty within the confines of a crushing force of oppression (García Pinto 1984, 40). Traba considered *Homérica latina* the climax of an externally oriented vision of her Latin American surroundings and of urban spaces (Garfield 1987, 136).

Her literary career was closely linked to her work as an art critic. She obtained a bachelor's degree in literature at the National University of Buenos Aires; later she began studying art. She met Jorge Romero Brest, the founder of the Escuela de Estudios de Artes Plásticas (School of Art Studies) and director of the magazine *Ver y estimar* (To See and Value, 1948–1955). Traba worked for the magazine and published her first writing in it. The late 1940s saw the inception of a specialized art criticism, spearheaded by Jorge Romero Brest, J. A. Payró from Argentina, and Mario Pedrosa and Ferreira Gullar from Brazil (Acha 1993, 150). Afterward Traba continued to study art in Italy and France.

Traba's research and analytical work came to be considered one of the most important and serious undertakings on Latin American art. She arrived in Colombia in 1953 with her husband, Colombian journalist Alberto Zalamea. There she started to make a systematic study of Latin American art. Her work was enriched by her experience as an art history professor at the University of the Americas (1954–1955) and at the University of the Andes (1956–1966), both in Santafe de Bogotá, Colombia, where she met Colombian painter Fernando Botero. She also taught Latin American art at the National University (1966–1967). In the second half of the 1950s, Colombia experienced an intellectual rebirth with the publishing of *Mito* (Myth), a magazine that played a crucial role in the cultural and art scene of the country. *Mito* aspired to become the opposite of the national myth the country was living, and consequently it stood for avant-garde nonconformity (Tellez 1975, 141). Colombia was under the military dictatorship of General Gustavo Rojas Pinilla, and *Mito* was important because it brought together individuals who shared a hatred for mediocrity and bureaucracy (Cobo Borda 1975, 8). In the field of art, the status quo was no longer an option. The abstract artists were opposed to the figurative ones. Geometric pieces reached high expression in the work of Omar Rayo and Eduardo Ramírez Villamizar. This is the context in which Traba made her name in just a few years. Her talent, theoretical strength, critical vision, and spirit of polemics contributed to the creation of a new, critical space in Colombian plastic art. **Beatriz González**, one of the best Colombian painters, and Traba's student at the University of the Andes, acknowledged that Traba's criticism was very convincing:

I think that Traba was the one to discover Botero. She found that Botero could fit well within an attitude of the world at that moment. If we think in Fellini's exaggeration or Bacon's, or even if we think of the figuration, this new attitude spread in Europe. Botero matched all of that. Traba explained it to us. (*El mundo rotundo*)

Traba criticized, innovated, proposed, and created. She was everywhere. She used all means she had at hand. In 1957 she founded *Prisma* (Prism) magazine. A year later, she published her first book about art: *El museo vacío* (The Empty Museum) and the essay "Problemas del arte en Latinoamérica" (Problems of Art in Latin America). In 1960 her third work came out: *Arte en Colombia* (Art in Colombia). In 1961 *La pintura nueva en Latinoamérica* (New Painting in Latin America) appeared. The first holistic vision of art in Latin America (Acha 1993, 161) was written by a woman. *La pintura nueva en Latinoamérica* was a turning point, according to Traba, in terms of her specialization in Latin American art (García Pinto 1984, 39).

Traba's body of criticism grew impressively both in theoretical and practical aspects. She arrived in Colombia during the dictatorship, a period during which many cultural venues, such as the national Art Exhibition Center, were closed. By the time the center enjoyed a second surge of importance, from 1957 to 1968, Traba's criticism had become very influential. On October 31, 1963, the Modern Art Museum of Bogotá opened under Traba's direction. Later, the museum moved to different places, including Colombia's National University, where she worked as the director of the Cultural Department. The university was a lively and open center where art, culture, and politics thrived.

In 1963 she published *Seis artistas contemporáneos colombianos* (Six Contemporary Colombian Artists). A year later *Los cuatro monstrous cardinales* appeared in Mexico. In 1966 Traba received the Casa de las Américas award. That year, she began working as the curator of the Organization of American States' permanent collection.

In 1967 the liberal Colombian president, Carlos Lleras Restrepo, decided to deport her from Colombia, which caused a national uproar. The Colombian newspapers recorded the protests of university students against a visit by Nelson Rockefeller, the governor of New York. Although Traba was an Argentine citizen when she was expelled, popular support and her two Colombian sons contributed to her being allowed to remain in the country but not at the university.

That same year, she divorced Alberto Zalamea, and everything became an exile within the exile. Her second novel, *Los laberintos insolados*, was published the same year. In 1968 she obtained a Guggenheim scholarship that helped her renew her historical and critical work on Latin American art.

In 1969 Traba left Colombia to start the third stage of her perilous odyssey. She lived temporarily with her two sons and her second husband, Angel Rama, the Uruguayan literary critic, in Montevideo. That

year she published her novel *La jugada del sexto día*. In 1970 they moved
to Puerto Rico, and she was hired at the University of Puerto Rico, Río
Piedras to teach Latin American art and to give seminars on aesthetics.
During her two-year stay in Puerto Rico, she published three books—
Propuesta polémica sobre arte puertorriqueño (A Polemical Proposal on
Puerto Rican Art, 1971), *La rebelión de los santos* (The Rebellion of the
Saints, 1972), and *En el umbral del arte moderno: Velázquez, Zurbarán, Goya
y Picasso* (On the verge of Modern Art: Velázquez, Zurbarán, Goya, and
Picasso, 1973)—and an essay, "El ojo alerta de José Campeche" (The
Alert Eye of José Campeche, 1972). She also started to write *Homérica
latina*. It is not clear why the University of Puerto Rico did not renew
both Traba's and Rama's contracts. They returned to Montevideo for a
short period of time and briefly visited Chile. Later on, they moved to
Caracas and lived there from 1973 to 1979.

Although the 1970s were years of instability and change for Traba,
they also turned out to be a productive decade. Besides her writings
about Puerto Rico, she published *Dos décades vulnerables en las artes plásticas latinoamericanas, 1950–1970* (Two Vulnerable Decades of Latin American Plastic Arts, 1973); *Historia abierta del arte colombiano* (Open History
of Colombian Art, 1973); *Mirar en Caracas* (To See in Caracas, 1974); *La
zona del silencio* (The Zone of Silence, 1975); *Los signos de vida* (The Signs
of Life, 1975); *Mirar en Bogotá* (To See in Bogotá, 1976); *Los muebles de
Beatriz González* (Beatriz González's Furniture, 1977); *Los grabados de Roda*
(Roda's Engravings, 1977); *Elogio de la locura, Alejandro Obregón y Feliza
Bursztyn* (In Praise of Madness, Alejandro Obregón and Feliza Bursztyn;
1978/1984); *Mirar en Nicaragua* (To See in Nicaragua, 1979).

In 1979 *Homérica latina* was published. Traba and Rama moved to Barcelona. Later that same year they arrived in the United States. Rama
worked at first as a visiting professor and then as a lecturer at the University of Maryland. Traba taught at Harvard University, the University
of Massachusetts, Oberlin College, the University of Maryland, Middle-
bury College, and finally at Princeton University. In 1982, in an interview
with Mexican journalist and writer **Elena Poniatowska**, Traba confessed:
"We enjoyed a period of stability by accepting to work at Maryland
University . . . a home, a library and a wonderful place to live. The Washington Museum and the Library of Congress looked to us like paradise."
Traba and Rama were unable to renew their visas. She was also facing
health problems and had to undergo cancer surgery. The risk of depor-
tation was looming. Traba accepted the proposal of Belisario Betancur,
the Colombian conservative president, to receive Colombian citizenship.
In March 1983, although in Paris, she renewed her ties with Colombia.
On November 27, 1983, Traba and Rama were invited to attend the Hispanic American Encounter of Intellectuals held in Colombia, but they

were both killed in the crash of an Avianca flight from Paris, a flight that left Latin American art and literature in mourning.

Further Reading

Acha, Juan. *Las culturas estéticas de América Latina; reflexiones*. México, D.F.: Universidad Nacional Autónoma de México, 1993.
Araujo de Vallejo, Emma, ed. *Marta Traba*. Bogotá, Colombia: Colombiana, 1984.
Bayón, Damián. "El espléndido no conformismo de Marta Traba." *Sin nombre 14*, no. 3 (1984): 92–96.
Cobo Borda, J. G., comp. *Mito, 1955–1962*, 8. Bogotá, Colombia: Instituto Colombiano de Cultura, 1975.
García Pinto, Magdalena. "Entrevista: Marta Traba." *Hispamérica* 38 (1984): 50–52.
———. "Marta Traba." *Hispamérica* 38 (1984): 39.
Garfield, Evelyn Picon. *Women Voices from Latin America: Interviews with Six Contemporary Authors*. Detroit, Mich.: Wayne State University, 1987.
González, Beatriz. "Termómetro infalible." *Gaceta* 6 (1990): 21–22.
———. *Botero: El mundo rotundo de Botero*. Bogotá, Colombia: Audiovisuales, 1994.
Tellez, Hernando. "Notas sobre *Mito*." In *Mito, 1955–1962*, compiled by J. G. Borda. Bogotá, Colombia: Instituto Colombiano de Cultura, 1975.

Oscar Rafael Jiménez González (translated by Alexandra Vincent)

MARÍA TERESA TULA
(April 23, 1951–   )

El Salvador: Political Activist

María Teresa Tula, a political activist and grassroots intellectual, is best known for her work with COMADRES (The Mothers and Relatives of Political Prisoners, Disappeared, and Assassinated of El Salvador Monseñor Romero). Born to a poor family in the community of Izalco, Tula was raised primarily by her maternal grandmother until she was thirteen or fourteen years old. She attended primary school for slightly less than two years and was a self-taught observer of Salvadoran rural life. Pregnant with her first child at fifteen, Tula became a single mother at an early age. Because the father of her first child never returned to live with her, she lived with her sibling and step-siblings.

A year later, she met a man who changed her life in important ways, and she built a loving marriage and partnership with him. José Rafael

María Teresa Tula. Courtesy of Kelley
Ready.

Canales Guevara was twelve years older than Tula, but he treated her
with respect and dignity. They became close friends long before they
lived together and had children. Rafael, who worked in a sugar refinery
as a blacksmith, became active as a labor organizer with the sugar-mill
workers. Initially, Tula was unaware of his work. This changed in 1978
when he was imprisoned and tortured for being a labor organizer. When
the sugar mill where he worked was stormed by the Salvadoran army
and the union leadership detained and imprisoned, Tula quickly learned
about his secret life as a labor organizer. Although upset that he had not
told her, Tula understood the need for secrecy in labor organizing. Most
grassroots organizing taking place in El Salvador in the 1970s had to be
done in secret.

Tula came of age politically in El Salvador just as the civil war between
the Salvadoran government and the armed left was getting under way.
In 1978 three important guerrilla groups were already working secretly
to achieve socioeconomic and political transformation. During this same
year the COMADRES was formed. When her husband became a political
prisoner, Tula met the COMADRES in the jail where he was being held.
Other women were visiting their imprisoned family members and working to free them. From the jail she began to attend COMADRES meetings
and to learn more about the deeply troubled political situation in El

Salvador. The COMADRES took over the Red Cross building and the United Nations building in El Salvador to draw attention to their cause that year. They occupied Catholic churches and held many public demonstrations as well. In 1979 they were invited to Costa Rica where they began a very effective campaign to build international solidarity for their work.

In 1980 several armed men, who said they were municipal police agents, came to Tula's home and took away her husband claiming he was a witness to a robbery. Two days later, his body was found dressed only in his underwear, and there was a .38 calibre bullet in his head. Tula defied the advice of many people and claimed his body. After the loss of her husband, she became a full-time activist in the COMADRES.

The year also marked the formation of the Farabundo Martí National Liberation Front (FMLN), which brought together four guerrilla groups and the Salvadoran Community party into a political and military coalition. The civil war heated up, and the climate of repression worsened. At that time, government and death-squad killings reached almost a thousand per month. Also in 1980, Archbishop Monseñor Romero was assassinated while saying Mass. The COMADRES were named for him; he had played a key role in founding and supporting the organization. In 1980 the country was clearly divided into revolutionary and counterrevolutionary camps.

That same year, the COMADRES themselves became the victims of repression. Their office was bombed for the second time, and the first COMADRES activists were captured and killed—the first of many. The COMADRES continued to do their very public work and to go to body dumps, where they took pictures of the bodies to show them to people looking for relatives who had disappeared. They also began to work with international delegations. When one woman escaped from jail and made it back to the COMADRES, she warned Tula that she would be next. Tula prepared to leave with her family, and in 1982 she took her four children with her to live in Mexico City, where she worked in the COMADRES office. In 1983 they traveled to Canada. In 1984 Tula returned to El Salvador after receiving a telegram informing her that her mother had died.

In January 1985, Tula traveled to Europe where she interacted with a wide range of feminists in the Netherlands, Switzerland, France, England, Italy, Greece, Spain, and Germany. It was there that she consolidated some of her ideas about what Salvadoran grassroots feminism meant, even if the label feminism was not used at the time:

You know, being a woman doesn't necessarily make for change. There are women in the positions of power, even presidents or prime ministers, who have the bodies of women, but the minds and hearts of oppressive men. It's a shame.

It just goes to show that it isn't enough to have women in power; we have to change the whole system—in El Salvador, the United States, and Europe. If we don't then we could die and another generation of feminists would be born with more ideas, but we would all continue to be oppressed. (Tula 1994, 126)

After she returned to El Salvador, Tula continued her work with CO-MADRES, and in 1986 she became a target herself. She was detained and tortured once in May and then picked up again shortly thereafter. She was again tortured and also raped, imprisoned for four months, and finally released in September after a great deal of international pressure and support. After an earthquake destroyed the house she was occupying, and living in fear of being recaptured, she decided to flee with her family to the United States.

In early 1987, Tula arrived in the United States with her two youngest children. She went first to Los Angeles and then to Washington, D.C., where the COMADRES had an office. She filed for political asylum in 1987, but her petition was denied. That same year she was accused of being a terrorist despite the support she received from forty-seven senators and congressmen after she gave testimony in the U.S. Senate. Finally, in 1994, Tula and four of her children were granted political asylum. She continued to work with the COMADRES office in Washington, D.C., and in 1995 she moved to Minneapolis where she works in an electronics factory, continues to make speaking tours, and carries out political work. She is well known for her testimonial titled *Hear My Testimony: María Teresa Tula, Human Rights Activist of El Salvador*, which contains her life story as well as many insights into the experience of women in El Salvador and elsewhere. She said of trying to raise U.S. awareness of the Salvadoran war in the 1980s:

It's interesting. When there are macabre crimes and murders committed in this country then people demand justice. . . . [A]nd yet when these same kinds of savage crimes are committed in El Salvador, no one demands justice. They don't believe what goes on in my country. Even journalists who have interviewed me use language that de-legitimates my experience. They write, María Teresa Tula "alleged" or "said" that she was tortured. The way they frame my responses makes it sound like there is some doubt about what happened or that I imagined what happened to me. This is very painful for me and anyone who gives testimony about their own torture. (175)

In the 1990s, Tula continued her work as an activist fighting for the rights of Salvadoran and other Latin American immigrants in the United States. She is also committed to continuing to publicize the role of the United States in militarizing and contributing to human rights violations in other countries. Since the mid-1990s, she has been working with Companion Communities in Development (COCODA), which links U.S. cities and towns to sister communities in El Salvador. The focus of the solidarity between U.S. and Salvadoran communities is to promote participatory grassroots economic development. Tula's skillful use of testimony as an organizing tool, as well as her analytical insights into politics and the potential that women have for participating in change, marks her as a major figure in El Salvador as well as in the United States. Her commitment to a model of cross-border solidarity in human rights work and in grassroots development are notable achievements.

Further Reading

Schirmer, Jennifer. "The Seeking of Truth and the Gendering of Consciousness: The COMADRES of El Salvador and the CONAVIGUA Widows of Guatemala." In *'Viva': Women and Popular Protest in Latin America*, edited by Sarah A. Radcliffe and Sallie Westwood, 30–64. London: Routledge, 1993.

———. "Those Who Die for Life Cannot Be Called Dead: Women and Human Rights Protest in Latin America." In *Surviving Beyond Fear: Women, Children and Human Rights in Latin America*, edited by Marjorie Agosin, 31–57. Fredonia, N.Y.: White Pine Press, 1993.

Stephen, Lynn. *Women and Social Movements in Latin America: Power from Below.* Austin: University of Texas Press, 1997.

———. "Women's Rights Are Human Rights: The Merging of Feminine and Feminist Interests Among El Salvador's Mothers of the Disappeared (COMADRES)." *American Ethnologist* 22, no. 4 (1995): 807–27.

Tula, María Teresa, and Lynn Stephen. *Hear My Testimony: María Teresa Tula, Human Rights Activist of El Salvador*, translated by Lynn Stephen. Boston: South End Press, 1994.

Lynn Stephen

VIRGINIA VARGAS
(July 23, 1945–   )
Peru: Sociologist, Feminist Activist

Feminist, sociologist, and founder of the Flora Tristán Center for Peruvian Women, Virginia Vargas was born in Lima, Peru. Vargas was a rebel and the second of four children born to an army officer and his very conventional but understanding wife. The family was always moving across the country owing to her father's work. After high school, Vargas attended Catholic University in Lima (1963–1968) where she became interested in drama and literature first, but finally she majored in sociology. In 1968 she married a Chilean, Juan Veas Rossi, moved to Chile, and started to support Leftist causes.

Upon joining Salvador Allende's Socialist party, she worked to elect a socialist president to change radically the social conditions of the poor and the working classes. In 1970 Vargas graduated with a bachelor's degree in sociology from the University of Chile; subsequently, she taught and did research at her alma mater for the next three years. The Unidad Popular's (Popular Unity's) collective socialist idealism energized Vargas and gave her opportunities to develop her leadership skills. In 1971 Vargas gave birth to her only daughter, and she continued her college teaching and political militancy. The appalling military coup d'état that ended Allende's government sent her and her family back to Peru in 1973, where Vargas worked at the National Cultural Institute and did solidarity work for Chile. From 1974 to 1976, she pursued graduate studies in economics at San Marcos and politics at the Social Sciences Studies School at Catholic University in Lima.

Vargas's independent personality and political participation in the Left had made her a liberal and a militant for social justice. In 1978 she had her first encounter with feminism while organizing a three-month seminar on women's role in economic development. This seminar was co-sponsored by the Institute of Social Studies of Holland and the Peruvian Institute of Culture. At the event, participants, who were beginning to write theory in the early days of feminism, included Magdalena León of Colombia, Marcia Rivera of Puerto Rico, Moema Viezzer of Brazil, **Julieta Kirkwood** of Chile, Kate Young of England, and Vicky Meynen of Holland. The three months of the seminar, including fieldwork in urban and rural communities, changed Vargas for ever because, right after the event, Vargas and several friends founded the Flora Tristán Center for the Peruvian Woman as a feminist space. The center allowed women to organize around social issues and support the struggles of the Teacher's Union, factory workers, miners, peasants, and others at a time of enormous social convulsion. This took place in 1979, the same year Vargas's husband died.

The 1980s were years of growing, learning, and activism for Vargas and for feminists in Peru and most countries in Latin America. In Brazil, Peru, and Chile, women's movements were a significant part of the resistance against dictatorships and helped develop organizations and women's groups of many kinds. Women's participation in politics was welcomed by Peruvian unions and political parties at first. Soon enough, however, when they started fighting for their own issues, women had to endure the ridicule and the distrust of the democratic movement. Feminist organizations like the Flora Tristán Center in Peru and La Morada in Chile, through their key combination of theory and practice, contributed to a healthy dialogue among women of different backgrounds. The first time women held a pro-choice demonstration in Peru, public criticism and attacks were directed in particular toward feminists. Vargas remembers how even her partner of those years, a university professor, often said he did not understand how an intelligent person such as Vargas could waste her time on women's issues. Vargas's passion for feminism was already anchored in her work and daily life. More and more groups slowly developed, became feminist groups, and took their demands to the street voicing forbidden issues, such as the violence inflicted on battered women. These same groups created cultural spaces of their own and shaped a pluralistic and diverse feminist movement.

In the effervescent social scene of the 1980s, the Flora Tristán Center grew as a strong feminist institution, offering programs on domestic violence, reproductive rights, abortion, and sexual freedom, as well as local empowerment and citizenship. The center also developed an excellent research institute and a strong communications program that edited the well-known *Viva* (Live) magazine for ten years. Vargas was first the coordinator and then the director of the center until 1990. Her research focused on women and economic development and social movements in the Southern Cone. She lectured, wrote, and published several research papers and two books on women. She conducted research on women's citizenship for UNICEF and for a state agency of Holland in Peru and Mexico; she participated in many non-governmental organizations' projects for women's economic development. During those years she founded the Latin American section of Development Alternatives with Women for New Era (DAWN) and helped organize the Latin American and Caribbean Women Meetings (*Encuentros*). The first *Encuentro* took place in 1981 and the second in 1983, in Peru. These events strengthened the development of local feminism, and Vargas's contribution, now well recognized, extended her influence to other countries. By now considered the most valid spaces of articulation for women of Latin America and the Caribbean, eight *Encuentros* have taken place. It is at these events that Virginia Vargas exercised a clear, legitimate leadership role. During this period, key contributions to international feminism were developed by Latin American feminists who embraced the notion of a plurality of feminisms and asserted that tolerance and pluralism were two crucial concepts women could incorporate into the social justice discourse of the times.

In that decade, working with the Red de Mujeres de Educación Popular de CEAAL (Latin American Council of Adult Education), Vargas traveled extensively in Peru organizing regional seminars on the women's movement, on theory and methodology. Also, she often found herself lecturing and organizing in Chile, Paraguay, and Ecuador. All that organizational frenzy was dissipated by twelve years of the Shining

Path crisis that terrorized Peru. In 1992, one of six years of open terror in the country, several leaders of the women's movement were assassinated, among them Elena Moyano, one of Vargas's closest friends. The 1990s brought political changes that precipitated the downfall of Shining Path and opened up a different dynamic for feminism.

Vargas now understood the need to work on building a new democratic discourse of citizenship. At this time, she started teaching in the Women's Program at the Social Studies Institute in The Hague for two months every year and has continued to do so. The experience of teaching in the Netherlands opened up Vargas's vision of feminism to new questions and perspectives because the contact with Dutch students transformed her research in many unexpected ways. In The Hague Vargas met her third partner, an Englishman with whom she kept a rich, mostly electronic relationship that has lasted for nine years.

The Latin American Association for Human Rights conferred on Vargas the Monseñor Proaño Award in 1995 in recognition of her work for human rights. She has continued her pursuit of scholarship and has published more articles. In 1995 the United Nations, in preparation for the Fourth Women's World Conference in Beijing, designated a Latin American conservative woman with no knowledge of the women's movement as its representative. Women in feminist organizations decided to fight back and sent more than 200 faxes in two days proposing Virginia Vargas as the representative for Latin America at the Beijing conference. The United Nations listened to the call, surprising even Vargas, who thought the position was certainly worthy but unreachable. Participation in Beijing was a most extraordinary achievement for Vargas, particularly because her presence secured the Latin American women's movements and non-governmental organizations a representation and a voice in the world conference. She considers the conference and the following processes her most significant learning experience of this last decade. In Beijing she received an award conferred by UNIFEM on women who have advanced the course of women in the world. She received a similar recognition by Spanish women who named her Mujer Progresista 1995 (1995 Progressive Woman).

Research and feminist activism constitute Vargas's days. She teaches in Peru and in the Netherlands, conducts research, writes, and participates in Peruvian politics through the recently created Women for Democracy group. She continues to be part of the board of the legendary Flora Tristán Center, where everyone knows and respects Vargas as a charismatic leader and an unconventional role model. At the regional level, she is part of a mentoring initiative that is forming a new generation of feminists in the Caribbean and Latin America. She has been a member of the Women's Council of the Interamerican Bank of Development, and since 1996 she has also been a member of the Council on

Gender of the World Bank. Continuing her work from the Beijing conference, she is one of the seven members of the board that coordinates regional post-Beijing initiatives in Latin America and the Caribbean. She has published seventeen scholarly papers in the last three years and many reviews, notes, reports, and articles in magazines, and lectures and gives speeches in Peru and other countries in Latin America. Vargas's research agenda is now focused on discursive strategies for Latin American feminism in the 1990s. Some of her latest research and her writing, which reflect on the Beijing experience, have been translated into English for the first time, allowing women and feminists around the world to read the research of this keen leader of Latin American feminism.

Further Reading

Nijeholt, Geertje Lycklama A., Virginia Vargas, and Sashia Weiringa, eds. *Women's Movements and Public Policy in Europe, Latin America and the Caribbean*. New York: Garland, 1998.

Liliana Trevizan

ANA LYDIA VEGA
(December 6, 1946–   )

Puerto Rico: Author

An author of distinctively Puerto Rican literature, Ana Lydia Vega was born in Santurce, Puerto Rico. Her parents are Virgilio Vega from Coamo and María Santana from Arroyo. Her mother was a grade school teacher in a public institution, and Ana Lydia followed in her footsteps. She studied for twelve years in a Catholic school, the Sacred Heart Academy (1952–1964). She began writing in English, and when she was only seven she began writing poetry; she later wrote eighteen mystery novels and a romance that remain unpublished. When she was a child she learned French from her neighbor and best friend. At age twenty-two, Vega obtained a scholarship to study for a master's degree in French literature at the University of Provence, in France. She finished in 1971 and in 1978 she received her doctorate in comparative literature from the same institution.

In France she met a poet and teacher named Robert Villanúa, who became her partner. Their daughter, Lolita, is a ballet dancer and studies foreign languages. As Vega explains in "Pulseando con el difícil" (Going at It with the Difficult), included in *Esperando a Loló y otros delirios generacionales* (Waiting for Loló and Other Generational Deliriums, 1994), her stay in France was one of the most decolonizing experiences of her life. It softened the linguistic tension she suffered between English and Spanish. She was able to familiarize herself with the liberal French intelligentsia, and the experience opened the doors of the French-speaking Caribbean islands to her search for a Caribbean identity. By learning French she reconciled herself with English as well. She began to conceive of it not only as a tool to have access to U.S. cultural production, but also as a threshold to universal knowledge and communication. It was especially useful, she admits, for the understanding of the English-speaking Caribbean and the Puerto Rican community in the United States. In this same essay, Vega exposes the acculturation suffered in a Catholic school and the repudiation, later in her life, of the transformation she underwent there. She proposes, however, to rid herself of the guilt about teaching and learning English. In her opinion, the first step would be to declare it a foreign language. Then it would be necessary to strengthen the teaching of Spanish.

Upon her return to Puerto Rico, she began teaching French at the University of Puerto Rico in Río Piedras, where she still works. There she met Carmen Lugo Filippi and Ruth Hernández Torres. Along with them and Robert, she published a French textbook entitled *Le français vécu* (Living French). She has also published numerous other textbooks. Together with Carmen Lugo Filippi, she published a collection of short stories, *Vírgenes y mártires* (Virgins and Martyrs, 1982), a feminist critique of Puerto Rican patriarchy.

Vega's second collection of short stories, *Encancaranublado y otros cuentos de naufragio* (Encancaranublado and Other Stories of Shipwreck, 1982), dedicated to "the future Caribbean confederation," was honored with the Cuban Casa de las Américas (House of the Americas) award. This book, which critiques the mass media manipulation of public opinion, protests the imprisonment of independence activists and contemplates a pan-Caribbean unity. In her characteristic style, peppered with colloquialisms and code switching, she criticizes the foreign policy of the Reagan administration and creates an apologetic vision of the "free and confederated Antilles."

As she explains in "Pulseando con el difícil," Vega enjoys reading detective stories and loves films. She created the script for Marcos Zuninaga's film *La gran fiesta* (The Big Party, 1987). In her articles published in 1985 in the column "Relevo" (Relief) of the weekly publication *Claridad* (Clarity), which were printed along with those of seven other young Puerto Rican authors under the title *El tramo ancla*, Vega questions stereotypical assumptions about Puerto Rico.

The stories in *Falsas crónicas del sur, colección de relatos* (Fake Chronicles of the South, a Collection of Stories, 1991), which take place on the southern coast of Puerto Rico, are inspired by oral tradition. Vega mixes romanticism and adventures with satiric social commentary to describe different national episodes and different Puerto Rican locations.

Once again, in *Esperando a Loló*, Vega combines different genres such as autobiographical essays, chronicles, and social commentary on issues like machismo, politics, emigration, and education. Daily life in contemporary Puerto Rico is represented from a variety of narrative perspectives. The new role of women in Puerto Rico, especially that of women writers, is one of the topics treated. Yet one of the most relevant issues studied in this collection and in her work in general is the Puerto Rican Spanish dialect and its struggle for survival vis-à-vis bilingual education and the dominance of English as the prestigious language. The idea of nationalism and the contradictions of Puerto Rican politics and culture emerge as a logical continuation of the debate on language. The tragicomedy of the sociopolitical uncertainty in Puerto Rico mirrors the alternation of humorous and more serious stories, as well as her approach to the history of Puerto Rican literature. Vega experienced her first contacts with the emancipation of women through a cousin from New York. She realized that the Puerto Rican in New York idealized an island that no longer exists. They talk about an eternal and motionless country that was indeed only a myth in their imagination. In light of the differences, Vega proposes to analyze together certain dilemmas, such as the subtle inferiority complex and the consequences of dependency.

In her first collection of short stories in English, *True and False Romances: Stories and a Novella* (the only book written by Vega translated into English thus far, 1994), Vega experiments once again with different genres. As in her previous works, the humorous tone, the references to popular food and culture, the use of code switching and Puerto Rican slang seem to serve the ultimate goal of locating a national language and cultural identity. The references to Puerto Rican reality, such as the mention of the newspapers *El vocero* (The Crier) and *Claridad*, are also common. This vague borderline between reality and imagination creates an open narrative for which the active reader must find responses. The separation of the real and the imagined, as well as the decision on the truth (or lack of) in the character's comments, are to be completed by the reader. Issues of gender roles, feminism, and sexuality are central. Machismo is criticized. Even those men who seem trustworthy eventually mistreat women. In the epistolary essay "La Gurúa Talía: Correo de San Valentín" (Gurúa Talía: Valentine's Day Mail), included in *El tramo ancla*, Vega revisits the contradictions between domestic machismo and leftist political activism.

In 1984 her third book, *Pasión de historias y otras historias de pasión* (Passion of History and Other Stories of Passion, 1987), was awarded the Juan Rulfo International Prize in Paris. Vega has received several honors for her short stories: "Pollito Chicken" (Little Chicken Chicken) received the Emilio S. Belaval award (1978); "Puerto Príncipe Abajo" (Down Puerto Principe) was honored with the Círculo de Escritores y Poetas Iberoamericanos (Circle of Iberoamerican Writers and Poets) award in 1979; and "Despedida de duelo" (Mourning Farewell) received third place in the Christmas contest of the Ateneo Puertorriqueño (Puerto Rican Atheneum, 1975). Vega received the Nemesio Canales Award for satiric literature presented by the magazine *Claridad* for "Cuatro selecciones por una peseta. Bolero a dos voces para machos en pena" (Four Selections for a Peseta. Bolero Duet for Machos in Sorrow), written in collaboration with Carmen Lugo Filippi. The same work received the P.E.N. Club de Puerto Rico award and that of the Instituto de Literatura (Institute of Literature) in 1983.

In her works, Vega mixes local language and events with cosmopolitanism. Her pages are generally seasoned with humor, nostalgia, political idealism, protest, and frustration. Over all, her writing has the ultimate objective of distinguishing a Caribbean identity and creating a distinctively Puerto Rican literature.

Further Reading

Den Tandt, Catherine Mary. "Tracing Nation and Gender: Ana Lydia Vega." *Revista de estudios hispánicos* 18, no. 1 (1994): 3–24.

Hernández, Elizabeth, translated by Consuelo López. "Women and Writing in Puerto Rico: An Interview with Ana Lydia Vega." *Callaloo: A Journal of African-American and African Arts and Letters* 17, no. 3 (1994): 816–25.

Labiosa, David J. *Ana Lydia Vega: Linguistic Women and Another Counterassault, or Can the Master(s) Hear?* Boston: William Monroe Trotter Institute, 1996.

Puleo, Augustus C. "Ana Lydia Vega, the Caribbean Storyteller." *Afro-Hispanic Review* 15, no. 2 (1996): 21–25.

Vega, Ana Lydia, Kalman Barsy, et al., eds. *El tramo ancla: Ensayos puertorriqueños de hoy*. Río Piedras, Puerto Rico: Editorial de la Universidad de Puerto Rico, 1991.

Ignacio López-Calvo

DELIA ZAPATA OLIVELLA
(April 1, 1926–   )

Colombia: Dancer, Choreographer, Educator

Delia Zapata Olivella, an Afro-Colombian dancer and choreographer born in Santa Cruz de Lorica, Colombia, pioneered the study and preservation of Colombian traditional dances through a unique anthropological approach. In addition, Zapata Olivella, who is now over seventy years old, continues to teach and tour with her internationally known Grupo de Danzas Folclóricas Colombianas de Delia Zapata Olivella (Delia Zapata Olivella's Folkloric Dances of Colombia).

Zapata Olivella is a descendant of Europeans, Zenús (an indigenous nation), and Afro-Colombians. She takes the history of cultural encounters that has shaped her family, a history often marked by violence and oppression, but also by creative resistance, as the starting point for reflecting on cultural identity. Zapata Olivella thinks of dance as the repository of that history and the embodiment of that reflection. As she claims, traditional dances are both the language with which to communicate with her ancestors and the living history of her country. She grew up in a tightly knit family in which her two grandmothers' spiritual view of the world tempered her father's rationalist and anticlerical influence. Furthermore, as the keepers of their respective oral traditions, the grandmothers, one of whom was a traditional Zenú ceramicist—Zapata Olivella's first love—and the other an Afro-Caribbean *rezandera* (healer), instilled in her a strong sense of connection with her cultural roots and provided her with a unique insight into the process of cultural *mestizaje* (racial and cultural mixing).

When Zapata Olivella was three, her family moved to the colonial city of Cartagena, once the major port of entry for black slaves in the Spanish colonies of South America. She grew up in a city that was awakening to its African roots (best exemplified by Jorge Artel's 1940 collection of poetry, *Tambores en la noche* [Drums in the Night]), surrounded by the drumbeats of the *cumbia* and the memory of resistance borne by the *palenqueros* (former runaway slaves) who had settled outside the city's walls. This sense of black cultural renaissance, of which her family was an important component, decisively shaped her life. Her father, Antonio Zapata Vásquez, a free spirit, was an educator and an actor who transmitted the love of learning and theater to his children. Her brother Manuel, a doctor, is one of Colombia's best-known writers. He is the author of one of the African diaspora's most powerful novels, *Changó, el gran putas* (Shango: The Greatest S.O.B.), as well as an eminent essayist and an interpreter of the African contribution to the continent. Zapata Olivella's younger brother, Juan, is a well-known poet, educator, and founder of Cartagena's Museo del Negro (Museum of Black Culture).

Zapata Olivella's father repeatedly emphasized the links among education, artistic expression, and cultural identity. When, in the early 1940s, Zapata Olivella rebelled against the traditional school system that permitted woman to pursue only teaching or secretarial positions, her father formally requested that she be accepted into the University of Cartagena's exclusive high school system, until then open only to male students. His request was accepted, and in 1947 Zapata Olivella, along with twenty-four other women, became the first graduates of the first coeducational school in the history of the city.

After finishing high school, Zapata Olivella began her formal education in sculpture and drawing, first in Cartagena and later in the capital, Bogotá, at the National University's National School for the Arts. After graduation, she moved back to Cartagena, and in 1954 she won first prize in a local exhibition: the Regional Exhibition of Caribbean Artists with a sculpture called "La Mendiga" (The Beggar). However, a deep-seated love for dance led her to renew her commitment to the performance and study of its history, or, as she puts it, "the art of sculpting living forms" (personal interview, May 1999). Already in 1950 she had conducted research into the local folklore of the Lorica region, and in 1952 she brought traditional Caribbean music and performers to the country's capital. In 1954 she persuaded Batata, a traditional sacred drummer from the centuries-old runaway settlement of Palenque de San Basilio, to accompany the *lumbalúes* (funerary songs) singers in a performance in Bogotá. Up until then, most people from the country's interior did not know about the existence of a distinct Afro-Creole culture in the country.

In 1954, at the suggestion of her brother Manuel, she formed her own dance group and recruited friends and colleagues who had worked with her in Cartagena's annual carnival. She rehearsed her dances on an empty lot (originally a cockfighting ring), a public space that made the local community spectators of its own culture for the first time. This experience led her to realize that there was a lot more to dancing than just performance. She began to develop an anthropological approach to dance designed to cultivate a sensibility for local history, oral traditions, music, and dress. Her methodology, which she still teaches, maintains that the choreography, assisted by peasants, elders, and local dancers, can be implemented only after having acquired a thorough understanding of the region and its dances.

In 1955 she and her brother Manuel embarked on a year-long research trip throughout the Pacific Coast in search of traditional Afro-Colombian dances. This trip marked the young Zapata Olivella for life, after which she felt convinced of and committed to her love for dance. Her acquaintance with important Afro-Colombians of the Pacific Coast, such as writers Carlos Arturo Truque and Arnoldo Palacios and politician Diego Córdoba, had already alerted her to some of the differences between the Caribbean and Pacific coasts and to the cultural riches ensconced in the small fishing villages scattered along the Pacific Coast. Since they had no financial support or institutional backing, Zapata Olivella and Manuel stayed in each region for a period of two to three months, working— Zapata Olivella as a seamstress and Manuel as a doctor—to earn a living. During this time, Zapata Olivella observed the local dances, learned their history and religious or secular function, and studied their choreography. With the help of a huge, old recording machine, for which they had to rent a mule to transport it, she recorded local lore and conversed with the elders. At night, she drew pictures of the dress and positions and described the steps with as much detail as possible in order to reproduce the dance later. Although Zapata Olivella became one of the foremost experts on Afro-Colombian dances, she continued with her research trips, including other regions of the country, including the Andes and the eastern plains.

After completing her research project, she toured the country, and in July 1957 Zapata Olivella and her group, Danzas Folklóricas Colombianas, embarked on a tour of Europe. They began their trip in Paris and were later invited to perform in Czechoslovakia, East and West Germany, the Soviet Union, and China. Upon their return to Paris, they were invited to participate in the Spanish-American Festival of Art and Folklore in Cáceres, Spain, where they were awarded first prize for their dances and performance. Their success led them to an extensive tour throughout Spain and, on their way back, Venezuela.

The following few years can be thought of as a time of consolidation and transition, as others began to take notice of her work. Zapata Olivella returned to her research and began to assimilate some of what she had experienced during her international tour. In 1959 she presented her group in the First National Folkloric Festival of Dance held in Ibagué, Colombia, and once again won first prize. From 1959 to 1961, she directed the workers' dance group in TELECOM (Colombia's national phone company), and in 1963 she became the main choreographer for the Institute of Popular Culture in Cali. Finally, in 1964, she was recognized by SAYCO (the Colombian Society of Authors and Composers) for her work with the Bandeja de Plata (Silver Tray) and the Medalla de Oro (Gold Medal), two of the society's most prestigious awards.

In 1965 Zapata Olivella was awarded a fellowship to study in the United States. She traveled to several cities, delivered a lecture at Indiana

University, and taught a course on Colombian dances in the Music Department of the Organization of American States. In New York, she studied African dance at the Dunham School of Arts and Research with the famous African-American dancer and choreographer Katherine Dunham, whom she had already seen in Cartagena years before. In fact, Zapata Olivella arrived in New York at a seminal and exciting moment in the history of modern dance in general and black dance in particular. Dunham, herself deeply interested in Caribbean dance forms, had become the first black woman to choreograph an opera, Giuseppe Verdi's *Aida*, for the New York City Metropolitan Opera. One year later, Dunham went on to represent the United States at Senegal's Festival of Black Arts. Alvin Ailey, another black American dance legend, had just retired from dancing and became the full-time choreographer for his American Dance Theater Company and Judith Jamison joined it. Other important dancers who were making their mark in New York at the time of Zapata Olivella's arrival are Trinidadian Pearl Primus, Agnes de Mille, and Antony Tudor. Though Zapata Olivella was fascinated by all of these dancers and absorbed as much as she could from them, she concluded that, before undertaking the process of reinterpretation through modern dance, it was essential to recover and understand her country's national heritage. It is precisely in contraposition to the liberties taken by modern dance and Broadway's musical tradition that she developed a sober style, loyal, and informed by tradition, with a scrupulous eye for accuracy in dress, proper musical instruments, particular steps, and dance sequences. Instead of the flashy and sharp movements of much of modern dance, Zapata Olivella strives to capture the rural, often slower fluidity of traditional dances. Never has she rejected modern dance—in fact, she has recently collaborated with dancers Alvaro Restrepo and Marie France Davalieu in the choreography of a modern dance group in Bogotá. However, Zapata Olivella points out that prior to experimentation, it is essential to delve into one's own cultural expressions (personal interview, May 1999).

After returning to Bogotá, Zapata Olivella combined teaching with dancing and directing. From 1967 to 1983, she taught dance at Bogotá's National University and directed the university's dance group. She reactivated the Danzas Folklórikas de Colombia de Delia Zapata Olivella and continued with her research into the understudied national dance traditions. In 1970 she spent two months in the Colombian islands of San Andrés and Providencia in the Caribbean, learning the Anglo-Creole culture and dances of the region. In 1974 she founded the Institute for Colombian Folklore with the purpose of training, researching, and preparing dance professors. Since 1983 she has been the director of the Faculty of Dance and Theater at the Antonio Nariño University in Bogotá.

During the last few years, Zapata Olivella has finally received the recognition and some of the support she so sorely lacked during most of her career. The government recognized her artistic career and contribution to Colombian culture in 1997 with the Orden del Mérito General José María Cordoba (Order of Merit). The House of Representatives awarded her the Orden de la Democracia (Order of Democracy) in 1998. In 1998 she also saw a longtime dream come to fruition when she published the first volume—*Manual de danzas de la costa Pacífica de Colombia* (Manual of Dances of the Pacific Coast of Colombia)—of what promises to be the most comprehensive manual of Colombian sacred and profane dances. The book includes a CD-Rom and a VCR tape that illustrate Colombian music and dance as performed by her company. This important work is the result of a lifetime of research and study, and hopefully it will promote the understanding of local cultures and suggest new paths for further research into Colombian folklore.

Further Reading

Zapata Olivella, Delia. *Manual de danzas de la Costa Pacífica de Colombia*. Santa Fé de Bogotá, Colombia: Patronato Colombiano de las Artes, 1998.
———. Personal interview, May 1999.
Zapata Olivella, Manuel. ¡*Levántate mulato!* Santa Fé de Bogotá, Colombia: Rei Andes, 1990.

Francisco Ortega

Appendix A: Notables by Fields of Endeavor

Fields of endeavor are listed under the following categories:

Actress

Architect

Artist

Attorney

Author

Choreographer

Composer

Critic

Culture Promoter

Dancer

Diplomat

Director

Educator

Ethnologist

Feminist Activist

First Lady

Government Administrator

Governor

Guerrilla Leader

Historian

Human Rights Activist

Journalist

Musician

Performance Artist

Physician

Playwright

Poet

Political Activist

Political Leader

Politician

Researcher

Screenwriter

Singer

Social Activist

Sociologist

Spiritual Leader

Surgeon General

Theologian

Translator

ACTRESS
María Félix
Fanny Mikey
Carmen Miranda
Eva María Duarte de Perón

ARCHITECT
Teresa Gisbert Carbonell de
Mesa

ARTIST
Débora Arango
Andrea Echeverri
Beatriz González
Frida Kahlo
Josefina Plá

ATTORNEY
Elizabeth Odio Benito

AUTHOR
Claribel Alegría
Isabel Allende
Albalucía Angel Marulanda
Laura Antillano
Domitila Barrios de
Chúngara
Gioconda Belli
María Luisa Bombal
Rosa María Britton
Julia de Burgos
Lydia Cabrera
Diamela Eltit
Rosario Ferré
Elena Garro
Ivone Gebara
Margo Glantz
Angela Hernández Nuñez
Carolina Maria de Jesus
Claudia Lars
Clarice Lispector

Carmen Naranjo
Victoria Ocampo
Cristina Peri Rossi
Elena Poniatowska
Beatriz Santos Arrascaeta
Armonía Somers
Marta Traba
Ana Lydia Vega

CHOREOGRAPHER
Alicia Alonso
Delia Zapata Olivella

COMPOSER
Chiquinha Gonzaga

CRITIC
Margo Glantz
Josefina Plá
Marta Traba

CULTURE PROMOTER
Victoria Ocampo
Haydée Santamaría

DANCER
Alicia Alonso
Rosa Luna
Delia Zapata Olivella

DIPLOMAT
Rosario Castellanos

DIRECTOR
María Luisa Bemberg
Nancy Cárdenas

EDUCATOR
Alicia Alonso
Laura Antillano
Hebe de Bonafini
Ivone Gebara
Teresa Gisbert Carbonell de
Mesa

Julieta Kirkwood
Antonia Novello
Elizabeth Odio Benito
Beatriz Santos Arrascaeta
Armonía Somers
Delia Zapata Olivella

ETHNOLOGIST
Lydia Cabrera

FEMINIST ACTIVIST
Julieta Kirkwood
Virginia Vargas

FIRST LADY
Eva María Duarte de Perón

GOVERNMENT ADMINISTRATOR
Carmen Naranjo
Elizabeth Odio Benito

GOVERNOR
Irene Sáez Conde

GUERRILLA LEADER
Commander Ramona
Major Ana María

HISTORIAN
Teresa Gisbert Carbonell de Mesa

HUMAN RIGHTS ACTIVIST
Rigoberta Menchú Tum

JOURNALIST
Laura Antillano
María Mercedes Carranza
Rosario Castellanos
Elena Garro
Josefina Plá
Elena Poniatowska

MUSICIAN
Chiquinha Gonzaga

PERFORMANCE ARTIST
Astrid Hadad

PHYSICIAN
Antonia Novello

PLAYWRIGHT
Rosa María Britton
Nancy Cárdenas
Elena Garro

POET
Claribel Alegría
Gioconda Belli
Julia de Burgos
María Mercedes Carranza
Rosario Castellanos
Angela Hernández Nuñez
Claudia Lars
Dulce María Loynaz
Alejandra Pizarnik
Josefina Plá
Magda Portal
Benedita da Silva

POLITICAL ACTIVIST
Claribel Alegría
Elvia Alvarado
Domitila Barrios de Chúngara
Gioconda Belli
Hebe de Bonafini
María Mercedes Carranza
Benita Galeana
Rosario Ibarra de Piedra
Lolita Lebrón
Patria, Minerva, and María Teresa Mirabal
Cristina Peri Rossi
Magda Portal
Haydée Santamaría
María Teresa Tula

POLITICAL LEADER
María Cano

POLITICIAN
Violeta Barrios de Chamorro
Nina Pacari
Eva María Duarte de Perón
Benedita da Silva

RESEARCHER
Julieta Kirkwood

SCREENWRITER
Elena Garro

SINGER
Celia Cruz
Andrea Echeverri
Astrid Hadad
Clementina de Jesús
Carmen Miranda

Beatriz Santos Arrascaeta
Mercedes Sosa

SOCIAL ACTIVIST
Elvia Alvarado
María Luisa Bemberg

SOCIOLOGIST
Julieta Kirkwood
Virginia Vargas

SPIRITUAL LEADER
Maria Escolástica da
Conceição Nazaré

SURGEON GENERAL
Antonia Novello

THEOLOGIAN
Ivone Gebara

TRANSLATOR
Alejandra Pizarnik

Appendix B: Notables by Country

ARGENTINA
María Luisa Bemberg
Hebe de Bonafini
Fanny Mikey
Victoria Ocampo
Eva María Duarte de Perón
Alejandra Pizarnik
Mercedes Sosa
Marta Traba

BOLIVIA
Domitila Barrios de
Chúngara
Teresa Gisbert Carbonell de
Mesa

BRAZIL
Ivone Gebara
Chiquinha Gonzaga
Carolina Maria de Jesus
Clementina de Jesus
Clarice Lispector
Carmen Miranda

Maria Escolástica da
Conceição Nazaré
Benedita da Silva

CHILE
Isabel Allende
María Luisa Bombal
Diamela Eltit
Julieta Kirkwood

COLOMBIA
Albalucía Angel Marulanda
Débora Arango
María Cano
María Mercedes Carranza
Andrea Echeverri
Beatriz González
Fanny Mikey
Marta Traba
Delia Zapata Olivella

COSTA RICA
Carmen Naranjo
Elizabeth Odio Benito

CUBA
Alicia Alonso
Lydia Cabrera
Celia Cruz
Dulce María Loynaz
Haydée Santamaría

DOMINICAN REPUBLIC
Angela Hernández Nuñez
Patria, Minerva, and María
Teresa Mirabal

ECUADOR
Nina Pacari

EL SALVADOR
Claribel Alegría
Claudia Lars
María Teresa Tula

GUATEMALA
Rigoberta Menchú Tum

HONDURAS
Elvia Alvarado

MEXICO
Major Ana María
Nancy Cárdenas
Rosario Castellanos
María Félix
Benita Galeana
Elena Garro
Margo Glantz
Astrid Hadad

Rosario Ibarra de Piedra
Frida Kahlo
Elena Poniatowska
Commander Ramona

NICARAGUA
Claribel Alegría
Violeta Barrios de Chamorro
Gioconda Belli

PANAMA
Rosa María Britton

PARAGUAY
Josefina Plá

PERU
Magda Portal
Virginia Vargas

PUERTO RICO
Julia de Burgos
Rosario Ferré
Lolita Lebrón
Antonia Novello
Ana Lydia Vega

URUGUAY
Rosa Luna
Cristina Peri Rossi
Beatriz Santos Arrascaeta
Armonía Somers

VENEZUELA
Laura Antillano
Irene Sáez Conde

Bibliography

LATIN AMERICA

Bethell, Leslie, ed. *The Cambridge History of Latin America*. New York: Cambridge University Press, 1984.

Black, Jan Knippers, ed. *Latin America: Its Problems and Its Promise*. Boulder, Colo.: Westview Press, 1998.

Guillermoprieto, Alma. *The Heart That Bleeds: Latin America Now*. New York: Vintage Books, 1994.

Skidmore, Thomas, and Peter Smith. *Modern Latin America*. Oxford, England: Oxford University Press, 1997.

Winn, Peter. *Americas: The Changing Face of Latin America and the Caribbean*. New York: Pantheon Books, 1992 and 1999.

WOMEN'S HISTORY

Bouvard, M. G. *On Revolutionizing Motherhood: The Mothers of the Plaza de Mayo*. Wilmington, Del.: Scholarly Resources Press, 1994.

Lavrín, Asunción. *Women, Feminism, and Social Change in Argentina, Chile, and Uruguay, 1890–1940*. Lincoln: University of Nebraska Press, 1995.

Miller, Francesca. *Latin American Women and the Search for Social Justice*. Hanover, N.H.: University of New England Press, 1991.

Paternostro, Silvana. *In the Land of God and Man*. New York: Plume/Penguin, 1998.

WOMEN AND POLITICS

Craske, Nikke. *Women and Politics in Latin America*. New Brunswick, N.J.: Rutgers University Press, 1999.

Jaquette, Jane, ed. *The Women's Movement in Latin America: Participation and Democracy*. Boulder, Colo.: Westview Press, 1994.

Jelin, Elizabeth, ed. *Women and Social Change in Latin America*. London: Zed Books, 1990.

Radcliffe, Sarah A., and Sally Westwood. *Viva: Women and Popular Protest in Latin America*. London: Routledge, 1993.

WOMEN AND ECONOMIC CHANGE

Beneria, Lourdes, and Shelley Feldman, eds. *Unequal Burden: Economic Crisis, Persistent Poverty and Women's Lives*. Boulder, Colo.: Westview Press, 1992.

Inter-American Development Bank. *Women in the Americas: Bridging the Gender Gap*. Washington, D.C., 1995.

UNICEF. *The Invisible Adjustment: Poor Women and Economic Crisis*. Santiago: Alfabeta Editores, 1987.

WOMEN IN LITERATURE AND THE ARTS

Biller, Geraldine P., et al., eds. *Latin American Women Artists. Artistas latinoamericanas: 1915–1995*. Milwaukee, Wisc.: Milwaukee Art Museum, 1995.

Franco, Jean. *Plotting Women: Gender and Representation in Modern Mexico*. New York: Columbia University Press, 1989.

Marting, Diane E., ed. *Latin American Women Writers: A Bio-Bibliographical Source Book*. Westport, Conn.: Greenwood Press, 1990.

Index

Since the Contents includes a comprehensive list of the entries, they are not included here.

About the Editors and Contributors

GASTÓN A. ALZATE is Codirector of Latin American, Latino, and Caribbean Studies at Gustavus Adolphus College in St. Peter, Minnesota.

NARA ARAÚJO, Professor of Comparative Literature at the University of La Habana, in Cuba, is currently teaching at the Universidad Autónoma Metropolitana in Mexico City.

MARC BECKER is Assistant Professor of Latin American History at Truman State University in Kirksville, Missouri.

CATHERINE M. BRYAN is Assistant Professor of Spanish at the University of Wisconsin-Oshkosh.

EVA PAULINO BUENO teaches Spanish and Portuguese at Mukogawa Women's University in Hyogo, Japan.

MARÍA CRISTINA BURGUEÑO is Assistant Professor of Spanish at Marshall University in Huntington, West Virginia.

HORACIO CAMPODÓNICO teaches Critical History of Cinema at the Universidad de Buenos Aires, Argentina.

GUADALUPE CORTINA is Assistant Professor of Latin American Literature at Texas A&M University College Station.

CLARICE DEAL teaches Portuguese at Arizona State University in Tempe.

RUBÉN D. DURÁN is a New York City–based artist educator.

ADRIANA FERNANDES is Associate Professor of Musicology at the Universidade Federal de Goiás in Goiânia, Brazil.

FABIOLA FERNÁNDEZ SALEK is a doctoral student at Arizona State University in Tempe.

DEBORAH FOOTE is a Ph.D. candidate at the University of Chicago.

MELISSA M. FORBIS is Coordinator of Proyecto Integral de Salud y Tecnologia Apropiada in Mexico City.

DAVID WILLIAM FOSTER is Chair of the Department of Languages and Literatures and Regent's Professor of Spanish, Humanities, and Women's Studies at Arizona State University in Tempe.

ROBERTO FUERTES-MANJÓN is Assistant Professor of Spanish at Midwestern State University in Wichita Falls, Texas.

SANDRA GARABANO is Assistant Professor of Spanish at the University of Texas, El Paso.

HEIDI ANN GARCÍA is a Ph.D. candidate at Arizona State University in Tempe.

MANUEL GARCÍA CASTELLÓN is Associate Professor of Spanish at the University of New Orleans.

ESTER GIMBERNAT GONZÁLEZ is Professor of Spanish at the University of Northern Colorado in Greeley.

M. CRISTINA GUZZO is Assistant Professor of Spanish at Ball State University in Muncie, Indiana.

JUDY HINOJOSA is an Honors College student in Psychology and Women's Studies at Arizona State University in Tempe.

ASUNCIÓN HORNO-DELGADO is Associate Professor of Spanish at the University of Colorado at Boulder.

LINDA S. HOWE is Assistant Professor of Spanish at Wake Forest University in Winston-Salem, North Carolina.

MIGUEL HUEZO MIXCO is the Publications Director of the Consejo Nacional para la Cultura y el Arte in San Salvador, El Salvador.

RAQUEL JACOBS teaches Spanish at the Catholic University of America in Washington, D.C.

FRANCES JAEGER is Assistant Professor of Spanish at Northern Illinois University in De Kalb.

JANE S. JAQUETTE is Bertha Harton Orr Professor in the Liberal Arts and Professor of Politics at Occidental College in Los Angeles, California.

CARLOS JÁUREGUI is a Ph.D. candidate at the University of Pittsburgh.

OSCAR RAFAEL JIMÉNEZ GONZÁLEZ is Professor of Sociology at the Instituto Tecnológico y de Estudios Superiores de Monterrey, Mexico City Campus.

BETH E. JÖRGENSEN is Associate Professor of Spanish at the University of Rochester in Rochester, New York.

KAREN KAMPWIRTH is Assistant Professor of Political Science at Knox College in Galesburg, Illinois.

LINDA I. KOSKI is Assistant Professor of Spanish at Santa Clara University in Santa Clara, California.

MICHAEL R. KULISHECK is a senior analyst with the political research firm of Talmey-Drake Research & Strategy in Boulder, Colorado.

GREGORY D. LAGOS-MONTOYA is Assistant Professor at Universidad de Los Lagos in Osorno, Chile.

ILSE ABSHAGEN LEITINGER is Coordinator of the Instituto Monteverde's Gender and Women's Studies Program in San José, Costa Rica.

DARRELL B. LOCKHART is Assistant Professor of Spanish at the University of Nevada-Reno in Reno, Nevada.

MARÍA DEL MAR LÓPEZ-CABRALES is Assistant Professor of Spanish at Colorado State University in Fort Collins.

IGNACIO LÓPEZ-CALVO is Assistant Professor of Spanish at California State University in Los Angeles.

DIANE E. MARTING is Assistant Professor of Spanish at the University of Florida in Gainesville.

ROSE McEWEN teaches Spanish at the State University of New York at Geneseo.

CHIARA MERINO PÉREZ is a graduate student at Arizona State University in Tempe.

JORGE VITAL MOREIRA is Visiting Lecturer of Spanish and Portuguese at Lawrence University in Appleton, Wisconsin.

ROBERT NEUSTADT is Assistant Professor of Spanish at Northern Arizona University in Flagstaff.

CECILIA OJEDA is Assistant Professor of Spanish at Northern Arizona University in Flagstaff.

FRANCISCO ORTEGA is a Ph.D. candidate at the University of Chicago and Dissertation Fellow at Boston College.

MYRIAM OSORIO is Visiting Lecturer at the University of Wisconsin, Green Bay.

GEMA P. PÉREZ-SÁNCHEZ is Assistant Professor of Spanish at the University of Miami, Coral Gables.

LEVILSON C. REIS is Assistant Professor of French at Otterbein College in Westerville, Ohio.

CARLOS MANUEL RIVERA is Visiting Professor of Spanish at Davidson College in Davidson, North Carolina.

RICARDO ROQUE BALDOVINOS is Professor of the Department of Letters at the Universidad Centroamericana de El Salvador, San Salvador.

ADRIANA ROSMAN-ASKOT is Assistant Professor of Latin American Literature at the College of New Jersey in Ewing, New Jersey.

PATRICIA RUBIO is Associate Professor of Spanish and Director of Women's Studies at Skidmore College in Saratoga Springs, New York.

LIZBETH SOUZA FUERTES is Assistant Professor of Spanish and Portuguese and Assistant Director of Latin American Studies at Baylor University in Waco, Texas.

LYNN STEPHEN is Professor of Anthropology at the University of Oregon in Eugene.

JUANA SUÁREZ is Assistant Professor of Spanish at the University of Mississippi in Oxford.

TOMÁS F. TARABORRELLI is a graduate student at the University of California, Irvine.

CYNTHIA MARGARITA TOMPKINS is Associate Professor of Spanish at Arizona State University in Tempe.

STEVEN TORRES is an Instructor of Spanish at the University of Nebraska at Omaha.

RHINA TORUÑO is Spanish Associate Professor at the University of Texas of the Permian Basin in Odessa.

LILIANA TREVIZAN is Associate Professor of Latin American Literature and Director of Women's Studies at the State University of New York at Potsdam.

MARÍA ELVIRA VILLAMIL is Assistant Professor of Spanish at the University of Nebraska at Omaha.

CAROLL MILLS YOUNG is Associate Professor of Spanish at the Indiana University of Pennsylvania in Indiana, Pennsylvania.

920
Not

Notable twentieth-
century Latin
American women.

DATE			